'He is fascinating about how [illegible]d the Foreign Office in particular, knew – and chose to ignore – of the Dirty War . . . The game of intelligence and diplomatic bluff is explained in piquant detail' *Guardian*

'Bicheno understands how battles are fought, and explains those of the Falklands perhaps better than any other writer has done . . . he knows how soldiers fight battles and has done us all a service by explaining them so well for a new generation' Max Hastings, *Daily Mail*

'It may seem impossible for anything original to appear about the Falklands War, so much has been written about it, but Hugh Bicheno's book is that thing . . . readers will find this book gripping and discomfiting' *Daily Telegraph*

'A wide-ranging and constantly engaging book, written under the pressure of real intellectual enthusiasm . . . anyone who opens this book will quickly be drawn into an extraordinary world of military rivalry and power politics' *Sunday Telegraph*

'As a narrative of the battle, *Crescent and Cross* is unlikely to be surpassed. Hugh Bicheno brings to his subject not only deep knowledge, but also an enviable ability to convey both the glamour and horror of sixteenth-century war' *Literary Review*

'In *Crescent and Cross*, Bicheno roves enthusiastically on a wide-ranging tour across the 16th-century Mediterranean. There are illuminating passages on oceanography and climatology together with well-researched studies of the fleets and their assorted weaponry. Graphic, pithy observations underline the awfulness of medieval war . . . cheerfully ideological, highly readable' *Financial Times*

Hugh Bicheno is himself something of a Renaissance man. He had careers as an academic, an intelligence officer and a kidnap and ransom negotiator before devoting himself to writing about men at war and how wars happen. Recent works include critically acclaimed histories of the Falklands War (*Razor's Edge*), the Battle of Lepanto (*Crescent and Cross*) and the American War of Independence (*Rebels and Redcoats*).

# VENDETTA

*High Art and Low Cunning at the Birth of the Renaissance*

HUGH BICHENO

PHOENIX

A PHOENIX PAPERBACK

First published in Great Britain in 2008
by Weidenfeld & Nicolson
This paperback edition published in 2009
by Phoenix
an imprint of Orion Books Ltd,
Orion House, 5 Upper St Martin's Lane,
London WC2H 9EA

An Hachette UK company

1 3 5 7 9 10 8 6 4 2



A CIP catalogue record for this book is available from the British Library.

ISBN 978-0-7538-2572-3

Typeset by Input Data Services Ltd, Bridgwater, Somerset

Printed and bound in the UK by CPI Mackays, Chatham ME5 8TD

The Orion Publishing Group's policy is to use papers that are natural, renewable and recyclable products and made from wood grown in sustainable forests. The logging and manufacturing processes are expected to conform to the environmental regulations of the country of origin.

*To the loving memory of my mother*

MAGGIE

*1913–2006*

*and to my friend and colleague*

ROBERTO DAMIANI

creator of the indispensable
*www.condottieridiventura.it*

I ask you, generals, whom will you defeat? I ask you, comrades, whom will you imprison? Is it not I who support you? It is I who bestow on you wealth, luxury, and power. While I am a captain in arms and disturbing the peace of the kingdom you are called out to war when otherwise you would be sitting idle. It is I who have got for you the gold with which you glitter, your arms, horses, dress; and you who were but now nameless I have made illustrious. Do you then persecute me who am the source of your safety? Suppose I am taken or fall in battle. What profit would be left for you? Will you take thought for yourselves or for others? Will Italy be at peace when I am dead? Who finds peace advantageous except merchants or priests? Our trade is to bear arms. Do not let them rust in idleness. Consult for the common good. Vote for war and arms. Why should priests have such wealth and power? Who can endure that the pride of the Venetians should lord it over land and sea? What more shameful than that the Florentines should rule Tuscany? It is fair that those who wield arms should be the ones to rule kingdoms.

CONDOTTIERE JACOPO PICCININO, 1463

# CONTENTS

# LIST OF ILLUSTRATIONS

Study of Federico da Montefeltro, Palazzo Ducale, Urbino[2]

Sigismondo Malatesta kneeling before his patron, St Sigismund of Burgundy, Piero della Francesca, 1451, Tempio Malatestiano, Rimini[3]

The Flagellation of Christ, Piero della Francesca, *c.* 1463–4, Galleria Nazionale delle Marche, Urbino[3]

Madonna with Child showing Federico da Montefeltro, Piero della Francesca, Pinoteca de Brera, Milan[1]

Detail from Procession of the Magi, Bennozo Gozzoli, Palazzo Medici-Riccardi, Florence[1]

Pope Pius II at Ancona blesses the fleet about to leave for the holy land on 15 August 1464, Pinturicchio, 1503–8, Piccolomini Library, Duomo, Florence[3]

Pope Sixtus IV appoints Bartolommeo Platina as Director of the Vatican Library, Melozzo da Forlí, *c.* 1477, Vatican Museum[3]

[1] Scala, Florence
[2] AKG images
[3] Bridgeman Art Library
[4] British Museum
[5] author's photographs

# MAPS AND DIAGRAMS

## MAPS



## DIAGRAMS



## GENEALOGICAL TABLES

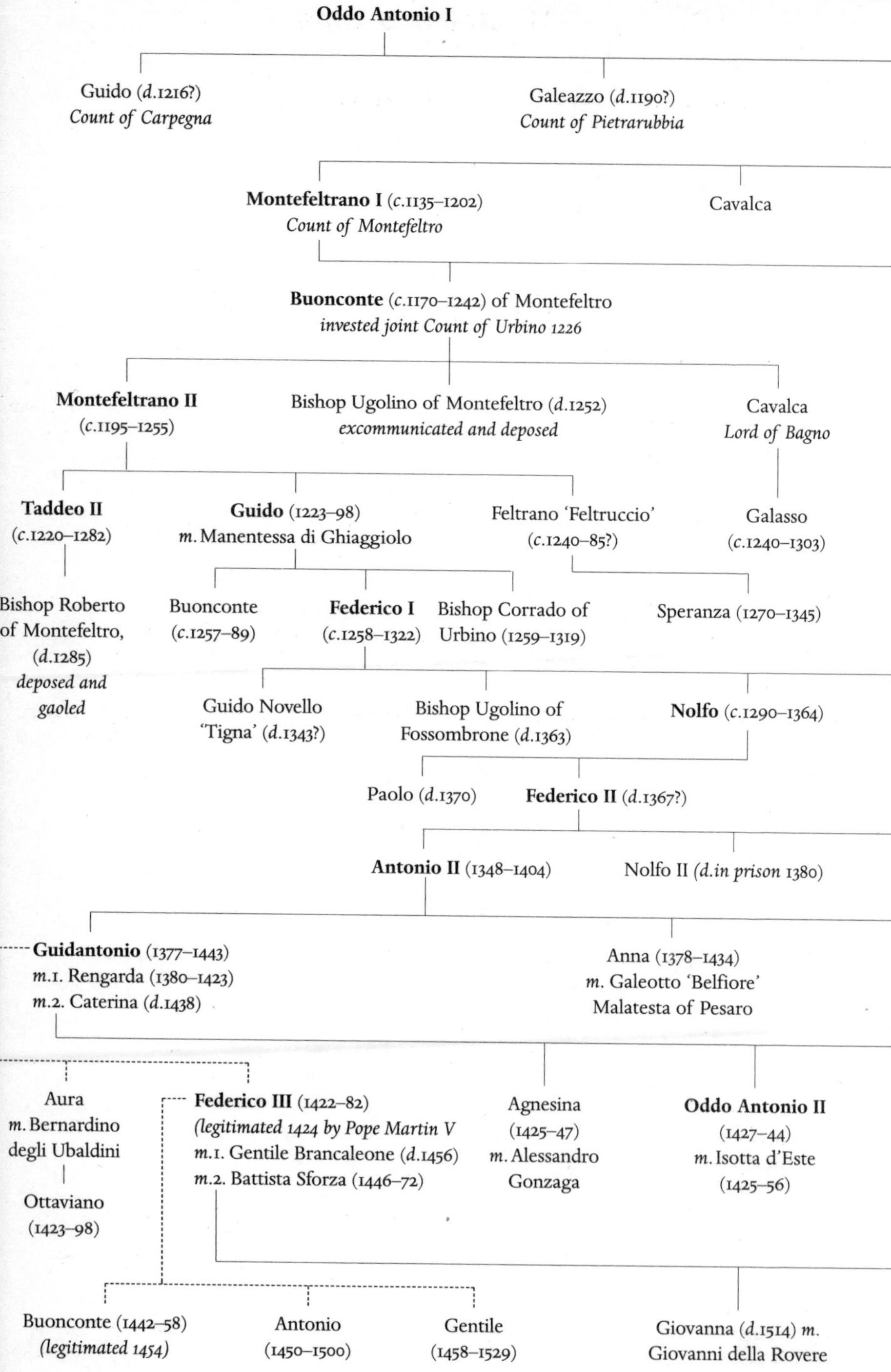

Oddo Antonio I
Guido (d.1216?)
Count of Carpegna
Galeazzo (d.1190?)
Count of Pietrarubbia
Montefeltrano I (c.1135–1202)
Count of Montefeltro
Cavalca
Buonconte (c.1170–1242) of Montefeltro
invested joint Count of Urbino 1226
Montefeltrano II
(c.1195–1255)
Bishop Ugolino of Montefeltro (d.1252)
excommunicated and deposed
Cavalca
Lord of Bagno
Taddeo II
(c.1220–1282)
Guido (1223–98)
m. Manentessa di Ghiaggiolo
Feltrano 'Feltruccio'
(c.1240–85?)
Galasso
(c.1240–1303)
Bishop Roberto
of Montefeltro,
(d.1285)
deposed and
gaoled
Buonconte
(c.1257–89)
Federico I
(c.1258–1322)
Bishop Corrado of
Urbino (1259–1319)
Speranza (1270–1345)
Guido Novello
'Tigna' (d.1343?)
Bishop Ugolino of
Fossombrone (d.1363)
Nolfo (c.1290–1364)
Paolo (d.1370)
Federico II (d.1367?)
Antonio II (1348–1404)
Nolfo II (d.in prison 1380)
Guidantonio (1377–1443)
m.1. Rengarda (1380–1423)
m.2. Caterina (d.1438)
Anna (1378–1434)
m. Galeotto 'Belfiore'
Malatesta of Pesaro
Aura
m. Bernardino
degli Ubaldini
Ottaviano
(1423–98)
Federico III (1422–82)
(legitimated 1424 by Pope Martin V
m.1. Gentile Brancaleone (d.1456)
m.2. Battista Sforza (1446–72)
Agnesina
(1425–47)
m. Alessandro
Gonzaga
Oddo Antonio II
(1427–44)
m. Isotta d'Este
(1425–56)
Buonconte (1442–58)
(legitimated 1454)
Antonio
(1450–1500)
Gentile
(1458–1529)
Giovanna (d.1514) m.
Giovanni della Rovere

## —*Montefeltro Clan*—

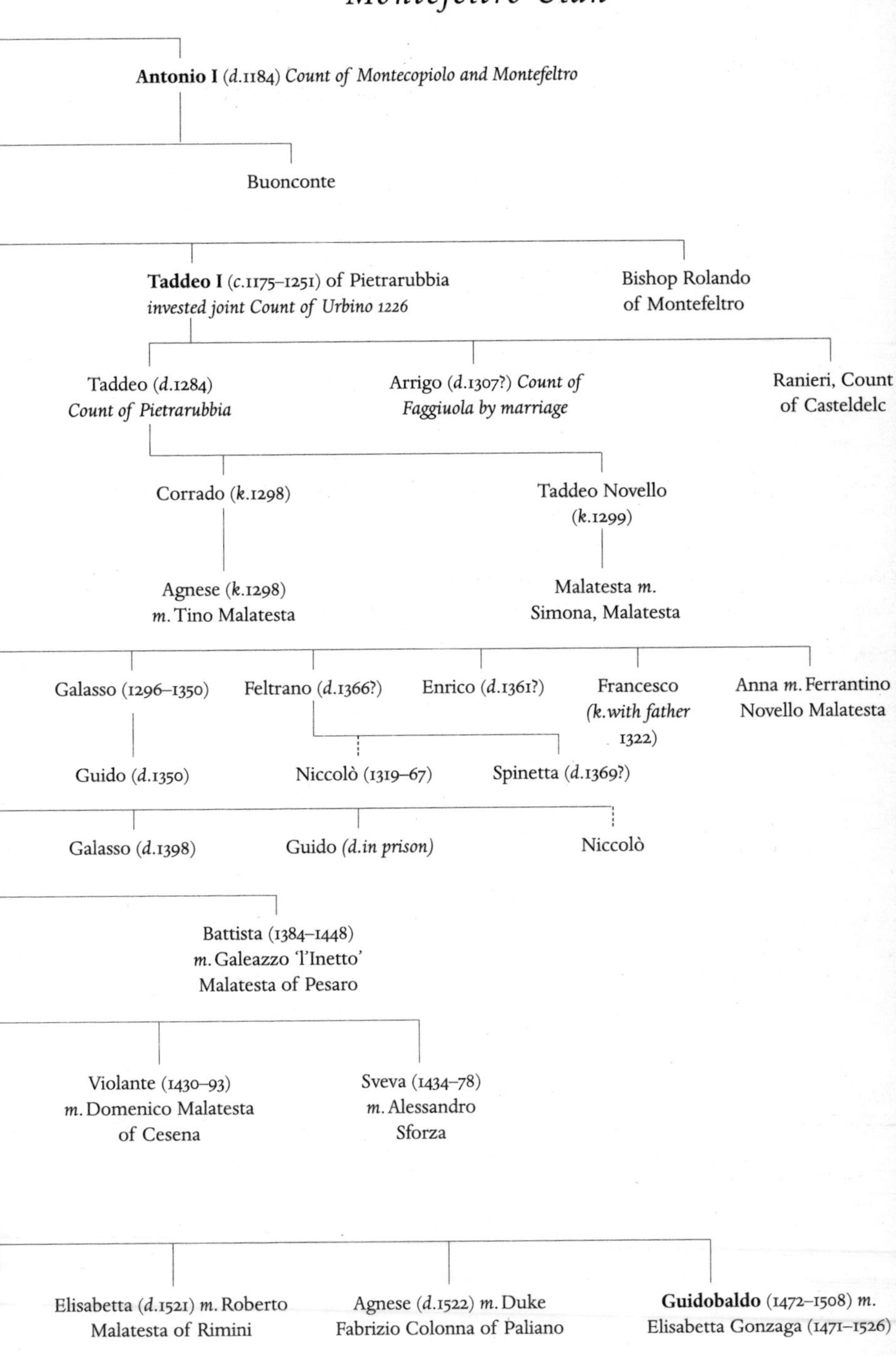

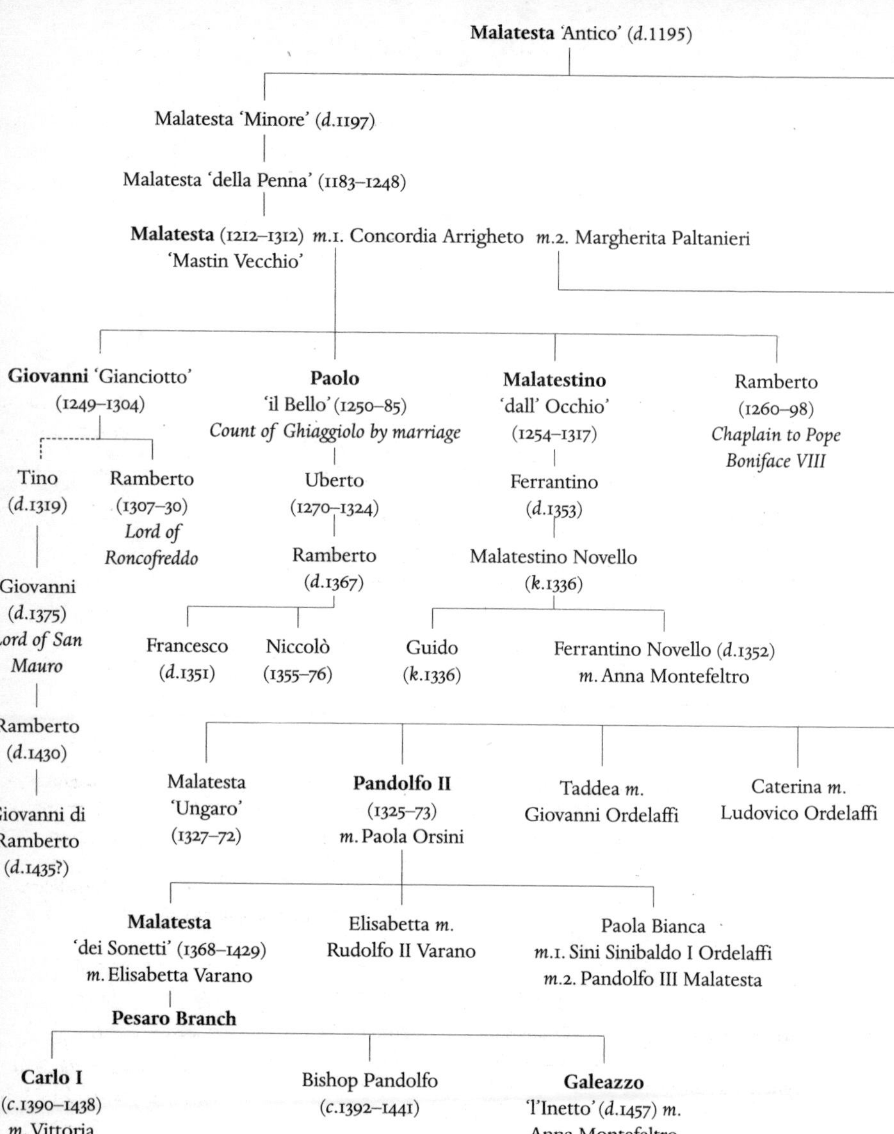


—*Malatesta Clan*—

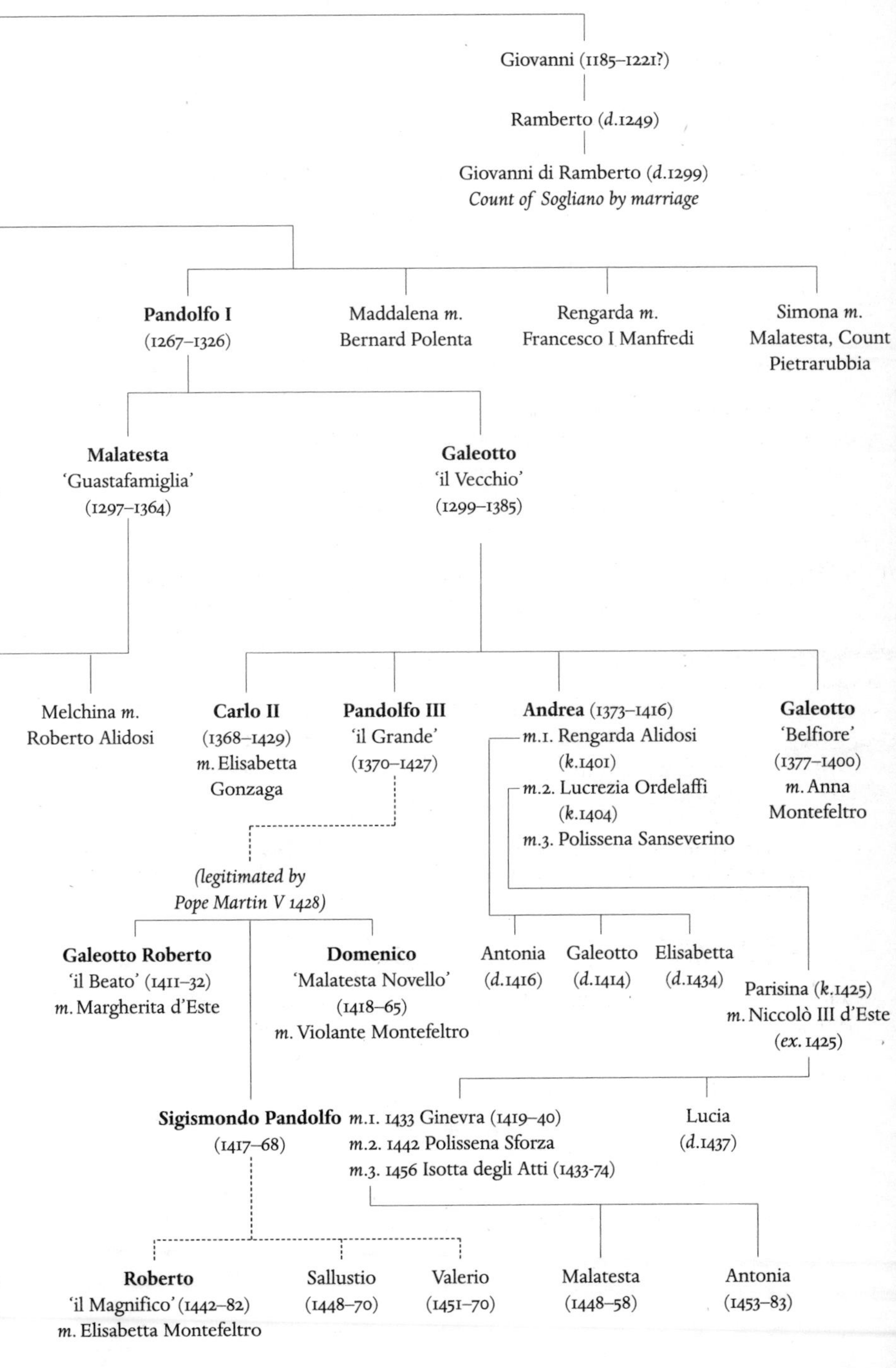

Giovanni (1185–1221?)
Ramberto (*d.*1249)
Giovanni di Ramberto (*d.*1299)
*Count of Sogliano by marriage*
**Pandolfo I** (1267–1326)
Maddalena *m.* Bernard Polenta
Rengarda *m.* Francesco I Manfredi
Simona *m.* Malatesta, Count Pietrarubbia
**Malatesta** 'Guastafamiglia' (1297–1364)
**Galeotto** 'il Vecchio' (1299–1385)
Melchina *m.* Roberto Alidosi
**Carlo II** (1368–1429) *m.* Elisabetta Gonzaga
**Pandolfo III** 'il Grande' (1370–1427)
**Andrea** (1373–1416)
*m.*1. Rengarda Alidosi (*k.*1401)
*m.*2. Lucrezia Ordelaffi (*k.*1404)
*m.*3. Polissena Sanseverino
**Galeotto** 'Belfiore' (1377–1400) *m.* Anna Montefeltro
*(legitimated by Pope Martin V 1428)*
**Galeotto Roberto** 'il Beato' (1411–32) *m.* Margherita d'Este
**Domenico** 'Malatesta Novello' (1418–65) *m.* Violante Montefeltro
Antonia (*d.*1416)
Galeotto (*d.*1414)
Elisabetta (*d.*1434)
Parisina (*k.*1425) *m.* Niccolò III d'Este (*ex.* 1425)
**Sigismondo Pandolfo** (1417–68)
*m.*1. 1433 Ginevra (1419–40)
*m.*2. 1442 Polissena Sforza
*m.*3. 1456 Isotta degli Atti (1433-74)
Lucia (*d.*1437)
**Roberto** 'il Magnifico' (1442–82) *m.* Elisabetta Montefeltro
Sallustio (1448–70)
Valerio (1451–70)
Malatesta (1448–58)
Antonia (1453–83)

# MAJOR PLAYERS

## THIRTEENTH CENTURY

### *Papacy*

**Innocent III** [Segni] (1198–1216), thanks to the death in 1197 of Emperor Henry VI Hohenstaufen and the minority of his son, Innocent III exercised more secular power than any other pope; he also preached crusades to the Holy Land in 1201 and 1217, and against the heretical Albigensians (Cathars) in 1209.

**Honorius III** (1216–27), a peacemaker whose good faith was abused by Emperor Frederick II and the Montefeltri, among others.

**Gregory IX** [Segni] (1227–41), upon accession excommunicated Frederick II, precipitating a bitter civil war in Italy.

**Alexander IV** [Segni] (1254–61), broke his oath as guardian of Frederick II's infant son Conradin and attempted to conquer the Southern Kingdom for the Papacy.

**Urban IV** (1261–64), French pope who declared Charles I of Anjou the rightful ruler of the Southern Kingdom in order to defeat, and kill, the heirs of Frederick II.

**Nicholas III** [Orsini] (1277–80), schemed against the House of Anjou with the Ghibelline lords to create a new kingdom in northern Italy for his family.

**Boniface VIII** [Caetani] (1294–1303), made the most extreme claim of papal sovereignty (over all mankind), kidnapped by rival Caetani clan and agents of the French king; his successors moved to France (Avignon) where the Papacy remained until 1377.

### *Empire*

**Frederick II Hohenstaufen** (d. 1250), heir to Southern Kingdom 1198, king of Germany 1212, Holy Roman Emperor 1220; his struggle with the Papacy ended in defeat in 1248.

**Conrad, Manfred & Conradin**, respectively son, illegitimate son and grandson of Frederick II, all died or were killed in a vain effort to recover the Hohenstaufen position in Italy.

## *Southern Kingdoms*

**Charles I of Anjou** (d. 1285), conquered the kingdom in 1268, lost Sicily to a popular rebellion (the Sicilian Vespers) in 1282; succeeded by **Charles II** (d. 1309).

**Peter I of Aragon** (d. 1285), elected king of Sicily 1282.

**Frederick III of Aragon** (d. 1337), elected king of Sicily 1285.

## *Malatesta Clan*

**Malatesta da Verucchio** [*Mastin Vecchio* – Old Mastiff] (d. 1312), centenarian who gained Savignano al Rubicone and Gradara by purchase and Ghiaggiolo by the marriage of son Paolo, defeated the Parcitadi clan to secure the overlordship of Rimini in 1295.

**Giovanni** [*Gianciotto* – the Lame] (d. 1304), eldest son of Mastin Vecchio, murdered his wife Francesca da Polenta and his younger brother **Paolo** [*il Bello* – the Handsome] in 1285, causing the estrangement of the Ghiaggiolo Malatesti; banished to a minor domain by his father and murdered in turn, probably by brother Malatestino.

## *Montefeltro Clan*

**Buonconte** (d. 1242), joint clan leader with brother Taddeo I.

**Taddeo I** (d. 1251), sole clan leader from 1242 who split the family by switching allegiance from the imperial (Ghibelline) to the papal (Guelf) cause.

**Taddeo II** (d. 1282), eldest son of Buonconte, who remained loyal to the Guelf cause and befriended Mastin Vecchio, killed leading an assault on Forlí, held by brother Guido.

**Guido** (d. 1298), second son of Buonconte, leader of the Romagna Ghibellines, renowned warrior who seemed to have lost everything by 1285 but who recovered most of the clan lands by 1294, only to become a monk and bequeath much of it to the Church; previously lost Ghiaggiolo and his allies the Parcitadi lost Rimini to the Malatesti.

**Galasso** (d. 1303), cousin of Taddeo II and Guido, leader of the Marche Ghibellines.

## FOURTEENTH CENTURY

### *Papacy*

**Innocent VI** (1352–62), sent Cardinal Albornoz to recover the Papal State from 1353.

**Gregory XI** (1371–78), returned Papacy to Rome.

**Urban VI** (1378–89), first Italian pope since 1303, his election precipitated the Western Schism, with Avignon antipopes elected in 1378 and 1395

### *Milan (Visconti)*

**Bernabò** (d. 1385), ruler of Milan and main mover of the war with the Papacy.

**Galeazzo II** (d. 1378), younger brother of Bernabò and ruler of Pavia.

**Gian' Galeazzo** (d. 1402), heir to Galeazzo II, killed uncle Bernabò to become ruler of a unified state, which he expanded by conquest; bought title of duke from the emperor in 1395.

### *Southern Kingdoms*

**Joanna I of Naples** (k. 1382), had first husband Andrew of Anjou–Hungary murdered in 1345, co–ruled with second husband Louis of Taranto 1352–62, backed Avignon in the Western Schism and declared Louis I of Anjou–Provence her heir, deposed by Urban VI in favour of Charles of Durazzo, backed by Hungary, who had her imprisoned and murdered. Her legacy was a long struggle among the three Angevin factions.

### *Malatesta Clan*

**Malatestino** [*dal'Occhio* – the One-Eyed], second son of Mastin Vecchio, clan leader until his death in 1317.

**Ferrantino** (d. 1353), **Malatestino Novello** & **Guido** (k. 1336) and **Ferrantino Novello** (d. 1352), line of Malatestino dal' Occhio who lost the struggle for clan leadership with the sons of Pandolfo I.

**Pandolfo I** (1267–1326), youngest son of Mastin Vecchio, clan leader until his death in 1326.

**Malatesta** [*Guastafamiglia* – family devastator] (d. 1364), eldest son of Pandolfo I, clan leader with brother Galeotto; humbled by Cardinal Albornoz in 1355, by 1357 they were fully rehabilitated and Galeotto was appointed *Gonfaloniere* (standard-bearer) of the Church.

**Galeotto** [*il Vecchio* – the Old One] (d. 1385), a notable warrior, joint clan leader with Guastafamiglia until 1364, with Guastafamiglia's sons until 1372–3, sole leader thereafter.

**Pandolfo II** (d. 1373) and **Malatesta** [*Ungaro* – the Hungarian] (d. 1372), sons of Guastafamiglia, joint clan leaders with uncle Galeotto.

**Carlo II** (d. 1429), acknowledged as *primus inter pares* by brothers **Pandolfo III** (d. 1427), **Andrea** (d. 1416) and **Galeotto** [*Belfiore* – beautiful flower] (d. 1400).

### *Montefeltro Clan*

**Federico I** (d. 1322), son of Guido, killed by an Urbino mob.

**Speranza** (d. 1345), cousin of Federico, leader of March Ghibellines.

**Nolfo I** (d. 1364), eldest son of Federico I, joint ruler of Urbino with brother Galasso; virtually dispossessed by Cardinal Albornoz in 1354.

**Galasso** and son **Guido** (d. 1350), conspired with Speranza and the Malatesti against Nolfo, expelled from Urbino in 1334.

**Antonio II** (d. 1404), leader when clan fortunes were at their lowest ebb, recovered them through brilliant diplomacy and military daring during the Eight Saints War (1375–78).

**Nolfo II** (d. 1380) and **Galasso** (d. 1398), disloyal brothers of Antonio II.

### *Condottieri*

**Werner of Ürslingen** (d. 1354), founder of the Great Company, mainly German knights.

**Montréal d'Albarno** [Fra Moriale] (k. 1354), led the Great Company when it was by far the largest military force in Italy.

**Conrad of Landau** (k. 1363), led a fragment of the Great Company until defeated and killed by Hawkwood.

**Sir John Hawkwood** [Giovanni Acuto] (d. 1394), led the White Company, including many English men-at-arms and longbowmen; ended his career as captain-general of Florence, honoured in death by a Paolo Uccello fresco in the Florence Duomo.

**Alberico da Barbiano** (d. 1409), founder of all-Italian Company of St George; proclaimed 'saviour of Italy' by Pope Urban VI for defeating Breton mercenaries fighting for Antipope Clement VII in 1379.

**Jacopo dal Verme** (d. 1409), field commander for the Visconti of Milan.

## FIFTEENTH CENTURY

### *Papacy*

**Martin V** [Colonna] (1417–31), his election marked the end of the Western Schism; devoted his papacy to advancing the cause of his family, mainly at the expense of the Malatesti.

**Eugenius IV** (d. 1447), Venetian who set out to undo Martin V's nepotism but was driven from Rome to Florence in 1434; sent Cardinal Vitelleschi (k. 1440) to restore papal authority in the Marche; recognised Alfonso of Aragon as king of Naples and returned to Rome 1443.

**Nicholas V** (d. 1455), founder of the Vatican Library who began to restore Rome to glory; showed considerable favour towards Sigismondo Malatesta.

**Pius II** [Piccolomini] (1458–64), brought about the undoing of Sigismondo Malatesta in close alliance with Federico III Montefeltro but was frustrated in his ambition to place a member of his own family in Rimini.

**Paul II** (d. 1471), Venetian whose attempt to seize Rimini on the death of Sigismondo was frustrated by Federico Montefeltro and Sigismondo's son Roberto.

**Sixtus IV** [della Rovere] (d. 1484), builder of the Sistine Chapel, involved the Papacy in assassinations and wars to advance his family, which ultimately came to rule an independent dukedom that encompassed the ancestral lands of the both Montefeltri and Malatesti.

### *Milan*

**Filippo Maria Visconti** (1412–47), extraordinarily devious ruler who combined with Alfonso of Aragon to divide Italy between them but whose life's work was undone by failure to produce a male heir and the marriage of his daughter to Francesco Sforza.

**Francesco Sforza** (1450–66), the most successful condottiere of them all, founded a dynasty that ruled Milan until 1535. The line of brother **Alessandro** (d. 1473) ruled Pesaro until 1512.

## *Southern Kingdoms*

**Joanna II of Naples** (1414–35), like her luckless namesake, her reign was plagued by strife among the Angevin factions, prompting her to adopt Alfonso of Aragon as heir; later she repudiated Alfonso and adopted Louis of Anjou–Provence.

**Alfonso** (d. 1458), king of Sicily (1411), of Aragon (1416) and of Naples (1435), mortal enemy of Sigismondo Malatesta, he made Federico III Montefeltro his captain-general.

**Ferrante of Naples** (d. 1494), legitimised son of Alfonso, allied with Pope Pius II to crush Sigismondo Malatesta.

## *Malatesta Clan*

**Malatesta** [*dei Sonetti* – of the Sonnets] (d. 1429), grandson of Malatesta 'Guastafamiglia' who felt fobbed off with Pesaro and Fossombrone by the heirs of Galeotto 'il Vecchio' and died preparing a coup against them, which failed in 1431 under his son **Carlo I** (d. 1438).

**Galeazzo** [*l'Inetto* – the Inept] (d. 1457), youngest son of Sonetti, sold Fossombrone to Federico III Montefeltro and Pesaro to Alessandro Sforza for a pittance in 1445.

**Galeotto Roberto** [*il Beato* – the Pious] (d. 1432), eldest legitimised son of Pandolfo III, ruled Rimini from 1429 until death from fasting and self-inflicted wounds.

**Sigismondo Pandolfo** (d. 1468), second legitimised son of Pandolfo III, ruled Fano from 1429, Rimini from 1432, brilliant soldier, extravagant lover and patron of the arts, but a ruinous politician who saw his domain reduced to Rimini alone by 1461.

**Domenico** [Malatesta Novello] (d. 1465), third legitimised son of Pandolfo III, ruled Cesena from 1429, as often as not in conflict with Sigismondo.

**Isotta degli Atti** (d. 1474), with Sigismondo, whom she married in 1456, protagonist of one of the great love affairs; with no surviving male issue she adopted two of Sigismondo's sons by another and tried unsuccessfully to ensure their succession against Roberto.

**Roberto** [*il Magnifico* – the Magnificent] (d. 1482), legitimised son of Sigismondo, in alliance with Federico III Montefeltro tricked Pope Paul II to gain control of Rimini and murdered the two half-brothers adopted by Isotta to ensure it; he was murdered by the della Roveres immediately after he destroyed the army of Ferrante of Naples on behalf of Sixtus IV.

## *Montefeltro Clan*

**Guidantonio** (d. 1443), after the death of childless Rengarda Malatesta in 1423 married Caterina, niece of Pope Martin V, and reopened hostilities with the Malatesti after a thirty-year truce; fearing that he might die heirless he claimed as his own Federico, child of his illegitimate daughter Aura and the condottiere Bernardino Ubaldini, and had him legitimised in 1424; by Caterina had Oddo Antonio and three daughters of whom Violante married Domenico Malatesta and Sveva married Alessandro Sforza.

**Oddo Antonio II** (k. 1444), gentle and ineffectual, murdered by agents of Federico.

**Federico III** (d. 1482), while his brother Ottaviano Ubaldini (d. 1498) governed Urbino during his many absences, in alliance with Pope Pius II and Ferrante of Naples he brought the long vendetta between Urbino and Rimini to a close with the complete defeat of Sigismondo in 1461; the highest-paid condottiere of his time, he and Ottaviano made Urbino one of the epicentres of the Italian Renaissance.

## *Condottieri*

**Muzio 'Sforza' Attendolo** (d. 1424), ended his days as grand constable of Naples, drowned in a river crossing on his way to confront lifelong rival Andrea Fortebraccio; sons Francesco and Alessandro became the lords of Milan and Pesaro.

**Andrea 'Braccio di Montone' Fortebraccio** (d. 1424), carved out a principality for himself in the Marche that did not survive his death in battle at the hands of Sforza's successors.

**Francesco 'Carmagnola' Bussone** (k. 1432), highly successful commander for Filippo Maria Visconti, earning his distrust; also successful after he defected to Venice but later his lacklustre performance aroused suspicion; tortured and executed for treason.

**Niccolò 'da Tolentino' Mauruzzi** (k. 1435), key figure in left-hand panel of Paolo Uccello's *San Romano* triptych, honoured in death by a fresco in the Florence Duomo.

**Bernardino 'della Carda' Ubaldini** (d. 1437), allegedly the black knight being unhorsed in the central panel of the *San Romano* triptych; real father of Federico III Montefeltro.

**Erasmo 'Gattamelata' da Narni** (d. 1443), loyal servant of Venice, his equestrian statue by Donatello stands in the main square of Padua.

**Niccolò Piccinino** (d. 1444), Filippo Maria Visconti's captain-general against the allied Papacy, Venice and Florence, extorted permission to maraud in Umbria and was defeated at Anghiari by Micheletto Attendolo; honoured in death by Filippo Maria, his monument in the Milan Duomo was destroyed by Francesco Sforza.

**Micheletto Attendolo** (d. 1451), key figure in right-hand panel of the *San Romano* triptych, which may portray his victory for Florence over Niccolò Piccinino at Anghiari in 1440; also grand constable of Naples and captain-general of Venice.

**Jacopo Piccinino** (d. 1465), adopted son of Niccolò and the last condottiere to win an independent principality for himself; his father-in-law Francesco Sforza conspired with Ferrante of Naples to disarm Jacopos caution, leading to his imprisonment and murder.

**Bartolomeo Colleoni** (d. 1475), outstanding military commander of his day, he fought for Filippo Maria Visconti and Francesco Sforza, and also against them on behalf of Venice, in whose service he died; a splendid equestrian statue of him by Verrocchio stands in the Piazza Giovanni e Paolo in Venice, which stole most of the rest of his estate.

S.Giorgio di Piano 1443
BOLOGNA
Casalecchio 1402
Zappolino 1325
Molinella 1467
Via Emilia
Santerno
Senio
Lamone
Lugo
Bagnacavallo
RAVENNA
Zagonara 1424
Cotignola (Sforza)
Barbiano
IMOLA
Sanguinario 1434
San Procolo 1274
FAENZA (Manfredi)
Montone
Ronco
(Polenti)
Savio
salt flats
Cervia
(Alidosi)
San Ruffillo 1361
Brisighella
FORLÌ (Ordelaffi)
Bussecchio 1393
1282
Castel del Rio
Lamone
Forlimpopoli
Cesenatico
Castrocaro
1423
Bertinoro
Monte Accianico
Firenzuola
Susinana (Pagani)
(Ubaldini)
Frassina
Palazzuolo
Marzeno
Modigliana
Meldola 1462
CESENA
Pisciatello
Rocca delle Caminate (Mussolini's castle)
Predappio
Polenta
San Mauro
Marradi
Savignano
Montiano
Mugello
Le Scallele 1358
Longiano
1389
Roncofreddo
Sant'Arcangelo
Montone
Rabbi
Bidente
Monleone
Rubicone
Poggio
GOTHIC LINE 1944
1276 1291
Ghiaggiolo
Civitella di Romagna
Sogliano
Scarperia
Montegelli
Scorticata
Torriana
Verucchio
ROMAGNA
Paderno 1287
Montebello
Marecchia
San Marino
Sarsina
Pietracuta
1390
Savio
Perticara
Talamello
San Leo
Sant'Agata Feltria
Maiolo
Bagno di Romagna
Montefeltro
M.Cerignone
Petrella Guidi
Macerata Feltria
Pennabilli
FLORENCE
TUSCANY
Pietrarubbia
Mercatino
Castelcavallino 1324
Casteldelci
1458
Montelocco 1441
Carpegna
Sassocorvaro
Campaldino 1289
Frontino
Lunano
Poppi
Foglia
See Map 9 for Arno valley battlefields
Sestino
Piandimeleto
Mercatello
Massa Trabaria
Metauro
Sant'Angelo in Vado
Arno
Tiber
San Sepolcro
Apecchio (Ubaldini)
Carda
Montevarchi
Anghiari 1440
Poggibonsi
AREZZO
UMBRIA (SPOLETO)
Montaperti 1260
Valdichiana
Citá di Castello (Vitelli)
Montone (Fortebracci)
SIENA
Fratta Umbertide 1387/88/89
Marciano

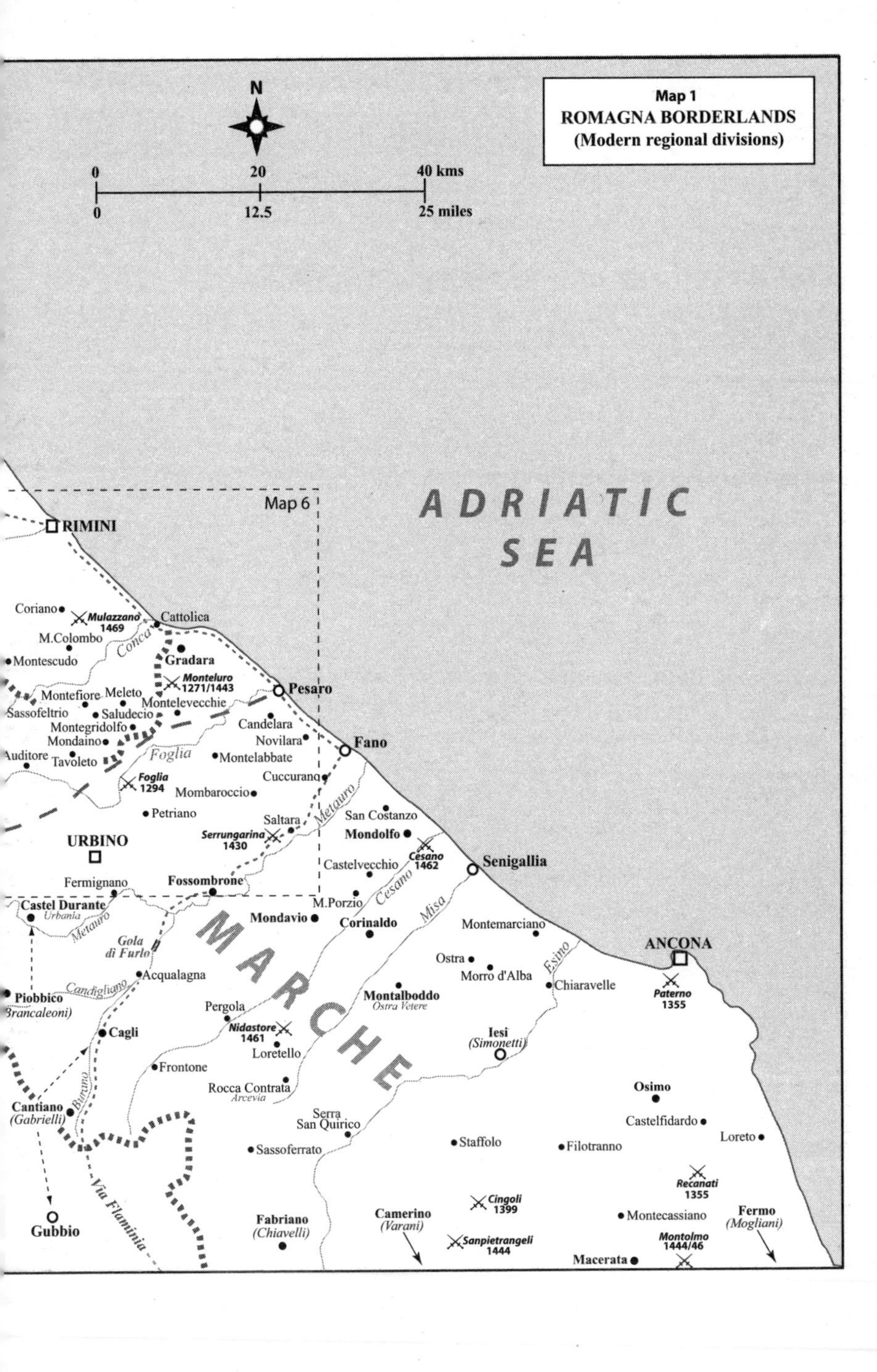

Map 1
ROMAGNA BORDERLANDS
(Modern regional divisions)
N
0
20
40 kms
0
12.5
25 miles
ADRIATIC
SEA
Map 6
RIMINI
Coriano
Mulazzano
1469
Cattolica
M.Colombo
Conca
Montescudo
Gradara
Monteluro
1271/1443
Montefiore
Meleto
Pesaro
Sassofeltrio
Saludecio
Montelevecchie
Montegridolfo
Candelara
Mondaino
Novilara
Fano
Auditore
Tavoleto
Foglia
Montelabbate
Foglia
1294
Cuccurano
Mombaroccio
Petriano
Metauro
San Costanzo
Saltara
Serrungarina
1430
Mondolfo
URBINO
Cesano
1462
Castelvecchio
Senigallia
Fermignano
Fossombrone
Castel Durante
Urbania
Metauro
M.Porzio
Cesano
Mondavio
Corinaldo
Misa
Montemarciano
Gola
di Furlo
MARCHE
ANCONA
Ostra
Morro d'Alba
Esino
Acqualagna
Chiaravelle
Candigliano
Paterno
1355
Piobbico
(Brancaleoni)
Montalboddo
Ostra Vetere
Pergola
Nidastore
1461
Iesi
(Simonetti)
Cagli
Loretello
Frontone
Osimo
Rocca Contrata
Arcevia
Cantiano
(Gabrielli)
Burano
Serra
San Quirico
Castelfidardo
Loreto
Staffolo
Filotranno
Sassoferrato
Recanati
1355
Via Flaminia
Cingoli
1399
Camerino
(Varani)
Montecassiano
Fermo
(Mogliani)
Gubbio
Fabriano
(Chiavelli)
Sanpietrangeli
1444
Montolmo
1444/46
Macerata

# INTRODUCTION

Strong, bold and proud they gaze from the walls and over the public places of Italy: the condottieri, the military impresarios who put their stamp on two centuries of Italian history, splendidly celebrated by the great artists of their time. Thanks to the frescos of them on adjacent walls of the Duomo in Florence, the two best known of these warriors are Sir John 'Giovanni Acuto' Hawkwood (Picture section 1, p. 4) and Niccolò 'da Tolentino' Mauruzzi. Donatello's portrayal of Erasmo 'Gattamelata' Narni, the first major equestrian bronze cast since antiquity, is somewhat lost in the expanse of Padua's Piazza del Santo, but Verrocchio's fierce bronze of Bartolomeo Colleoni, defying unseen enemies and time alike, dominates Piazza Giovanni e Paolo in Venice.* These great works of art represent the payment of an unwritten contract of honour, in most respects more binding than the commissions *(condotte)* from which the condottieri took their name. For although it was an age when belief in life after death was strong, it was no less a time when men pursued secular glory in the hope that future generations should remember them.

Their spirits must be content: no other cohort of soldiers has attracted anything like as much attention. The most distinguished families of Italy look back to condottieri ancestors but none has been more written about than Federico III Montefeltro and Sigismondo Pandolfo Malatesta, respectively lords of Urbino and Rimini, who brought the centuries-old vendetta between their clans to a climax in the mid fifteenth century. Montefeltro is a title dating from an investiture by Emperor Frederick 'Barbarossa' in 1150 and is properly

* Life or reign dates follow names in the Index.

'da Montefeltro', but I have dropped the 'da' for convenience. Malatesta, 'bad head', was the name – or more probably the nickname – of the founder of the family fortune, who was born in the Montefeltro district and by the time of his death in 1195 had acquired significant holdings by purchase and marriage within the Montefeltro and around Rimini. Usually one member of every succeeding generation was christened Malatesta and to avoid confusion I use their individual nicknames.

The two families were destined to be prickly neighbours, but what turned their rivalry into an all-consuming feud was the struggle for supremacy between the Papacy and the Holy Roman Emperor in the thirteenth century. Even had they wished to stand aside the Montefeltri and Malatesti could not have been neutral in the greater struggle because the title, the very terms under which they held their lands, was fiercely disputed between Church and Empire. As we shall see, mere skill at arms was never enough to secure the warring clans' hold over their lands – the crucial quality was *furbizia*, the intelligent cunning that distinguishes successful businessmen and politicians from the herd.

The Age of the Condottieri overlapped with an era that has become of obsessive interest to academics and, as tends to happen when scholars get the bit between their teeth, the result has been to lay down a foundation of semantic flypaper, full of historical judgements about the period. Thus the late fifteenth through sixteenth centuries are tagged with the French term 'Renaissance' because some believe it witnessed a rebirth of human creativity after a long period of stagnation after the extinction of the Western Roman Empire in AD 476, dubbed

**FRANCESCO PETRARCA (1304–74)**

**Scholar born in Arezzo who spent his early life at the papal court in Avignon. He wrote poetry (*Canzoniere* and *Trionfi*) in Tuscan dialect and popularised the sonnet. He was crowned Poet Laureate at Rome in 1341 in a ceremony revived from the Classical era. He was a pioneer of the cult of antiquity and his major works (among them *De Viris Ilustribus*, an imaginary dialogue with St Augustine) were in Latin. He spent his last years at the Visconti court in Padua.**

the 'Dark Ages' by the Tuscan poet and scholar Petrarch. There is a strong case for regarding both terms – Renaissance and Dark Ages – as misleading clichés, not least because St Thomas Aquinas wrote *Summa Theologiae* in the darkest of the 'Dark Ages'.

Petrarch is considered the father of 'Humanism', summarily defined as the quest for truth and morality by human means, particularly reason. The concept begs the question why the study of humanity for its own sake should be considered a thing apart from, or in conflict with, the spiritual dimension that has inspired so much hope and artistic expression. False dichotomy or not, the reason there are more than 14,000 titles listed under 'Renaissance' on Amazon.com is that the term 'university' was born of the Humanist belief that an elite community of scholars might aspire to learn all there is to know, so in a broad sense Renaissance research is an affirmation of traditional academic life. Scholars who argue that the era is distinguished mainly because it is so much better documented than preceding centuries have made little impression on the academic juggernaut and, to judge from the phenomenal success of *The Da Vinci Code*, none at all on popular consciousness.

In the mid fifteenth century Flavio Biondo coined the term 'Middle Age' to describe the period between the Classical Age and a Modern Age of Humanism, which might have provided a neutral alternative to the judgement explicit in the term 'Dark Ages'. Unfortunately over time the adjective 'medieval' acquired the old semantic baggage and is now synonymous with all that is ignorant, cruel and reactionary. Sadly Humanism itself in due course mutated into the arrogant, genocidal and 'Progressive' ideologies that made the twentieth century such a severe trial for those who wished to believe well of humankind. This said, as a way of thought Humanism remains the prism through which we in the West observe our world, and perhaps the quintessential Humanist pursuit is the study of history as a fact-based attempt to understand the past.

Humanism is said to have rediscovered the cultural values of Classical Antiquity, although it is highly debatable whether or not those values were ever really lost or, indeed, whether they were regained in the late Middle Ages. The medieval code of chivalry would seem to be in direct line of descent from the Homeric warrior's overarching desire for public esteem and his willingness to die rather than suffer dishonour. Not so the soldiers and rulers of the Renaissance, who desired principally money and ostentatious power on one hand, and on the other were unconstrained by considerations of honour in their business and personal lives. They were in fact very modern in outlook and employed the trappings of Classical Antiquity mainly to ornament – or perhaps more accurately to disguise – a subversive outlook on life that welcomed innovation in art, architecture and philosophy. One of the threads woven loosely through the following pages is that while the Age of the Condottieri was destructive, it was a highly creative destruction that cleared the ground for the flowering of the imagination generally known as the Renaissance.

'History with its flickering lamp stumbles along the trail of the past,' said Winston Churchill, 'trying to reconstruct its scenes, to revive its echoes, and kindle with pale gleams the passions of former days.' History's lamp gleams paler still when presenting an English-speaking readership with a theme taken from the past of another culture, which makes it essential to explain the complex background, the deep context without which any historical work is merely anecdotal. Academics writing for other academics and Italian scholars writing for Italians can assume their readers will be familiar with the broad outlines, the geography and with many of the rulers (Appendix A) and I could not have written this book without the works starred and double starred in my Bibliography. I seek to address a broader audience, however, and to that end I have leavened the text with graphics to assist the process. Not even Italians are likely to be familiar with all the towns and villages in Map 1, the most significant of which are revisited in the last chapter, the 'Coda', where I guide the reader through the historical landscape of the Romagna–Marche borderlands. Maps 2–3 (pp. 8–9) show the topographical armature that underlies the political divisions of Italy and Map 4 the Roman infrastructure that has considerable bearing on our story. Later maps and diagrams illustrate more specific points.

My purpose is also polemical and if it inspires others to pound out rebuttals of this or that aspect of my overview, then so much the better. There is undoubtedly a need, across the board, to emerge from the shadow of a generation of scholars who deprecated individuality and embraced, openly or tacitly, the theory of history proposed by Karl Marx and Friedrich Engels. The collectivist school tried to identify deep currents in which individuals are little more than the puppets of vast impersonal forces, to arrive at supposedly inevitable conclusions. Their agenda was always clear and their falsification of history often flagrant. They also made it stupefyingly dull. History, like biological evolution, is contingent and if you could rerun the tape you would get a different outcome every time. Great schemes collapse, small ones bear disproportionate fruit, winners lose and losers win according to unpredictable circumstances alone.

When dealing with the late Middle Ages it is also necessary to swim against a more recent historicist current, which has crept in since the long overdue collapse of the Marxist world-view. Americans are conditioned to believe the rise to dominance of their society was as historically inevitable as Marx thought the rise of the proletariat would be.* Their desire to perceive a Dark Ages to Renaissance to Enlightenment progression, crowned by the emergence of the Great Republic, found its clearest expression in Francis Fukuyama's 1992 'End of History' thesis, which boiled down to a blithe belief that all the great ideological issues were resolved and the 'American Way' would henceforth reign supreme.

Along with the American Way has come a high colonic of intellectual fads generally known as 'Political Correctness', in origin little more than an effort by leftist US academics to shrink all of human existence to fit within their own parochial agenda. While researching this book it became apparent that many modern academics do not let their often wide research impinge on the foregone conclusions dictated by their sadly limited personal and institutional agendas. For example, Anderson and Zinsser, in the introduction to their otherwise valuable two-volume study of women in European history, state that 'the central thesis of this book is that gender [by which they mean sexual asymmetry as a social construct] has been the most important factor in shaping the lives of European women'. More important than endemic death in childbirth, heartbreakingly high infant mortality and holocausts like the Black Death?

---

* See my *Rebels & Redcoats* (2003) for a discussion of the US Foundation Myth.

The ruling-class women who appear in *Vendetta* were counters in a dynastic game but they were often also full partners in the struggle for survival, capable in their own right of ruling a state, defending a fortress or plotting the downfall of rivals. The proper corrective to history written with women as wallpaper is not to write a 'History of Women in the Middle Ages' but to write one in which they are active participants alongside the more headline-capturing men. While it is true that women are marginalised in much of the source material, usually written to exalt and flatter male patrons, it does not require much historical imagination to fill in the blanks. Even if only when their men were away, a great deal of state administration and diplomacy must have been conducted by and among women. No one should doubt that women were, are and ever more shall be as able, ambitious and even more devious than men, and that although sexual dimorphism ruled them out of actual combat in the era of muscle power they were probably braver as a sex and certainly no more gentle and peace-loving than men.

**NICCOLÒ MACHIAVELLI (1469–1527)**

**Florentine scholar and government official best known for *The Prince*, a treatise on political pragmatism written in 1513 to curry favour with the recently restored Medici dynasty, although at the same time (1512–17) he wrote *Discourses on Livy*, which revealed strong republican sympathies through an idealised vision of pre-imperial Rome.**

Anyone writing about the condottieri must also labour against the highly influential legacy of Niccolò Machiavelli, who argued in his *Discourses* and in his 1520 book *The Art of War* that mercenaries were a waste of money and that those with a stake in their community should have formed militias. Merchants, manufacturers and bankers could no more become warriors on demand than they could design attractive buildings, paint beautiful frescos or write learned treatises. They understood money, which is why they hired specialists across the board. The real watershed between the period known as the Renaissance and preceding centuries was the emergence of the cash economy, but the will for it to have been otherwise lingers. Victor Davis Hanson's *Why the West Has Won* includes the judgement that after the battle of Lepanto in 1571 'the future of military dynamism . . . returned to the old paradigm of classical antiquity: superior technology, capital-creating economies, *and civic militias*' (my italics). The last time a militia was successful prior to the guerrilla wars of the nineteenth century was when the Swiss won their independence in the late fourteenth century – but having done so they became highly effective mercenaries, their militia origins a very dim memory by the time Lepanto was fought.*

In terms of classical economics the condottieri phenomenon was straightforward. First, skill at arms was the most valued of all the specialist talents unleashed by the late medieval commercial and industrial revolutions. Second, supply boosted demand as buyers who had not previously contemplated military adventures were tempted by the availability of 'freelance' soldiers for hire, and early suppliers made their fortunes easily. Third, as the market clearing point approached, buyers became more discriminating and the cost of entry rose steeply, while some condottieri made hostile takeovers upstream to become buyers in their own right. Fourth, the 1454 Peace of Lodi, which presaged the end of the Age of the Condottieri, was an attempt to create a buyers' cartel but broke down because, before welfare became the preferred mechanism, warfare was the main method by which rulers could justify centralising power and increasing taxation. Finally, following the French invasion of Italy in 1493, the system suffered the fate of all closed markets when exposed to international competition and the days of the independent Italian military entrepreneur were numbered.

While it is important to make allowance for the manner in which contemporary concerns tend to shape the interpretation of history, humankind's recidivism in matters of mass folly makes it historically valid to identify occasions in the past that clearly prefigure some of the Gadarene stampedes of our own time. It is no less desirable to show how perceptions of the past have shaped the present and of these perceptions probably the most important has been the legacy of imperial Rome, the tent pole of Western culture. The cultural ramifications

* For a more detailed discussion see my *Crescent and Cross* (2003).

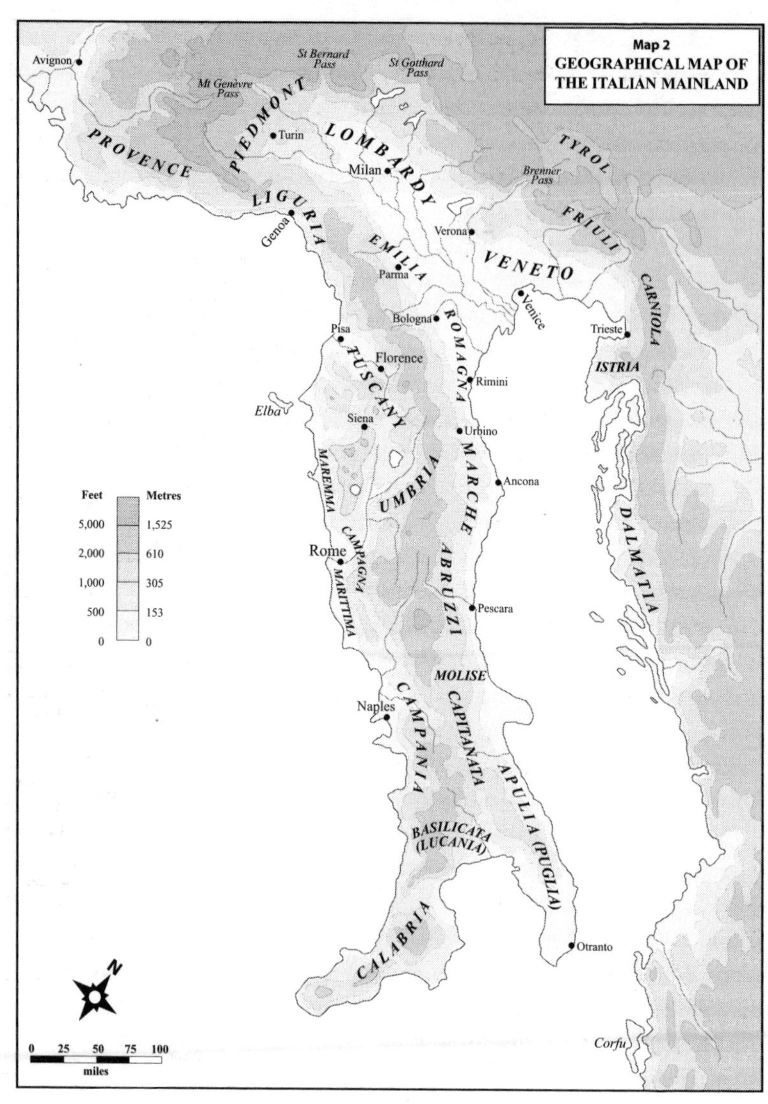

Map 2
GEOGRAPHICAL MAP OF THE ITALIAN MAINLAND
Avignon
St Bernard Pass
St Gotthard Pass
Mt Genèvre Pass
PIEDMONT
Turin
LOMBARDY
PROVENCE
Milan
TYROL
Brenner Pass
LIGURIA
Genoa
EMILIA
Parma
Verona
VENETO
FRIULI
CARNIOLA
Venice
Bologna
ROMAGNA
Trieste
Pisa
Florence
TUSCANY
Rimini
ISTRIA
Elba
Siena
Urbino
MAREMMA
UMBRIA
MARCHE
Ancona
Feet
Metres
5,000
1,525
2,000
610
1,000
305
500
153
0
0
CAMPAGNA
Rome
MARITTIMA
ABRUZZI
Pescara
DALMATIA
MOLISE
Naples
CAMPANIA
CAPITANATA
APULIA (PUGLIA)
BASILICATA (LUCANIA)
CALABRIA
Otranto
N
0 25 50 75 100
miles
Corfu

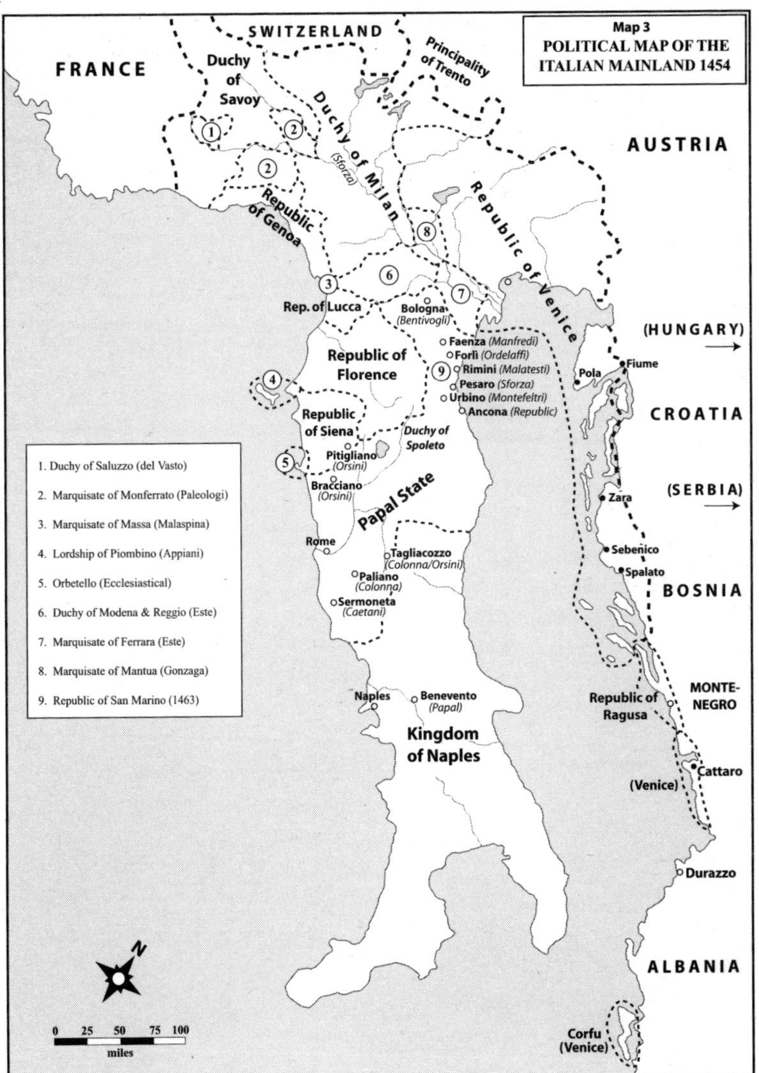
Map 3
POLITICAL MAP OF THE ITALIAN MAINLAND 1454
SWITZERLAND
FRANCE
Duchy of Savoy
Principality of Trento
Duchy of Milan
(Sforza)
AUSTRIA
Republic of Genoa
Republic of Venice
Rep. of Lucca
Bologna (Bentivogli)
(HUNGARY)
Faenza (Manfredi)
Forlì (Ordelaffi)
Rimini (Malatesti)
Pesaro (Sforza)
Urbino (Montefeltri)
Ancona (Republic)
Republic of Florence
Pola
Fiume
CROATIA
Republic of Siena
Duchy of Spoleto
Pitigliano (Orsini)
Bracciano (Orsini)
Papal State
(SERBIA)
Zara
Rome
Tagliacozzo (Colonna/Orsini)
Sebenico
Spalato
Paliano (Colonna)
Sermoneta (Caetani)
BOSNIA
1. Duchy of Saluzzo (del Vasto)
2. Marquisate of Monferrato (Paleologi)
3. Marquisate of Massa (Malaspina)
4. Lordship of Piombino (Appiani)
5. Orbetello (Ecclesiastical)
6. Duchy of Modena & Reggio (Este)
7. Marquisate of Ferrara (Este)
8. Marquisate of Mantua (Gonzaga)
9. Republic of San Marino (1463)
Naples
Benevento (Papal)
Republic of Ragusa
MONTE-NEGRO
Kingdom of Naples
Cattaro
(Venice)
Durazzo
N
ALBANIA
0 25 50 75 100
miles
Corfu (Venice)

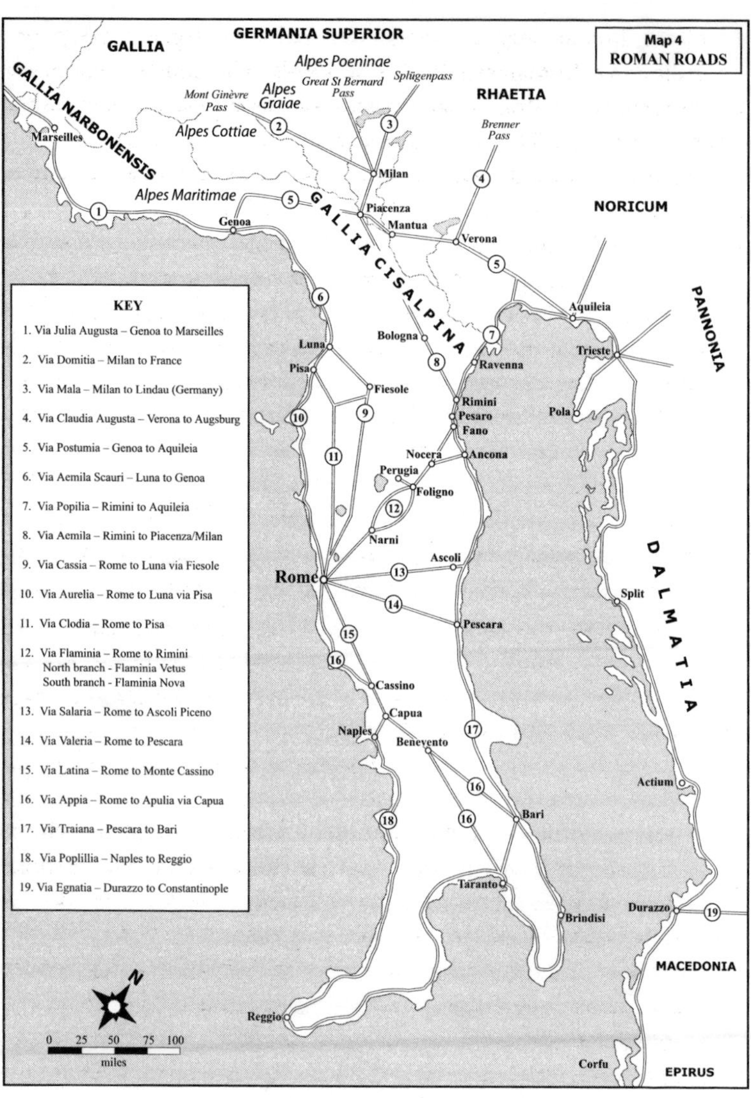
Map 4
ROMAN ROADS
GALLIA
GERMANIA SUPERIOR
RHAETIA
NORICUM
PANNONIA
DALMATIA
MACEDONIA
EPIRUS
GALLIA NARBONENSIS
GALLIA CISALPINA
Alpes Poeninae
Great St Bernard Pass
Splügenpass
Mont Ginèvre Pass
Alpes Graiae
Alpes Cottiae
Alpes Maritimae
Brenner Pass
Marseilles
Genoa
Milan
Piacenza
Mantua
Verona
Aquileia
Trieste
Pola
Bologna
Ravenna
Luna
Pisa
Fiesole
Rimini
Pesaro
Fano
Ancona
Nocera
Perugia
Foligno
Narni
Ascoli
Rome
Pescara
Split
Cassino
Capua
Naples
Benevento
Actium
Bari
Taranto
Brindisi
Durazzo
Reggio
Corfu
KEY
1. Via Julia Augusta – Genoa to Marseilles
2. Via Domitia – Milan to France
3. Via Mala – Milan to Lindau (Germany)
4. Via Claudia Augusta – Verona to Augsburg
5. Via Postumia – Genoa to Aquileia
6. Via Aemila Scauri – Luna to Genoa
7. Via Popilia – Rimini to Aquileia
8. Via Aemila – Rimini to Piacenza/Milan
9. Via Cassia – Rome to Luna via Fiesole
10. Via Aurelia – Rome to Luna via Pisa
11. Via Clodia – Rome to Pisa
12. Via Flaminia – Rome to Rimini
North branch - Flaminia Vetus
South branch - Flaminia Nova
13. Via Salaria – Rome to Ascoli Piceno
14. Via Valeria – Rome to Pescara
15. Via Latina – Rome to Monte Cassino
16. Via Appia – Rome to Apulia via Capua
17. Via Traiana – Pescara to Bari
18. Via Poplillia – Naples to Reggio
19. Via Egnatia – Durazzo to Constantinople
N
0 25 50 75 100
miles

of the Roman legacy include the Arthurian legend, based on the exploits of Romanised British warlords who fought against Saxon invaders after Roman administration withdrew from the islands. Thanks to Sir Thomas Malory, whose *Le Morte d'Arthur* first gave the myth its modern form in 1469–70, then to romantic Victorian illustrators and finally to Hollywood, King Arthur and the Knights of the Round Table will forever inhabit a late medieval era of sword, shield and plate armour. The myth of course was much older – 150 years before Malory, in *L'Inferno* V, 127–38, Dante linked the doomed thirteenth-century passion of lovers Francesca da Polenta and her brother-in-law Paolo Malatesta to their reading about Lancelot and Guinevere (see Picture section 1, p. 3).

**DANTE ALIGHIERI (1265–1321)**

**Poet who wrote *La Divina Commedia* (*The Divine Play*), the first major literary work to be written in the Tuscan dialect, which became the basis for the Italian language. *Commedia* is an epic of a hundred cantos divided into *Inferno, Purgatorio* and *Paradiso*, of which the first in particular contains open or veiled allusions to a number of individuals who shaped Italian history in the late Middle Ages.**

The reputation of the condottieri owes much to depictions by some of the greatest artists in history but, like Malory's literary creation, the portraits and statues represent a romantic ideal. An early example is Simone de Martini's 1330 fresco of Guidoriccio da Fogliano in Siena's Palazzo Pubblico (Picture section 1, p. 4). The artistic convention of heroes in soft raiment showing their faces and armoured villains dehumanised in closed helmets was laid down in Paolo Uccello's *The Battle of San Romano* (Picture section 1, pp. 6–7), perhaps the most famous depiction of a battle in the history of art. Now divided among the National Gallery in London, the Louvre in Paris and the Uffizi in Florence, Uccello's triptych reflects a time when the Age of the Condottieri was at its apogee. *San Romano* is closely linked to our story because the Darth Vader-like knight unhorsed in the central panel is supposed to be Bernardino 'della Carda' Ubaldini, the biological father of

Federico III Montefeltro whose lifelong confrontation with Sigismondo Pandolfo Malatesta was the climax of the feud around which this book is written.

The fires of vendetta are fuelled by cherished memories of wrongs done by the warring parties' ancestors to each other. To outsiders it may all seem pointlessly destructive, but mutual hatred becomes almost genetically programmed in the families involved and may become the defining feature of their existence. This was certainly the case with the Montefeltro and Malatesta clans, which, with one tantalising but ultimately sterile hiatus in the late fourteenth and early fifteenth centuries, tore at each other over three centuries until both were exhausted. At the climax of the vendetta Federico and Sigismondo fought it out as though goaded by ancestral armies of unquiet warrior souls. And what souls they were! Surely no other rivalry has featured so many colourfully desperate characters, or so much crime, treachery and passion.

Federico built a fairy-tale palace at Urbino, where a glittering court flourished, and enjoyed the support and counsel of his brother, Ottaviano degli Ubaldini, who had acquired the reputation of being a magus. The parallels between Federico's castle and retinue with the mythic Arthur's court at Camelot, his counsellor Merlin the Magician and Arthur's conception by trickery could hardly be more exact. Edward IV of England, who emerged the victor from the renewed struggle for the throne during which Malory was in prison writing *Le Morte d'Arthur*, made Federico a Knight of the Garter in 1474, so clearly his fame had long transcended the borders of Italy. While it is not impossible that Malory drew some inspiration from what he heard about Federico, by far the most likely explanation for the coincidences is that Malory's fictional creation and Federico's cultivated image both reflected chivalrous conventions and golden-age myths common across contemporary European cultures. The main reason why historians have tended to portray Federico as the virtuous and honourable exception to the condottieri rule is that he consciously encouraged them to draw the Arthurian parallel. 'Spin' is not a modern invention. The facts behind the image are that he became lord of Urbino by an act of fratricidal usurpation and achieved eminence more by the exercise of treacherous *furbizia* than by military skill.

Every hero needs a villain and, again according to the canonical accounts, Federico drew one of history's best. Sigismondo Malatesta was the illegitimate son of Pandolfo III, lord of Fano and a notable condottiere, lover and patron of the arts. When Pandolfo III died in 1427 his childless brother Carlo II, lord of Rimini and Cesena and the Papal Rector of Romagna, became the guardian of Pandolfo's three sons. When Carlo II died two years later he left Rimini to the monkish Galeotto Roberto, while Fano went to Sigismondo and Cesena to the youngest son, Domenico, known as Malatesta Novello. Sigismondo became lord of Rimini after the ascetic Galeotto died of self-inflicted punishment and privation in 1431. Unlike Federico and his Merlin-like brother Ottaviano in Urbino, however, Sigismondo and Domenico, the surviving Malatesta brothers, harboured little affection for each other and were more often enemies than allies.

Domenico had good reason to disassociate himself from his brother. Sigismondo was a human earthquake who relished his evil reputation, describing himself as 'more wild beast than man' – although he probably did so because the fear of his name enhanced his price in the condottieri market. He was indeed among the foremost field commanders of his time, his presence worth a thousand men in battle, but a reputation for wild savagery proved a bad business choice and enabled his enemies to paint him as a psychopath. Wild he was, but psychopaths cannot love and one of the defining features of Sigismondo's life was that he adored his mistress Isotta degli Atti, finally marrying her at a time when his circumstances urgently demanded a dynastic wedding accompanied by a large dowry. Perhaps the most telling refutation of his black legend is that the area his family once ruled still proudly proclaims itself 'Malatestaland' on signs bearing the distinctive silhouette taken from Piero della Francesca's portrait of Sigismondo (Picture section 2, p. 3).

Although Pope Pius II, born Aeneas Silvius Piccolomini, was the man most responsible for blackening his reputation, even he recognised Sigismondo's charisma:

> Sigismondo, of the noble family of Malatesta but illegitimate, was very vigorous in body and mind, gifted with great eloquence and military ability. He had a thorough knowledge of history and no

slight acquaintance with philosophy. Whatever he attempted he seemed born for, but in him evil inclinations were always uppermost. He was such a slave to avarice that he was ready not only to plunder but to steal. His lust was so unbridled that he violated his daughters and his sons-in-law. As a youngster he dressed as a woman and sometimes he played the woman to men, sometimes made men women to him. No marriage was sacred to him. He polluted sacred virgins and coupled with Jewish women. He had boys and girls who did not submit to him killed or cruelly beaten. He had no belief in another world and thought the soul died with the body. Nevertheless he built at Rimini a splendid church dedicated to St Francis, though he filled it so full with pagan works of art that it seemed less a Christian sanctuary than a temple of heathen devil-worshippers. He outdid all barbarians in cruelty. His bloody hands inflicted terrible punishment on innocent and guilty alike. He oppressed the poor and despoiled the rich of their goods, sparing neither widows nor orphans. Nobody could feel secure under his dominion. . . . Such was Sigismondo: intolerant of peace, devoted to pleasure – although able and willing to endure the hardships and avid for war – the worst of all men who have ever been or shall be, the dishonour of Italy and the disgrace of our century.

Ecclesiasts of the time commonly employed extremes of vituperation, which opened the door to one of the most celebrated jibes in *The Decline and Fall of the Roman Empire*, Edward Gibbon's late eighteenth-century masterpiece of dry scepticism. With reference to the impeachment of Antipope John XXIII in 1415 Gibbon wrote: 'the most scandalous charges were suppressed; the vicar of Christ was only accused of piracy, murder, rape, sodomy, and incest.'* Pius II, the only pope to have written a published autobiography, took the practice to extremes in his denunciation of Sigismondo and his prejudice has heavily coloured the historiography. Pius II is also generally praised as a Humanist, although if the term has any meaning beyond a desire not to be too beastly to one's fellow man it must involve scepticism about

* In the 1420s Cosimo de' Medici had Donatello and the young Michelozzo create a magnificent tomb for the first John XXIII in the Florence Baptistery.

the supernatural – a difficult feat for one professing to be the representative of the heavenly Father, Son and Holy Ghost. My curiosity about Sigismondo dates from reading, long ago, that he once responded to the insolence of Pius II's young nephew and legate by publicly sodomising him in the presence of his cheering troops. Unfortunately I cannot recall the source and have been unable to verify what would certainly explain, if true, Pius II's hysterical vindictiveness.

The struggle to destroy Sigismondo, which led to the apotheosis of his mortal rival Federico, defined Pius II's Papacy. Most histories portray it, fairly but inadequately, as simply one episode in the long struggle of the late medieval Papacy to turn nominal sovereignty into effective government over the Papal State, of which Rimini and Urbino formed a part. The secular authority of the Church, never undisputed and in practice usually based on the principle of divide and rule, became almost entirely dependent on hired soldiers from 1305, when the Papacy moved to Avignon. The institution returned to Rome in 1377 but did not begin to recover prestige and authority until the end of the Western Schism in 1417, when three shameful decades during which there were two and finally three rival popes were brought to a close by the drastic expedient of sacking all three incumbents, including John XXIII, and electing a new pope. By the time Pius II was elected in 1458 the Papacy had been for many years a major employer of condottieri to enforce, always selectively, the legal rights husbanded over centuries.

Although the period 1305–1417 marked the nadir of the Papacy, the Church continued to enjoy broad spiritual authority not only among humble people looking forward to a better life beyond the grave but among the wealthy and well-educated as well. Spiritual authority was not, however, easily transferred to the political sphere and because the Papacy was also a sovereign secular power, divine appeals or holy summons were often devalued by suspicions that their true purpose was simply to increase papal territory and revenues. Added to which the feature of life in the Papal State was uncertainty about all except that Rome, no matter how weak or desperate, would never relinquish sovereignty over any territory to which it had even the most tenuous claim. As Machiavelli put it in *The Prince,* 'only [the popes] have dominions and do not defend them, have subjects and do not govern them; and although their dominions are undefended they are not taken from them and their subjects, although they are not governed, pay no attention to the fact; nor do they, nor can they secede from papal dominion.'

In the following pages the greater aspirations and problems of the Papacy are interwoven with the Malatesta–Montefeltro vendetta because the origins of the feud cannot be understood in isolation from, in particular, the titanic clash between the Papacy and the Holy Roman Empire. Shakespeare based his story of the star-crossed lovers Romeo Montague and Juliet Capulet on a real vendetta between the two families in medieval Verona, identified by Dante as part of the Guelf–Ghibelline conflict that kept Italy devastated by civil wars during the greater part of the later Middle Ages. The names Guelf and Ghibelline came from the contest for the title of Emperor between the house of Welf (dukes of Bavaria) and the house of Hohenstaufen (dukes of Swabia), whose battle cry was 'Waiblingen' from their seat in Franconia. Waiblingen being unpronounceable in Italian, it became *Ghibellin*. The struggle between the Hohenstaufen dynasty and the Papacy from the mid twelfth to the mid thirteenth centuries led to the names being adopted by pre-existing factions in Italy, with *Guelfos* theoretically supporting the popes and *Ghibellinos* the emperors. In most places they might as well have been 'Red Team' and 'Blue Team', but in Romagna and the Marche, where much of our story unfolds, the issue of whether legitimate authority came from imperial decree or papal appointment was of vital significance.

Since the medieval Papacy favoured the emergence of republican communes in defiance of imperial authority, in principle the Guelfs should have been urban and commercial, the Ghibellines rural and aristocratic. Marxist historians have tried to make it so with a devotion worthy of a better cause but the bedrock of Italian culture is the family, from which rings of allegiance ripple out to encompass neighbourhood, commune and region, with an identity as a people persistently shimmering beyond. Religion matters – it always has – but except when in conflict with an alien ideology confers no greater legitimacy on the political machinations of the Papacy than on those of any secular power. Even the totalitarian sledgehammers of the twentieth century failed to crack the bedrock of Italian clannishness, so it is no surprise to find that family affiliation, even more than local politics and intercity rivalries, decided what banner people followed in the Middle Ages. It was against this background of misleadingly labelled opportunistic partisanship that the Montefeltro–Malatesta vendetta was fought out.

The Malatesti were usually and profitably affiliated with the Guelf cause until Sigismondo violently broke with tradition after one too many acts of papal bad faith. Mainly, one suspects, to insult the clergy, in 1451 he commissioned a doubly provocative fresco for his 'pagan temple' showing him kneeling in front of the Burgundian St Sigismund (Picture section 2, p. 6), who became the patron saint of Bohemia after Emperor Charles IV moved his remains to Prague. The insult lay in the fact that the saint was depicted with the face of Emperor Sigismund, Charles IV's second son, who knighted both Sigismondo and Federico in 1433. In a mirror image of the Malatesta family trajectory the Montefeltri could scarcely have been more associated with the imperial cause. They paid a very high price for their Ghibelline affiliation and by the time Federico seized power it had long been clear that the Montefeltri could not stand against Rome. Federico wisely set out to make himself the Papacy's favourite son and as a result the Montefeltri replaced the Malatesti as the dominant clan in the Romagna–Marche borderlands.

The political, social and cultural background to the Montefeltro–Malatesta rivalry has been well researched but their most enduring legacy to the land over which they fought, their fortifications, has been less so, and the natural topography scarcely at all. Yet one cannot visit Malatestaland and the hill country of the Montefeltro without being struck by the manner in which geology shaped the boundaries of their dispute. The amount of human energy and expense represented by all the works reviewed in 'Touring the Borderlands', the last chapter of this book, highlights some of the less examined aspects of the Age of the Condottieri. The first is the centripetal effect of small state anarchy, which obliged the rural population to coalesce into more easily defensible concentrations and was a factor in the emergence of the lords (*signori*) who could provide stability in a world of violence and uncertainty. The second is that while it may have been cheaper to pay extortion than to endure the depredations of invaders, the better but more expensive option was to build the fortifications to deter and to hire the soldiers necessary to combat the predators. There was, therefore, an economic imperative behind the emergence of the condottiere-lord, who could supplement the revenues from the lands that submitted to his rule by hiring out his own and his retainers' services to others.

### VLAD DRACULA (1431–76)

**Among Federico's and Sigismondo's contemporaries was the Wallachian Prince Vlad III 'the Impaler', also known as Dracula (little dragon), who was at times the subject and at others the savage enemy of the Ottomans in their inexorable conquest of the Balkans. The big dragon was his father Vlad 'Dracul', so called because he was a knight of the Imperial and Royal Dragon Court and Order, founded in 1408 by soon-to-be Emperor Sigismund.**

As well as geology, the history of the region was shaped by geographical proximity to the Christian outposts clinging to the edges of the Ottoman Empire across the Adriatic, sometimes in conflict but usually coexisting with their Muslim neighbours. The French historian Fernand Braudel speculated that the Apennines are as much a cultural as a physical watershed and one cannot fail to note that the unique signature of Federico Montefeltro's Urbino palace is the twin minarets flanking the balconies of the duke's private quarters (see p. 249). The minarets no doubt reflect the fact that the architect responsible, Luciano Laurana, was born in Dalmatian Zara. At the end of his life Sigismondo bought property in the Republic of Ragusa (today Dubrovnik) and his reputation has something of a Balkan flavour.

When Sigismondo's son Roberto murdered his younger siblings after their father's death he was following standard Ottoman practice in removing future foci of subversion, something earlier generations of Malatesti might have done more systematically to the benefit of their dynasty. As, indeed, might all the ruling families of Europe, although the experience of Richard III in England suggests that murdering one's relatives was no guarantee of an untroubled succession. That Roberto Malatesta became the *Gonfaloniere* (standard-bearer) of the Church and was known as 'il Magnifico' while his highly comparable contemporary Richard III became Shakespeare's evil hunchback simply illustrates that as far as posterity is concerned winning isn't everything – it's the only thing.

The contrast between the unfinished Tempio Malatestiano in Rimini, where Sigismondo and his beloved Isotta are buried, and massive Castel Sismondo that symbolised his potency in life, underlines that whatever late medieval rulers spent on decorating their environment, or even on the ecclesiastical works perhaps intended to shorten their stay in Purgatory, it was a drop in the ocean by comparison with what they were compelled to spend to defend their authority over their lands and towns. Leonardo da Vinci and Michelangelo Buonarroti, the greatest of the Old Masters, wished for nothing more than to win military contracts because that was where there was serious money to be made. In 1482 Leonardo wrote to Ludovico il Moro, Duke of Milan, detailing his ingenuity in designing machines that could bring decisive military advantage. Only at the end of the letter does he note that in time of peace, 'I can do whatever can be done in painting as well as anyone else'. In 1528, when competing for the reconstruction of the perimeter defences of Florence, Antonio da Sangallo sneered that Michelangelo was a 'mere' painter and sculptor, to which Michelangelo replied that although he had won 'some renown' in these fields, his principal interest lay in military engineering.

Thus our story combines many themes and my aim is to guide the reader through a landscape of memory where the hills, crags and their masonry adornments are reminders of an era full of passion – of lust, indeed – for life and for the thrill of risking it. Many believe that life was cheaply held because death by disease or violence could strike at any time, but the exact reverse was true: life was far more highly prized, and lived to the full by those able to do so, precisely because it was so precarious. At a time when knighthoods and titles of nobility are commonly awarded to individuals of unimpeachable mediocrity it is refreshing to study the lives of those with much to lose, who nonetheless gambled their skill and intelligence against the world. One could wish the castles and palaces they built were still venues of exuberant celebration rather than worthily dull civic museums; but a small effort of historical imagination can easily populate them with their creators, flaunting, feasting, fornicating and above all fighting their way from the pages of the history books into the heart of our culture.

# ONE

# *Birth of the Vendetta*

## CHAPTER SUMMARY

*The Montefeltri traced their origins to a Saxon knight granted a fief by the Holy Roman Emperor in 962, which included the district of Montefeltro. Their great rivals were descended from a parvenu known as 'Malatesta' (Bad Head) who acquired large land-holdings in Romagna by marriage and purchase in the later twelfth century. The key Malatesta holdings nearest Rimini had once been Montefeltro property. The ancestral lands of both clans lay in an area whose sovereignty was fiercely disputed between the empire and the Papacy, and their vendetta was nurtured by the fact that the Montefeltri were strongly identified with the imperial (Ghibelline) cause, while the Malatesti leaned towards the papal (Guelf) party. For much of the thirteenth century the Malatesti were led by the centenarian Malatesta de Verucchio, known to history as 'Mastin Vecchio' from a reference to him in Dante's* Inferno. *In the same period the main Montefeltri holdings were shared by brothers Buonconte and Taddeo I, briefly reunited under Montefeltrano I and then shared among his sons Taddeo II, Guido and Feltrano. The final showdown between the Papacy and the German–Sicilian Hohenstaufen dynasty under Emperor Frederick II split the Montefeltri, with Taddeo II leading the Guelf faction and Guido the Ghibelline. The breach only began to close after Taddeo II was killed leading an assault on Forlì, held by Guido, in 1282. Mastin Vecchio's leadership kept the Malatesti politically united but an affaire between his favourite son, Paolo 'il Bello', and the wife of his eldest, Giovanni 'Giancotto', ended with Giancotto killing them both in 1285. Giancotto was murdered in turn, probably by his one-eyed brother Malatestino, in 1304. In 1233 another prominent Rimini clan, the Parcitadi, was instrumental in making effective an imperial grant of strongly papal Urbino to the Montefeltri. Guido Montefeltro lost Urbino in 1286 but recovered it in 1294, overcoming the armed opposition of the Malatesti. In 1295 the Parcitadi, supported by Guido, tried to drive the Malatesti out of Rimini and were decisively outmanoeuvred, after which the Malatesti became the unquestioned lords of the city and its hinterland.*

The legacy of the prolonged struggle for power between the Papacy and the Holy Roman Empire, known as the 'Caesaro-Papal' conflict, has been scarcely less important for Europe than the inheritance of the old Roman Empire. We shall be examining the conflict mainly as it affected Italy but it impacted perhaps even more negatively on the political development of Germany: the tomb of Emperor Frederick II Hohenstaufen in Palermo is a place of pilgrimage for German tourists, testimony to a suspicion that their history took a horribly wrong turn after his death. Popes and emperors alike had daggers at their breasts, in Germany held by dynastic rivals and in Rome by local barons – and the mob, which did not see why priests and aristocrats should have all the fun. Christ's teaching to 'render unto Caesar the things that are Caesar's and to God the things that are God's' could be construed to work in favour of either party, but in practical terms the main advantage enjoyed by the Papacy was that while imperial authority rested on the personal dynamism of a given emperor, the Roman bureaucracy provided an iron continuity regardless of the personal qualities of the pontiffs. A fanatical commitment to the minutiae of the law, with which anyone who has been involved in a mainland European legal process will be painfully familiar, led to a ratchet-like process of incremental gains by which any concession by an emperor, however circumstantial, was held to be permanent, while any surrender of rights by a pope was not binding on his successors.

The Montefeltri claimed descent from the Saxon knight Udalric, invested Count of Carpegna and Pietrarubbia by Otto I, the first unarguable Holy Roman Emperor (962–73), in a deed signed at Viterbo in August 962. The deed granted Udalric all the fortified places between the Conca and the Marecchia rivers, including San Leo where at the time Berengar II, the last Frankish king of Italy, was under siege, plus Sestino, Carpegna and Pietrarubbia in the upper Foglia–Isauro basin (Map 6). The territory lay within Otto's donation to the Papacy and although the document is suspect it is dated after the emperor had learned that his donatee Pope John XII was scheming against him with Berengar's son. Other imperial grants were made at this time to the Brancaleoni, Dadei, Faggiuolini, Gaboardi and Olivieri in 'Flaminia', which suggests Otto wished to guard the old Roman road, still the main avenue from central to northern Italy, with his own men as insurance against further papal ingratitude. Something similar happened during the reign of Emperor Otto III (996–1002). He aspired to recreate the unified empire of Charlemagne and when he oversaw the election of his tutor to the Papacy they chose the name Sylvester II in evocation of the first Pope Sylvester who, in legend, founded the Christian Empire with Emperor Constantine in AD 313. Although Otto III renewed the donation of the eight counties of Byzantine Pentapolis (Marche) to Rome, he also confirmed the overlapping right of the Archbishopric of Ravenna, an imperial vassal and Rome's principal ecclesiastical rival, to the lands from the Reno to the Foglia rivers (Romagna) in succession to the Byzantine Exarchate of Ravenna. From the beginning, therefore, the Romagna–Marche borderlands were potentially at the front line of the Caesaro–Papal conflict.

Matters came to a head in the conflict between Pope Gregory VII and King Henry IV over the king's right to invest German bishops and abbots with the spiritual as well as secular symbols of their office. The best-known episode of the Investiture Conflict was the midwinter penance by Henry in 1077, still uncrowned and facing a major revolt in Germany, at the gates of Canossa in northern Italy, where Gregory had taken refuge, to beg revocation of the pope's edict of excommunication. Although highly dramatic, the episode resolved nothing and after consolidating his position in Germany Henry marched on Rome in 1084. Gregory refused to crown him emperor unless he paid feudal homage to him – that is, to acknowledge publicly that the pope was the emperor's secular as well as spiritual master. The Roman cardinals, happy to be rid of a reforming pope who threatened their comfortable lifestyles, deposed Gregory and elected Henry's antipope, the Archbishop of Ravenna, who as Pope Clement III placed the imperial crown on Henry's head. Gregory died soon afterwards with the bitter words 'I have loved justice and hated iniquity, therefore I die in exile' on his lips. However, Gregory had also set in motion a stratagem that simultaneously provided an outlet for the violence of Europe's mass of land-poor minor nobility and enhanced, too, the Church's moral authority: the Crusade. From the Synod of Clermont in 1095, where Pope Urban II issued the call to arms, eight crusades to the Holy Land and several more preached against Rome's Christian foes punctuated the Caesaro–Papal dispute.

**MAJOR CRUSADES**

**First Crusade 1095–99**
**Second Crusade 1145–49**
**Third Crusade 1189–92**
**Fourth Crusade 1201–04**
***Albigensian Crusade 1209–29***
**Fifth Crusade 1217–21**
**Sixth Crusade 1228–29**
***Stedinger Crusade 1232–43***
**Seventh Crusade 1248–54**
**Eighth Crusade 1270–72**
***Aragonese Crusade 1284–95***

The Investiture Conflict was put on hold by treaty in 1122, to grumble on until the next time the issue tore Europe apart in the sixteenth century, but it was not long before new protagonists found fresh cause to claw at each other. Round two came after the Welfs of Bavaria lost the struggle with the Swabian Hohenstaufen of Waiblingen for the kingship of Germany at the battle of Weinsburg in 1140. The reign of Frederick I Hohenstaufen, known as 'Barbarossa', was punctuated by expeditions to Italy starting in 1155 when he supported Pope Hadrian IV against republican forces led by the radically anti-materialist priest Arnold of Brescia, after which the pope crowned Barbarossa as Holy Roman Emperor. Unfortunately Barbarossa was disrespectful of papal prerogatives within the lands donated to the Church by previous emperors, for example by investing Antonio, one of Udalric's descendants, as Count of Montefeltro in 1150 and as imperial Vicar of Urbino in 1155. Pope Hadrian, for his part, broke the generous terms of the coronation treaty agreed with the emperor by allying with the rival Byzantine Empire against the Norman Hauteville dynasty of southern Italy, which the Papacy regarded as its own territory.

There followed the struggle to restore imperial authority over the Lombard communes, which were supported by the Papacy. Barbarossa's second expedition to crush a Milanese revolt led to his excommunication in 1160. Further unsuccessful expeditions followed in 1163 and 1168 but the fifth proved a disaster for the imperial army, culminating in crushing defeat by the papally blessed Lombard League at Legnano in May 1176. The emperor made peace with Pope Alexander III the following year and recognised Rome's sovereignty, in principle, over most of the territory that was to become the Papal State. Strife with the Lombard cities continued until 1183, when Barbarossa recognised their right to elect their own magistrates. To cement peace with the Church, in 1189 Barbarossa marched overland on the Third Crusade. Pausing to have a mortal illness cured by St Sava in Serbia, he drowned crossing a river in southern Anatolia.

The watershed of the Caesaro–Papal struggle came when Barbarossa's son Henry VI successfully claimed the succession to the Norman Kingdom of the Two Sicilies through his wife after the failure of the male Hauteville line. Among those who marched south with Henry was Montefeltrano I, Count of Montefeltro and Pietrarubbia. The imperial cause suffered a devastating double blow when Henry died in 1197 and Pope Innocent III was elected the following year. Nothing was more certain than that the Papacy would commit every resource at its disposal to prevent being gripped on either side by the imperial nutcracker, and the Roman aristocrat (Segni) Innocent was the hardest nut ever to occupy the throne of St Peter (Picture section 1). To compound the damage, Henry VI had appointed the Papacy guardian of his infant son Frederick, which permitted Innocent to play emperor-maker. Once more the battle-cries of 'Welf and 'Waiblingen' rang out over bloodstained German fields as the ruling houses of Bavaria and Swabia fought it out and it was at this time that, for no easily discernible reason, pre-existing Italian factions chose to style themselves *Guelfos* and *Ghibellinos*.

## KEY

**A. Achaia/ Morea** - Latin county, Angevin by marriage 1338, sold to Venice 1408, Ottoman conquest 1460-1503.

**B. Armagnac** - major player in Anglo-Franco-Burgundian wars.

**C. Artois** - Burgundian/Hapsburg county.

**D. Athens** - Latin duchy, won by Catalan Company 1311, sold 1388, Ottoman conquest 1460-64.

**E. Avignon** - Papal See from 1309, sold to Clement VI by Joanna I of Provence/Naples 1348.

**F. Brabant** - Burgundian/Hapsburg duchy.

**G. Calais** - English coastal enclave 1347-1558.

**H. Dauphiné** - chronic feud with Savoy, sold to France 1349.

**J. Ferrara** - Este domain 1240-1597 (and Modena 1288-1796).

**K. Flanders** - Burgundian county, constantly fought over.

**M. Hainaut** - Burgundian/Hapsburg county.

**O. Lorraine** - bone of endless Franco-German contention.

**P. Luxembourg** - dynasty subsumed by Hapsburgs 1437.

**Q. Lucca** - mainly sovereign republic until 1805.

**R. Majorca** - taken by crusade 1229, ruled by cadet line of Aragon until 1343.

**S. Mantua** - Gonzaga domain 1328-1707.

**T. Montpellier** - ruled by Aragonese kings of Majorca, sold to France 1349.

**U. Mystra** - Byzantine despotate, fell to Ottomans 1460, sacked by Sigismondo Malatesta 1464.

**V. Rhodes** - held by Knights of St John 1309-1522.

**W. Roussillon** - Mainly Aragonese/Spanish until 1642.

**Y. Siena** - sovereign republic absorbed by Florence 1559.

**Z. Thessalonika** – Byzantine, sold to Venice 1423, Ottoman conquest 1387-1405, and 1430.

## EARLY MONTEFELTRI

*(see Appendix B for full genealogy)*

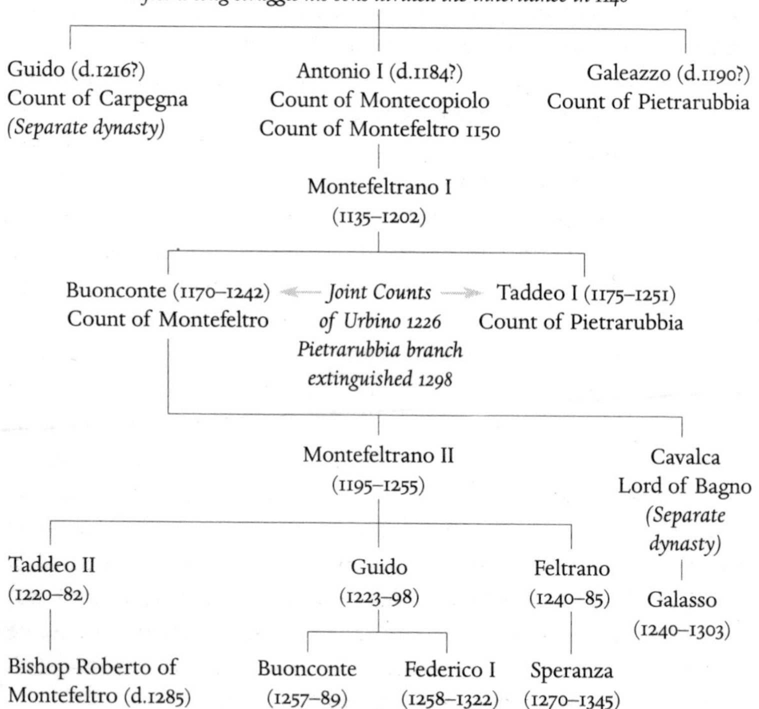


Following the death of Montefeltrano I in 1202 his eldest son Buonconte became Count of Montefeltro and the younger, Taddeo I, became Count of Pietrarubbia. Little is known of the third brother, Cavalca, except that his son, Galasso, was briefly the leader of the clan at the turn of the century. Ironically the clan's land tenure, based on imperial investitures not recognised by the Church, was in fact strengthened by an act of papal imperialism designed to dislodge them. Part of the price Innocent III extorted for the coronation of Emperor Otto IV in 1209 was imperial recognition of full papal sovereignty over a new trans-Apennine province of Massa Trabaria. To make it effective Innocent urged the authorities of papal Città di Castello, in the upper Tiber valley, to move against the Montefeltri and the Brancaleoni. The gambit misfired, as it prompted the authorities of Rimini, who had a mutually profitable association with Città as the Adriatic outlet for its goods, to make common cause with the threatened clans. Città, consequently, did nothing to disturb the status quo and its representatives became the advocates of the Montefeltri and Brancaleoni in Rome. Thus the best-laid plans of mice and popes.

In 1216, there being at the time no emperor, the two older Montefeltro brothers accepted confirmation of their titles from the peaceable Pope Honorius III (Picture section 1, p. 3), whose reign spanned the period between Innocent III and the second Segni Pope, Gregory IX. This was the first acknowledgement of even nominal papal sovereignty by any of the Montefeltri. Shortly afterwards Henry VI's son became king of Germany after Otto IV died in 1218, and Emperor Frederick II in 1220. The basic allegiance of the Montefeltri remained unchanged and in 1226, at a ceremony in San Leo allegedly attended by St Francis of Assisi (if so it was one of his last acts, for he died the same year), Buonconte and Taddeo were jointly invested with the County of Urbino as an imperial fief. Few places were more loyal to the Papacy than Urbino, however, and the citizens refused to recognise the brothers' investiture. The Urbino investiture was one of many provocations, but during Honorius's lifetime the tension between the Papacy and the Empire merely smouldered. It flared into the endgame of the Caesaro-Papal conflict with the election in 1227 of Gregory IX, one of whose first acts as pope was to excommunicate Frederick even though the emperor was about to embark on the Sixth Crusade, in which he recovered Jerusalem without fighting.

### ST FRANCIS OF ASSISI (1182–1226)

**It would be hard to overstate the importance of St Francis to the lords of the Romagna–Marche borderlands, who favoured the order he founded over all others. Many of them chose to be buried in the habit of the order and their widows commonly chose to enter the Franciscans' sister order of the Poor Clares. That some of the most bloody-handed men in history were drawn to one of the gentlest is not the least of the miracles attributed to the saint.**

The revival of the imperial cause led Rimini to grant citizenship to Buonconte and Taddeo I as well as their Carpegna cousins. Città di Castello, in turn, not only made the brothers citizens but also elected Buonconte chief magistrate *(podestà)* in 1231. The office remained in the family until 1246, during which time they built a palace, concluded alliances with nominally papal Cagli and Gubbio, and were the hosts and lieutenants to Frederick II in 1240 when Città became the base for his operations in central Italy. In Rimini the Montefeltri became associates of the Parcitadi (from the Latin for 'father of the city', a defunct civic office), a prominent Romagna merchant family. In a *furbo* (adjective of *furbizia*) deal the Montefeltri made the Parcitadi the beneficiaries of the market rights to the produce of Montefeltro and Urbino, which they had granted to Rimini in return for citizenship. Of course Urbino's market rights were not, at this time, in the gift of the Montefeltri – but it was now in the interest of the Parcitadi to make it so and when Ugolino Parcitade became *podestà* of Urbino in 1232–3 he was instrumental in negotiating the peaceful assumption of overlordship by the Montefeltri.

The Malatesti first appear in the history of Rimini in 1197 when Giovanni Malatesta, after a period of hostilities, made submission with a symbolic rope round his neck to grant the commune sovereignty over the lands inherited from his father, Malatesta 'Antico', and in his sole possession following the death of his older brother, Malatesta 'Minore'. Malatesta Antico had acquired the holdings by purchase and through marriage with a daughter of Pietro Traversari, a leading citizen of Ravenna, but how he rose from obscurity in the hard-scrabble Romagna highlands is not known. If, as family lore had it, he began life in Pennabilli, then he was born a subject of the Montefeltri and may have acquired properties mortgaged to pay for the long fratricidal struggle that ended in 1140 with the break-up of the Montefeltro inheritance into three separate domains: Carpegna, Pietrarubbia and Montecopiolo. Antonio of Montecopiolo was invested as the first Count of Montefeltro in 1150 and inherited Pietrarubbia from his uncle in 1190, but it was during the time of the Montefeltro clan civil war that Malatesta Antico put together his holdings. Four of the towns Giovanni Malatesta submitted to Rimini were part of the original Montefeltro patrimony: Scorticata, Saiano and Verucchio, which together control the mouth of the Marecchia valley, and Pennabilli itself in the upper valley. Possibly relations between the clans were soured from the start by lender-borrower animosity, exacerbated by social tension between a prosperous parvenu and spendthrift aristocrats.

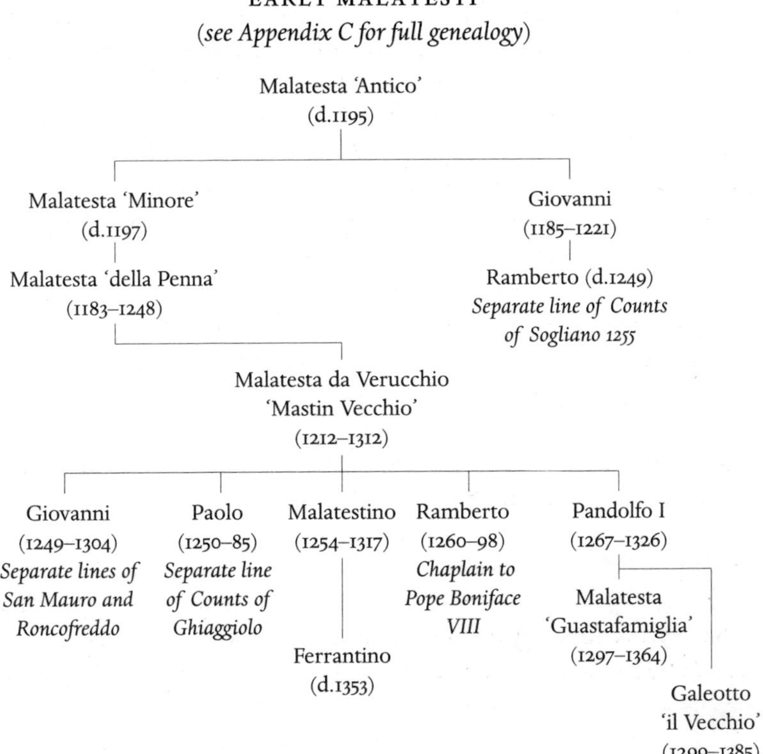


In 1216 Rimini made Giovanni and his nephew Malatesta 'della Penna' citizens, in a deed specifying that they must live in Rimini for three months of the year in peace and full-time if the city were at war, when they were to make war as directed by the commune and to commit all their castles *(rocche)* and fortified towns *(castelli)* to the defence of the city. In return they were declared immune from all taxes, which the deed noted with pointed irony 'they were not accustomed to pay', and their jurisdiction over their lands was confirmed by an undertaking that none of their subjects could become a citizen of Rimini. Giovanni died in the early 1220s

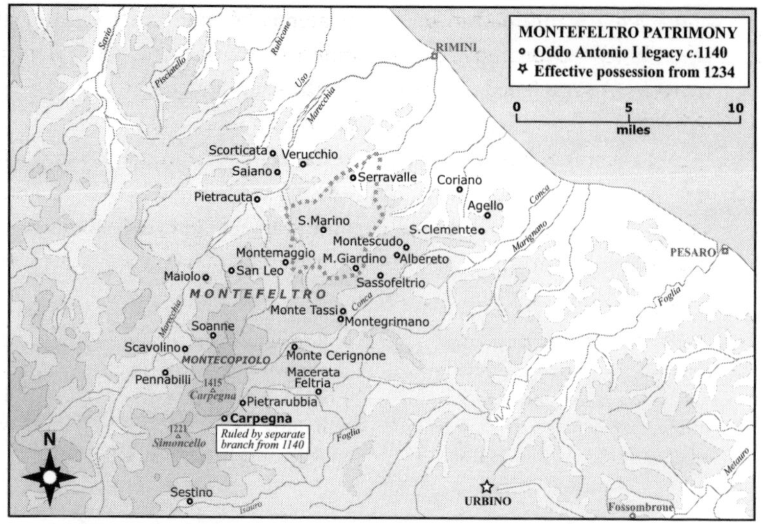


Map 6: PATRIMONY OF THE MONTEFELTRO AND MALATESTA CLANS

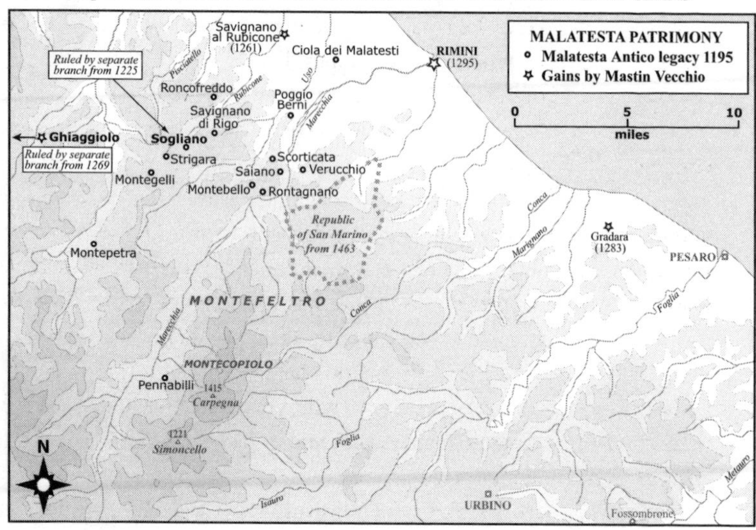

and his line continued in the backwater Rubicone valley, consolidated when his grandson Giovanni di Ramberto became Count of Sogliano by marriage in 1225. The line of primogeniture continued through Malatesta della Penna, who was elected *podestà* of Rimini in 1239 and died in 1248. He was succeeded by his son Malatesta da Verucchio, who was dubbed 'Mastin Vecchio' by Dante in *L'Inferno* XXVII, 37–8 and 46–8. In a passage where the ghost of the great Ghibelline warlord Guido Montefeltro asks him whether Romagna was at peace or war, Dante replies:

| | |
|---|---|
| *Romagna tua non è, e non fu mai* | Your Romagna is not, and never was |
| *Senza guerra ne' cuor de' suoi tiranni;* | Without war in the heart of its despots; |
| *E 'l Mastin vecchio, nuovo da Verucchio* | The old Mastiff, latest of the Verucchio line |
| *Che fecer di Montagna il mal governo,* | Which misrules there, in the mountains where |
| *Là, dove soglion, fan de' denti succhio.* | Even when aged, their teeth draw blood. |

At a time when life expectancy was low, Mastin Vecchio spanned a century during which he is said to have been ill only in the last few days. Born in 1212, he saw off eighteen popes, lived through the entire period when the power of the Empire peaked and crashed under Frederick II, and died in 1312, the year when the coronation of Emperor Henry VII marked an end to over fifty years during which Germany, under disputed or absentee kings, influenced Italian affairs scarcely at all. Mastin had many children and married them well, only for his eldest son Giovanni 'Gianciotto' (the Lame) to murder his wife, Francesca da Polenta, and his handsome brother Paolo for adultery in 1285. Local lore has it that Gianciotto himself was murdered at Scorticata in 1304: if true, the 'who benefits' rule puts his one-eyed younger brother Malatestino 'dal Occhio' in the frame. Pandolfo I, Mastin's youngest son by his second wife, wisely kept his head down while his half-brothers tore the family apart and as a result the main line of succession passed to Pandolfo's offspring.

Mastin was perhaps particularly fortunate to have lived through the period when the Montefeltri divided bitterly into Guelf and Ghibelline factions. Had the rival family remained united it is unlikely that Mastin would have been able to outmanoeuvre Dante's interlocutor Guido Montefeltro and make himself lord of Rimini in 1295. Guido was the leading Romagna Ghibelline and perhaps the most renowned Italian warrior of the second half of the thirteenth century. So great was his posthumous fame that Dante did not feel it necessary to identify by name the spirit that proudly proclaimed his *furbizia* in *L'Inferno* XXXVII, 76–8:

| | |
|---|---|
| *Gli accorgimenti e le coperte vie* | Shrewd tricks and hidden stratagems |
| *io seppe tutte, e sì menai lor arte,* | I knew them all and mastered them, |
| *ch'al fine della terra it suono uscie.* | Such that my fame was known worldwide. |

The 'emperor has no clothes' moment for the Ghibellines came in 1248 when Emperor Frederick II's army, besieging Parma, was shattered by a sortie by the garrison and his lavish camp, hubristically named Victoria and pronounced the new capital of a Northern Italian kingdom, was sacked and burned. Until then the lords and communes of Romagna were prudently imperial and in Rimini Mastin Vecchio had allied with the Ghibelline Omodei and Parcitadi, increasing the family holdings by his own well-timed marriage in 1247 to the daughter of the imperial Viscount of Rimini by a Parcitade wife. But at the same time he was in secret contact with Cardinal Legate Ottaviano degli Ubaldini, sent by Pope Innocent IV to take control of Massa Trabaria and the Foglia valley. When this was discovered the Omodei-controlled *podestà* of Rimini sent a letter to the imperial Count of Romagna, under whom the local lords were assembled at Imola, to arrest Mastin. Mastin's agents intercepted the letter and then came news of Frederick II's defeat at Parma.* Mastin, Taddeo I Montefeltro, the Malatesta Count of Sogliano and the Montefeltro Count of Carpegna instantly became Guelfs and marched from Imola to overthrow the Omodei in Rimini, in which they were greatly assisted by the clergy acting on the orders of Cardinal Ubaldini. Innocent IV immediately lifted his interdict from the city and conferred his particular blessing on Mastin.

The Parcitadi did not share in the wreck of the Ghibelline cause at Rimini because of their links of marriage with Mastin and their friendship with Taddeo I Montefeltro. However, Taddeo's grand-nephew, Guido, fast emerging as the new leader of the Romagna Ghibellines, allied with the exiled Omodei to make punitive raids into the Rimini hinterland. In a brilliant act of *furbizia* Mastin brokered a power-sharing agreement with the Omodei in 1252 using the Gambancerri family as a front, thereby

* The capture in 1249 of Frederick's designated heir Enzo, King of Sardinia, and his imprisonment until his death in 1272 was even more devastating to the Hohenstaufen cause than Frederick's defeat at Parma.

reactivating Guelf–Ghibelline discord among the rival Rimini clans while himself sitting on the fence. In contrast Montefeltrano II, who had been joint Count of Urbino until Taddeo I died in 1251, was obliged to renounce the title by the Guelf citizens of Urbino the following year. Montefeltrano II's death in 1255 left his sons Guido and Taddeo II facing each other in arms across the divide between Church and Empire.

The divide yawned following the attempt to conquer southern Italy for the Papacy in 1255 by the third Segni pope, Alexander IV, in breach of his sacred oath to uphold the succession of Frederick II's infant son Conradin. The papal army was defeated at Foggia by Manfred, Frederick's bastard son, who usurped Conradin's claim and had himself crowned King of Sicily in 1258. In response Alexander set in motion the negotiations to 'call in Beelzebub [Charles of Anjou, younger brother of the French king] to defeat Lucifer (Manfred)' brought to fruition by his successor, the French Urban IV. In the north Alexander declared a successful Crusade against Ezzelino III da Romano, despot of Verona and Vicenza, but in central Italy he saw his life's work undone. In 1260 a host assembled by the Guelfs of Tuscany was shattered at Montaperti by a smaller Sienese force reinforced by heavy cavalry sent by Manfred.

### BATTLE OF MONTAPERTI, 1260

**The battle turned on the treachery of Bocca degli Abati, a Ghibelline serving in the Guelf army, who hacked the standard-bearing arm off the Florentine *Gonfaloniere* to coincide with an attack by Manfred's cavalry and as a signal to others like him to sow confusion in the Guelf ranks. In *L'Inferno* XXXII Dante trips over Bocca's head, jutting from the frozen lake of the ninth circle of hell.**

The commune of Rimini, in the meantime, prudently declared for Charles of Anjou when he marched south through Romagna in 1265 and elected Mastin Vecchio's friend Taddeo II Montefeltro as *podestà*, which saved the Malatesti from a combination among the Parcitadi, Gambancerri and Omodei to expel them from Rimini. Taddeo II's brother Guido remained a Hohenstaufen partisan even after Manfred's defeat and death at Benevento in 1266 and was excommunicated by

Cardinal Ubaldini along with his cousin Galasso after they smashed a detached French column in 1268. Later that year Guido held the fortified Capitoline Hill in Rome for Conradin when he marched south to defeat at Tagliacozzo; however, he then closed the gates to the fleeing youngster (who was handed over to Charles of Anjou and judicially murdered in Naples) and surrendered the Capitoline Hill in return for safe conduct and 4000 gold florins.

In the midst of all this, upon the death of the Count of Ghiaggiolo in 1263 without a male heir, the ecclesiastical right-holders awarded Mastin Vecchio the title to the strategically important district, although Guido Montefeltro had a prior claim by marriage to the late count's sister. Guido must have had a very strong case because despite being under papal interdict he submitted his claim to an ecclesiastical court. There it remained under review until 1269, when Mastin married his son Paolo to the daughter of the late Count of Ghiaggiolo, after which the court found in Paolo's favour. In 1271 Guido marched to the relief of Monteluro, a Montefeltro town besieged by Mastin Vecchio, and although he routed the besiegers he was captured when his horse fell and pinned him. There were only two ways of dealing with such a man and Mastin could not kill him because it would have started a blood feud with Taddeo II, therefore he released Guido promptly. Perhaps as a quid pro quo Guido did not attempt to overthrow the Ghiaggiolo judgement in 1276, when he was the overlord of Forlì and Cesena downstream from the county and defeated a Florentine Guelf army at Civitella, the main town in Ghiaggiolo. It would be hard to find a better example of the respect for the forms of legality that coexisted with the survival of the ruthless that often makes the politics of the late Middle Ages so opaque to modern understanding.*

The substitution of the Angevin dynasty for the Hohenstaufen in southern Italy nurtured a new viper in the papal breast and proved a very temporary fix to the problem of Naples and Sicily. Following three short-lived popes in 1276–7 there was an intriguing three-year hiatus under the Orsini Pope Nicholas III, who set a benchmark for nepotism

* Perhaps not any more – we have, after all, quite recently seen the British government bend itself into a sordid pretzel to find a shysterish justification for invading Iraq rather than admit it was practising *realpolitik*: but that was a product of moral cowardice and personal inadequacy, which are not charges one can level against the warlords of the late Middle Ages.

when he turned against the Angevins and made common cause with the Ghibellines as part of a grand scheme to create a new kingdom to be ruled over by his family. Guido Montefeltro fell in with Nicholas III's plan and made homage to the pope for Cesena and Forlì in 1280, only to see the scheme fall apart when the pope died later the same year. Charles of Anjou in person ensured the succession of French Pope Martin IV by imprisoning the leading Roman cardinals. Charles and the new pope sent an army to claim the rights over Cesena and Forlì that Guido had conceded to the Church and put it under the command of Guido's brother Taddeo II, presumably to test his loyalty to the Angevin cause. Greatly outnumbered and besieged at Forlì in 1282, Guido ordered his men to fall back from the walls in the face of an assault, luring the attackers into the city where they were ambushed and slaughtered. Taddeo was probably not deceived by his brother's stratagem but he had limited authority over the French troops nominally under his command. Certain to be accused of treachery if he survived, he died fighting. Unable to send another army, Martin IV bombarded Guido's cities instead with excommunications, interdicts and threats of a Crusade until the citizens regretfully asked their popular lord to move on.

### ORSINI HUBRIS

**Pope Nicholas III schemed to unite Tuscany, Umbria and Romagna under his nephew Bertoldo Orsini as part of a new northern Italian kingdom, including Lombardy and Piedmont, which was to be put under an Orsini prince. In *L'Inferno* XIX Dante made Nicholas III chief among the simoniacs, those who bought ecclesiastical offices, in the foot-burning eighth circle of hell.**

The reason Charles and his puppet pope could not reconquer lost ground in the north after Forlì was because of the near-simultaneous 'Sicilian Vespers' rebellion, which drove the French from Sicily. The Sicilian rebels invited Peter III of Aragon, who was a direct descendant of Robert 'Guiscard' Hauteville and was married to Frederick II Hohenstaufen's granddaughter, to assume the throne as Peter I of Sicily.

Peter's Hauteville and Hohenstaufen connections made him a papal nightmare and Martin IV declared a Crusade against him, to no avail. Meanwhile Guido Montefeltro went back to Urbino where he was again besieged. In another display of *furbizia* Guido saved the town from assault in 1283 by making a seemingly desperate appeal to Rome for reconciliation. When the overconfident besiegers returned the following year, Guido made a sortie that destroyed their siege engines and scattered them. He capitulated in 1286 on generous terms to Cardinal William Durand, legate for Martin IV's successor Honorius IV, who needed peace in the north to concentrate his resources on the Aragonese Crusade.

Guido went into exile at Asti while Cardinal Legate Durand set about consolidating the Papacy's hold on the lands between the Foglia river and the Via Flaminia. To that end Durand allied with Mastin Vecchio, which in turn ended a tentative rapprochement between the Malatesti and the Montefeltro counts of Pietrarubbia, who were outraged when Durand favoured the Malatesta interest over their own in Urbino. Durand's partiality also brought an end to the Guelf–Ghibelline split within the main branch of the Montefeltri. Corrado, the eldest of Taddeo II's sons, and his brother, Taddeo Novello, gave up posts elsewhere in the Papal State and returned to defend the family interest. One of Taddeo II's bastard sons even tried to murder Mastin in a Cesena street. Possibly Durand was given an impossible task but a memorial to his failure is the fortress he built in the Metauro valley at Castel Durante, now Urbania, which became the seat of another ousted clan, the Brancaleoni, not long after Durand's death in 1296. Just as in Pope Innocent III's time, the strategically located Massa Trabaria remained a graveyard for papal schemes.

Guido's capitulation at Urbino in 1286 had another paradoxically adverse effect on the power of the Malatesti, because their usefulness as a Guelf counterbalance to the Montefeltri abruptly declined. In 1283 Mastin Vecchio had bought the stronghold of Gradara, located midway between Rimini and Pesaro, and became *podestà* of Pesaro from 1285. The Papal Rector of Romagna viewed this with alarm and correctly perceived that a peace treaty negotiated in 1287 by Mastin, then also *podestà* of Rimini, with the leading families of rebel Forlì and Faenza was a tacit alliance against resurgent papal power. The Rector sent troops to ambush Mastin's party at Paderno as they returned from Forlì and although Mastin escaped, other family members were captured. They were ransomed by the payment of a large indemnity cunningly levied against the commune of Rimini, not the family, and the Rector continued trying to drive a wedge between Malatesti and the commune with further fines and by placing Rimini under an interdict.

Ironically Mastin was deposed as *podestà* and the Malatesti expelled from the city in 1288 by a faction led by Montagna Parcitade – not because of papal pressure, but for showing too great a desire for reconciliation with Rome. The Papal Rector now allied with Mastin in a war against the commune, which ended in 1290 with the surrender into the hands of the Church of the villages each party had seized from the other. The Malatesti and the Parcitadi then submerged their differences in an alliance to expel the provocative Rector, whose unsuccessful effort to divide and rule was tacitly repudiated by Rome in 1294 when it lifted an interdict placed on Rimini by the Rector and restored the city's communal privileges. This left the Parcitadi and the Malatesti face to face and a final reckoning could not be long delayed.

Guido Montefeltro, meanwhile, had escaped from exile to become the *podestà* of Pisa, while Arezzo elected his distant cousin, Galasso of Begno. Arezzo had a debt of honour with the Montefeltri because Guido's son Buonconte had been killed fighting for the city at Campaldino in 1289. With Guido fully occupied with the war between Pisa and Florence, it was left to Galasso to carry the family banner in Romagna, where he defeated Mastin in a skirmish near Civitella in 1291. Guido, meanwhile, prosecuted his war so successfully that by the terms of a 1294 peace treaty Florence paid his fees and gave him safe passage across Tuscany. The availability of a proven war leader inspired the citizens of Cagli, on the Via Flaminia between Gubbio in Umbria and Fano on the coast, to overthrow their papal governor and to elect Guido their *podestà*. Guido and Galasso sank their differences with the Pietrarubbia branch of the clan and together they returned in triumph to Urbino. A papal counter-attack was mounted from the coast by Malatestino 'dal Occhio', Mastin's second son, but he was soundly defeated and pursued down the Foglia valley by Galasso, who followed through to storm Pesaro.

**BATTLE OF CAMPALDINO, 1289**

**In a rare display of tactical skill a coalition of Tuscan Guelfs under the French condottiere Amaury, Viscount of Narbonne, double-enveloped and almost annihilated a Ghibelline army led by Guglielmino degli Ubertini, Bishop of Arezzo, who was killed along with Buonconte Montefeltro. One of the Guelf combatants was Dante, who mentions the bishop and Buonconte in *Purgatorio* V.**

Although Martin IV and his two successors had failed to recover Sicily from the Aragonese, despite exhausting the resources of the Papacy, fate intervened when Peter III's son James gave the kingdom back to the Papacy in 1295. The recently elected Pope Boniface VIII snatched defeat from the jaws of victory by awarding it to Charles II of Anjou, at which the Sicilians again rebelled and elected James's younger brother, Frederick, to the throne. To free his hands to deal with what he saw as the greater threat in the south, Boniface instructed Cardinal Legate Durand to make peace with the Montefeltri and their Ghibelline allies by granting them ten-year papal vicariates for all their traditional titles, honours and lands, during which they were to refrain from war. Not much hope of that. In October 1295 Durand came to Rimini accompanied by Guido Montefeltro as Exhibit A in Boniface VIII's pacification policy, but Guido took the opportunity to plot a coup against the Malatesti with the Parcitadi.

Rimini was a powder keg and in December a street battle between Parcitade and Malatesta partisans erupted while Guido was standing by in nearby San Marino with 300 horsemen. According to the *Cronaca malatestiana*, written in the late fourteenth century, Mastin appealed to Giovanni, the head of the Parcitade clan, to join him in stopping the fighting, and the two patriarchs agreed that if Mastin sent his own troops out of the city, Giovanni would send a message to Guido that his intervention was no longer required:

> Mr Malatesta [Guido] divided his following. One part he concealed in his house while the other with trumpets and banners left in the direction of Verucchio . . . but at nightfall they turned back to the city,

> entering at the Gattolo [Malatesta palace] gate. Then Mr Malatesta's company charged out, shouting 'Long live Mr Malatesta and the Guelf party, death to Mr Parcitade and the Ghibellines'. Mr Parcitade, being without support, sought safety in flight with his family ... [and] made for San Marino, where Count Guido greeted him with the words 'Welcome, Mr Perdecitade [Lose-a-city]'.

The Rimini Ghibellines were decimated and Montagna Parcitade, scion of the house, was captured. There followed an episode out of *The Godfather.* Mastin asked his son Malatestino dal Occhio if he had taken care of Montagna. Malatestino, who appears to have been a dim bulb, replied that he had indeed and that even should Montagna wish to harm himself, he could not. Mastin patiently asked again, and again, until finally he said, 'I begin to doubt whether you do know how to take care of him.' The bulb lit and Malatestino departed to have Montagna strangled. Not only was all Parcitade property declared forfeit to the commune, but when Cardinal Durand arrived ten days later, outraged that his peace mission had been used to plot the coup and acutely aware that Mastin's son Ramberto was Pope Boniface VIII's private chaplain, he added the censure of the Church to the utter ruin of the defeated Parcitadi.

Thanks to a century of careful acquisitiveness during which they spent comparatively little of their own money in warfare the Malatesti had become the richest clan in the Romagna borderlands. They were now also the most powerful. The first generations could not match the Montefeltri as warlords, but by building up their personal holdings in the towns and cities of the region they extended their power more inexorably. Mastin and his heirs also fathered countless illegitimate children, who were bound to the family interest by small endowments. If such a thing were practicable, mass sampling of DNA in 'Malatestaland' might still find a predominance of the family genetic endowment. What this meant, in the century to come, was that even when relations with the Church broke down the papal authorities were compelled to treat the Malatesti generously as the only realistic rulers of their domain.

# TWO

# *Chaos*

## CHAPTER SUMMARY

*When Guido Montefeltro died in 1298 his bequests to the Church were so generous that his son Federico I was compelled to earn his living as a soldier of fortune. In the same year the Pietrarubbia branch of the Montefeltri was massacred in a popular uprising. The Malatesti were unable to benefit from the eclipse of their rivals, or from the collapse of papal authority following the removal of the Papacy to France in 1305, because of murderous competition among Mastin Vecchio's heirs following his death in 1310, until the line of Pandolfo I emerged victorious under the leadership of his sons. His eldest, Malatesta, earned the sobriquet 'Guastafamiglia' (family devastator) by a brilliant coup in 1331, when he betrayed his cousin and clan leader Ferrantino to Papal Legate Pouget. He then turned against Pouget and finally in 1334 imprisoned Ferrantino along with his eldest son and grandson, who were later killed. Pandolfo I had also won great good will in Rome by leading a papal crusade against Federico I Montefeltro in 1322, which ended with the brutal murder of Federico and his youngest son Francesco by a priest-inspired popular uprising in besieged Urbino. After little more than a year of papal misgovernment, Federico's eldest son Nolfo returned to power in Urbino by popular acclaim. Nolfo's brother Galasso and their uncle Speranza schemed against him with Malatesta Guastafamiglia, but the plot was undone in 1334 when Ferrantino's surviving grandson, Ferrantino Novello, betrayed it and provided Nolfo with the troops to drive Speranza and Galasso from Urbino. Nolfo made a marriage alliance with Ferrantino Novello and together they made war on Guastafamiglia and his long-lived brother Galeotto, during which Nolfo recovered much ground previously lost to the Malatesti, including the citadel of San Leo. In contrast, by 1348 Ferrantino Novello had been driven from his last outpost within the Malatesta domain. Two years later the threat to Nolfo posed by his brother Galasso and Galasso's son Guido was removed when they both died of the plague.*

Following the loss of Rimini the surviving Parcitadi and Galasso Montefeltro, joined by the Sogliano Malatesti, ravaged the surrounding countryside for a while; but the mainspring of the Montefeltri broke in a very medieval way when Guido underwent a spiritual conversion and became a Franciscan monk in 1296. When he died two years later he left such generous gifts of land and revenues to the Church that the family fortunes did not recover for a century. Guido had been at war most of his life, during which he had been responsible for the death of his brother Taddeo II at Forlì and had lost his elder son Buonconte at Campaldino. He was sick of it, and there also appears to have been no love lost between him and Federico I, his next son, who was closer to Guido's cousin Galasso. Guido's donations may have been intended in part to advance the career in the Church of his youngest, Corrado, who eventually became Bishop of Urbino, but on balance it seems more likely that his intention was to force the eldest, Federico I, to govern in harmony with the Church. Perhaps he might have, but the ecclesiastical authorities froze him out and Federico became a rootless soldier of fortune.

Oddly, considering their Guelf inclinations, the Malatesti did not follow the sensible dynastic practice of committing a member of each generation to the Church and Ramberto, Pope Boniface VIII's chaplain, was to prove the only prelate produced by the clan who achieved a position where he might have been able to advance family interests. However, Ramberto died in 1298 and even if he had lived it is unlikely he could have restrained the megalomaniac Boniface, who proclaimed a Jubilee in 1300 and decreed indulgences for all who made the pilgrimage to Rome during the Holy Year, cash in hand. Many thousands heeded the call, perhaps the first example of mass mobilisation for a political end in European history. The unlimited nature of Boniface's pretensions were revealed in the Bull *Unam Sanctam* in November 1302, which proclaimed it 'necessary for salvation that every living creature be under submission to the Roman pontiff'. The matter immediately at issue was a dispute over revenues with French King Philippe IV, whom the pope excommunicated in 1303. An interdict on France would have followed, but before Boniface could announce it Philippe's agents stormed the palace the pope had built at his home town of Anagni, slaughtered his retinue and captured him. The plan was to take Boniface to France for ecclesiastical trial and formal deposition, but the local population rose up and freed him. Boniface died shortly afterwards and two years later the Papacy moved to Avignon, where it remained until 1377 under seven French popes.

**IMPEACHMENT OF BONIFACE VIII**

**In a remarkable display of concern for the forms of legality French King Philippe IV persisted in impeachment proceedings against Boniface VIII for ten years after the pope's death. The chief witnesses for the prosecution were French prelates and the cardinals from the Colonna clan, bitter rivals of the Orsini. Philippe IV's court predictably concluded that Boniface had grossly exceeded his authority and divine mandate.**

Guido Montefeltro's belated embrace of the Church undermined the family finances, but his cousins were responsible for losing part of the remaining Montefeltro domain by an act of gratuitous cruelty. Galasso became the leader of the Montefeltri following the death of Guido and, while remaining *podestà* of Arezzo, was elected war captain and *podestà* of Cesena, where a tradition of resisting the hegemony of Rimini overcame the town's Guelf inclination. Having blocked the expansion of Malatesta power to the north, Galasso allied with Count Corrado of Pietrarubbia to do the same in the west by consolidating family holdings in the Marecchia valley. In 1298 they besieged the village of Piego near San Leo held by the Olivieri, a clan as old as the Montefeltri. When the place fell they impaled two of the Olivieri and dismembered a third to intimidate the other small landowners in the Montefeltro area. The opposite occurred and later that year the citizens of Pietrarubbia, many with family ties to the Olivieri, slaughtered Corrado, his daughter, his infant son, one of his brothers and a sister, and in a particularly macabre touch imprisoned and would have murdered Corrado's wife if she had proved to be pregnant, which fortunately she was not. The following year Corrado's younger brother Taddeo Novello was captured in Macerata Feltria by the Gaboardi, another old family, and murdered in prison. There remained only Taddeo Novello's son, christened Malatesta at the time when the families had been allied in the Guelf cause, who years later married the widowed Simona, Mastin Vecchio's youngest child, after which the Pietrarubbia Montefeltri disappear from the record.

The slaughter of the Pietrarubbia branch, Taddeo II's reproductive parsimony and the death of Galasso in 1303 reduced potential leaders of the Montefeltro clan to Federico I and his cousin Speranza, which was to prove an advantage in the chaos to come. Towards the end of his life Galasso, his vigour undermined by illness, ensured that Federico I became captain of Cesena in his place, while their distant relative Uguccione della Faggiuola took over in Arezzo. After inviting him to share power as *podestà* of Cesena, Federico found that Uguccione, whose personal following was a prototype of the freebooting companies that came to dominate warfare in Italy during the fourteenth century, was not one to share power with anyone. The ensuing struggle for dominance ended with both men expelled by the citizens of Cesena in 1301. Uguccione became the leading Ghibelline in Italy and was drawn out of our story by the lure of greater prizes in Tuscany and Liguria, leaving Federico I to pick up the pieces in Romagna. Speranza was an outstanding warrior but his area of operations was to the south, where he became the leader of an anti-papal association of local lords known as the 'Friends of the Marche'.

On paper the Malatesti were in a far stronger position, but Mastin Vecchio's get was cursed. During Mastin's lifetime three new branches of Malatesti hostile to the main line of succession came into being. The enmity of the Counts of Sogliano under Mastin's envious cousin Giovanni di Ramberto may have been inevitable, but the other two were the result of his son Giancotto's murder of his wife Francesca and his younger brother Paolo in 1285. It seems likely that their parents' favouritism towards handsome Paolo over ill-favoured Gianciotto lay behind the tragedy, and Mastin's angry grief may explain why he did not pursue the promising alliance with the Montefeltri of Pietrarubbia that began with the marriage of Gianciotto's son Tino to Count Corrado's daughter Agnese – who was one of those slaughtered with

Corrado in 1298. Mastin also excluded Gianciotto's sons from the main line of succession, which left a legacy of hostility between their heirs and the rest of the family that was to have adverse repercussions as late as 1430. Despite Mastin's punishment of Gianciotto, the murder of Paolo also created a lasting blood feud between the Malatesti of Ghiaggiolo and the rest of the clan.

When considering politico-military developments in Italy during the first half of the fourteenth century it is easy to resist the temptation to impose retrospective order on events: one could go mad trying. Even following the vagaries of papal policy is no mean task, veering as it did from the unlimited aspirations of Boniface VIII through a two-year interregnum to the Angevin-cringing Clement V and, after another protracted election process, back to papal absolutism (based on Angevin power) in the papal Bull *Si fratrem* promulgated by John XXII in 1317. The Bull declared that when there was no duly crowned Holy Roman Emperor – a distinction in the gift of the pope – the powers of the Empire devolved to the Papacy, and that even pre-existing imperial appointments required papal reconfirmation. Declaring that any subversion of papal authority was heresy completed the conflation of secular and spiritual power. Heresy was taken far more seriously than mere excommunication because the penalties included the expropriation of the heretics' assets by secular rulers – who were only too ready to oblige, most notoriously in the Europe-wide dispossession of the wealthy Knights Templar in 1307–14. However, the first victims of the new doctrine were the Franciscan 'Spirituals', who argued that the Church should follow the example of Christ and the Apostles by renouncing earthly goods and abandoning the contest for secular

### THE NAME OF THE ROSE

**The setting for Umberto Eco's best-selling murder mystery is a Benedictine abbey in the year 1327. The fictional detective (Sean Connery in the movie) is the Franciscan friar William of Baskerville, a combination of William of Ockham and Sherlock Holmes. A sub-plot involves the deadly tension between Michael of Cesena, a leading Franciscan 'Spiritual', and the sinister Inquisitor Bernard Gui, both real historical characters.**

power. Many were burned at the stake for this flagrant heresy; others, including the English philosopher William of Ockham, fled to Germany.

Boniface VIII had undone the Guelf alliance by attacking its Angevin underpinning, but his Avignon successors made the papal cause hated by gross partiality towards their compatriots, in particular by appointing French prelates to Italian sees where they behaved like conquerors and provoked frequent rebellions. However, the Ghibellines were unable to profit from the Guelf disarray. When German King Henry VII descended on Italy in 1312, he thought it necessary to disown those claiming to act in his name in order to ensure his coronation as emperor. He said he was acting in the name of peace, but all he did was make things worse. In addition Henry VII's intervention on behalf of the pope against the Visconti of Milan, which was historically the commune most hostile to imperial pretensions in northern Italy, created something relatively new in Italy: a regional great power under an able and ruthless dynasty determined to extend its borders at the expense of papal territories. After Henry VII died the German throne was disputed by Louis the Bavarian and Frederick of Austria, and it was the resulting period of imperial vacancy, during which Germany was absorbed by civil war, that emboldened John XXII to issue *Si fratrem*.

Unfortunately for the Papacy, the Angevins of Naples under King Robert, unaccountably known as 'the Wise', were a military broken reed. The battle of Montecatini (Map 7) in August 1315, during the papal interregnum before the election of John XXII, provides a breakdown of the opposing forces at that time. The large army led by Philip of Taranto, King Robert's brother, included contingents from Florence and Pistoia, Bologna, Siena, Perugia, Gubbio, Città di Castello, Volterra and Prato. Castruccio 'Castracane' Antelminelli, who ruled Lucca as the lieutenant of Pisa-based Uguccione della Faggiuola, commanded the opposing Ghibelline force with strong contingents from Arezzo, Visconti Milan, della Scala Verona and Este loyalists from Mantua and Ferrara. The Guelfs were defeated with great slaughter and among the dead were the younger brother of King Robert and Philip of Taranto, and also Philip's eldest son. The salvation of the Guelfs was that their opponents fell to fighting among themselves: in 1316 Uguccione tried to eliminate his lieutenant, at which the citizens of Lucca rebelled and elected native son

Castruccio their lord. Why Castruccio was known as 'Dog-gelder' is something of a mystery, but he held the city against all comers until his death in 1328 and had he left an heir would have founded a dynasty with a family name even more intriguing than 'Malatesta'.

Montecatini serves as a reminder that Tuscany and Lombardy were the main areas of conflict over the coming century, and that events in Romagna–Marche often merely reflected the struggle among the main players. Thus in 1307 we find Federico I and Speranza Montefeltro in the service of Papal Legate Napoleone Orsini against the Black Guelfs of Florence, in which they were thwarted by Malatestino dal Occhio's son Ferrantino. The Malatesti returned to papal allegiance after Orsini was recalled and King Robert of Naples was nominated Papal Rector of Romagna, and they stood almost alone with the Angevins during the resurgence of Ghibellinism that occurred during Emperor Henry VII's blundering descent into Italy. Following the emperor's death their reward included armed Church support against their troublesome Sogliano relatives, but the main prize was that they received papal blessing to become the rulers of Cesena, Cervia and, briefly, Forlì. One-eyed Malatestino died in 1317 and Pandolfo I became the undisputed leader of the clan. Under him, still with full papal backing, Malatesta authority extended far into the Marche. In 1324, when Pandolfo's son Galeotto married the niece of Cardinal Legate Amelio de Lautrec, with guests and gifts flowing in from Guelf communes across northern Italy, Pandolfo may have thought that the future of the dynasty was secure. Fate, sandbag in hand, lurked just around the corner.

When the Papacy was able to focus on Romagna, however briefly, the consequences for its foes could be drastic. Federico I Montefeltro unwisely threw salt in an old wound by proclaiming his right to Urbino on the basis of the 1226 imperial investiture. He did so in the expectation that Louis the Bavarian would defeat his papally supported cousin and rival Frederick of Hapsburg in the struggle for Germany and revive Ghibellinism in Italy – which he did, but too late to save Federico I. From 1319 Pope John XXII condemned Federico I with annually renewed anathemas, culminating in charges of heresy and idolatry, and finally the preaching of a Crusade against him in 1321. Trapped in Urbino by papal forces led by Pandolfo I Malatesta, Federico and his son Francesco were imprisoned after a popular uprising in April 1322 and four days later were dragged through the streets and beaten to death, their remains daubed with dung and buried with the carcass of a horse in unconsecrated ground. Federico's son Nolfo was saved to become the Montefeltro clan leader by Cante Gabrielli, lord of Gubbio and later Nolfo's father-in-law. The atrocious outcome caused the Guelf lords of Romagna, after collecting their share of the spoils (Pandolfo also took the opportunity to raze the walls of Urbino), to reconsider. Time and again the Papacy assembled a coalition against a given lord, only to see it dissolve once the other lords perceived it as an attack on their class.

## MALATESTI – THE NEXT GENERATIONS

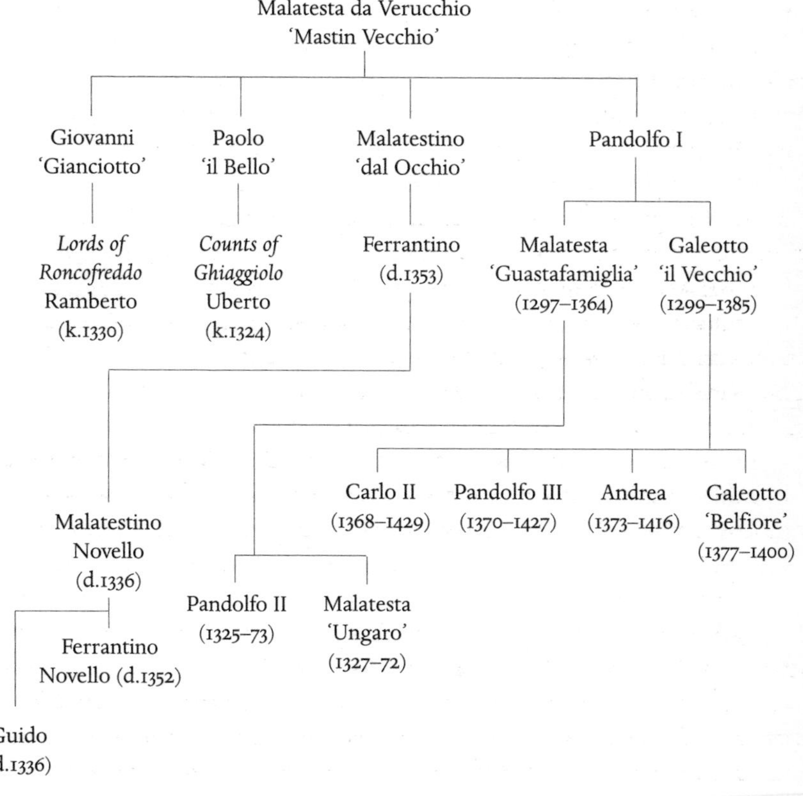

In 1324 Pandolfo I Malatesta and his sons deepened the breach with the Ghiaggiolo branch by luring their kinsman Count Uberto to a gathering at the family estate of Ciola dei Malatesti with the prospect of conspiring with him against the heirs of the fratricide Gianciotto. Instead they murdered Uberto and dumped his body in the village midden. After Pandolfo I died in 1326 clan leadership passed to Ferrantino, Malatestino dal Occhio's eldest, and Pandolfo's sons Malatesta and Galeotto emulated their patient grandfather and waited for the dust to settle while the heirs of Gianciotto and Malatestino tore at each other.* In July 1326 Gianciotto's surviving son Ramberto, lord of Roncofreddo and Castiglione, kidnapped Ferrantino, his son Malatestino Novello and grandson Ferrantino Novello. Malatestino Novello's young wife, Polentesia, raised the citizens of Rimini against the coup, but in Cesena the populace took the opportunity to throw off Malatesta rule altogether. Ramberto freed his captives but the matter was not settled until January 1330, when Malatestino Novello stabbed Ramberto to death as he knelt at his feet for pardon at a Church-sponsored meeting of reconciliation. Such behaviour was not unusual among the lords of Romagna – during the fourteenth century fratricide, filicide and parricide winnowed the ruling families of Imola, Faenza, Forlì and Ravenna.

In September 1325 an all-star Guelf army was defeated at Altopascio, midway between Florence and Pisa (Map 7), by Castruccio Castracane of Lucca and Azzone, scion of the Milanese Visconti. Leading a second Guelf offensive, against the Este of Ferrara, Pandolfo's eldest, Malatesta, and Ferrantino's son Malatestino Novello were defeated and captured in October when their fortified camp at Zappolino was stormed. Azzone Visconti was also present at this battle and the release of the captives under parole enabled the Malatesti to evade papal service in the renewed struggle against Milan and Ferrara. The Malatesti had problems of their own, including a Ghibelline assault on Rimini in 1328, but they committed the unpardonable offence of deducting the costs of defending their lands from the dues they owed the Church.

Clan leader Ferrantino incurred the odium for these actions and Papal Legate Bertrand du Pouget secretly combined with Pandolfo I's sons to commit a brilliant coup against him. Pouget had earlier recovered Imola,

---

* A glance at Appendix C would undoubtedly be helpful at this point.

Faenza and Forlì with columns converging from the papal bastions at Bologna and Cesena, and in April 1331 he demanded the surrender of Rimini. Ferrantino wanted to resist but Malatesta di Pandolfo, who ever afterwards was to be known by the sobriquet 'Guastafamiglia' (family devastator), piously declared that he would not rebel against the Church and drove Ferrantino and his family out of the city before himself surrendering it to Pouget, as agreed. For one golden moment Pouget must have believed he had returned the whole of Romagna to obedience and he rewarded Guastafamiglia by fully supporting him in the ensuing family civil war, with Ferrantino limited to a few strongholds along the Rubicon and, further south, Mondaino held by Ferrantino's namesake grandson, with support from the Montefeltri. The latter circumstantial alliance flowered into a marriage between Ferrantino Novello and Anna, younger sister of Nolfo and Galasso Montefeltro.

Pouget's card-castle came down when he summoned the supposedly pacified lords of Romagna to march on Este Ferrara in 1333, where they were roundly defeated at Porta San Pietro and surrendered en masse to Count Rinaldo II d'Este. As well as Guastafamiglia and his brother Galeotto, the list of captives included Ferrantino's son Malatestino Novello and the leaders of the Alidosi (Imola), Manfredi (Faenza), Ordelaffi (Forlì) and Polenta (Ravenna) clans (Appendix D), all of whom went over to the Este and were set free to undo Pouget's work. The full extent of Guastafamiglia's *furbizia* was now revealed as he feigned reconciliation with his cousins and combined forces with them to retake Rimini. Each faction of the family and their armed retainers occupied separate parts of the city, but Guastafamiglia conspired with the Ordelaffi to send reinforcements from Forlì and in a surprise attack in June 1334 captured Ferrantino, his son Malatestino Novello and grandson Guido.

Guastafamiglia's coup against his cousins caused another of his plots, against Nolfo Montefeltro, to fail. Guastafamiglia had been in secret contact with Nolfo's brother Galasso and cousin Speranza to take control of Urbino, but Ferrantino Novello doomed his captive father and sibling by betraying the conspiracy and by providing the troops that permitted Nolfo to drive Galasso and Speranza out of his domain. Much might have been forgiven, but not that. The older Ferrantino was released in 1336 but Malatestino Novello, still excommunicate for the murder of Ramberto six years earlier, died along with his son Guido in the dungeons of Fossombrone. Over the next twelveyears Ferrantino Novello and Nolfo Montefeltro allied to wage war against the Rimini Malatesti, but while Nolfo recovered much previously lost to the rival clan, Ferrantino Novello's holdings were reduced one by one until the last, Mondaino, fell in 1348. He was killed fighting someone else's war in Umbria four years later and when his grandfather died the following year the line of Malatestino dall'Occhio was extinguished.

MONTEFELTRI – THE NEXT GENERATIONS

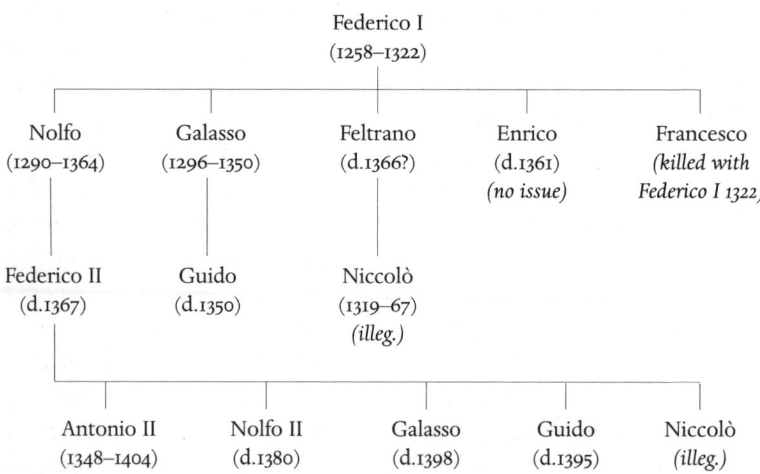


Perhaps the most significant factor that kept much of Italy in chaos long after the nominal reason for the great Guelf–Ghibelline divide had disappeared was that each time a state fell to one faction or the other the embittered exiles took up residence in some nearby town and allied with whoever seemed most likely to make war successfully against their place of origin. Thus the importance of Sogliano and Mondaino to the sons of Pandolfo I and later of Sassocorvaro to the Montefeltri. If to this we add a host of conflicting family and individual interests even among the victors, it can readily be appreciated why communes increasingly clamoured for lords *(signori)* and despots *(tiranni)* to keep the peace. The clamour was particularly loud in the towns of the Papal State, where citizens were desperate for an end to the domestic factionalism that flourished under the fragile authority of ecclesiastical representatives, who had every reason to exacerbate the strife in order to divide and rule.

Few places illustrate better than Urbino how rapidly Church rule could make almost any alternative seem preferable. In 1323, little more than a year after the people of Urbino beat Nolfo's father and brother to death, they expelled the papal governors and acclaimed Nolfo their lord. Although he and his brother Galasso were nominated co-rulers of Urbino by Louis the Bavarian in 1328, Nolfo was careful not to repeat his father's mistake and based his authority on the consent of the citizens, abandoning the claim based on the old imperial title that had for so long bedevilled the clan's relations with the Papacy. Behind this was the practical consideration that the Avignon popes had become leading employers of mercenaries and the Montefeltri were now almost wholly dependent on their income as condottiere.

With regard to the Montefeltro–Malatesta vendetta the highlights of this period are Nolfo's expulsion of Speranza and Galasso, and his restoration of clan hegemony in the Montefeltro region with the recovery of San Leo citadel in 1338, which his illegitimate nephew Niccolò accomplished by a daring escalade of the rock face. But as far as the depleted family finances were concerned his more important achievements were his substantial earnings as an officer in the papal army in 1333, Captain of the People at Pisa in 1341, Captain (and the election of his family to the patriciate) of Venice in 1348, Captain-General of Milan in 1351 and of Siena from 1358. Since the Malatesti also began to depend more and more on their income as hired soldiers during the fourteenth century, it is the appropriate moment to review the roots of the condottieri phenomenon and to explain why the lords of the Romagna–Marche borderlands came to dominate the market.

# THREE

# *Dogs of War*

## CHAPTER SUMMARY

*The very word 'soldier' derives from the name of a Roman coin and the phenomenon of men fighting primarily for pay cannot be separated from the emergence of military professionalism. For rulers the attraction of mercenaries is that they are an 'on demand' option: cheaper and, if treated correctly, safer than raising and maintaining a standing army. The precursor of all the mercenary companies was the Greek 'Ten Thousand' made famous by Xenophon's* Anabasis. *The Catalán 'Great Company' that conquered the principality of Athens from a treacherous employer in 1311 is generally considered the model for many that followed, but a more influential example may have been the Normans who conquered kingdoms for themselves in southern Italy and Sicily in the late twelfth century. German knights who stayed behind after imperial incursions into Italy formed the first independent companies in the 1340s, followed in the 1360s by English, Flemish and others temporarily unemployed during a long lull in the Anglo-French Hundred Years' War. The first formal contract, from which military entrepreneurs in Italy took the name condottieri, dates from the late thirteenth century. The hiring of specialist military skills was simply one manifestation of the emerging cash economy that transformed Italy in the late Middle Ages and was comparable to the commissioning of architects, artists and scholars that gave birth to the Renaissance. From the beginning the petty lords of the Romagna were prominent among the Italian swords for hire because they were raised to warfare from birth, could contribute skilled troops from their own domains and, perhaps most important of all, because the need to look after their own lands provided a guarantee that they would go home at the end of a contract.*

In 1976 the Diplock Commission, reviewing the involvement of British mercenaries in the endemic wars of post-independence Africa, listed rapacity last in its thoughtful list of reasons why a man might become a soldier of fortune. The Commission concluded that 'a spirit of adventure, an ex-soldier's difficulty in adjusting to civilian life, unemployment, domestic troubles, ideals, fanaticism, greed – all these may play some part in the individual's motivation'. More broadly, men may be driven to arms in times of chaos, when joining one or other of the warring bands is the only sane choice for those who would otherwise be the undifferentiated victims of all. But the Diplock Commission failed to highlight the most important factor of all: opportunity. For independent mercenary bands to prosper the preconditions include unconstrained political rivalry, weak states, rulers lacking legitimacy and a submissive civilian population. While it is true that soldiers make war but seldom make the wars they fight, mercenaries are like the guns that do not kill people of the US National Rifle Association slogan: it is indeed people who kill people – but they do so more readily if there are guns to hand.

In more volatile societies hiring military expertise at need reduces the risk of Praetorianism. The term comes from the Praetorian Guard, the imperial bodyguard created by the Roman Emperor Augustus, which during its 300-year existence assassinated fourteen emperors, appointed five and on one occasion sold the office to the highest bidder. In contrast to mercenary bands, men normally join regular armies for stability and regular pay. Once armed, however, their first loyalty is not to their employer but to their comrades, intensified by the fact that they generally live apart from the civilian community, further distanced by mutual incomprehension and distrust. For insecure rulers Praetorianism is an ever-present threat and hire-on-demand soldiers, particularly foreigners with homes elsewhere to go to, are a cheaper and safer option – so long as the insecure rulers do not commit the folly of trying to cheat the soldiers they hire.

The first mercenary leader of whom we have a detailed record is Xenophon the Athenian, whose epic *Anabasis* is the foundation stone of military history. Xenophon joined the Greek contingent led by Clearchus the Spartan to serve the cause of Persian Prince Cyrus the Younger against his older brother, Emperor Artaxerxes. A large number of men skilled in war but not much else were available for recruitment at the end of the Peloponnesian War (431–404 BC), in which Sparta and her allies, crucially including a fleet provided by Prince Cyrus, crushed Athens. Xenophon formed part of Cyrus's retinue until the prince was killed during the pyrrhic victory of his forces at Cunaxa in 401 BC. Shortly afterwards Clearchus and his lieutenants were treacherously killed and the Greeks (the 'Ten Thousand') elected Xenophon as one of their new generals, judging that his intelligence and learning outweighed his lack of military experience. This made him the prototype of the successful condottiere, distinguished as much by *furbizia* in politico-financial matters as by skill in combat. Xenophon led the Ten Thousand in a retreat from Mesopotamia to the Black Sea, whence they were taken by galleys to Thrace where he tried unsuccessfully to found a permanent settlement.

Seventeen hundred years later, following defeat at Nicomedia in 1302 by the Turkic tribe of Othman, Byzantine Emperor Andronikos II hired the services of a 'Great Company' of Catalonian light infantry *(almogavares)* who were unemployed at the end of the 1282–1302 Sicilian war between the Aragonese and Angevin dynasties. The Company, led by the sometime Knight Templar and pirate Roger de Flor, became an independent power in its own right until in 1305 the emperor had Roger assassinated. The surviving *almogavares* elected a new leader, the erudite and astute Ramón Muntaner, whose *Crónica* bears comparison with Xenophon's epic. Under Muntaner the Great Company defeated the Byzantine army in 1306 and even attempted to blockade Constantinople, until in 1308 it moved to Salonica. In 1310 the Company accepted employment by Walter de Brienne, Duke of Athens (among the last remnants of the Frankish Latin Empire that supplanted the Byzantine from 1204 to 1261). A year later Brienne decided it would be cheaper to kill the Catalans than to honour the contract, but his surprise attack failed and the Company killed him and most of his knights, took over the duchy and asked the house of Catalonia–Aragon to provide them with a figurehead duke. The heirs of the Great Company ruled Athens until they sold it to the Acciaiuoli, a Florentine banking family, in 1388.

Although the Catalan Company is usually cited as the precursor of the Italian mercenary companies of the later Middle Ages, an earlier and arguably more influential example was the Norman Conquest of southern Italy. The remarkable story starts around 1030, when the first of the minor Norman noble Tancred d'Hauteville's seven sons joined other Normans fighting as mercenaries for the Papacy against the rump of the Byzantine Empire in Apulia, Basilicata and Calabria. The brothers succeeded each other as leaders of the quarrelsome Normans and, having conquered the heel and toe of Italy, worked up the boot into Capitanata and Campania. In 1053 the reforming Pope Leo IX personally led a German mercenary army south to defeat and capture at Civitate. In 1059 Pope Nicholas II made terms with reality and, in exchange for recognition of the Papacy's nominal sovereignty, formally proclaimed Richard d'Hauteville as Count of Capua and Robert 'Guiscard' (the Norman word for *furbo)* the ruler not only of Apulia and Calabria but also of Sicily – he could reconquer it from the Saracens.

### THE FIRST NORMAN CONQUEST

**The Hauteville conquest of Sicily produced an extraordinarily fruitful synergy among the Byzantine, North African Islamic and Norman Gothic artistic traditions, to be seen most notably in the Palatine Chapel and several churches in Palermo, the abbey at Monreale and the cathedral at Cefalù.**

Led by Roger, the youngest of Tancred's sons, the Normans stormed Messina in 1061. Aided by dissension among the Saracens and supported by some of the indigenous Greek population they fought their way across northern Sicily and captured the Saracen capital of Palermo in 1072. But it was not until 1090 that they completed the conquest and not until 1127 that the two greater parts of the Hauteville empire were united, when Roger's namesake son, Count of Sicily since 1105, succeeded his childless uncle as Duke of Apulia and Calabria. He was crowned King Roger II of the Two Sicilies in 1130. The Hauteville dynasty only lasted until 1194 when, as we have seen, failure of the legitimate male line permitted Hohenstaufen Emperor Henry VI to claim the throne in the name of his wife, Roger II's daughter Constance.

Elsewhere in Europe the late Middle Ages were a period of endemic warfare, fallow ground for skilled soldiers prepared to serve any master, in particular the *routiers* (men of the road) from the Netherlands who were mainly infantry equipped with the crossbow, the medieval 'equaliser'. The civil war during King Stephen's reign in England sucked in many such and in the usual confusion between cause and effect that attends the appearance of mercenaries in history they were blamed for the savagery of the Anarchy. The *routiers* and their weapon of choice were condemned in the Third Lateran Council of 1179, as they were by the English barons in the Magna Carta of 1215, which demanded the expulsion of the *routiers* employed by King John. It is ironic that a charter of aristocratic privileges (among them not to have their expensive armour perforated by plebeian crossbow bolts) became the cornerstone of a uniquely English concept of a citizen's inalienable rights against the exercise of arbitrary state authority – until the legal principles based on it were subverted and Common Law supplanted by a statist model imported from Europe in the late twentieth and early twenty-first centuries.

There was a relative lull in the employment of mercenaries in northern Europe during much of the thirteenth century, but the Hohenstaufen dynasty made great use of them in their wars for Italy, as did the opposing northern Italian cities and the Papacy. Seeking to find a less pay-sensitive alternative, Frederick II established a colony of Sicilian–Saracen archers at Lucera in south-eastern Italy, who were forbidden conversion to Christianity in order to keep their loyalty uncontaminated in his ultimately doomed struggle with the Papacy. Following the collapse of the imperial cause after 1250, small state anarchy within Italy fed the aspiration of daring soldiers of fortune to win lordships for themselves and also drew from abroad the fearsome Free Companies, described in 1366 by Pope Urban V as 'a multitude of villains of various nations associated in arms by the greed to appropriate the fruits of labour of innocent and unarmed people, let loose to every cruelty, to extort money, methodically devastating the countryside'.

The Free Companies were distinguished by their ability to give formal battle rather than merely raid and run: in a word, their military professionalism. The first group to demonstrate this ability was the Company of St George, formed after Mastino della Scala, lord of

Verona, hired German mercenaries away from Venice, with which Mastino was at war. The most prominent were the Swabian Werner of Ürslingen, the Württemberger Count Conrad of Landau and the Swiss Rinaldo de Giver. In 1339 the Company of St George invaded Milanese territory and in February at Canegrate, after defeating the (also mainly German) knights employed by Count Azzone Visconti, the Company dispersed to loot and was driven from the field by a late-arriving Viscontean contingent from Bologna.

After Canegrate Ürslingen proposed that the German knights, who had stayed behind after the ill-fated imperial interventions in 1327–31 and had been hiring themselves out piecemeal to the warring city-states, should combine instead of fighting against each other. In 1342 the new association adopted the name Great Company and marauded under Ürslingen until his retirement in 1351, then under the Provençal Montréal d'Albarno (Fra Moriale) until 1354, when it numbered 8–10,000 fighting men and double the number of camp followers, a mobile city and a far greater force than any Italian state could match. The company went where it wished, extorted money at will from Lombardy to Naples and may also have received a papal retainer to guide its perambulations. If so it was of a piece with the Papacy's *furbizia* in sponsoring the return to Rome at this time of the demagogue Cola di Rienzo, where he not only reminded the turbulent local barons that there were worse things than papal rule, but also cancelled whatever contract there was with Fra Moriale by beheading him (after he entered the city expecting a welcome), before himself being butchered by the demos he had gogued.

Thereafter the Company split into smaller bands, the most significant under Conrad of Landau and his sons. Conrad was heavily defeated in a peasant ambush as La Scallele in 1358 and was finally killed in 1363 at the battle of Canturino by the White Company, a new arrival in Italy, which was a product of the Hundred Years War between France and England. The lull that followed the Peace of Brétigny in 1360 left many soldiers unemployed and some moved to pastures green in Italy, pausing to extort protection money from the Papacy at Avignon. The company was named for the polished armour worn by its members and employed the tactics developed by the English in France, in which dismounted men-at-arms fought with longbowmen on their flanks.

Although the first leader of the White Company was the German Albrecht Sterz, whose faithlessness finally led to his decapitation by the Perugians in 1366, thereafter it was led by the English knight Sir John Hawkwood, known in Italy as Giovanni Acuto (John the Sharp). Hawkwood's cadaverous image adorns a wall of the Duomo in Florence, where he ended his days as captain-general.

The term condottieri properly applies only to those mercenaries, in Italy, who agreed to detailed, written commissions *(condotte)* with their employers. Contractual agreements of this kind began in the thirteenth century and were attempts by city-states to make their endemic warfare more cost-controllable. Commissions would specify not only how many men, when and for how long the military entrepreneur must provide, but also how they must be equipped. The contracts might be for specified active service *(ferma)*, or to maintain forces in reserve *(in aspetto)* until activated under specified circumstances. The most revealing was the exclusive availability commission (*di respetto*), by which an employer might pay an individual a pre-emptive retainer: in essence the 'protection money' made infamous more recently by the Mafia. Hundreds of *condotte* survive and no two are alike. The condottieri's representatives might specify whom their principals would and would not fight against, but the crucial issue was how much upfront money *(prestanza)* they could obtain because, although these were legal documents, there were no courts to enforce them. The most common examples of bad faith were by employers who felt no urgency to honour contracts after a peril had passed, or who in desperation offered sums they never had a realistic prospect of being able to pay.

Hawkwood was really the only foreign man-at-arms to make a successful transition to the new entrepreneurial paradigm. Chief among the Italians was Alberico da Barbiano who, along with Hawkwood and the notoriously savage Bretons, perpetrated atrocities in Faenza and Cesena on behalf of Cardinal Robert of Geneva in 1376–7. In 1378 Barbiano formed a new, wholly Italian Company of St George and entered the service of newly elected Pope Urban VI. At Marino the following year he defeated the dreaded Breton Company, still fighting for Robert of Geneva, who was now Antipope Clement VII. After a triumphal entry to Rome Barbiano was dubbed a Knight of Christ by his grateful employer and presented with a banner bearing the cross of St George embroidered with the words 'Italy liberated from the Barbarians'. The Papacy only returned to Rome, uneasily, in 1377 and it was prudent of the Neapolitan Urban VI to emphasise that he represented a break with his seven French predecessors of the Avignon Papacy, and to evoke the old Roman division of the world into Italians and barbarians.

### HAWKWOOD THE SHARP

**On meeting Sir John Hawkwood on the road, a wandering mendicant friar greeted him with the words, 'Peace be with you.' 'May your begging bowl remain empty,' replied Sir John. Astonished, the friar enquired the reason for this incivility. Sir John replied that to wish peace on a condottiere was to desire for him hunger and misery.**

As Alberico da Barbiano learned his trade under Hawkwood so he in turn schooled Jacopo del Verme, Braccio da Montone and Muzio 'Sforza' Attendolo, whose careers flow into the period covered in later chapters. Before entering the Age of the Condottieri it is as well to highlight some of the themes in the events we have examined. The most obvious is the relationship between the proliferation of mercenaries and the ability of states to raise money. It was the enormous new wealth of the Italian city-states that drew mercenaries like ants to syrup, with the added attraction of endemic, if essentially petty warfare where well-trained men could make a significant impact. On the demand side, bearing in mind that the condottieri era was a period when anyone of means could and often did aspire to political power, it is obvious why wealthy rulers chose to hire military expertise when needed rather than maintaining standing armies within their walls, which might seize power for themselves.

Somebody had to maintain a reserve of men at arms, however, and since rootless, freebooting companies were a danger to all it was desirable to reward faithful service with peacetime stipends and land grants, both to tie deserving condottieri to a particular cause and also to give them the means to provide for their men when they were not required to fight. The republican communes could not match a significant incentive available to hereditary rulers, which was to honour a successful field commander with marriage into the ruling house. The bride's dowry was a means of rewarding the groom with real estate as well as cash, and as a two-for-one introduced a blood tie into the relationship between the military contractor and his employer. The only drawback was that such a marriage might, if the main line of succession became fragile, nurture usurping ambition in the breast of the favoured condottiere.

The petty lords of the Romagna borderlands made ideal condottieri. Raised to war in an area where families were large, land scarce and strong codes of personal honour prevailed, they commanded small armies of highly professional and dependable men, who returned home to alternative occupations in the rare periods of peace. They were also socially acceptable spouses for the daughters of the grander houses and although their own dynastic ambitions often distracted them from their employers' service at critical moments, their own lands provided a 'tail' that could be stepped on if they got too badly out of line.

Spanish Cardinal Legate Gil Álvarez Carrillo de Albornoz, who came to enforce submission in the Papal State from 1353.

A period of global warming, accompanied in Europe by dependable summers and mild winters, peaked in the period 1100–1250. The start of the atmospheric trend reversal into the 'Little Ice Age', which reached its lowest temperatures between 1650 and 1850, coincided with a period in which population growth levelled off and in places declined some decades before the Black Death. After heavy rains ruined three successive harvests, northern Europe suffered a severe famine between 1315 and 1322, and disease finished off animal herds already weakened and diminished by lack of feedstock. Trade had made Europe economically as well as epidemiologically interdependent and the knock-on effect of, for example, the collapse of English wool exports and consequently of the Flemish weaving industry, contributed to the eclipse of Flanders as a commercial rival to the northern Italian cities. There were swings and roundabouts, of course. The florin (3.5 grams of gold) first minted by Florence in 1252 rapidly became the standard unit of international currency, reflecting and reinforcing the wide reach of Florentine financial and commercial activity. However, the same wide reach meant that while Florence made commercial gains when its competitors collapsed, it also suffered from the overall contraction of trade and bore the brunt of loan defaults across Europe. There were other factors at work, including overpopulation relative to available land, which left the rural economy horribly vulnerable to the Black Death.

No great effort of historical imagination is required to understand the mood generated by all these catastrophes. Our own time has been washed by successive waves of apocalyptic prophecy, of which currently the one that has achieved the greatest resonance is global warming. The climatological phenomenon is undeniable and the anthropogenic contribution may indeed be critical, but the finger-pointing and debate-precluding orthodoxy of the tenured modern priesthood contributes a great deal more heat than light and is in no important detail different from the response of its tonsured late medieval predecessor to the calamities of the fourteenth century. In both cases natural phenomena were portrayed as punishment for sin, while offering the rich and powerful an opportunity to lubricate the biblical eye of the needle along the lines of 'leave the praying/thinking to us and give us your money'. The general public will always be swayed by suspicion that if there is a great deal of smoke then hell's portals must indeed be gaping; some will respond by living austerely but most will live for the day because those to whom they have delegated the task of augury seem to be telling them it is futile to provide for the future.

**GIOVANNI BOCCACCIO (1313–75)**

**Poet probably born in Tuscany and raised in Florence and Naples best remembered for the *Decameron*, a Tuscan dialect compilation of one hundred popular tales written in 1349–52 and extensively revised twenty years later. In 1350–1 he formed a close bond with Petrarch and by 1359, when he undertook a diplomatic mission to Avignon on behalf of Florence, either pragmatism or religious conversion had caused him to turn away from vulgar themes to concentrate on scholarship.**

Doom-mongering is a two-edged blade: in Boccaccio's *Decameron* the narrative frame is provided by the Black Death, from which seven young men and three young women flee Florence for healthier Fiesole, where they pass the time by telling stories. A common theme is the lascivious greed of the clergy, and the book shows that the metropolitan elite of Boccaccio's day regarded the priesthood with contempt and rejected the idea that human will could prevail against the blind working of impersonal fate. The coda, however, is that Boccaccio later stopped writing in the vernacular and may have repudiated his earlier work. It is hard to see how he could have been well received at the Avignon court of Pope Innocent VI without doing so, although Innocent's views on the clergy whose corrupt incompetence undermined his Italian policies were probably similar to those of Boccaccio's young storytellers. However, faith floats above the often squalid doings of those self-selected to administer it to the faithful and there were always enough decent, even holy, prelates to save the Church from the total disrepute into which the more common run of churchmen might otherwise have brought it.

Unfortunately the best of the clergy took a deadly hit from the Black Death, which in its almost invariably fatal pneumonic form cruelly struck down the most diligent among them as they tended to the dying, while the bubonic plague wiped out even cloistered communities that cut themselves off from the outside world – one infected rodent was all it took, and the grain stores of monasteries were magnets for *Rattus rattus*. Secondary consequences included a precipitous decline in rental income as the countryside became depopulated, which compelled landlords to enter into share-cropping agreements with the reduced labour force under which the landlords assumed all the capital costs and most of the risks in return for, typically, half the produce. In practice this meant however little the peasants thought they could get away with. On the other hand, many wealthy men thought to leave life no longer rich and thus qualified to enter the kingdom of heaven by willing their estates to the Church. The massive transfer of wealth from taxpaying secular hands to the tax-exempt clergy provides the backdrop to the next phase of confrontation between the Church and its unwilling subjects.

Church wealth may have declined in absolute terms for the reasons given, but relative to the civil power it increased sharply at precisely the time that money could buy a decisive military advantage. Even the Angevin kings of Naples went from being the patrons of the Papacy to being its paid retainers, not always a guarantee of obedience but closer than ever before to the control of the southern kingdom sought by popes since the early days of the Hauteville conquest. The great cities also had a broad enough economic base to emerge from under the apocalyptic hooves with their relative wealth enhanced and could therefore compete for the services of mercenaries: but lesser states were ground down. Perhaps the best example was Siena, once the equal of Florence, but which fell behind during the fourteenth century. One of the reasons was that Siena was forced to pay the mercenary companies protection money thirty-seven times between 1342 and 1399, a constant drain on her finances that in conjunction with the hostility of Florence drove the city to surrender its independence to Duke Gian' Galeazzo Visconti of Milan.

**DUCCIO DI BUONINSEGNA (*c.*1257–1319)**

**Siena's victory at Montaperti in 1260 was preceded by massed prayers to the Virgin Mary, which strengthened a unique cult that gave rise to local artist Duccio's *Maestà*, an epic storytelling altarpiece painted in 1308–11 that far outshone anything the city's hated rival Florence could show and gave Duccio a secure place alongside Cimabue and Giotto in the pantheon of European art.**

Perhaps even more tellingly, when Siena chose to fight – in 1363 against the ephemeral all-Italian Company of the Hat led by Niccolò Montefeltro, the escalader of San Leo – it cost the city 48,500 florins for troops alone and at least a further 8000 for incidentals, without computing the damage done by the Hats before and after the battle. These sums must be compared to a total of 16,300 in bribes and defensive costs in 1359 to buy off Conrad of Landau. Nor did the victory over the Hats, despite being immortalised in Lippo Vanni's fresco *Battaglia della Val di Chiana* (Picture section 1, p. 5) in the map room of the Palazzo Pubblico, win the Sienese any respect: the following year they had to pay off the Company of the Star with 38,650 florins, plus 13,600 to hire their own mercenaries to provide a fig leaf of deterrence. Siena may have been particularly victimised because it resisted the general trend towards government by warlords. Barring the desperate submission to the Visconti at the turn of the century, the city persisted in communal government until Pandolfo Petrucci became absolute ruler in 1487, by which time the city's independence was doomed no matter what form of government it chose.

# FIVE

# *White Rider*

## CHAPTER SUMMARY

*By the middle of the fourteenth century, their expansion to the north blocked by the Ordelaffi of Forlì and to the west by Nolfo Montefeltro, the duumvirate Guastafamiglia–Galeotto Malatesta extended their rule over lands stretching far south into the Marche, including the prosperous ports of Pesaro, Senigallia, Fano and Ancona. Some of their gains resulted from hiring the mercenary 'Great Company', but in 1353 the company was hired against them by an alliance of Marche lords and the Ordelaffi, backed by the Visconti of Milan. Hard on the heels of their defeat by the Ordelaffi and the Great Company, the Malatesta brothers were confronted by Cardinal Legate Albornoz, who arrived in 1353 with an army of French mercenaries to recover the states of the Church on behalf of the Papacy, resident at Avignon since 1309. Albornoz's forces defeated the Malatesti in 1355 and the brothers made submission to him, after which they were stripped of all save their core possessions, for which they had to pay a high rent and perform military service. The Montefeltri had already been virtually dispossessed and after the Malatesti were humbled the Polenti of Ravenna, the Alidosi of Imola, the Este of Ferrara and the Carrara of Padua also bent the knee to the implacable cardinal. The Ordelaffi of Forlì were the last to capitulate, in 1359. Albornoz's achievement was undone when he sought to round off his recovery of the Papal State by accepting Bologna from a governor who had rebelled against the authority of the Visconti of Milan. A grinding war ensued during which the lords of Romagna recovered many of their lost rights and lands in payment for their services against the Visconti. The chief beneficiaries were Guastafamiglia and Galeotto Malatesta, but the Montefeltri were by now so inconsiderable that they failed to benefit from the bonanza.*

In 1334 the commune of Rimini bestowed outright dictatorship on Guastafamiglia and Galeotto Malatesta and their descendants in perpetuity. The brothers' attempts to expand to the north were checked at Cesena by the Ordelaffi lords of Forlì, and to the west by the Montefeltri, but in the south they already held Pesaro and Fossombrone, and in 1340 took control of Senigallia. This was followed by Fano in 1342, for which they hired part of the Great Company, then led by Werner of Ürslingen. By 1350, aided by the devastation of the Black Death – which spared the Malatesti even as it hollowed out their dominions – the brothers governed Ancona, Cingoli, Iesi, Osimo and many lesser communes in the Marche, some by invitation, others by intimidation and mainly at the expense of discredited papal governors. Their expansion was challenged in 1348 by an alliance of lesser lords led by Count Gentile da Mogliano of Fermo, but he was defeated, captured and compelled to accept humiliating terms.

Guastafamiglia besieged Fermo in 1353 but in doing so he broke a private undertaking with Francesco II Ordelaffi of Forlì and with it an alliance cemented in 1338 by marriage between two of Francesco's sons and Guastafamiglia's daughters. Ordelaffi, backed by the Visconti of Milan who were displeased with the Malatesti for other reasons, made common cause with Gentile da Mogliano and together with part of Fra Moriale's horde devastated the Malatesta dominions, starting with the relief of Fermo. Between November 1353 and March 1354 the combined companies ravaged the countryside around Iesi, Fano and Rimini, sacked forty-four Malatesta *castelli* ranging from Montefiore in the north to Castelfidardo in the south, and finally compelled Guastafamiglia to give up his son, Malatesta 'Ungaro', as a hostage against payment of 6000 ducats (Venetian equivalent of the florin, first minted in 1284) to Moriale and a further 3000 to Ordelaffi and Mogliano.

Meanwhile Cardinal Albornoz was imposing papal rule in Umbria with the army of French mercenaries brought from Avignon, before setting off for Romagna in late 1354 with the over-mighty Malatesti at the top of his 'to do' list. What, if any, role Albornoz played in forming the anti-Malatesta alliance is unclear: the other lords of Romagna and the Marche had abundant reasons of their own to combine against the hegemony of Rimini. Guastafamiglia had also made the fateful decision to throw in his lot with King Louis of Hungary when he marched through eastern Italy in 1347 on his way south to avenge the death of his brother Andrew, whose marriage to Queen Joanna I of Naples ended two years earlier when he was thrown from a palace window. This was a high-stakes game in which the lords of Rimini were unwise to take a hand, attracting as it did the hostility of Venice to add to their store of enemies. We will not delve further into the complicated situation that developed in southern Italy (and, indeed, all around the Adriatic), other than to observe that the gains the Malatesti made at the Marche–Abruzze borders were more than offset by becoming the tallest poppies in the eastern Papal State, and thus the first to fall to Albornoz's sword.

### JOANNA I OF NAPLES (1343–82)

**The reign of Joanna was torn by strife between the Anjou–Durazzo and Anjou–Taranto factions. Joanna may have been complicit in the murder of Andrew of Durazzo and after Louis of Taranto beat back the first Hungarian invasion she became pregnant by him before their marriage in 1448. After Louis defeated a second Hungarian invasion in 1352 he was crowned King of Naples, in Joanna's right. None of their children survived.**

Albornoz's career reflected the fact that he was born of royal blood in the Crusader state of New Castille. In 1340, as the warrior Archbishop of Toledo, he saved the life of King Alfonso XI in battle against the Moors. When Pedro the Cruel succeeded to the Castilian throne in 1350 Albornoz denounced the king's public and private behaviour, and was compelled to flee for his life to Avignon, where Clement VI made him a cardinal. As a rare warrior prelate who was also loyal to the Papacy, in June 1353 Innocent VI appointed him plenipotentiary Legate and Vicar-General of the Papal State, and charged him with restoring papal authority. It was understood that the task encompassed both the humbling of those who had usurped papal power and the reform of papal administration, without which no settlement would stand. As

Early fourteenth-century *Crucifixion* attributed to Giotto, but possibly by the Rimini School; St Francis kneels with the donors, who may be Malatesta da Verucchio and his wife Margherita.

Early fourteenth-century *Deposition from the Cross* by Pietro da Rimini; the stylistic similarities with the *Crucifixion* attributed to Giotto are striking.

Illumination of Dante with the doomed lovers Francesca da Polenta and her brother-in-law Paolo 'Il Bello' Malatesta, from a fourteenth-century Venetian manuscript of Dante's *L'Inferno*.

Pope Innocent III dreaming that St Francis will save the church from collapse and Pope Honorius III confirming the new monastic order, from Benozzo Gozzoli's 1450–2 fresco cycle *Scenes from the Life of St Francis* in San Francesco church, Montefalco.

Simone de Martini's splendid 1328 fresco in the Palazzo Pubblico, Siena, honouring the condottiere Guidoriccio da Fogliano.

Paolo Uccello's 1436 fresco in the Florence Duomo honouring Sir John Hawkwood; the cadaverous face suggests the artist worked from Hawkwood's death mask.

Lippo Vanni's 1363 monochrome *Battaglia della Val di Chiana* in the Map Room of the Palazzo Pubblico, Siena, celebrating a rare victory over the marauding mercenary companies.

What a difference a century makes: Antonio Pollaiuolo's 1465 engraving of a stylised battle among naked men, reflecting conventions employed on ancient Greek vases.

Paolo Uccello's 1438 *Battle of San Romano*

*(left)* Florentine captain Niccolò 'da Tolentino' Mauruzzi rides into battle while messengers ride away to summon help from fellow captain Micheletto Attendolo.

*(below left)* The symbolic overthrow of the enemy commander Bernardino 'della Carda' Ubaldini, who was not, in fact, unhorsed.

*(below)* Long believed to be Micheletto Attendolo arriving at San Romano, now thought to be a later work celebrating his victory for Florence at Anghiari in 1440.

Illuminated letter 'U' from a 1420 antiphonal by Bartolomeo di Fruosino shows Pope Martin V flanked by cardinals from his Colonna clan, to whose advancement and enrichment he devoted the best efforts of his papacy.

with most great military commanders, Albornoz was lucky. We have seen how the coincidence of the Black Death and the mercenary companies strengthened relative Church power, but in addition Albornoz found Milan in the hands of Archbishop Giovanni Visconti, and on his death in 1354 divided among three heirs. Bernabò and Galeazzo II murdered their brother Matteo, after which Galeazzo kept his head down in Pavia while Bernabò ruled Milan – but during the first crucial years of his reconquest Albornoz enjoyed respite from the hostility of the greatest secular power in northern Italy, whose interests were inimical to a unified Papal State.

The first shot in the offensive against the Malatesti was a summons from Innocent VI in July 1354 to appear before a papal court in Avignon, to answer charges that they had illegally occupied Church territories. They made no reply and after petitions on their behalf by the crown of Naples and by Florence proved unavailing they were declared in rebellion, a necessary precondition for Albornoz to take armed action against men who could produce dozens of papal missives sent over the preceding thirty years lauding them as faithful defenders of the Church. They knew what to expect because in 1354 Albornoz had humbled Giovanni di Vico, Prefect of Rome and Lord of Viterbo, who had usurped a domain stretching from Civitavecchia on the Tyrrhenian coast to Orvieto in the duchy of Spoleto. Vico was besieged at Orvieto in March and made submission in June, in a treaty that granted him a twelve-year appointment as papal vicar for the port of Corneto (today Tarquinia), a small part of his previous holdings. This was more than Innocent VI thought he should have received, but Albornoz argued that he needed Vico's support in Rome and that to dispossess him entirely would arouse furious resistance from his peers across the Papal State. As it was, the humbling of Vico undid the anti-Malatesta alliance in Romagna, with Francesco II Ordelaffi and Guastafamiglia reconciled, and Gentile da Mogliano persuaded to desert Albornoz's cause.

Many other minor lords remained in the legate's camp, however, and in March 1355 several towns in the Ancona hinterland rebelled against the Malatesti, pinning down their forces. Albornoz's army under Ridolfo II Varano of Camerino drove Galeotto away from Recanati before bringing him to battle outside Paterno, near Ancona.

Galeotto was wounded and captured, which ended Malatesta resistance.* Ascoli was surrendered while Iesi and Macerata separately submitted to papal rule, but Ancona reverted to a republic under papal sovereignty, a peculiar status it was to enjoy until 1532. Galeotto was taken to Gubbio, where Guastafamiglia went in June under safe conduct to seek terms from Albornoz. These were the surrender of all Malatesta holdings except Rimini, Fano, Pesaro and Fossombrone, for which they would be granted a ten-year probationary vicariate. Other conditions included personal submission to the pope at Avignon (which Guastafamiglia performed in 1358) and an annual *census* (tribute) of 8000 florins plus 150 knights for three months' service at papal discretion. Guastafamiglia could only accept the terms under protest that they were more burdensome than he could have sustained even in possession of all his former territories. Rimini submitted separately, confessing that the Malatesti had been granted powers that were not in the gift of the commune. Innocent VI was pleased to confirm the settlement, lifted the excommunications and interdicts laid on the Malatesti and the communes that had invited them to rule over them, and in recognition of former services reduced the annual tribute to 6000 florins and 100 knights.

The Montefeltri also enjoyed a brief moment of glory before being eclipsed by Albornoz. Nolfo had a stroke of luck when the plague carried off his brother Galasso and Galasso's son Guido in 1350. In 1352 Nolfo seized Cagli, midway between papal Gubbio and Malatesta Fossombrone, while fighting for Archbishop Giovanni Visconti against Florence and settled the lordship jointly on his brothers Enrico and Feltrino, possibly calculating that mutual rivalry would keep them too busy to scheme against him. All his *furbizia* could not save him from Albornoz: noting that their sworn enemy Bishop Francesco Brancaleone of Urbino was among the legate's closest associates, Nolfo and Enrico obeyed Albornoz's summons and in June 1354 made submission to him in Rome, publicly confessing their sins against the Church. Urbino and Cagli separately asked forgiveness for having granted the

* Twelve years later Galeotto married Ridolfo II Varano's daughter Gentilina, who bore him Carlo II, Pandolfo III, Andrea, Galeotto and three daughters who married into the ruling families of Faenza, Imola – and Montefeltro.

Montefeltri powers that infringed on papal sovereignty. The relative insignificance of the Montefeltri at this time was underlined when Albornoz did not grant them a vicariate, as he did other lords of the Borderlands, but simply recognised their right to exercise the civil power in those places that elected them. Albornoz further complicated their existence by requiring the return and reinstatement of those exiled from Urbino and Cagli. In return for these small favours the Montefeltri swore to provide prompt and wholehearted support against other rebellious Romagna lords.

The Polenti of Ravenna made submission after the Malatesti were humbled, leaving the Manfredi of Faenza and the Ordelaffi of Forlì as the outstanding rebels. Albornoz preached a Crusade against them during the winter of 1355–6, promising full remission of sins for those who took up arms against them. Guastafamiglia and his son Ungaro, with 600 retainers, were among the first to take the cross, bringing with them the Count of Carpegna and the Alidosi of Imola, with the Este of Ferrara and the Carrara of Padua also bowing to the prevailing wind. Albornoz appointed Galeotto Malatesta, so lately his captive, captain-general and *Gonfaloniere* at a monthly salary of 300 florins. The Manfredi surrendered Faenza but Francesco II Ordelaffi and his fierce wife Marzia were still defiant in April 1357, when Albornoz summoned the vicars of the Papal State to a parliament at the Fano palace of 'the magnificent lord Galeotto of the Malatesti of Rimini'. Rehabilitation could hardly have been more complete. It was here that Albornoz revealed the *Constitutiones Sanctae Matris Ecclesiae*, known as the 'Egidian Constitutions' from the Italian rendering (Egidio) of the legate's unpronounceable Spanish name. It was among the first books printed in Italy (Iesi, 1373) and set out the rules under which the Papal State was governed, when possible, until 1816.

Albornoz also announced that he was returning to Avignon, to be replaced by a monk with no military experience. The assembled papal vicars were appalled and begged him to stay long enough to see Ordelaffi reduced to submission, but Albornoz felt compelled to leave his work unfinished and hastened back to Avignon to secure his political base against the enemies his success had bred. Pronounced 'Father of the Church' by Innocent VI upon arrival in October, Albornoz was sent back to Italy a year later because his achievement was unravelling, with Ordelaffi still defiant, Giovanni di Vico intriguing to recover his lost domain and Rome once more in chaos. Albornoz at once began operations against Ordelaffi, outbidding him for the services of Conrad of Landau, and in July 1359 Forlì surrendered. In what was by now a familiar formula Ordelaffi was granted a conditional papal vicariate over Forlimpopoli and Castrocaro, to the east and south of Forlì. This was a mistake: he had been condemned as a heretic and by that judgement deserved condign punishment. Guastafamiglia may have intervened on behalf of his once and future friend and the father-in-law of his daughters, but the episode illustrates how the unbending righteousness that Albornoz brought with him from Spain had finally succumbed to Italian *realpolitik* and moral relativism.

The historic papal patrimony was now entirely returned to obedience with the exception of Bologna, much the largest city in the Papal State, whose purchase in 1350 by Archbishop Giovanni Visconti had been recognised by the pope in 1352 with the grant of a twelve-year vicariate against an annual tribute of 12,000 florins. Albornoz, ultimately backed by Avignon, cynically took advantage of a rebellion by the Visconti governor of Bologna to break the agreement by accepting the city from the rebel governor in 1360, despite previous papal undertakings to help restore Bologna to its legitimate ruler. This was another, more serious, error: the deadly Bernabò had by now established himself as the supreme lord of the Visconti domain in Lombardy and a ferocious war ensued, whose effects rippled through the Papal State and undid Albornoz's achievement. His moral authority was destroyed by a massacre of 170 captive rebels and their wives at Corinaldo in 1360 and the levelling of Forlimpopoli in 1362, but the principal damage was done by the cession of many of the secular rights he had recovered for the Papacy in order to maintain an alliance among the other northern lords against Bernabò Visconti.

Pope Urban V, who continued to prosecute the war after the death of Innocent VI in 1362, pronounced Bernabò a heretic. But the ruinous cost, perhaps also a dawning realisation that the free companies ravening around the walls of Avignon were drawn by the draught of war in Lombardy, caused the pope to reconsider. The deal made with Milan in 1364 has been ascribed either to Bernabò's wholesale bribery of the Curia or to Urban V's desire to persuade the free companies to join a

Crusade against the Turks. There is a less florid explanation: the pope was one of the foremost Church lawyers and the usurpation of Bernabò's Vicariate of Bologna had been blatantly illegal even by the elastic standards of the time. Urban was a Benedictine monk, not even a cardinal at the time of his election, and it took him a while to find his feet at Avignon; once he did it could not be long before he concluded that the war being waged in his name was unjust. Although not finally beatified until 1870, Urban V was widely regarded as saintly even in life, which would seem to offer an adequate explanation why, despite having Bernabò at his mercy, the pope agreed to pay him an indemnity of half a million florins and granted him the Vicariate of Bologna until the sum was paid.

White Rider Albornoz, of whom it could fairly be said that he made a wasteland and called it peace, was disowned in 1364 – but by serving him long, loyally and lucratively the Malatesti emerged from the struggle strengthened to an extent none could have imagined when they made submission in 1355. Not only was their probation revoked prematurely in 1362, but also they and their heirs were then confirmed as papal vicars for a further ten years. In addition their price in the condottiere market was boosted by their military successes. Guastafamiglia's eldest son Pandolfo II outmanoeuvred the fearsome Company of the Star at Campo delle Mosche in the Arno valley in 1359, Galeotto and Guastafamiglia's younger son Ungaro defeated a Visconti army at San Ruffillo near Faenza in 1361, Ungaro defeated Bernabò himself and captured Bernabò's bastard son and lieutenant Ambrogio at Salaro, near Modena, in 1363, and finally Galeotto, as Captain-General of Florence, defeated a Pisan army led by Hawkwood and his White Company at the extremely bloody battle of Cascina in 1364.*

By contrast Nolfo Montefeltro did not, perhaps could not, honour his pledge to support Albornoz and by 1359 was just another citizen of papally ruled Urbino, his son Federico II inheriting little except the empty title of Count of Montefeltro when Nolfo died in 1364. Guastafamiglia also died in 1364, a few days before Cascina. Although jointly

---

* For Campo delle Mosche and Cascina, see Map 7. Both were defeats of 'foreigners' by 'Italians' a generation earlier than Alberico da Barbiano's more celebrated victory over the 'barbarian' Bretons at Marino.

appointed with Galeotto, Guastafamiglia disposed of the vicariate as though his own, dividing it by lot to avoid rancour between his sons. Pandolfo II received Pesaro, Fano and Fossombrone, with Rimini going to Ungaro. However, Galeotto remained the overall papal vicar and outlived both of his nephews, earning the sobriquet 'il Vecchio'. After Ungaro died without a male heir in 1372 Galeotto took over administration of Rimini, and when Pandolfo II died the next year he ruled in Fano as the guardian of his five-year-old grand-nephew Malatesta 'dei Sonetti'. Given the family history it was remarkable – and was to prove imprudent – that Galeotto did not unite the inheritance in his own line. But by resisting the temptation to dispossess his brother's offspring he continued to display a loyalty that had done as much as Guastafamiglia's often flawed *furbizia* to sustain the clan through a time when the wheel of fortune spun out of control.

SIX

# Creativity

## CHAPTER SUMMARY

*The direct exercise of secular power by the Church led to the erosion of its spiritual and intellectual hegemony, arguably an essential precondition for the individual empowerment that Jacob Burckhardt identified as the defining spirit of the era in* The Civilisation of the Renaissance in Italy. *The abject submission Albornoz sought to inculcate, if backed by a secular power to bear the opprobrium of enforcing it, might have condemned the West to the intellectual stagnation that came to characterise the Islamic world under the Ottoman caliphate.*

The concept of submission as applied by Cardinal Albornoz during his reconquest of the Papal State was quite unlike the feudal ceremony of homage. What Albornoz required was almost modern, a precursor of the show trials to which the secular religion of Communism subjected selected sacrificial adherents in the twentieth century. The ceremony involved genuine abasement and the penitents knew that limiting their public confession merely to the sins they were formally charged with would prejudice their prospects – they had to heap coals on their own heads. Considering Albornoz's background it is perhaps not surprising that the submission he required owed much to cultural cross-fertilisation in the Iberian Peninsula during the long struggle between Christian and Muslim kingdoms. A radical sect within 'Islam', the word defining a faith that demands the submission of humankind to the will of God as told to his messenger Muhammad, has recently reminded us that the principle of absolute submission governs a large proportion of mankind. Today's suicide bombers resemble the sect of assassins (*Hashashiyyin*) who occupied the fortress of Alamut in north Persia from 1090 until destroyed by the Mongols in 1256. The reappearance of the sect has uncovered an incomprehension mixed with cognitive dissonance in post-Christian Western societies that may stem from a psychological divide more unbridgeable than the more obvious cultural chasm.

For much of the Islamic world the institution of the (Sunni) Ottoman Caliphate in 1517 created a relationship of close collaboration between the spiritual and secular spheres similar to that developed between the Eastern Christian Church and the Byzantine Empire. In both the Empire was the protector of religion, and religion guided its protector. Circumstances led the Western Christian Church to take another course, with a paradoxical outcome. The direct exercise of secular power by the Roman Church, with all its attendant ethical compromises, corruption and abuse, played a significant role in the erosion of its spiritual and intellectual hegemony, arguably an essential precondition for the individual empowerment that Jacob Burckhardt identified as the defining spirit of the era in his landmark *The Civilisation of the Renaissance in Italy*. The abject submission Albornoz sought to inculcate, if backed by a secular power to bear the opprobrium of enforcing it, might have condemned the West to the stagnation that gradually came to characterise the Islamic world. It has been illuminating to observe the reaction to the new Islamist threat by those in the West rendered bereft by the recent collapse of the Communist Caliphate. The otherwise incomprehensible solidarity of Western leftists with Islamists whose world-view is violently hostile to their own may stem from a common psychopathology: submissives need to submit – to what or to whom appears to be immaterial.

Having jemmied open the door to a discussion of psychological determinism, it seems the appropriate place to review a hypothesis about the relationship between creativity and sexuality that has become a taboo subject of late. It should be unarguable that the relatively recent decline of infant mortality and death in childbirth, and the ability of men and women to satisfy the mating instinct without procreating, has had a revolutionary effect on human society: but to project the implications back in time helps us to understand neither the past nor the present. The hypothesis in question is that while traditionally some men proved themselves in battle, all women who did not or could not choose chastity had to confront the more certainly dangerous test of childbirth, while a surprising number also knowingly risked their lives in extramarital dalliance. It follows that physical courage was the norm for women, perhaps less so among men. The second part of the hypothesis is that desire for immortal glory was more urgent in men because they were denied women's intimate bond with posterity. We can be sure most women encouraged ambition and bravery in their husbands and sons – Latin *machismo/maschilismo* is notoriously mother-driven – but it is likely that their men would have indulged in public works and ostentatious artistic patronage regardless of female influence. The theory has the merit of calling into question what we mean by 'hard' and 'soft' power.

These considerations may help to explain why the patrons who made possible the surge of literary and artistic creativity in the period we are about to enter were also responsible for chronic, destructive warfare. The career of Giotto, the second artist after Pietro Cavallini – who has priority but was far less influential – to imbue a flat surface with something akin to the depth later achieved with geometric perspective, provides an illustrative anecdote. Giotto intersects with our story in an intriguing sojourn at Rimini that preceded his famous stay in Padua, where in 1303–5 he painted the wonderful fresco cycle of the life of Christ that adorns the Scrovegni chapel. While in Rimini he painted an altarpiece of which only the central crucifix remains, hanging over the altar in the Tempio Malatestiano. Some unknown hand sawed off the flanking figures of Mary and St John, now lost, and a headpiece depicting God the Father that has been traced to a private collection in England by Professor Federico Zeri, furious critic of 'the cretins and the corrupt' who are charged with looking after Italy's artistic heritage.

Mastin Vecchio probably commissioned Giotto's crucifix for the old Franciscan church in which he was buried. Sadly, when Sigismondo remodelled the church he destroyed fresco cycles painted by the Rimini School, artists of whom little is known and of whose early work, clearly modelled on Giotto, little of certain attribution remains except

**GIOTTO DI BONDONE (1267–1337)**

**Florentine painter and pioneer of perspective who invented the device of framing his work with painted architectural features (*grisaille*), Giotto was acclaimed by Dante in *Purgatorio* XI as having surpassed his teacher, the great Cimabue (1240–1302). If not the fathers, Cimabue, Giotto and their Sienese contemporary Duccio were certainly the grandfathers of the artistic Renaissance.**

a Giovanni da Rimini crucifix dating from 1309 in the Franciscan church-museum at Mercatello sul Metauro, and a fresco of the Resurrection of Drusiana in the church of Sant'Agostino in Rimini with many faces, alas unidentified, clearly modelled from life. Sigismondo almost certainly destroyed more of their work when he demolished the Gattolo palace to build Castel Sismondo. The English art historian Dillian Gordon has suggested that the cycle of seven paintings of the Life of Christ attributed to Giotto and held by museums in New York, Boston, Munich, London and the Berenson collection in Settignano, near Florence, may have been painted by the Rimini School; if so, the donors kneeling with St Francis at the base of the cross in the Munich *Crucifixion* (Picture section 1, p. 1) could be Mastin and his last wife Margherita, portrayed in youthful guise.

For our purposes it suffices to know that among the earliest patrons of Giotto, the grandfather of the artistic Renaissance, was Dante's blood-sucking mountain dog, Mastin Vecchio. When I revisited the Scrovegni chapel after its painstaking and glorious restoration I was amused to learn that the haloes on the lesser figures are black because the Master ran low on funds and cheated by using gold paint instead of gold leaf. This suggests that his patron, Enrico Scrovegni, drove as hard a bargain as his father, a notorious usurer also denounced by Dante, for the expiation of whose sins the chapel was built. Mastin Vecchio and Enrico Scrovegni were social outsiders, self-made men living in uncertain times, and perhaps for this reason they had the confidence in their own judgement to break with the flat, symbolic style of iconography that remained the norm in Venice and the Byzantine Empire, culturally and geographically far closer to Rimini and

Padua than the artistic epicentres of Florence or Rome. It is reasonable to conclude that men with no investment in the status quo were instinctively attracted by the new in other areas of human endeavour.

Despite being the leading Ghibellines of Romagna, the Montefeltri were more generous to the Church than their Guelf rivals in Rimini. Their patronage fits the pattern, common to many cultures, of the warrior's desire to atone for homicide; from the endowment of the archbishopric and rebuilding the cathedral of San Leo in the Romanesque style by Antonio I in 1173, through Guido's posthumous endowments and many subsequent donations by his frequently excommunicated successors, notably Nolfo's contribution to the new church of St Francis in Urbino completed in 1350. It bought them no earthly favour: when Pope John XXII purged the Franciscan order of those heretically advocating poverty and humility, he specifically denounced the Franciscan lay brotherhood of Saint Mary of Mercy, devoted to caring for orphans and the sick in Urbino, as a 'blasphemous' organisation set up by soon-to-be-murdered Federico I to affirm his dominion.

When even charity was regarded as potentially subversive by a Papacy obsessed with secular power, it is not remarkable that secular princes moved away from the devout patronage that built the cathedrals and endowed the foundations that were the glory of the medieval Church, and towards works that more directly immortalised their own names. The popes did not lag behind, and the prize for self-glorification must surely go to Pope Paul V, who had his name inscribed in enormous letters across the façade of St Peter's basilica in Rome. Pius II cut to the heart of the matter in his autobiographical *Commentaries:* 'while men live they take pleasure in the glory of the present, which they hope will continue after death. It is this which sustains the most brilliant intellects and even more than the hope of a celestial life, which once begun shall never end, cheers and refreshes the heart of man.' The paradigm shift these words convey would not have taken place when it did, if at all, without the struggle to define the boundaries of secular and spiritual power during the late Middle Ages, making it perhaps the most important single factor in the liberation of the human imagination that shaped the early modern era in the West.

Thus although the constant warfare in which the Papacy played such a central role may seem a thing apart from the new forms of

# SEVEN

# *Anarchy*

## CHAPTER SUMMARY

*Pope Urban V attempted to return the Papacy to Rome in 1367, in the midst of renewed war with the Visconti, but gave up in disgust and died in Avignon in 1370. His successor, Gregory XI, restored the freeholds previously confiscated from the Montefeltri to the new clan leader, Antonio II. The Malatesti continued to prosper in the service of the Church. Galeotto 'il Vecchio' became the sole clan leader after the death of Guastafamiglia in 1364 and of his sons in 1372–3. The War of Eight Saints in 1375–8 between Florence and the Papacy saw the final undoing of Cardinal Albornoz's work and after Gregory XI died in 1378 there was a schism in the Church, with the Italian cardinals electing one pope and the Avignon cardinals another. The chief beneficiaries of the schism and of the split between Rome and her long-time ally Florence were the Visconti of Milan. Galeazzo Visconti had been careful never to challenge his deadly brother Bernabò and when Galeazzo died in 1378, his son Gian' Galeazzo posed as a harmless dilettante until, in 1385, he ambushed his uncle and put him to death. Under Gian' Galeazzo the unified Visconti state reached the peak of its power and in 1395 he bought the title of duke from the Holy Roman Emperor. Upon his sudden death in 1402, however, Gian' Galeazzo's empire fell apart. The expansion of Visconti power provoked a reaction from Venice, which began to expand its mainland dominions aggressively in the early 1400s to create a permanent counterbalance to Milan in northern Italy. Although some border bickering persisted, the Malatesti and Montefeltri refrained from serious mutual aggression and both clans prospered while the major players were otherwise engaged. After the death of Galeotto il Vecchio in 1385, however, Malatesta clan unity was broken, with the disgruntled heirs of Guastafamiglia dissatisfied with Pesaro while Galeotto's sons shared Rimini, Fano and Cesena. In the early 1390s a new Roman pontiff, Boniface IX, made a series of territorial concessions to the Montefeltri and the two branches of the Malatesti that would in time set them all at each other's throats.*

To return to our narrative, it is likely that the Visconti would have made war on Albornoz's reunified Papal State anyway, but the legate's overstretch in the matter of Bologna made conflict certain and the 1364 settlement provided only the briefest of lulls before hostilities recommenced. Pope Urban V sought to unite the Italian lords against the mercenary companies, but Bernabò and his brother Galeazzo of Pavia chose to use them as proxies, covertly funding a new Company of St George to maraud in Tuscany and Liguria. In 1366 Urban V pronounced anathema against the Visconti condottieri, calling down the vengeance of Archangel Michael the Exterminator on them. More practically, he also made preparation for a return to Rome and put together a new anti-Visconti alliance with Queen Joanna I of Naples, Emperor Charles IV, the Este of Ferrara, the Gonzaga of Mantua and the Carrara of Padua. Galeotto, Pandolfo II and Ungaro Malatesta were also in close attendance when Urban V entered Rome in October 1367, where the pope made Galeotto a Roman Senator.

Federico II Montefeltro died in 1367 and his brother Paolo and nephew Spinetta had to borrow money and horses to obey the papal summons to Rome, where they were consigned to the undifferentiated mass of riders trailing behind the papal cortège in which the Malatesti had pride of place. To add injury to insult Urban then sent his brother, Cardinal Legate Anglic Grimoard, to Romagna where he abolished the instruments of self-government at Urbino and Cagli and with it the tithe paid by the towns to the Montefeltri for defence. Even before the death of the older generation, the younger Montefeltri abandoned the submission that had served them so ill and reverted to Ghibelline type. Summoned to serve against Perugia in 1369, Antonio II and his brothers Nolfo, Galasso and Guido made a show of obedience but soon negotiated a commission with the Perugians. This cost the family their properties in Urbino, which Paolo was compelled to surrender to Grimoard for his nephews' treachery. The Montefeltro palace was demolished to make way for a new building to house the Church officials (Priors) and other houses were given to the faithful.

Disillusioned, Urban V returned to Avignon to die in 1370 and his successor, Gregory XI, did not return to Rome until 1377. Paolo Montefeltro also died in 1370 and Antonio II became the new clan leader. After the Perugian war ended in 1370 Antonio and his brothers cleverly joined a delegation sent by Bernabò Visconti to make submission at Avignon to Gregory XI; perhaps impressed by the company they kept Gregory restored the Montefeltri freeholds, confiscated by Grimoard, who commented that 'this excessive clemency to those who have departed from Our Lord damages the interests of the Church and provides material for future rebellions and scandals'. Bernabò was simply seeking a breathing space and the Papal–Visconti war dragged on, punctuated by two further treaties, until mutual exhaustion brought about a sullen truce in 1374. The war completed the undoing of Albornoz's fragile achievement, with papal authority so reduced that in 1372 Bernabò forced legates sent with Gregory's Bull of excommunication to eat it. The gesture won him much admiration in the Papal State, where popular resentment of the French governors sent from Avignon was reaching boiling point.

The Malatesti profited greatly from the war without playing a notable part in it, with Pandolfo II appointed governor of Città di Castello in 1368–9 and of Urbino in 1370. Papal finances were so overdrawn by the grinding war with Milan that in 1371 Galeotto was able to buy San Sepolcro in lieu of 18,000 florins in unpaid commissions. He earned further kudos by his participation in the May 1373 victory over the Visconti at Montichiari, near Brescia. Pandolfo II died in 1373, leaving Galeotto as sole clan leader when in 1375 a long series of small but cumulatively significant acts of double-dealing by the Church finally alienated Florence, its most constant ally. Florence did not merely form a new alliance with its mortal rival Milan: in preparation for the breach with Rome Florentine agents in Romagna cultivated rebellion among the dispossessed Montefeltri, Ordelaffi and Manfredi.

Thus it was that in late 1375 Florentine cavalry joined with Antonio II Montefeltro's infantry to drive the papal governors and Galeotto Malatesta out of Urbino. Galeotto retreated to Cagli but was promptly driven from there as well by Antonio's supporters. In response Galeotto improvised a blocking alliance in the upper Metauro and Foglia valleys by backing the return to power of the Gabrielli to Gubbio, the Brancaleoni to Castel Durante and the Olivieri to Piandimeleto, clans with no desire to see the Montefeltri resurgent, and held Cesena when the rest of the Po valley cities rebelled. Galeotto was seventy-six years old yet between October 1375 and January 1376, starting in Verona where as executor he secured the succession of his wards, Bartolomeo and Antonio della Scala after the death of their father, he rode to Urbino, thence to Cagli, to Piandimeleto and Castel Durante, to Fano and Rimini and from there to Cesena, wearing out a string of horses and fighting several skirmishes along the way.

The War of Eight Saints, so called from the popular designation of the eight War Councillors of Florence, lasted until 1378 and overlapped with the Chioggia War of 1376–81 between Venice and Genoa. Both overlapped with the final collapse of papal authority to a level of impotence considerably more abysmal than it had been before Albornoz's reconquest. Upon the death of Gregory XI in 1378 there was a schism in the Church, with the Roman cardinals electing another Italian, Urban VI, and the Avignon cardinals an antipope, the French Clement VII. Prior to his election Clement, then Cardinal Legate Robert of Geneva, was responsible for an atrocity that shocked even the dull sensibilities of the times. Under his orders a company of Bretons brought with him from France and Hawkwood, who had been awarded the lordship of Bagnacavallo and a complementary sack of Faenza in lieu of commissions, slaughtered the citizens of Cesena – the only city loyal to the Church along the Via Emilia – after they rose up against the brutality of the Bretons. Galeotto Malatesta refused to act against Cesena and gave asylum to the survivors. He was awarded the papal vicariate of the town in 1378, which was rebuilt by the Malatesti and remained notably loyal to them until the heirless death of Malatesta Novello in 1468, when it passed unhappily under papal rule.

The Western schism created a situation of such frantic disorder in Italy that the details become wearisome. Much the most significant development was that Florence, by shattering the residual Guelf alliance, weakened itself in the face of the more deadly threat to its autonomy posed by the Visconti, to whom we must turn for a moment. Bernabò only ruled the eastern part of the Visconti domain, the western rump remaining under his brother Galeazzo II at Pavia. The two collaborated, but Galeazzo was careful to do nothing to challenge his brother's supremacy and when Galeazzo died in 1378 his son Gian' Galeazzo adopted an even lower profile, cultivating an image of harmless dilettantism so that his uncle Bernabò should not think it necessary to eliminate him. While Bernabò made himself hated by the brutal nature of his regime and the heavy taxation required to sustain his wars, Gian' Galeazzo taxed his subjects lightly and bided his time. Because 'virtue' in English has acquired another meaning, the sobriquet *Conte di Virtù* enjoyed by Gian' Galeazzo Visconti causes confusion in translation. In Italian, as Gracie Fields put it in another context, goodness has nothing to do with it: *virtù* means manliness, and it is a grim commentary on the time in which he lived that Gian' Galeazzo, inventor of the forty-day execution he called the 'Lenten treatment', should have been thought outstandingly manly: *Conte di Furbizia* would have been nearer the mark.

### THE HANGED MAN

**Tarot cards first took their modern form at the Milanese court of the highly superstitious Filippo Maria Visconti. The 'Hanged Man' card illustrates an innovation decreed in 1398 by his father, Gian' Galeazzo, for the exemplary public punishment of notable wrongdoers, who might be hanged by one foot and given food and water until they died.**

There was no doubt that Bernabò, with fifteen legitimate and at least as many illegitimate children to provide for, would move against Gian' Galeazzo eventually, but the final straw was the imminent marriage of Bernabò's granddaughter Isabella of Bavaria to King Charles VI of France. Bernabò's son Carlo had also married into the French royal family in 1382, the intent being to trump Gian' Galeazzo's claim to French protection through his daughter Valentina, only surviving child of his marriage to Isabella of Valois, herself the daughter of King Jean II of France. In 1385 Gian' Galeazzo ambushed and captured the unwary Bernabò, then rounded up his wife and such children as remained in Milan. Bernabò was put to death and the danger that

France might intervene was allayed when in 1387 Valentina married Charles's brother Louis, Duc d'Orléans. The immediate risk of French intervention vanished after Charles VI succumbed to madness in 1392, giving rise to a *coup d'état* by his brother Duke Philippe of Burgundy and a division of the kingdom until Philippe's descendant Charles the Rash fell to Swiss pikes in 1477. Nonetheless Valentina's marriage ultimately provided the pretext for the French crown to claim Milan after the Orléans branch succeeded to the French throne with Louis XII in 1498.

Gian' Galeazzo united the Visconti dominions and set out to transform them into a unitary state by administrative reforms and by training a new generation of recognisably modern civil servants at the University of Pavia. He began to build the Milan Duomo in 1386, a Gothic extravaganza not consecrated until 1577, and also founded the Carthusian monastery at Certosa di Pavia in 1396, although it was not completed until 1473. It is said that Gian' Galeazzo was influenced by the yearnings for a united Italy of the poet Petrarch, who lived at the Milanese court and directed the collection of the great Visconti library. Whether or not this was the case, Gian' Galeazzo's ambitions were made explicit in 1395 when he paid 100,000 florins to uncrowned Emperor Wenceslaus to be made a hereditary prince of the Holy Roman Empire with the titles of Duke of Milan and Count of Pavia.

In politics as in physics, for every action there is an opposite and equal reaction and Gian' Galeazzo's expansionism provoked the Republic of Venice to abandon its centuries-old tradition of limited involvement on the Italian mainland (*terraferma*). The immediate circumstances were that after Gian' Galeazzo allied with Venice to overthrow the Carrara of Verona and the Scala of Padua in 1388, he overreached by claiming Treviso and the mainland north of Venice. In 1390 the Venetians backed the return of the Carrara to power in Verona and Padua, where they continued to be troublesome neighbours until 1404 when the Venetians, emboldened by the death of Gian' Galeazzo two years earlier, conquered Padua, Vicenza and Verona to create a permanent counter-balance to Milan in northern Italy. Before he died Gian' Galeazzo took Bologna in 1395, while Pisa, Siena and Perugia sought his protection in 1399–1400. In 1402 he formally annexed Bologna and concentrated his forces against an alliance among Florence, Padua and the Bolognese exiles. 'Decisive' battles are often an illusion, but the victory of the Visconti army at Casalecchio on 26 June 1402, with its enormous haul of the few prominent condottieri not already on the Milanese payroll, might have proved to be one had Gian' Galeazzo not died less than two months later. His eldest son Gian' Maria was only thirteen years old and the Visconti empire promptly fell apart.

While the big cats fought, the Malatesti mice did rather well for themselves. Galeotto il Vecchio was among the few lords who tried to prevent the papal schism, the more typical reaction being that of his father-in-law Rodolfo II Varano, who wished for the Papacy 'to have so much on its hands with its own affairs that it will keep them off ours'. As a result Pope Urban VI granted Galeotto vicariates over Cesena, Meldola, Mondavio, San Leo, Sant'Arcangelo, Senigallia and San Sepolcro in the upper Tiber valley. The acquisition of Meldola risked incurring the enmity of the Ordelaffi brothers, Guastafamiglia's grandsons, who had recovered Forlì during the Eight Saints War. Galeotto arranged the marriage of his niece Paola, Pandolfo II's daughter, to Sinibaldo I Ordelaffi as part of a broad agreement that included using his influence to obtain the Forlì vicariate for Sinibaldo. While Galeotto lived the two clans supported each other at the expense of the Polenta of Ravenna, from whom Galeotto took Cesenatico, Cervia and the clan birthplace of Polenta in 1382–3. Galeotto's vicariates were reconfirmed in 1380 when he was also made Papal Rector for the whole of Romagna, an honour later extended for three generations in return for 15,000 florins. It lasted only two, but the Malatesta clan leaders held the office uninterruptedly until the death of Carlo II in 1429.

Antonio II Montefeltro followed a path more representative of the Romagna–Marche lords and in 1377 married the daughter of Giovanni di Vico, prefect of Rome, and sister to Francesco, the foremost Umbrian rebel against papal authority, who in 1375 was invited to return to power by the citizens of Viterbo and soon recovered the vast family domain lost to Albornoz. One result of Antonio II's shrewd marriage alliance was that in 1384 he became lord of Gubbio, gateway to the passes from Spoleto to the Marche, over the determined resistance of the incumbent Gabrielli, who were backed by the Malatesti. The Gabrielli must have thought they had trumped Antonio when in 1377 his brother Nolfo married the daughter of Cante Gabrielli II, as his namesake grandfather had married the daughter of the first Cante Gabrielli fifty years earlier. They were soon disillusioned: Nolfo schemed against them as well as his brother and died in Cagli prison around 1380, one suspects not of natural causes.

In 1390 the new Roman Pope Boniface IX nominated Antonio II as Papal Vicar of Urbino and Gubbio, and recognised his title as Count of Montefeltro. In 1391–2 Boniface nominated Antonio II and his brother Galasso joint Papal Vicars of Cagli and also awarded Malatesta 'dei Sonetti' an independent vicariate for Pesaro. The arrangement left the Trabaria Pass and the upper Metauro under the control of Galeotto il Vecchio Malatesta and his allies the Brancaleoni, the lower Apennine passes and the stretch of the Via Flaminia along the Burano in the hands of the less than mutually supportive Montefeltro brothers, and the lower Via Flaminia and Metauro valley under the sole heir of Guastafamiglia's eldest son Pandolfo II. The latter's rights of primogeniture seem to have been recognised by his uncle Galeotto's heirs only in the formality of accepting that Sonetti's eldest son should be designated Carlo I, although he was twenty-two years younger than the Rimini Carlo.

The tensions Boniface sought to exploit within the Malatesta clan arose because the close working relationship between Guastafamiglia and his brother Galeotto emphatically did not carry over to the next generation. Of Guastafamiglia's two legitimate sons Malatesta Ungaro arranged a double marriage alliance with Ferrara in 1362–3, marrying his daughter Costanza to Alberto I d'Este's younger brother and himself to Alberto's daughter. Both marriages were barren and as Ungaro was estranged from his illegitimate son Niccolò he did not seek to have him legitimated, so his line died with him in 1372. Guastafamiglia's eldest, Pandolfo II, produced an heir in Malatesta 'dei Sonetti' who was long-lived and also produced four legitimate sons. Sonetti was, however, fobbed off with Pesaro while Galeotto's sons took the rest of the Malatesta patrimony. The Pesaro Malatesti provided a focus for other dissatisfied members of the clan, including the descendants of Gianciotto, sidelined since the beginning of the fourteenth century.

## MALATESTI – THE FATAL DIVISION

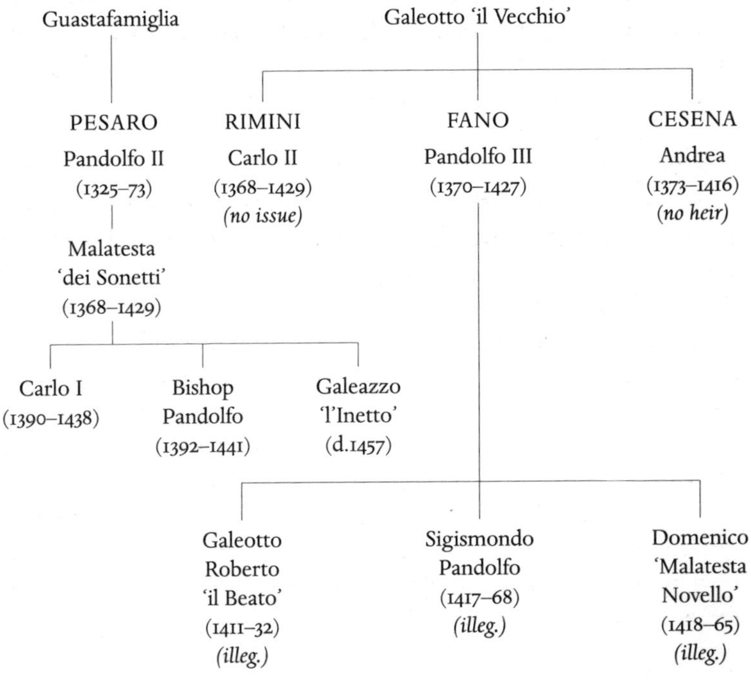


The split would not have proved so damaging if Galeotto's sons had been able to produce legitimate heirs. The line of Andrea, Galeotto's third son, seemed to be particularly cursed. In 1401 he returned his first wife Rengarda Alidosi for adultery to her family in Imola, who poisoned her. Rengarda bore him Galeotto (who predeceased him and was the only legitimate heir produced by Galeotto il Vecchio's sons) and Antonia, who married the impotent sadist Duke Gian' Maria Visconti in 1408. Andrea was next married for little more than a year to Lucrezia Ordelaffi, who bore him Parisina before being poisoned by her father Francesco III (another Guastafamiglia grandson) for conspiring with Andrea against him. Nobody doubted there was such a thing as 'bad seed', or that a lack of healthy children was a sign of divine displeasure. Andrea's track record, in conjunction with the sterility of his brothers Carlo II and Malatesta 'Belfiore', and Pandolfo III's ability to engender only bastards, may have contributed more than is generally recognised to the fall of the house of Malatesta. Certainly a combination of low fertility and reckless passion, the opposite of *furbizia*, was not a recipe for dynastic success.

**PARISINA MALATESTA**

**Parisina, daughter of Andrea Malatesta and the ill-fated Lucrezia Ordelaffi, married Niccolò III d'Este in 1418 and bore him twin daughters. She later fell in love with his illegitimate son Ugo and in 1425, when their liaison was discovered, demanded to be beheaded along with him instead of being sent to a monastery. Niccolò, who had possibly hundreds of bastards, may not have wanted to execute either of them but probably felt he had to draw the line at incest.**

Boniface IX's calculation with regard to the Montefeltri misfired: after the papal settlement of 1390–2 Antonio entrusted the administration of Gubbio to his illegitimate but loyal half-brother Niccolò. In Cagli Galasso tried to reactivate the Gabrielli connection without success and after his death in 1398 the family holdings were all firmly in Antonio's hands. Boniface's ploy was more successful – admittedly only in the long term, although playing for time was always the great strength of the Papacy – in sowing dissension among the Malatesti. Although Boniface could not have foreseen the precise details of the self-destructive elements that were to bring about the downfall of the clan, it was always safe to bet that the sinfulness of humankind in general and the Romagna lords in particular would eventually produce a situation that Rome could exploit.

# EIGHT

# *Golden Age*

CHAPTER SUMMARY

*The condottieri enjoyed their period of greatest success from the last decade of the fourteenth century until the Peace of Lodi in 1454. It was a period of fluid alliances and indecisive wars during which a number of condottieri carved out independent principalities for themselves. Many of them learned their trade under the lifelong rivals Muzio 'Sforza' Attendolo and Andrea 'Braccio di Montone' Fortebraccio, whose followers were known as 'Sforzeschi' and 'Bracceschi'. The two men died within five months of each other in 1424. Muzio's sons became lords of Milan and Pesaro, but Braccio's power died with him. Mounted knights became practically invulnerable with improved armour and the increase of the basic cavalry 'lance' from three to six, with the additional men providing a bodyguard for their principal in battle. Strategically, rulers waged war not so much for territorial gain as to increase their own domestic power of taxation and convocation, while operationally there was a premium on speed and mobility, which limited the use of infantry and field artillery.*

The era of marauding companies came to an end with the second Company of the Star originally formed by Astorre I Manfredi in 1379 to return him to power in Faenza. Instead the company elected to accept a commission from the Visconti and Venice for war against the Genoese, with whom the Stars settled secretly for 19,000 florins. Returning for more in August the entire company was captured in a surprise attack by a scratch Genoese force, after which most were massacred by the populace. The Golden Age of the Condottieri that followed was more orderly because the major players offered more secure employment while excluding and persecuting individuals who indulged in freelance banditry; but it was golden because the collapse of papal authority, the implosion of the Visconti empire following the death of Gian' Galeazzo and chronic turbulence in the south led the more successful and ambitious men-at-arms to carve out states for themselves.

There were many such and their fate varied. One of the nastiest, both in his life and the manner of his death, was red-haired Ottobuono Terzo, who in 1404 became lord of his native town Parma and took Reggio from the Este of Ferrara. In 1408 he committed the fatal error of torturing Michele Attendolo, who bribed his way out of the cell in which Ottobuono had left him to starve. The following year, in a surprising lapse, Ottobuono accepted a safe conduct to meet Niccolò III d'Este of Ferrara, famed as a Humanist and patron of arts and letters, and was murdered by Michele and his older brother Muzio Attendolo, who kept his ears as trophies. His body was dismembered and such parts not fed to dogs were displayed prominently at Ferrara and Modena. Ottobuono's killer Muzio Attendolo was the most successful condottiere of all. He won a considerable domain in the southern kingdom as Queen Joanna II's Grand Constable, after a shaky start during which he was imprisoned and tortured by those fighting for control of the queen. He was saved by his sister Margherita who held the town of Tricarico for him, took hostage a high-level delegation sent from Naples under safe conduct to demand her surrender and threatened to kill them slowly and horribly should any further harm come to her brother. After Muzio's death in 1424 his sons Francesco and Alessandro adopted their father's nickname, 'Sforza', as their family name and founded dynasties that ruled as dukes of Milan from 1450 to 1535 and lords of Pesaro from 1445 to 1512. How they achieved their eminence plays a significant part in our story.

Muzio Attendolo's great rival was Andrea Fortebraccio, known as Braccio di Montone, who at the apogee of his power ruled Perugia and much of the Marche. Like Muzio he was drawn into the maelstrom swirling around Joanna II and achieved the rank of Prince of Capua and Grand Constable before being killed at the battle of Aquila in 1424, five months after Muzio was drowned crossing a river on the way to challenge him. Braccio was not blessed with heirs of fighting age and his domain fell apart, but he left a legacy of condottieri known as 'Bracceschi' who learned their trade under him. These included Niccolò 'Piccinino' (so called because he was very short) and his adopted sons Francesco and Jacopo. Another who learned his trade under Braccio was Erasmo 'Gattamelata' (Honeyed Cat) da Narni, whose equestrian statue by Donatello stands in the main piazza of Padua. Braccio's tight control of his forces and his ability to feed squadrons into battle for brief periods before withdrawing them to regroup while fresh units took their place was much remarked upon and suggests the norm before him was a pell-mell engagement.

The leading 'Sforzeschi' were Muzio's sons, their cousin Micheletto Attendolo, Niccolò 'da Tolentino' Mauruzzi and Bartolomeo Colleoni, whose equestrian statue by Verrocchio stands in the Piazza Giovanni e Paolo in Venice. There is no evidence that the Sforzeschi represented an alternative school of combat tactics and at Aquila each army had 4000 cavalry divided into twenty or more squadrons. Some attributed Braccio's defeat to the decision of Niccolò Piccinino to leave Aquila unguarded, permitting the Aquilani to sortie and attack Braccio's army from the rear, but in fact Piccinino was drawn away from the walls of Aquila by a deteriorating battlefield situation brought about by Micheletto Attendolo, commanding some 1300 infantry, who ordered them to kill their opponents' chargers. Equinicide was a highly unusual tactic at a time when horses were the principal booty and Micheletto's ruthlessness completely disrupted Braccio's battle plan. One would have thought that after Aquila the writing was on the wall for armoured horsemen, but they chose to ignore it because to do otherwise would rob their profession of glamour and bring their golden age to an abrupt end. They could not have done so, however, without the consent of their employers, which argues that they served the purpose for which they were hired in a way that infantry could not.

The main reason for the survival of heavy cavalry was that strategy remained a process of sending punitive expeditions into enemy territory to loot and to shake the allegiance of the opponent's subjects. Speed was of the essence and fortified villages that held out until taken by storm were brutally sacked and sometimes destroyed to encourage others not to be so obstinate. In the field the game was to provoke the

## Italian Armour late XIV century

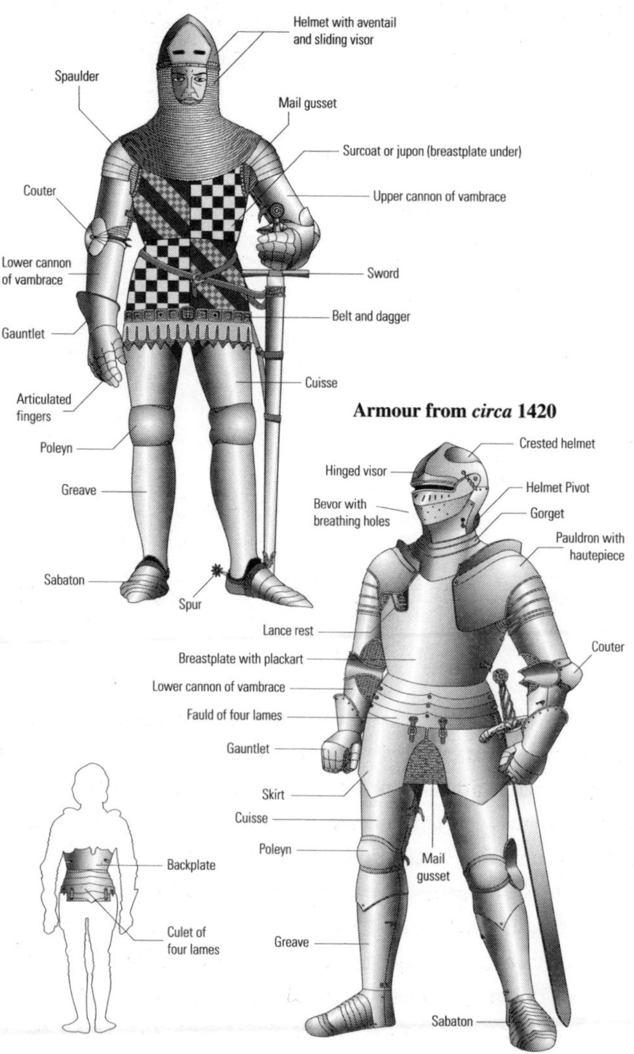

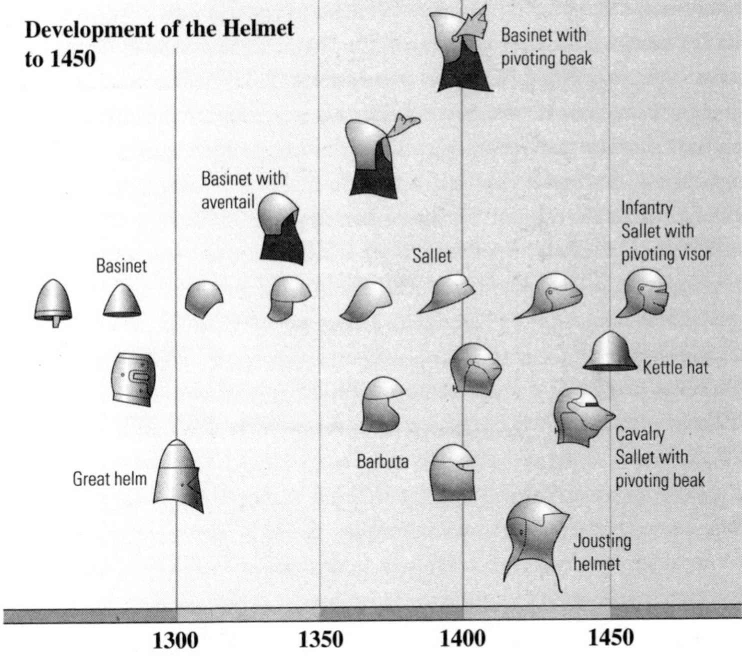


enemy into a false move, with a premium on intelligence gathering by light cavalry and spies in the enemy camp. Tactically everything depended on mobility and most non-siege-related battles of the era were either surprise attacks or involved false flight to draw the enemy into a prepared ambush. 'Showdown' battles were rare but when they took place were as bloody in Italy as anywhere else. Machiavelli spoke for most employers when he sneered at the reluctance of the condottieri to crush a beaten foe, but many condottieri at one point or other in their careers had over-pursued to defeat, while all of them were disinclined to force an opponent to fight to the death. There were two reasons, the first that a cornered enemy might seriously deplete the victor's assets before succumbing, the other that mounted men could usually escape and the golden rule of reciprocity would condition any future encounter, where the wheel of fortune might turn to another outcome.

Fatal battle casualties among the condottieri were rare in part for the reasons mentioned but also because as metallurgy improved they were able to armour-plate themselves from head to toe (Diagram 1). Arms and legs had long been covered by plate, but it was not until armourers could devise a workable neck pivot that a fully enclosed helmet firmly attached to the body armour (which also became not only stronger but lighter too) could replace the armoured cap with mail aventail. By 1420 full suits of 'white armour' were available with articulated joints further protected with additional layers of armour such as the spaulder on the shoulder of the sword arm. Men thus equipped were difficult to wound, and to increase their chances of survival the basic 'lance' of knight, bodyguard and a page to look after the string of horses grew to six men with several horses each. They were accompanied by infantry who rode with the cavalry and dismounted for battle, for without infantry support armoured knights were as vulnerable as the tanks of the first half of the twentieth century. Their particular problem was that they could be unhorsed by humble foot soldiers armed with billhooks, and if not promptly rescued might not be taken prisoner for ransom but instead dispatched with a dagger through the eye slit.

The infantry had only leather or, exceptionally, chain mail for the body and rather simple iron basinets for the head, although during the first decades of the fifteenth century the sallet evolved, providing greater protection for the face and incorporating an extension to cover the back of the neck (Diagram 2). The infantry elite were the crossbowmen and later handgunners, accompanied by men carrying a large rectangular shield behind which the crossbows or guns could be reloaded. Apart from the crossbowmen the professional infantry cadre consisted of men equipped with swords and round bucklers who went forward with the armoured knights, captured valuable prisoners and covered tactical retreats. The English longbowmen who made such an impact when they first arrived in Italy around 1360 had no local imitators – it was a skill requiring lifelong dedication. The *arceri* of late medieval Italian armies used less effective hunting bows and enjoyed a status not greatly superior to the rank and file equipped with a variety of pole arms, at this stage hooks, halberds and lances – the pike wall did not become a feature of warfare in Italy until the end of the century. Another, crucial, reason for the relative insignificance of infantry during the Age of the Condottieri was that communal military service was traditionally limited to taxpayers, which greatly reduced a levy pool whose usefulness was limited to wall defence and expeditions of a few days.

A general populace skilled at arms would have posed a considerably greater threat to rulers than to the professional soldiers they hired and therein lies the two-part explanation for the incessant scheming and petty warfare that permitted the condottieri to flourish. In his 1452 treatise on architecture Leon Battista Alberti commented that 'neither public bodies nor private persons can ever set bounds to their insatiable desire of getting and possessing still more and more; from which one source arises all the mischiefs of war'. In his brilliant analysis of the phenomenon Michael Mallett added a modern appreciation that 'the principal driving force in the growth of organised bureaucracy, of fiscal and credit institutions, and ultimately of centralised political power was the rising cost of warfare, and nowhere was this more clear than in Italy'. To this day, regimes seeking to extend their powers of coercion and taxation are inclined to warlike rhetoric if not to war itself. 'Wars' on poverty or drugs are commonly used to justify the extension of state power, but much the most effective excuse will always be to rally public opinion against its own objective interest by conjuring up an external enemy. Little conjuring was necessary in late medieval Europe.

# NINE

# *Lull Before The Storm*

## CHAPTER SUMMARY

*Between 1394 and 1423 peace reigned between the Malatesti and Montefeltri, based on the great respect felt towards Carlo II Malatesta by Antonio II Montefeltro and his son Guidantonio, and cemented by Guidantonio's betrothal to Carlo II's sister Rengarda. Antonio's daughters Anna and Battista also married Carlo's brother Galeotto 'Belfiore' and Galeazzo 'l'Inetto' of the Pesaro Malatesti. Only the last of these marriages had issue, a single daughter whose marriage into the Varani of Camerino was to light the fuse that eventually led to the fall of the Malatesta clan. Paradoxically, another factor in the long truce between the two families may have been that neither produced a talented military leader during this time. Despite their history of almost unbroken defeat in the field, they continued to win plum commissions and the most obvious explanation is that Carlo II, in particular, was highly valued for his diplomatic skill. This was much in evidence in his successful effort to bring about an end to what was by now a double schism in the Church, with three popes making war on each other. The outcome of Carlo's diplomacy was that all three resigned or were deposed and the Colonna Pope Martin V was elected in 1417. The marriage of Martin V's niece to Guidantonio Montefeltro following the death of Rengarda in 1423 put the last nail in the coffin of the truce between the clans.*

As we have seen, before Galeotto il Vecchio Malatesta died in 1385 he divided his holdings among his sons: Carlo II became the Rector of Romagna and got Rimini, Pandolfo III got Fano, Mondavio, Mondolfo and Scorticata, Andrea got Cesena, Fossombrone and Roncofreddo, and Belfiore (in trust until his fifteenth birthday in 1392) got Cervia, Meldola and San Sepolcro. The division was one of income rather than domain – when one was called away by business elsewhere his administrative duties were taken over by another. Continuing their father's tradition they never broke ranks with each other and as a result family power reached its apogee during the first decades of the fifteenth century.

Among the Montefeltri, although Antonio II was nearly fifty years younger than Galeotto Malatesta he lived just nineteen years longer and had only a single heir. His reproductive parsimony fortuitously proved a blessing: it affirmed the principle of primogeniture in his line precisely at the time when the old system of power shared among brothers, even when not riven by sibling rivalry – as in the cases of the Manfredi of Faenza, the Ordelaffi of Forlì and the Varani of Camerino – was strained to breaking point when individuals sought to create independent niches. Those who attempted to do so found that while the larger states might be prostrate at a given moment, when their traditional rulers possessed the advantage of dynastic legitimacy – the absence of which caused chaos in the southern kingdom – they could command the loyalty and resources to expel usurpers relatively easily.

Even after the Malatesti and Montefeltri became Visconti retainers in 1388, low-intensity warfare periodically flared up between them until 1393, when Pope Boniface IX brokered an agreement to be sealed by the marriages of Antonio II's heir Guidantonio to Carlo II's sister Rengarda and of Malatesta Belfiore to Antonio's daughter Anna. Residual friction revolved around the fate of the Malatesta client Gabrielli of Cantiano and the Ordelaffi of Forlì, Montefeltro clients since Sinibaldo II's sons killed their father and repudiated the Malatesta alliance in 1386. During 1393 Antonio II Montefeltro bought Cantiano from the pope while Carlo II and Pandolfo III Malatesta smashed the Ordelaffi at Bussecchio, but it still took a year for the Montefeltri and the Malatesti to arrange compensation for their clients before finally meeting at Montelevecchie in October 1394, where the betrothals were confirmed amid much merry-making and vows of mutual affection. Malatesta Belfiore married Anna the following year but the dynastically more significant wedding of Guidantonio Montefeltro and Rengarda did not take place until 1397, the bride's dowry including some of the

which he achieved by an act of *furbizia* in a way that may not have been as straightforward as it is usually reported.

In 1397 Gian' Galeazzo sent a river fleet of about 600 vessels carrying a siege train of heavy cannon to win control of the Po, escorted by an army of 11–12,000 cavalry, among them Antonio II Montefeltro and a contingent from Urbino, and 15,000 infantry under the overall command of Captain-General Jacopo del Verme, the best-regarded condottiere in Italy. In August, having overcome several checks to his advance – including a letter from Gian' Galeazzo ordering a withdrawal that was in fact a forgery sent by Francesco I Gonzaga of Mantua (doubly linked to Carlo II by the marriage of each to the other's sister) –Verme laid siege to Governolo, a powerful fortress complex guarding the confluence of the Mincio, Mantua's river, and the Po. Verme's army was reduced by malaria but was still stronger than the force assembled by Carlo II and his three brothers for Florence, Bologna, Padua and Mantua, which was held in check east of Governolo. A surprise attack by Venetian galleys on Verme's supply ships caused him to pull back across a bridge of boats over the Serraglio canal, a key element in Governolo's defences. Carlo II fell on the rearguard, which surrendered when the bridge was fired by Venetian combat swimmers, and a sortie by the besieged garrison completed the rout. Verme lost about 6000 infantry, 2000 cavalry, 5000 remounts, a third of the fleet and his entire siege train.

Carlo II Malatesta wanted to march on Brescia but the victorious allies fell out with each other and permitted Verme to recover the initiative. In May 1398 Verme for Gian' Galeazzo and Carlo II for Francesco negotiated a ten-year truce during which Carlo II was to have custody of the territory in dispute between Mantua and Milan – a startling enough mark of trust, made more so by the manner in which Gian' Galeazzo's confidence was won. It appears Carlo II subtly intimated that the duke's hard-line councillor, Pasquino Capello, was responsible for the forged letter that robbed Verme's campaign of momentum in 1397. Capello was executed and Gian' Galeazzo not only agreed to make Carlo II the arbiter of his dispute with Mantua but also drew up a will in which Carlo was nominated head of a Council of Regents including Pandolfo III, Malatesta dei Sonetti, Antonio II Montefeltro – and Francesco I Gonzaga. Gian' Galeazzo was one of the shrewdest men who ever lived and it is impossible to believe he was deceived: it is more likely that he judged the *furbizia* displayed by Carlo and

Francesco to be precisely the qualities required to hold his domain together for his heirs should he die prematurely, and Capello became a pawn to be sacrificed in a swiftly formed plan to win them to his cause.

Perhaps Carlo II's greatest merit in Gian' Galeazzo's eyes was that despite being the trusted Rector of Romagna for the Roman popes his word was valued in Florence as well as Milan, a tightrope act nobody else came close to performing in a time of more than usually fluid political combinations. Carlo's principal virtue seems to have been that he was an honest broker who rigorously resisted the temptation to turn his status as an intermediary to personal advantage. He also enjoyed a solid reputation as a condottiere associated with several notable battlefield victories, although closer inspection suggests he contributed little to them. The Venetians delivered the killer strokes at Governolo and only a very inept commander would have failed to seize the opportunity they created. Carlo II was among the leading condottieri in the Viscontean armies that defeated a German–Florentine army in October 1401 at Nave, near Brescia, where he was wounded, and that won Bologna at the battle of Casalecchio in June 1402, but in neither case was he the overall commander.

### BATTLE OF CASALECCHIO, 1402

**Casalecchio was won by the vanguard under the obscure Ludovico Cantelli – or perhaps more accurately lost by the enemy commander Bernard de la Serre, a reckless Gascon (the terms are traditionally synonymous) who accepted Cantelli's challenge to single combat and was captured before the battle began, and whose troop dispositions were so flawed that the Florentines accused him of deliberately losing the battle. Cantelli spent his last years as poet in residence at Pandolfo III's glittering court in Brescia.**

A decade later, while Captain-General of Venice, Carlo II was seriously wounded at the battle of Motta di Livenza north-west of Venice in August 1412. The Venetians had been driven back from the border area by a Hungarian army under Filippo 'Pippo Spano' Scolari, who introduced his native Italy to the light cavalry tactics and cruelty of Balkan warfare during this campaign. Carlo had twenty-two miles of earthworks erected along the Livenza, yet despite this and Venetian galleys patrolling the river Scolari's men made a crossing and stormed Carlo's camp. His men were able to get him away because the Hungarians succumbed to premature plundering, but Ruggiero Cane Ranieri, one of Carlo's sub-contractors, delivered the decisive counter-stroke on his own initiative. In 1416, when commanding for Perugia, Carlo was roundly defeated and captured by Braccio da Montone at San Egidio, halfway between Perugia and Assisi, and in 1424 for Florence he was again defeated and captured by Angelo della Pergola for Milan at Zagonara, near Lugo in Romagna. It would seem his organisational and diplomatic skills, not his military prowess, explain why he continued to obtain important commissions.

Widening the focus to include the other Malatesta brothers and the Montefeltri, we see that neither clan produced commanders of the first rank during their long period of détente. Pandolfo III and Andrea Malatesta were with Carlo II at Nave, joined by Antonio and Guidantonio Montefeltro at Casalecchio. After Antonio died in 1404 Guidantonio became Captain-General of Naples in 1408 for Ladislas of Hungary and Grand Constable in 1409, when the Roman Pope Gregory XII also appointed him *Gonfaloniere*. He and Ladislas were defeated at Roccasecca halfway between Naples and Rome in May 1411 by an all-star army including Braccio, Sforza and Niccolò Piccinino acting for Louis II of Anjou–Provence and Antipope John XXII, after which Carlo II Malatesta replaced him while Guidantonio became John XXIII's captain-general – without in any way disturbing the peace between them. Pandolfo III replaced Carlo as Captain-General of Venice and won a minor victory over a detachment of Scolari's Hungarians near Vicenza in 1413, but acting for himself as lord of Brescia he was defeated and wounded in a skirmish with Braccio near Bologna in 1415, beaten by Carmagnola for Milan at Olginate near Bergamo in 1418 and crushed by him at Montichiari near Brescia in 1420.* As a captain of Florence Pandolfo III was beaten by a Milanese force near Forlimpopoli in 1423 and he shared Carlo's crushing defeat at Zagonara the following year. In sum, Pandolfo III earned the sobriquet 'il Grande' for the splendour of his lordship of Brescia (1404–21) and Bergamo (1408–19), not for his military accomplishments.

---

* Site of the battle won by Pandolfo III's father and Hawkwood over Bernabò Visconti in 1373.

The Pesaro Malatesti fared little better. Sonetti was Captain-General of Florence in 1409–10 and in 1412–14 served Naples and Antipope John XXIII under other commanders, but these were low-intensity wars that never really put his battlefield skills to the test. His only significant territorial gain came from the redistribution of lands after his brother Andrea died in 1417, when Sonetti received Fossombrone. Sonetti's sons Carlo I and Galeazzo were captured when they surrendered Gradara to Angelo della Pergola, sent by Filippo Maria Visconti to ravage the Malatesta domains after Carlo II's defeat at Zagonara. This brought about the enforced allegiance of the Malatesti to the Viscontean cause and, after Carmagnola defected to the Venetians, Carlo I was prematurely promoted to Captain-General of Milan in 1427. In October at Maclodio, facing Carmagnola for Venice–Florence, he committed the beginner's error of pursuing a false retreat, along a causeway to boot, and was captured along with the bulk of his men, all his remounts and his supply train. As we shall see, he was no more successful when he tried to seize Rimini in 1430. Younger brother Galeazzo was dubbed 'the Inept' and features in the military history of his era only when captured at San Egidio in 1416 and at Gradara in 1424.

The long détente between the two clans and the peace and prosperity of their domains owed much to the personal qualities and generally benevolent rule of the clan leaders, which to a considerable degree outweighed their military shortcomings and sheltered their corner of the peninsula from the storms sweeping through the rest of Italy. While not great generals, they were strong enough in their own not very wealthy domains to make the cost-benefit of a serious assault on them discouraging, especially when there were far richer pickings elsewhere. In addition the intricate web of dynastic alliances spun by Carlo II made him virtually unassailable. His close friendship with Niccolò III d'Este survived the tragic waywardness of his niece Parisina, while after his double brother-in-law, Francesco I Gonzaga, died in 1407 Carlo's wise and unselfish management of the principality during the minority of Gian' Francesco Gonzaga earned him his nephew's devotion. In addition he gave generous shelter to the Manfredi during their 1405–10 exile from Faenza and was instrumental in obtaining the restoration to power of his brother-in-law, Gian' Galeazzo I Manfredi. Carlo's nephew, Guidantonio Manfredi, ruled Faenza from 1417 to 1443 and while his uncle lived he was a loyal ally of the Malatesti. The stain of Andrea's meddling in the affairs of the Ordelaffi through his wife Lucrezia, which caused her murder in 1404, was expunged when his sons killed her filicide father Francesco III the following year. Carlo helped Giorgio Ordelaffi to recover Forlì in 1411 and in 1413 dissuaded his nephew-in-law, Guidantonio Montefeltro, from attacking Forlì on behalf of Florence. Carlo also arranged the marriages of Andrea's two daughters from his first marriage to the young Duke Gian' Maria Visconti in 1408 and to Obizzo da Polenta of Ravenna in 1414.

If the barrenness of the Malatesta–Montefeltro marriages represents one of the ways in which a dynastic combination may fail, the close marital bonds between the Malatesti and the Varani of Camerino illustrates the problem of excessive fecundity. Carlo II and his siblings were the offspring of their father's second marriage to Gentilina Varano, while the Pesaro Malatesti were born of Sonetti's marriage to Gentilina's sister Elisabetta, the two women being the only offspring of Ridolfo II of Camerino. Sonetti's sister, who was also named Elisabetta, married Ridolfo II's nephew Ridolfo III and bore him the first ten of his twenty-two legitimate children. In 1421 Pandolfo III Malatesta married one of Ridolfo III's legitimate daughters but the union became a 'what if' when she died giving birth to their only child, who was stillborn. In 1425 another Elisabetta, the daughter of Sonetti's son Galeazzo and Guidantonio Montefeltro's sister Battista, married Pier Gentile, son of Ridolfo III by his second marriage, and bore him Ridolfo IV and Costanza. From this, in time, came the crucial marriage, between Galeazzo's granddaughter Costanza and Alessandro Sforza in 1444, which cemented a convergence of interests among the Varani, the Sforzas, the Montefeltri and the Pesaro Malatesti.

### VARANO BLOOD BATH

**Pier Gentile I was beheaded in 1433 by the Bishop of Recanati, Giovanni Vitelleschi. In 1434 Pier Gentile's popular brother Giovanni II was murdered by his half-brothers Gentile IV and Berardo III (Appendix D), who wished to simplify the succession. Some weeks later the perpetrators and Berardo's six sons were massacred by a Vitelleschi-inspired mob in Camerino. The Varani did not recover lordship of Camerino until Giovanni II's son Giulio Cesare I was invested by Pope Nicholas V in 1447.**

While it is confusing to track all the marital alliances we may be sure all those involved were acutely aware of their interrelationship – as we may also assume that an untold back story of cooperation and rivalry among the Varani women was probably a significant factor in the downfall of the Malatesta dynasty. When men spent so much time away from home, in the absence of evidence that they appointed a deputy it is fair to assume their wives handled day-to-day administration. This was the reason – additional to the dynastic problem of cuckoldry – why discovered infidelity was sometimes punished by death: the same fate awaited any male chancellor suspected of less than total loyalty. However, their wives were also daughters and sisters, and barring manifest conflicts of interest – or sibling rivalry – would have encouraged social and political closeness between their families. There is abundant evidence of genuine reciprocal affection and deep respect between Guidantonio Montefeltro and Rengarda Malatesta, to the point that when her brother Carlo II was taken prisoner at San Egidio it was Guidantonio who took the lead in organising his ransom and stood surety for a large part of it. The mutual devotion of childless Carlo II Malatesta and Elisabetta Gonzaga is no less striking – although Carlo II may have been sterile, a more likely explanation for his lack of bastard children was an almost unheard-of marital fidelity.

Of Carlo II's loyalty to the Church there can be no doubt, but it is sad to conclude that what earned him great respect in life was dynastically disastrous. It was objectively very much in his interest, as a lord, that the Papacy should be divided and weak; yet he devoted the greater part of his diplomatic effort to healing the papal schisms. He was instrumental in obtaining the belated consent of the querulous Roman Pope Gregory XII, who sought asylum at Rimini in 1408, to the assembly of bishops summoned at Constance in 1414 by German King Sigismund, who was a supporter of Antipope John XXIII, thereby turning it into an official Ecumenical Council. The opportunities for reform spurned by the Council of Constance, the condemnation of the ideas of John Wycliffe and the treacherous imprisonment and judicial murder of the Wycliffean Jan Hus in July 1415 have had such far-reaching consequences that one cringes to dwell only on its success in ending the papal schisms. Even that success came about not through any merit of the assembled prelates but thanks to the lonely efforts of Carlo, who presented his credentials as Gregory XII's proxy in July 1415 and then renounced the Papacy on behalf of his principal in return for the recognition of all Gregory's nepotistic appointments and his election as the senior cardinal. The Pisa Antipope John XXIII was deposed and imprisoned but the Avignon Antipope Benedict XIII was not formally excommunicated and deposed until July 1417.

The Council, in no hurry to relinquish the power and excitement of the process, took another five months to elect a successor but finally settled with suspicious unanimity on Ottone Colonna, previously a prominent member of the Council of Pisa and a leading supporter of its antipopes, who in his family and person represented everything that was divisive, corrupt and reactionary in the Church (Picture section 1, p. 8). He took the name Martin V and, resisting invitations from the kings of Germany and France to reside in their territory, meandered back to Rome between May 1418 and September 1420. In due course Martin V rewarded Carlo II's devotion to Church unity by setting in motion the ruin of the Malatesti for no higher reason than a desire to benefit the extended Colonna clan. Ottone's niece Vittoria married Sonetti's heir Carlo I in 1416, and from the time her uncle became pope the Pesaro Malatesti broke ranks with their northern cousins until finally they openly attacked them after Carlo II's death. However, the more fateful marriage was between the pope's niece Caterina and Guidantonio Montefeltro after the death in 1423 of his first wife, Rengarda Malatesta. Following the marriage Martin V broke every undertaking made by his predecessors with Carlo II and missed no opportunity to favour the Montefeltri, with whom he had a long and close association dating from his appointment as the twelve-year-old bishop of Urbino in 1380.

# TEN

# *Bastards*

## CHAPTER SUMMARY

*With the birth of Federico, falsely claimed as his own illegitimate son by Guidantonio Montefeltro, and of Pandolfo III's illegitimate sons Galeotto Roberto, Sigismondo Pandolfo and Domenico, the pieces were in place for the endgame of the Montefeltro–Malatesta vendetta and the action becomes too intricate for chapter summaries. One of the purposes of this book is to underline the contingent nature of human history, in which relatively small factors can have disproportionate consequences, while apparently major episodes may have none. The passage of time reveals that personalities, who married whom, their reproductive success or failure and other domestic details often prove to be more important than grand political designs, battles won or lost and the allegedly great themes of history. The fifteenth century in Italy probably provides as good a laboratory to test Chaos Theory as any in history: what follows is a small but circumstantially crucial part of the whole.*

The defeat and capture Carlo II along with his nephew Galeazzo of Pesaro at San Egidio in July 1416, coinciding with the fatal illness of Andrea Malatesta of Cesena, marks a watershed in the Malatesta family fortunes. Pandolfo III was compelled to negotiate a two-year truce with Duke Filippo Maria Visconti, who was seeking to recover Bergamo and Brescia from him, and to resign his commission as Captain-General of Venice. Agreement to both was forthcoming with surprising ease, which suggests that neither Visconti nor the Venetians were happy to see Braccio, the victor at San

Egidio, omnipotent in central Italy. In addition to demanding an exorbitant ransom for his hostages, Braccio embarked on a programme of conquest in the Marche that eliminated all the gains recently made by Andrea around Osimo and Iesi, and threatened Fano as well. The Migliorati of Sulmona and the intermarried Varani of Camerino and Malatesti of Pesaro tried to abandon the sinking ship but soon realised that Braccio neither needed them nor intended to respect their domains. Accordingly they coalesced around Pandolfo III when he arrived from Lombardy with his captain Martino da Faenza and 3000 heavy cavalry. It was perhaps as well for them that Braccio was called away to deal with unrest in his Umbrian domain and decided the solution to his problems lay in Rome, always a strategic chimera but particularly so at a time when the Church heavyweights were all in Constance.

Through the good offices of Florentine and Church ambassadors, and of Guidantonio Montefeltro who stood surety for a third of the ransom, Carlo and Galeazzo were freed by Braccio in February 1417 against a payment of 60,000 ducats with half down and 10,000 more annually for three years. The Malatesti also surrendered Iesi, Montalboddo, Montecassiano and Recanati to Braccio, while allied Ancona surrendered Senigallia. In an episode that does not fit with Carlo II's reputation, one of the first things he did after recovering his freedom was to arrest Martino da Faenza, who had contributed a large loan towards the down payment of the ransom. Martino confessed under torture to having conspired with Braccio and in October was beheaded in the piazza at Fano. Pandolfo seems to have washed his hands of the matter and went back to Lombardy in April. Most historians believe the execution was a charade but it is curious that a middle-ranking condottiere with no family fortune had accumulated the enormous sum he loaned the Malatesti, variously estimated between 10,000 and 20,000 ducats.

Sigismondo Pandolfo Malatesta was born to Pandolfo III's mistress Antonia Barignano on 19 June 1417, which means Antonia must have accompanied Pandolfo during his foray into the Marche to confront Braccio. It comes as no surprise to find that Sigismondo was conceived at a time of extreme stress, nor that he was born on the eve of his father's rash decision to break the truce with Filippo Maria by marching to the relief of Piacenza, where the citadel was besieged by Carmagnola. In August, after Carmagnola abandoned the siege, Pandolfo entered the town and found it evacuated and stripped bare. The message could not have been clearer: nobody holding any part of the Visconti empire would profit from it – Filippo Maria was not going to play the traditional game and there was no hope of financing a war against him through conquest. A wiser man would have come to terms with such an implacable foe, but Pandolfo overestimated his importance to the Venetians and chose to fight instead. Although Martin V interceded on his behalf, the help Pandolfo hoped to receive from Venice did not materialise. He lost Bergamo and many Brescian villages to Carmagnola after defeat at Olginate in 1418, and after being trounced at Montichiari in 1420 sold Brescia itself back to Visconti for a mere 34,000 florins.

Pandolfo's lordship in Lombardy had come about because once Gian' Galeazzo died many communes of the Visconti empire reverted to civil strife under the old Ghibelline and Guelf banners. He came to power, as the *signori* invariably did, to restore order and if Gian' Galeazzo's older son, Gian' Maria, had not been psychotic Pandolfo might have remained true to the oath he took as one of the young duke's guardians. But by the time Gian' Maria was assassinated in 1412 and his brother Filippo Maria became Duke of Milan, Pandolfo had made such a large personal investment in Brescia and Bergamo that conflict was inevitable. It was the new duke's great good fortune that Facino Cane, the condottiere who replaced Verme as the Viscontean captain-general and who had been at the heart of the conflict between Gian' Maria and their mother, died within days of Gian' Maria's assassination. Filippo Maria was well served by his new captain-general, Carmagnola, thanks to whom he recovered the entire Visconti domain by 1423. He then exploited his guardianship of Teobaldo Ordelaffi, the young heir to the lordship of Forlì, to embark on a war of conquest in Romagna, seizing Imola as well as Forlì. Carlo II and Pandolfo III – who resigned as Captain-General of the Church over the protests of Martin V – became captains of Florence in opposition to Filippo Maria, which led to their defeats at Forlimpopoli and Zagonara in 1423–4. With Carlo once again in enemy hands, Pandolfo III scrambled to save Cesena and Rimini from Filippo Maria.

**BEATRICE CANE-VISCONTI (1392–1418)**

**Facino Cane's dying wish was that his widow Beatrice should marry Filippo Maria Visconti, who was twenty years younger than she. To make the match more appetising Facino endowed Beatrice with a dowry that included lordship of Alessandria, Novara and Tortona, and about 500,000 gold florins. Filippo Maria married her and took the dowry but ignored his unfortunate bride, whom he beheaded on a trumped-up charge of adultery in 1418.**

It was precisely at this time that Rengarda née Malatesta died and Guidantonio married Pope Martin V's niece, creating a situation where the highly nepotistic pope, already offended by Pandolfo's desertion, had every reason to encourage Montefeltro expansion at the expense of the Malatesti. The flashpoint was the domain of the Malatesta-allied Brancaleoni in the Metauro and Foglia valleys. In about 1410 the Brancaleoni divided their holdings with one branch of the family ruling the Massa Trabaria and the other Castel Durante, Sassocorvaro, Lunano and Montelocco. The first became vulnerable when Count Bartolomeo Brancaleone died without a male heir in 1424, at which Martin V took the opportunity to reassert Church sovereignty over all the Brancaleoni holdings and appointed Guidantonio Rector of the Massa Trabaria, Papal Vicar of Castel Durante and guardian to Bartolomeo's daughter Gentile. As happened so often when the Montefeltri obtained the title to a new possession, Brancaleone loyalists drove Guidantonio's representatives out of Castel Durante the following year.

Guidantonio also took advantage of Carlo II's imprisonment by Filippo Maria to open old wounds with a campaign of conquest in the Montefeltro region and by recapturing Montalboddo in the Senigallia hinterland, taken in 1399 by Carlo from the Paganelli, allies of the Montefeltri, and lost to Braccio in 1420. The Pesaro Malatesti probably also intended to attack their cousins, but Sonetti was compelled to join them in becoming retainers of Filippo Maria Visconti after his sons were captured at Gradara. Carlo II returned to Rimini in January 1425 and Guidantonio Montefeltro did not wait for the inevitable: in July, through the mediation of Martin V, he surrendered all his conquests and the 1393 agreement between the clans was reconfirmed and enshrined in a papal Bull, with the pope reserving Castel Durante, Pietrarubbia and Pennabilli for himself. Sonetti was excluded from the new agreement, as he had been from the arrangement among Visconti, Carlo II and Pandolfo III, and had to make his own terms with Filippo Maria and Pope Martin V. The slighting of the Pesaro Malatesti can only have been a statement of Carlo II's displeasure and also suggests that papal nephew-in-law Carlo I, who had failed to produce an heir, was no longer a significant factor in Martin V's dynastic plans.

Pandolfo III died at Fano in 1427. His eldest illegitimate son Galeotto Roberto, born in 1411 to Allegra de' Mori, had long been in the care of Carlo II and Elisabetta in Rimini, and he was now joined by his half-brothers Sigismondo and Domenico, the latter also known as Malatesta Novello. Under the tutelage of Elisabetta, Galeotto Roberto became the nearest thing to a saint ever produced by the Malatesta clan, a tendency only reinforced by his never-consummated marriage to the similarly devout Margherita, one of Niccolò III d'Este's illegitimate daughters. Sigismondo was the polar opposite. He was his father's favourite and everything a warrior-lord could wish for in a son: handsome, fearless, a brilliant horseman and adept at arms. Born on the cusp between the astrological signs of Gemini and Cancer, he had many of the characteristics associated with the first. The astrological bas-reliefs he commissioned for the Tempio Malatestiano include the crab of Cancer hovering menacingly over Rimini, but this was probably just an aesthetic or symbolic preference: many of his contemporaries were slaves to astrology, but Sigismondo was raised a freethinker in the Humanist hothouse of Pandolfo III's court at Brescia and believed individuals made their own destinies. From a medallion made by Pisanello in 1445 we know Sigismondo's younger brother Domenico had a decidedly delicate face before he became bloated by over-indulgence and dropsy. He was also a far more conservative individual than Sigismondo and personal incompatibility made the brothers as often enemies as allies in the years ahead.

The future Federico III Montefeltro's parentage defined his life and career. He was almost certainly the son of Bernardino degli Ubaldini della Carda and Guidantonio Montefeltro's illegitimate daughter Aura. In 1419–20 Bernardino was Guidantonio's principal captain, during which time they made a daring assault on Braccio's Assisi through a picket gate left open by a priest and later beat off a furious counter-attack by the Bracceschi against Gubbio. Bernardino's marriage to Aura followed and Federico was born at Gubbio on 7 June 1422 – another Gemini. The evidence of the paternity claimed by Guidantonio is not strong: the mother was alleged to be an unidentified noble lady and the boy to have been conceived after Rengarda's death in 1423, enabling Guidantonio to evade the stigma of adultery that might have been an obstacle to Federico's legitimation by the pope, whose niece Guidantonio had just married. The reason Guidantonio claimed Federico as a son instead of as his grandson most likely lay in the dynastic threat posed by the legitimate line through his sister Battista's marriage to Galeazzo Malatesta of Pesaro, whose only daughter Elisabetta was betrothed to Pier Gentile Varano in 1424 – the year Guidantonio claimed Federico as his son. The subterfuge pre-empted any claim the Varani might make to the Urbino succession should he fail to produce a legitimate son.

There is a strong family resemblance between Federico and Bernardino della Carda's son Ottaviano, born at Gubbio in 1423, in a pair of marble tondos at Mercatello sul Metauro. It was perhaps even more forcefully displayed in a sadly deteriorated semicircular stone bas-relief attributed to Francesco Martini in the ducal palace at Urbino, where they face each other as though the armoured Federico, with a Roman standard behind him, is looking at the other half of his personality, unscarred Ottaviano dressed in a robe with law books behind him. However, the strongest evidence of Federico's true paternity came when Bernardino died in 1437, by then lord of Castel Durante for Guidantonio and the commander of a standing force of 800 *lance* (2400–3200 cavalry), which he willed in equal parts to Federico and Ottaviano. The bookish Ottaviano was at Filippo Maria Visconti's court and, as his father must have anticipated, renounced his share to Federico, who thereby became a major condottiere at the age of fifteen.

The Ubaldini were an old clan that in the seventh century took up residence in the Mugello, the mountainous area north-east of Florence, controlling the upper Santerno valley and the Futa and Faetino passes between Tuscany and Imola–Bologna (Map 1). Like the Pagani, another robber baron clan that controlled the parallel Santerno valley from their stronghold at Susinana, the Ubaldini were violently Ghibelline and the two clans merged through the marriage of the infamous Maghinardo Pagani's daughter and heiress to successive Ubaldini counts of Frassino (today Palazzuolo). At the turn of the thirteenth–fourteenth century the Republic of Florence razed the Ubaldini stronghold at Monte Accianico and built the new fortified towns of Scarperia and Firenzuola on either side of the Apennines. By that time, however, Cardinal Legate Ottaviano Ubaldini, whose involvement in the Romagna borderlands we saw in Chapter One, had established a new base for a branch of the clan at Carda and Apecchio, in the upper Candigliano valley south of the Massa Trabaria.

Bernardino della Carda was among the many middle-ranking condottiere of his time. His early career was spent fighting for and against several of the Marche lords before being hired by Pandolfo III Malatesta and sharing his defeat at Olginate in 1418. In 1422, when in the service of Guidantonio Montefeltro, he was sent to support Pandolfo and they were again defeated at Montichiari. He was wounded and captured in 1425 when fighting for Florence and in 1427 escaped from prison thanks to opiates sent him by Guidantonio, with which he drugged his gaolers. Later that year he distinguished himself at the battles of Castelsecco and Maclodio while fighting for Venice under Carmagnola. In December 1430 he and Guidantonio, then Captain-General of Florence, were trounced at the Serchio by Niccolò Piccinino for Lucca and Milan (Map 7). A month later, after defeating a Milanese incursion along the Elsa valley, he quit Florentine service at the end of his commission and became a Visconti retainer. In 1432 he was defeated at San Romano (see following chapter), but despite this Filippo Maria Visconti appointed him to the lordship of Vespolate on the border with hostile Savoy, on condition that young Ottaviano take up residence at the Milanese court as a hostage to his father's loyalty.

In November 1424 Federico was legitimated by Pope Martin V as Guidantonio's heir (if no legitimate heir were born later) and brought to the court of Urbino. Caterina Colonna accepted the situation with good grace and even consented to Federico's legitimation; but her attitude changed after she gave birth to a short-lived boy in 1425, when Federico was sent to Mercatello sul Metauro to be raised by Bartolomeo Brancaleone's widow, Countess Giovanna (née Alidosi).

Thus Federico was raised in a place where the very stones were seeped in the centuries-old triangular conflict among the Montefeltri, the Malatesti and the Papacy. Even after Caterina bore him Guidobaldo in 1427, Guidantonio still regarded Federico as the spare to his heir and in 1425 successfully petitioned Martin V to bless the betrothal of three-year-old Federico to Gentile Brancaleone, eight years older and his acting sister. The union, solemnised ten years later, secured the Brancaleone freeholds in the Massa Trabaria for the Montefeltri. The other Brancaleoni branch was doomed when Carlo II Malatesta died in September 1429, after which the pope invested Guidantonio Count of Castel Durante, with a commission to seize the town and its dependencies at Sassocorvaro, Lunano and Montelocco. This he did with a lightning campaign in June 1430, driving the Brancaleoni to exile in Rimini.

Martin V's conspiracy against the Malatesti went much further. Carlo II petitioned for the legitimation of Pandolfo III's sons after his brother died in 1427 and part of the price extorted for the papal Bull making them eligible to inherit Carlo's holdings was an agreement that Cervia in the north and the Rimini Malatesta holdings south of the Metauro in the Marche should revert to the Papacy on Carlo's death. For his part, Carlo's last effort to secure the succession was to arrange the marriage of Galeotto Roberto to Niccolò III d'Este's daughter Margherita, who brought back with her the lands given as dowry to the ill-fated Parisina. In January 1430 the pope unmasked his guns and declared all the Malatesta lands forfeit for failure to pay the tribute, not only a cynical pretext but also blatantly false accounting given the enormous amounts still owed Carlo II for his services to the Papacy. The Malatesta holdings in the Marche seem to have accepted a return to papal rule with dull resignation, while Guidantonio repossessed San Sepolcro in the upper Tiber valley for Rome – he was not, however, granted title to the town, which would have secured both sides of the Trabaria Pass for the Montefeltro domain.

Of the repossessed Marche holdings Martin V promptly ceded Senigallia to the Pesaro Malatesti, whom he also funded covertly to attack Rimini. Sonetti died in December 1429, his last act being to prepare a military campaign in support of a claim lodged with Rome to the whole of the domain held by Carlo II's widow Elisabetta and a Council of Regents on behalf of the three newly legitimated Malatesta heirs. The Council included Guidantonio Montefeltro, Elisabetta's brother Gian' Francesco I Gonzaga of Mantua, Niccolò III d'Este, Guidantonio Manfredi of Faenza and Obizzo Polenta of Ravenna. The Council also enjoyed the support of Braccio da Montone's nephew Niccolò Fortebraccio, Captain-General of Florence at the time, who hated Martin V for the dishonest dispossession of his uncle's widow in 1425. Venice also weighed in on Elisabetta's side and the pope was forced to make a hasty retraction. Carlo I marched north from Pesaro after the pope declared the Rimini Malatesta lands forfeit but retreated on finding himself diplomatically isolated and faced by several thousand armed men rapidly gathered by thirteen-year-old Sigismondo. Sigismondo then led his ragtag force in a lightning march south to Serrungarina, where he stormed the fortified camp of condottieri hired by Guidantonio Montefeltro, who were ravaging the Fano hinterland, then north again in response to the storming of Sassocorvaro by Guidantonio himself.

The haplessness of the Pesaro Malatesti was further revealed in 1431 when Carlo I marched north again to support a coup in May by members of the Council of Regents led by Giovanni di Ramberto Malatesta, a descendant of the long-marginalised line of Giovanni 'Gianciotto'. Once again events made Carlo I's timing exquisitely bad, as Pope Martin V died in February and his successor the Venetian Eugenius IV made it his first priority to undo all his predecessor's nepotistic arrangements. The Rimini coup had failed even before Sigismondo arrived from Cesena with a scratch force of retainers. Carlo slunk back to Pesaro and the disloyal Regents were exiled at the insistence of Venetian and papal envoys. Other attempted coups in Fano and Cesena found no popular support and were easily suppressed. Not so a further revolt in Fano led by Matteo Buratelli, priest of the nearby parish of Cuccurano, which began with the assassination in early November of the authorities who ruled the town for Domenico including Count Giovanni Malatesta of Carpegna (footnote Appendix B). Sigismondo marched from Rimini to recover the city for his brother and was roughly handled in a street fight before restoring order. Buratelli was sent to Rimini, defrocked by an episcopal court and hanged.

The Buratelli revolt may have been a belated product of the conspiracy by the Pesaro Malatesti, but by the time it erupted they were prostrate. Priest-inspired revolts drove them out of Fossombrone and Pesaro itself immediately after the failure of the Rimini coup, and had the leadership of the main Malatesta line been in the hands of anyone other than the unworldly Galeotto Roberto, the sons of Pandolfo III might have taken possession of their cousins' domain. Galeotto Roberto even refused an invitation by the church and citizens of Fossombrone to become their lord. He died of self-flagellation and privation in October 1432 but by that time the opportunity to settle accounts with the Pesaro Malatesti had passed. Eugenius IV's determination to undo his predecessor's legacy threatened far too many vested interests and in 1432 a new schism robbed him of much of his authority, culminating in his flight from Rome in a boat along the Tiber in May 1434, pelted with stones and offal from the banks of the river.

The pope took up residence in Florence and appointed Giovanni Vitelleschi, the warlike bishop of Recanati and governor of Bologna and Romagna with a free hand to restore order in the Papal State, where the hydra-like Prefetti di Vico in alliance with the Colonna clan had seized the opportunity to reclaim lost lands. Vitelleschi's style was demonstrated in the murderous revolt he sponsored against the Varani of Camerino in 1434, which he was to repeat against the Trinci of Foligno in 1439. However, he was a native of Corneto and bent his savage talents preferentially against Giacomo di Vico, lord of the town, whom he crushed in battle and executed in 1435. He also demolished the Colonna stronghold of Palestrina and other fortified villages held by them and their Savelli allies, and terrorised Rome into submission. Vitelleschi hired many condottieri, among them Antonio da Pontedra who in 1434 defeated and killed Niccolò Fortebraccio, whose support had been crucial in thwarting the designs of Pope Martin V against the sons of Pandolfo III Malatesta in 1429–30. Pontedera then switched sides to the Colonna and was captured and hanged by Vitelleschi in 1436.

In the north an alliance between Florence, the Papacy and Venice kept Milan in check throughout the 1430s and beyond, ending with the establishment of something close to permanent borders in 1454.

Meanwhile events in the southern kingdom moved towards the outcome all popes dreaded with Alfonso 'the Magnanimous' of Aragon, heir to Sicily in 1411, claiming the kingdom of Naples after the death of Joanna II in 1435. Defeated and captured by the Genoese, allies of Milan, at the naval battle of Ponza that year, Alfonso was sent to the court of Filippo Maria Visconti. To the astonishment of all they became friends and agreed that Italy was best divided between them. To abbreviate the greater complexities, suffice it to say that Vitelleschi, by then Cardinal Archbishop of Florence, was imprisoned and died in Castel Sant'Angelo in 1440 after the Florentines intercepted treasonous correspondence with Milan, while in 1443 Alfonso of Aragon and Sicily won recognition from Eugenius IV of the title to Naples for himself and legitimation for his bastard son Ferrante. The deal permitted the definitive return of the Papacy to Rome, although Milan continued to sponsor the bizarre Antipapacy of Felix V, the retired Duke Amadeus VIII of Savoy. This, the last papal schism, was not finally healed until the deaths of Eugenius IV and Filippo Maria in 1447.

Following the flurry in 1430–2 the Montefeltri and the Malatesti refrained from mutual backstabbing until 1439. The main reason was that the 1433 Peace of Ferrara between Milan and Florence stipulated that Federico should be sent to Venice as a hostage to Guidantonio's good behaviour, which precluded any further hostility towards Venice's Malatesta clients. It proved to be the making of Federico, because after fifteen months as an honoured guest in Venice an outbreak of the plague caused him to be sent to the Gonzaga court in Mantua. There he spent two years enrolled in the *Ca' Gioiosa* (Joyous House), a boarding school run by the remarkable Vittorino da Feltre. The Gioiosa had a profound influence on Federico, who included Vittorino among the marquetry portraits of the twenty-eight wisest men in history that decorate the upper walls of his study in the Urbino palace. It had perhaps an even more profound influence on historical perception of his legacy through Elisabetta Gonzaga, another of Vittorino's pupils and Federico's daughter-in-law, who was the hostess of the Renaissance Camelot in Baldassare Castiglione's highly influential 1528 treatise *The Courtier.*

**VITTORINO DA FELTRE (1378–1446)**

**Vittorino's legacy illuminates every corner of Castiglione's *The Courtier*. The Ca' Gioiosa created an idealised home environment where the new Humanist curriculum was seamlessly merged with traditional Christian teaching and combined with sports and training in the gentlemanly arts. As well as the children of the Gonzaga and other leading Mantuan families, the school welcomed the offspring of other notable Humanist scholars and promising youths from poor families.**

While Federico was acquiring the polish that banishment from his official father's court had denied him, the Malatesta brothers were learning about the real world. Among those executed after Giovanni di Ramberto's failed coup was one of the two scholars (the other mysteriously disappeared) to whom Pandolfo III had entrusted the education of Sigismondo and Domenico at the Brescia court, the tutor thus providing his pupils with one last harsh lesson. In late 1431 soon-to-be Marquis Gian' Francesco Gonzaga of Mantua arranged the betrothal of Sigismondo to the daughter of the great Carmagnola, a few months before the Venetians beheaded Carmagnola for treasonous dealings with his old master Filippo Maria Visconti. As soon as word of Carmagnola's arrest reached Rimini the match was repudiated. Some have judged Sigismondo harshly for keeping the dowry, but this is a canard. The Council of Regents handled the matter and they arranged to repay the dowry in instalments to the Venetians, their most powerful ally, who had confiscated Carmagnola's estate.

After Galeotto Roberto died the Regents made a new administrative division along the line of the Marecchia, with Sigismondo getting the lion's share comprising Rimini, Fano and all lands south of the river plus, on the northern side, the strategic fortresses of Sant'Arcangelo, Scorticata and Sant'Agata Feltria, while Domenico received Cesena, its port Cesenatico, and the detached counties of Bertinoro and Meldola. In the beginning Eugenius IV addressed Domenico as Rector of Romagna, which paid lip service to the 1380 contract that the office should be hereditary for three generations but also suggests that the Regents, who may have nominated Domenico for the title, were tolerably sure Sigismondo was not destined to be a loyal servant of the Papacy.

Carlo II's widow Elisabetta also died at about the same time as Galeotto Roberto, both in due course to feature in the long list of those allegedly poisoned by Sigismondo, and the Council of Regents played no further role in the administration of the state, which was now governed by the two teenagers and their councillors of choice. There was in principle no reason why the brothers should not have exercised joint rule over the whole domain, as their father, Carlo II, and Andrea had done, but it would have required superhuman forbearance for Domenico not to resent being so comprehensively outshone. The crowning humiliation must have been that he was impotent, whereas Sigismondo was a throwback to earlier generations and, starting young, fathered many anonymous bastards in addition to at least fifteen recognised offspring.

In 1434 Sigismondo married Ginevra, daughter of his ill-fated cousin Parisina and Niccolò III d'Este, and in 1435 he negotiated Domenico's betrothal to Violante, five-year-old daughter of Guidantonio Montefeltro. The formal betrothal took place five years later and the marriage two years after that, in Guidantonio Montefeltro's last year of life, by which time he must have known that his own heir Oddo Antonio lacked the mettle to fight the Malatesti. This helps to explain why Violante did not finally join her husband in Cesena until 1447 – she was a hostage to Domenico's good behaviour. Ironically, in 1444 she became the prisoner of her brother's murderer, Federico III, and the *casus belli* for Sigismondo and Domenico to sink their differences and to attack the usurper. It is quite possible that the insider knowledge contained in Sigismondo's later denunciation of Federico's dubious parentage and his lack of legitimacy as a ruler came from Violante, his teenaged sister-in-law.

The 1430s were a testing period for small state rulers, who in addition to conducting a balancing act among the greater powers also had to deal with roving condottieri armies larger than any seen since the heyday of Fra Moriale's Great Company. The glacier from which these icebergs calved was Filippo Maria Visconti, whose gift for choosing brilliant generals was matched only by his ability to make them feel so insecure that they seldom remained on his payroll for long. After driving Carmagnola into the arms of Venice in 1425, resulting in the loss of the eastern reaches of the Visconti empire including Brescia and Bergamo, Filippo Maria tried again with a stable of condottieri including the brothers Francesco and Alessandro Sforza, heirs of the great Muzio Attendolo, and Niccolò Piccinino, foremost among the Bracceschi. Having first tried to bind Francesco Sforza to his cause by betrothal (in 1432, when she was seven years old) to his eldest, legitimated, daughter Bianca Maria, Filippo Maria sent the Sforzas to maraud the Marche in late 1433 with orders to attack only lands ruled by the Church, and within a few months they had conquered most of the province. But then, of course, they decided to go into business for themselves and so great was Pope Eugenius IV's anxiety to detach them from Filippo Maria that in March 1434 he appointed Francesco Sforza lifetime Marquis of Ancona, with all secular rights, against a promise of military service that was to be separately paid for and which did not even commit the Sforza brothers themselves to fight for the Church. The pope also prevailed on Queen Joanna II to appoint Francesco Grand Constable of Naples. Thus, to all practical effect, a new state was created – to the indescribable fury of Filippo Maria Visconti.

The military history of greater Italy during the years when the final showdown between the Montefeltri and Malatesti took place resembles one of the old Hollywood bar-room brawls, where an apparently peaceful scene erupts after the first punch is thrown, with every man breaking a chair over his neighbour's head and all furniture except the bar and piano rapidly reduced to matchwood. Following in the steps of Machiavelli many historians have judged that it was all sound and fury signifying very little, but somehow the lasting boundaries of Milan, Florence, Venice and even the Papal State emerged from the shambles. Unfortunately there was little reliable reporting on how campaigns were conducted and battles fought, but we do have detailed information on one, so let us now turn to examine the campaign that culminated in the battle of San Romano, and the paths taken by the condottieri who fought there.

## ELEVEN

# *San Romano*

Paolo Uccello's *The Battle of San Romano* (Picture section 1) was the subject of an excellent programme in the series *The Private Life of a Masterpiece* aired by BBC2 in April 2005. The work, consisting of three 10 foot by 6 foot poplar panels, is currently displayed at the National Gallery in London, the Uffizi in Florence and the Louvre in Paris. It celebrates a battle fought on 1 June 1432 between Florentine forces under the command of Niccolò 'da Tolentino' Mauruzzi and Micheletto Attendolo, and a Siena–Lucca–Milanese army led by Federico III Montefeltro's father Bernardino della Carda and by Antonio 'da Pontedera' Gambacorta. Long believed to have been commissioned by the Medici, it was a puzzle to military historians why they should have wished to celebrate a battle with no great consequences, in a war begun by Florence with the intention of subduing Lucca, which drew in Siena and Milan against Florence and which ended in 1333 with the parties returning all towns taken from the other. The only beneficiary was Filippo Maria Visconti, who took the opportunity to make Florence exhaust its energy apart from the alliance with Venice that had thwarted his imperialism over the preceding decade.* Yet there it is, a work considered among the most artistically influential of all time, with references to it even in Pablo Picasso's *Guernica*, the only painting

* Although as Machiavelli observed, 'in this war the Florentines [had] expended three and a half million ducats, extended the territory and power of the Venetians and brought poverty and disunion on themselves'.

to challenge *San Romano* as the most famous depiction of battle in history.

In fact Uccello's triptych only came into the possession of the Medici around 1484, when Lorenzo I 'the Magnificent' part-bought and part-stole the panels from the original owners. They were the sons of Leonardo Bartolini Salimbeni who, according to a document dating from 1495 discovered by Professor Francesco Caglioti in 2000, commissioned the work *circa* 1438 to decorate his bedroom on the occasion of his second marriage. Therein lies the explanation both of how the work came into being and why Lorenzo felt he had to have it, for Bartolini Salimbeni was one of Florence's War Commissioners in 1432 and disputes about the conduct of the war contributed to the exile of Cosimo de' Medici by the Albizzi faction in 1433. Cosimo returned in triumph the following year and, barring a republican interlude in 1494–8 and a subsequent French occupation, the Medici ruled Florence until the line died out in 1737. *San Romano* was propaganda, designed to glorify an event in which the man who commissioned it took pride, but which also might have aborted the transformation of the Medici from increasingly troubled bankers to lords of Florence. By the time the panels passed into the hands of the city the story behind them and even the identity of the artist had been forgotten. Florence kept the central panel, but the other two passed through dealers to Paris and London in the nineteenth century.

The triptych owes much of its artistic fame to being the first example of one-point perspective in an entirely non-architectural painting, with the litter of broken lances and the fallen knights in the first two panels drawing the viewer's attention to the technique. But its stylistic influence ironically owes a great deal to an act of vandalism committed by Lorenzo the Magnificent. The panels were originally arch-topped and after Lorenzo secured them he had the arches sawn off and the top corners squared with spandrels, to make them fit the rectangular wall spaces between the vaults of Lorenzo's room in the Medici palace. Lance tops and banners were amputated along with background land- and skyscape, probably including the battle's signature tower at San Romano built by Sir John Hawkwood during one of his last campaigns in 1391 and demolished by the Germans in 1944. The mutilation of the panels created a striking but stylistically anachronistic foreground concentration, whose influence art historians detect in the work of several First World War artists as well as in Picasso's *Guernica*.

Sir John Hale's *Artists and Warfare in the Renaissance* and Peter Paret's *Imagined Battles* were both written before Caglioti's discovery, but their appreciation of the triptych as battle art remains valid. Uccello had never witnessed combat and despite many technically accurate details what he painted was an allegorical tournament: the knights wear parade helmets and the horses are not protected, as they would have been in battle. Pietro Roccasecca, with whose *Paolo Uccello: le Battaglie* it would be unwise to disagree, argues that the Louvre panel was painted later and portrays the more significant victory of Micheletto Attendolo for Florence at Anghiari in June 1440. So it is only by chance that in juxtaposition with the other two it conveys a time-elapsed third phase and the turning point of the battle of San Romano, when Attendolo arrived to save Tolentino's exhausted army. Although outnumbered, Tolentino launched repeated charges over the preceding three hours of a very hot day, during which four of his captains were captured and 400 horses lost. After Attendolo attacked them from the rear Carda and Pontedera retreated in reasonably good order but lost their reserve herd of 600 horses. The majority of the 500–600 men killed during the battle were Sienese militiamen and most of their losses must have come after the cavalry abandoned them. Francesco Piccinino, who rode with Carda and Pontedera, abandoned the siege of nearby Montopoli that had kept him from the battle (in the background of the second panel).

Perhaps the single most important – but most awkward – thing military historians must bear in mind is that even front-line soldiering is in most respects a job like any other. What sets it apart from most others is that physical courage is a fundamental requirement and that errors can be fatal; but beyond that the desire for peer approval, recognition by management and career advancement work no less powerfully than in any other occupation. So, also, do issues such as pride, envy and resentment that may cause men to do things contrary to their objective interest. Since armies became bureaucratic many of the old rules no longer apply and far too many time-serving mediocrities rise to the top, but for most of human history warfare has been a constant, and a constant winnower of the unfit and the incompetent.

Never was this truer than in the Age of the Condottieri. A military entrepreneur might command followers from his own lands but they still had to be paid, or in the absence of steady wages needed a reasonable assurance of compensation in the form of loot. Every head contractor in the San Romano campaign had to balance the conflicting priorities of employers who wanted to pay by results and followers who might refuse to deliver those results unless paid.

We have seen how some condottieri maintained their market value despite defeats that in principle should have reduced it substantially, the most likely explanation being that their employers were well aware that financial attrition was the real purpose of the wars they initiated. Even an apparently unsuccessful campaign could oblige an opponent to spend money he could not afford and ultimately force him into a settlement beneficial to the apparent loser. The war waged by Florence against Lucca in which San Romano was an episode shows money at work in its crudest form: Florence could outspend even Lucca and Siena combined, but once Milan weighed in the equation became more balanced. Filippo Maria's interest, in turn, was not to preserve the independence of the smaller city-states but to keep Florence so busy in Tuscany that she could not interfere with his plans for Lombardy and Romagna. The strategic background helps to explain much that seems so inconsequential at the operational level of many campaigns, with much to-ing and fro-ing apparently signifying little except to the unfortunate non-combatants cruelly caught up in it.

Niccolò Mauruzzi was born around 1395 into a prominent family of Tolentino in the Marche and left home because of conflict with his father over his stepmother. He learned his trade in the Free Companies before becoming an official in the service of Pandolfo III Malatesta in 1407. In 1412 Pandolfo invested him with the hereditary title of Count of Stacciolo, a manor in the Fano hinterland somewhere along the Cesano valley. By 1423 Tolentino was a *maresciallo* (a lower rank than its literal translation of 'marshal' suggests) in Pandolfo's army but it was in a private capacity that he served Florence, with one interruption, between 1424 and 1434. During 1431, the year before San Romano, he first received a commission from Filippo Maria Visconti for 400 *lance* (a minimum of 1200 cavalry) and 200 infantry, with a personal guard of ten crossbowmen. In March with Francesco Sforza he ambushed

Carmagnola at Soncino, twenty-two miles from Cremona, and captured over a thousand horses and 500 infantry. In June he was joined by Niccolò Piccinino and together they inflicted a severe defeat on Venice at Casalmaggiore, equidistant from Parma, Mantua and Cremona, where they destroyed or captured the enemy river fleet and seized enormous booty, including the Venetian payroll of 60,000 ducats. Tolentino prevented the Venetian army from intervening to save the fleet, a failure that was to prove the principal nail in Carmagnola's coffin. After the battle, offended that Piccinino was appointed captain-general (therefore presumably entitled to the lion's share of the booty), Tolentino accepted a commission of 20,000 ducats from Venice – to return to the service of Florence, which would carry the burden of the war with Milan while Venice regrouped. The Florentines in turn lent him reinforcements to go to the aid of Pope Eugenius IV, who made him captain-general. Tolentino performed his new duties to such good effect that the pope confirmed his hereditary title to Stacciolo and also appointed him lord of San Sepolcro, taken from the Malatesti by Pope Martin V a year earlier. However, Tolentino made no effort to exercise the new lordship and it was revoked the following year.

In April 1432 he negotiated a commission of 52,000 florins with Florence and at the insistence of Cosimo de' Medici was appointed captain-general in May. There followed the San Romano campaign, dealt with in detail below. His commission was renewed in 1433 but he did not formally receive the baton of captain-general until June. Based at Pisa, when news reached him that Cosimo de' Medici had been arrested he marched on Florence but was persuaded to return by Cosimo's emissaries. The briefly dominant Albizzi were happy to lend him back to Venice and in November he was in Romagna blocking Sforza when he learned that the Varani had seized Tolentino, where he had built a basilica in anticipation of the canonisation of the town's patron Saint Nicola (which finally took place in 1446). Niccolò was persuaded not to march south and was rewarded with the lordship of his home town following the Vitelleschi-inspired massacre of the Varani in July 1434. He was not granted time to savour his triumph over the shade of his long-dead father for in August, still serving the Venetian–papal cause in Romagna, he was ambushed and captured along with half his army by Niccolò Piccinino and Bernardino della Carda while crossing the River Sanguinario, midway between Imola and Faenza. Taken to Milan, despite Florence's efforts to ransom him and the pleas of Piccinino for mercy, in March he 'fell' from a rock to his death while being taken to another place of imprisonment. His estate included over 200,000 ducats in cash and 2000 pounds of silver ingots. His body is buried at the Florence Duomo and his heart at the basilica he built in Tolentino.

Micheletto Attendolo was an extremely prickly and superstitious individual. Born around 1370, he was a cousin of the Sforzas and followed their banners in the service of Naples and the Church until Muzio's death in 1424. He served under Francesco Sforza at the battle of Aquila later that year, but afterwards became an independent contractor. His company was in continuous existence until 1448, during which time 512 condottieri signed sub-contracts with him ranging from 50 *lance* to individual signings. He served the Church until May 1431 when he became Captain-General of Florence with a commission for 600 *lance* and 200 infantry. 'We know very well how you behave when you no longer have need of us,' he said to the Florentine commissioners, before demanding a guarantee of long-term employment. In June he received the captain-general's baton from Rinaldo degli Albizzi in Arezzo, followed by a full ceremonial investiture in Florence later that month on the day his astrologers declared auspicious. Thus reassured he marched to Pisa to evict the Viscontean Antonio da Pontedera from a fortified village south of the city and defeated him in a battle at Ponsacco (Map 7).

In October Micheletto required another ceremonial parade in Florence before marching south along the Arno valley to retake the village of Caposelvi from the Sienese. He returned to Florence for another triumph and was awarded a silver helmet, a horse and a banner with the insignia of Florence. Things did not go so well in 1432. In March a plan to capture Lucca by a night escalade with the help of bribed members of the garrison failed because Attendolo did not arrive in time and when he marched south to confront Antonio da Pontedera in the Arno valley he was defeated at Marti, where 400 of his men were captured. Without permission from Florence he negotiated a truce and withdrew to the outskirts of Pisa, after which he was stripped of the captain-generalcy and Tolentino appointed in his place, although

Attendolo refused to surrender the baton. His arrival at San Romano was in breach of the terms of the unauthorised truce.

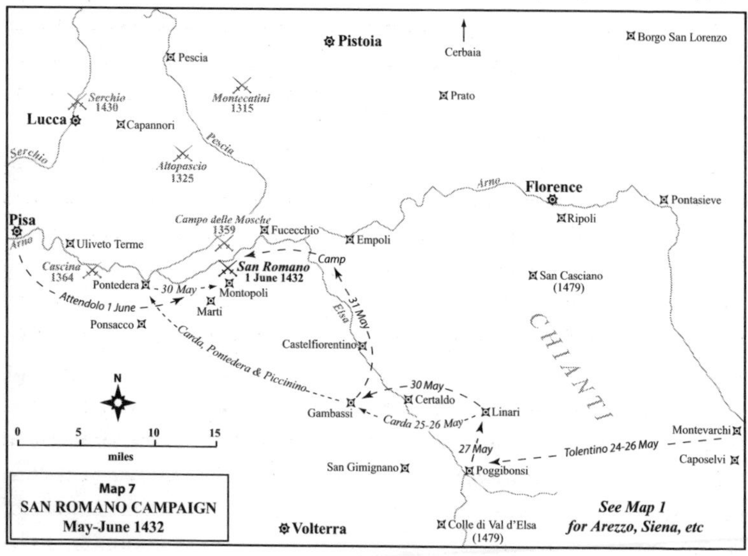

**Map 7**
**SAN ROMANO CAMPAIGN**
**May-June 1432**

After the battle Attendolo would not serve under Tolentino and was sent on an independent commission into the Val di Chiana south of Arezzo where he went on strike, claiming back pay of 30,000 florins. In November he was given the honorary title of Governor-General at a monthly salary of 1000 florins in addition to a commission for 650 *lance* and 400 infantry for nine months' active service and two years in reserve. He returned to Pisa and gave up the baton in 1433, but after the two years in reserve were not confirmed he went south to fight for the Church against Niccolò Fortebraccio. Micheletto's subsequent career was extraordinary. To mention only the highlights, he was Captain-General of the Church in 1433–4, Grand Constable of Naples in 1435–8, Governor-General of Ancona for Francesco Sforza in 1439, a post he delegated to Alessandro Sforza in order to accept a commission from Florence during which he defeated Niccolò Piccinino at Anghiari. Far from basking in the glow of a victory that gave Florence San Sepolcro and the eastern extension of Tuscany that persists to this day, in 1441 he joined his cousins to fight against the Aragonese in the

Abruzzi until mid year, then became Captain-General of Venice in opposition to them, replacing the ailing Gattamelata. He remained in overall command of the Venetian army until 1448, when against his better judgement he was persuaded by Bartolomeo Colleoni to attack Francesco Sforza's fortified camp at Caravaggio and was crushed, with most of his men captured and the loss of more than 10,000 horses. He was pensioned off and died in 1451, at least eighty years old.

Bernardino della Carda we have already met. In 1430 Guidantonio Montefeltro became Captain-General of Florence as a third choice because Bernardino and Niccolò Fortebraccio, both under contract to Florence, would not serve under the other. Guidantonio led them all to resounding defeat at the battle of the Serchio, where he failed to contain Lucca when offering battle to a Milanese army led by Niccolò Piccinino and was undone when the garrison made a sortie to his rear. Fortebraccio was captured and treated generously by Piccinino, not so by Florence when he was released, after which he never again bore arms for Florence or against Milan. Bernardino thus became captain-general by default, a commission that barely lasted the month of January 1431, during which the town of Marradi (Map 1) capitulated to him on terms that included the release from prison of one of its leading citizens. When the Florentines refused to release the man Bernardino resigned his commission and took service with Milan. Filippo Maria immediately sent him to help the Pesaro Malatesti against the Church at a time when the election of Pope Eugenius IV had forced Guidantonio Montefeltro to pull back from supporting them. Bernardino's intervention helps to explain how the heirs of Malatesta dei Sonetti survived the consequences of their inept attempts to seize Rimini and Fano – there were/are always wheels within wheels in the politics of Italy. Siena requested his services and he led their contingent during the San Romano campaign. Convention has it that Carda is the knight being felled in the Uffizi panel of Uccello's triptych, but there is no evidence he was unhorsed during the battle. Afterwards Filippo Maria invested him lord of Vespolate, which as mentioned earlier required his son Ottaviano to take up residence in Milan as a guarantee of good behaviour. Bernardino's last battle was at the Sanguinario in 1434, where he defeated Tolentino, after which he became seriously ill. He seems never to have recovered good health and died in 1437.

Francesco Piccinino, born at Perugia in 1407, was the adopted son of Niccolò Piccinino and brother to Jacopo, born sixteen years later. The key to understanding his lacklustre career is that he seems to have been an alcoholic, a genetic predisposition far less common in Italy than in northern European cultures. Troops under his command frequently got out of control, notably in a spiteful massacre of men, women and children at San Sepolcro after their defeat at Anghiari. He commanded no regular following and the indiscriminate looting that marked his passage suggests he attracted the condottieri dregs to his banner. The poor quality of his troops in turn may be the reason why he avoided battle whenever possible, which might also explain why he was absent from the field at San Romano. His many subsequent acts of bad faith are more readily explained by indecisiveness and lack of confidence in his men than by any positive intent. On the only occasion when he was forced into battle with a first-rate opponent, at Montolmo in the Marche in 1444 after his father had been recalled to Milan, he was routed and captured by Francesco Sforza. Francesco Piccinino died of congestive heart failure in the forty-first year of a life in which his adoptive name seems to have been all that redeemed him from obscurity.

Antonio Gambacorta was born at Pontedera in the Arno valley, a factor that was to impinge on the San Romano campaign. His family may have moved there after their kinsman Piero Gambacorta, the last independent lord of Pisa, was assassinated in 1392. One of many made rootless by the conquest of Pisa by Florence in 1406, he first enters the record in 1425 when in breach of a commission with Florence to conquer the Bidente valley he took service with the Malatesti of Ghiaggiolo, for which he was painted hanging by his feet on the wall of the war office in Florence, the traditional punishment for those the Florentines were unable to hang in person. Niccolò Piccinino was similarly depicted in 1428 and Pontedera was one of his captains at the Serchio, after which he was sent to take possession of several fortified villages around Pisa that had taken the opportunity to expel their Florentine rulers and begged for the protection of Milan, an example followed by other villages around Volterra. His followers were mainly Pisan exiles, joined during the San Romano campaign by a contingent from Lucca. As we have seen, he defeated Attendolo at Marti and the fury of the Florentines when Micheletto negotiated a truce was fuelled by their hatred of Pontedera, which may also explain why Attendolo felt free to break his own oath – or more likely was forced to do so on pain of forfeiting his accumulated back pay.

Later in 1432 Pontedera uncovered yet another attempt by Florence to bribe a gate guard at Lucca, after which the citizens attempted to retain his services with fine promises – and a house worth a mere 600 florins. Offended, Pontedera took service with Niccolò Fortebraccio against the Church in September 1433, and against Fortebraccio for Vitelleschi in October. In May 1434 he killed Fortebraccio in battle, reportedly in single combat, but afterwards tried to become a power in his own right, switching allegiances frequently amid the multifaceted war in the Roman Campagna and Marittima among Vitelleschi, the Sforza brothers, the Colonna, the Orsini, Alfonso of Aragon and the Anjou–Provence pretenders. Highlights included a foray into Rome in August 1435 and being paid by the defenders of Capua to lift a siege when he was on the point of forcing their capitulation in October. Finally, in 1436 when leading a villainous personal following of 600 cavalry and 2000 infantry, he was defeated and captured by troops loyal to Vitelleschi, who hanged him and left his body to be consumed by the wolves that had made a notable comeback in the Patrimony of St Peter amid the human chaos.

This quick review of the senior captains at San Romano offers us the full condottieri spectrum from the dependable, honourable and even pious Niccolò da Tolentino to the outright brigand Antonio da Pontedera, and from the famously brave Bernardino della Carda to the cautious at best Francesco Piccinino. Their performance during the San Romano campaign is better reported than most others thanks to the diary kept by Luca degli Albizzi, special envoy of the Florentine republic to Niccolò da Tolentino. Luca was the younger brother of Rinaldo, who was to exile Cosimo de' Medici in 1433 and was exiled by him in turn the following year, and was sent to keep an eye on Tolentino because he and Cosimo were friends, while Cosimo's kinsman Bernardetto de' Medici accompanied the party in order to keep Luca honest. The delegation arrived near Montevarchi on 18 May and the following day went on to the captain-general's camp near Arezzo. Tolentino was away, having set out the previous day on an expedition down the

Chiana valley to ambush a recruiting party led by Francesco Piccinino. Warned by his own spies, Piccinino evaded the ambush and joined forces with Carda in the upper Elsa valley. Tolentino rode further down the Chiana to send supplies and reinforcements into Montepulciano, a small town that had rebelled against Siena and was loosely besieged by militia, before returning to Arezzo. It was not considered remarkable for Tolentino's detachment to have ridden more than fifty miles in twenty-four hours.

When Luca Albizzi and Tolentino met on 20 May the commander asked for pay, mules to carry supplies, two or three bombards with stonemasons to cut balls for them and militia labourers for siege work. Luca sent a dispatch to Florence but it appears most of Tolentino's requirements were satisfied locally, for on the 24th he set off for the Elsa valley with about 2000 cavalry, the same number of infantry, some militia and the bombards. Although marching to the relief of Gambassi and Linari, Florentine towns besieged by Carda and Piccinino, Tolentino was slowed by the bombards and covered less than twenty miles in two days, arriving at Poggibonsi after both towns had capitulated. Carda and Piccinino left garrisons to hold the towns while they marched to the lower Arno valley, joining up with the Milan–Lucca contingent on the way, and occupied Pontedera's home town on the 29th. Tolentino was in a quandary – he could not leave Linari and Gambassi in enemy hands for fear of contagion along the Elsa, but the thrust into the Arno valley was strategically far more serious. His desperate haste, plus the background of rebellion against Florentine rule across southern Tuscany, helps explains the barbarous treatment of Linari after he breached the walls and stormed it on the 30th. The small Sienese garrison refused to surrender on terms and could have been put to the sword, but Tolentino spared them; however, he ordered his troops to take away their pick of the women, demolish the walls and burn half the village.

The Sienese garrison at Gambassi promptly surrendered, no doubt with considerable encouragement from the villagers, and Tolentino left the militia behind to make a lightning ride down the Elsa to the Arno confluence, where he camped the night of 31 May. The enemy meanwhile had marched east from Pontedera to besiege Montopoli and on 1 June Tolentino advanced along the Arno to relieve the town.

In the background of the first *San Romano* panel two messengers can be seen riding to tell Attendolo that battle was imminent but we may be sure Tolentino would not have attacked an army twice the size of his own without an assurance that his fellow commander was on his way. Matteo Palmieri, on whose account of the battle Uccello appears to have based his paintings, states that Tolentino 'sent three companies through the vineyards and brambles toward Montopoli, under orders to wait until, after the battle had begun, the others had all descended on the plain, and then to launch their own attack'. He left three more companies in reserve on the hill under the tower and advanced himself with two in order to draw the enemy out of their defensive position. Carda and Pontedera seem to have fought the battle with some of their heavy cavalry forming a line with crossbowmen posted on the flanks. Sienese accounts attributed the setback to a dispute between Carda and Pontedera, which fatally delayed a counter-attack by the cavalry reserve that might have driven Tolentino from the field before Attendolo could arrive.

Tolentino's attack was designed to pin the enemy until Attendolo could come up behind them and the three hours he spent doing so must have been a very anxious time for him, as the overlong delay suggests Attendolo was in no hurry to fulfil his part of the plan. Carda and Pontedera were taken by surprise because Attendolo's intervention was in breach of the terms he had agreed after being defeated at nearby Marti in April, but despite the title 'rout' traditionally attached to the Uccello triptych the mounted men withdrew in good order, taking their prisoners and captured horses, and left the Sienese infantry to their fate. While an earlier commitment of their reserve cavalry might have secured victory over Tolentino, the reserves were able instead to hold Attendolo long enough for the rest to escape. The only named condottieri captured at San Romano were four Tolentino sub-contractors. Of these, Pietro Torelli had surrendered before at the Serchio and did not work again until 1438. Niccolò 'Attaccabriga' Sameroli went over to Milan and eventually to Francesco Sforza, who appointed him lord of Corinaldo in 1443. Attaccabriga robbed and raped the citizens and also betrayed Sforza, allying with Sigismondo and Domenico Malatesta in 1447. In 1448 the Corinaldese overthrew and, according to some accounts, beheaded him. Niccolò da Pisa, another exile, had a career indistinguishable from brigandage and in 1442 was assassinated in Bologna on the orders of the Manfredi of Faenza. Florence would not have paid ransom for any of them and the fact that they survived capture at San Romano and were released unharmed can only be attributed to professional courtesy.

I began by saying that nothing of great importance followed from the battle, but that is not to deny there might have been dire consequences if Tolentino had been defeated. We may deduce how tenuous Florence's hold on her own territory had become from the fact that in July Pontedera escorted emperor-elect Sigismund, on his way to Rome for coronation, from the fortress of Cerbaia, north of Prato, through Florentine territory to Siena, where he was met by an honour guard led by Bernardino della Carda. Sigismund appears to have released some of his retinue to fight for his hosts because later that month Micheletto Attendolo killed a Hungarian captain outside Lucca. Tolentino tried to retake Pontedera but he had left his bombards far behind and on instructions from Florence he moved to Capannori as a base from which to ravage the Lucca hinterland. Before then Luca degli Albizzi returned to Florence and our window into what seems to have been a representative summer campaign closes.

The main impression to emerge from Albizzi's account is of the breathtaking speed with which operations were conducted, which argues that the captured horses may have been the herds of blown mounts following behind the fast-moving cavalry. No less impressive was the rapidity of decision-making, made all the more remarkable by the complexity of the problems facing Tolentino. In a few days he had reinforced a rebel town deep in the Siena hinterland, countered an enemy thrust into the Elsa valley while making a deterrent example of Linari to discourage rebellion elsewhere, and took a calculated risk that their mutual employer would persuade Micheletto Attendolo to put money before pride. As a result he won a handy victory that prevented the enemy from blocking communications between Florence and Pisa. Perhaps the battle itself did not deserve to be immortalised, but Niccolò da Tolentino certainly earned the fresco by Andrea del Castagno, commissioned to honour his memory in 1456, which adorns the wall next to Uccello's fresco of Sir John Hawkwood in the Florence Duomo.

## TWELVE

# *Sigismondo*

During the nineteenth century the historical reputation of Federico III Montefeltro was burnished by hagiographers but during the twentieth century the stock of his crushed and humiliated rival Sigismondo Malatesta soared, the former submerged and the latter borne up by the tidal wave of Nationalism and Modernism that swept disastrously over Europe. The process began when Burckhardt in *The Civilisation of the Renaissance in Italy* selected Sigismondo as an exemplar of the 'new man', one who combined action and learning, the arts of war and of peace, for whom state building itself was a work of art. Sigismondo's rehabilitation gathered momentum when Gabriele d'Annunzio was drawn to the drama of Rimini, beginning with his 1886 poem *The Book of Isotta*, inspired by Sigismondo's love affair with Isotta degli Atti, followed by the tragedy *Francesca da Rimini*, written in 1901 for his own lover the actress Eleanora Duse, and the opera *Parisina* written in 1913 about the doomed love of the eponymous Malatesta wife of Niccolò III d'Este and her stepson Ugo. However much d'Annunzio and the anarcho-syndicalist Alceste de Ambris later shrank from their offspring they were the fathers of Mussolini's Fascist Party, which borrowed the title 'Duce', the black shirts, the anti-capitalist rhetoric, the corporativism and even the repellent technique of force-feeding castor oil to opponents from de Ambris and d'Annunzio's flamboyant 1919–20 occupation of Fiume, today Croatian Rijeka.

Arguably the strongest thread binding the image of Sigismondo with Fascism was Mussolini's birth in Malatestaland and a childhood spent in the shadow of the ruined Rocca Belle Caminate, which overlooks his birth and burial place in Predappio. However, it was probably Friedrich Nietzsche's vision of the Renaissance as a frustrated promise of modernity, a moment marked by 'positive forces which have up to now, in our contemporary modern civilisation, never been so powerful again', that most directly affected Fascist thought through Antonio Beltramelli's 1912 A *Temple of Love*, which contained the crucial phrase 'the mere presence of Sigismondo was enough to impose subjection, and in this lay the secret of his fascination over the masses'. Beltramelli later wrote the first biography of Mussolini, *The New Man*, published in 1923 after Mussolini had seized power, which explicitly identified the Fascist leader as heir to the Malatesta tradition. On a parallel course Ezra Pound was gestating *The Cantos*, regarded by many as the most important work of Anglo-American literary Modernism. Lawrence Rainey's book on the core *Malatesta Cantos*, which are essentially a hagiography of Sigismondo, contains a description of Pound's motivation too rich to summarise:

> ... distaste for the world engendered by capitalism is structured through a radical anti-materialism that rejects both the historicist trend of elite bourgeois culture and the repetitious uniformity of an urban lower class public associated with socialism. Meanwhile the middle (read also mediocre) socioeconomic strata are rejected in favor of an imaginary cultural aristocracy that embodies and is unified with the vitality of a traditional-rural folk, and this imaginary construct becomes the vehicle for values uncontaminated by the [ethos] that has engendered the culture of capitalist industrialism, materialism, or its academic exponent, philology.

If there is a hell, the raving spirit of Ezra Pound is locked for eternity in a library filled with the output of modern literary criticism. The historical person whom Pound chose to idealise of course bears little relation to the Sigismondo of the *Malatesta Cantos*, but it is peculiarly pointless to belittle an historical event because it was not 'really' as significant as people believed it to be, more useful to identify why they believed it was and how that belief influenced events. Within the broader framework of the fascination that men of action have always exercised over intellectuals, Federico Montefeltro and Sigismondo

Malatesta are the archetypes respectively for those who need to perceive natural if not divine order and justice in the world, and those whose inner turmoil finds solace in the arbitrary chaos of human affairs.

The real Sigismondo was what we now call a 'Thatcherite'. He inherited a domain in apparently terminal economic crisis with nothing in the coffers, no prospect of replenishing them from traditional industries (agriculture and related activities), a declining population base and the ports at Rimini and Fano silting up as seaborne trade was throttled by Venetian dominance of the Adriatic. One of his first measures on becoming lord of Rimini and Fano, aged fifteen, was to abolish all restrictions on the purchase of property and on the setting up of new enterprises by outsiders. It was a radical departure to attack the vested interests upon whose consent all *signori* depended for their power, and argues that Sigismondo understood how reduced levels of taxation can increase state revenues by encouraging greater economic dynamism, a principle many still find impossible to accept. However, Anna Falcioni's study of the economy under Sigismondo in the splendid multi-volume *Storia delle Signorie dei Malatesti* shows that his reforms were undone by the financial demands of the wars in which he was involved. Although the situation became critical under Sigismondo, the Malatesta state was not economically viable without condottiere income and Sigismondo was forced to earn in arms the money that might have been forthcoming from peaceful economic development. Peace, however, was never a realistic option for a state located at the strategic elbow of the Papal State and at the choke point of the easiest route to and from central and northern Italy; if the Papacy had not self-destructed during the fourteenth century the end for the Malatesta dynasty would probably have come much earlier.

If we accept that even a more prudent lord would probably have been crushed by the historical forces closing in on the Malatesta state, much that seems perverse and self-defeating in Sigismondo's behaviour begins to look like an accurate appreciation that while he might lose all by gambling, he would certainly lose it all if he refrained from doing so. His overarching strategic aim was to recreate the Malatesta domain as it was under his father and uncles, and in particular to close the gap created between Rimini and Fano when the Pesaro branch of the clan went its separate way. With regard to Pesaro he was probably mistaken to believe that the whole would be greater than the sum of the parts because Pesaro was in far worse shape than Rimini or Fano. In addition to a house in Florence and a lifetime pension, Galeazzo 'the Inept' sold Pesaro in 1445 for a mere 20,000 florins, with Fossombrone fetching a further 13,000, although Sforza also paid off Pesaro's cumulative tribute debt to Rome. Even these paltry sums, less than an average year's commission for a first-rate condottiere, are reckoned an exaggeration by some chroniclers, although the transaction took place under circumstances highly favourable to the seller. The lordship was valueless without the assent of the pope, which Galeazzo could not guarantee, so the price shows how pitifully small the freeholdings of the Pesaro Malatesti had become after decades of alienating property in favour of the retainers without whom there would have been no effective territorial authority to sell.

Although considered a big man by his contemporaries, measurement of Sigismondo's skeleton revealed that he was only 1.70 metres, not quite five and a half feet tall. He had dark red hair and the very white skin that often accompanies it and although Piero della Francesca's 1451 portrait of him when thirty-four years old (Picture section 2, p. 3) has suffered at the hands of a restorer who thought he knew better, it does capture the cold and rigid expression he showed the world. In private he could be charming and he was very attractive to women, but the gaping fault line in his character was lust. Cosimo de' Medici was inclined to believe an accusation of rape made against Sigismondo because 'Lord Sigismondo is well known to be so unbridled in his appetites that when he desires something he must have it at once without the patience to let it come to him in good time, and will do whatever it takes to satisfy his hunger'. Even more damaging were the judgements of Filippo Maria Visconti and Francesco Sforza, employers whose good opinion was vitally important to Sigismondo in the middle decades of the century, who both wrote to their other captains ridiculing his propensity to unconsidered schemes. In sum he was neither wise nor *furbo*, a deficiency compounded by his unshakeable belief that he was. Philip Jones put his finger on Sigismondo's carotid artery when he wrote, 'his fickle changes of allegiance were partly those of a captain in search of a sure and lucrative contract. But only partly. They proceeded just as much from a native simplicity which hoped to follow and profit by immediate advantage, indifferent to agreements broken or animosity aroused.'

Sigismondo's first commission came from Pope Eugenius IV as early as 1431, for 200 *lance* to police the payment of the annual papal tribute by other Romagna lords, which hints that the post of Rector might have been renewed if either of the Malatesta brothers had considered it worth having. They were instead more inclined to recover by force the lands taken from their family by Martin V, and in December 1433 Sigismondo took Cervia and its valuable salt flats, for which Eugenius declared him in rebellion. In the same year Sigismondo recovered some more ancestral lands by marrying fourteen-year-old Ginevra, one of Niccolò III d'Este's twin daughters by the ill-fated Parisina, who brought her mother's dower estates back to the Malatesta domain. The Louvre collection includes a portrait by Pisanello of a wan girl-princess of the house of Este, possibly Ginevra (Picture section 2, p. 1). If so, it may have been commissioned by her father as a memento. Her dress bears the Este livery and she is shown against a background of butterflies and columbines, symbolic of fleeting happiness and abiding sorrow.

The pope, as we have seen, was soon immersed in far greater troubles and the charge of rebellion was dropped after a face-saving transfer of Cervia from Sigismondo to Domenico in 1434. The nominal nature of the transfer was revealed early the next year when Sigismondo paid homage to Pope Eugenius IV in Florence and was awarded the Cervia vicariate along with a monthly retainer of 100 florins, followed a few months later by command of all papal forces in Romagna and the Marche. He made war on Antonio Ordelaffi, who was trying to re-establish his family's lordship of Forlì with the support of Niccolò Piccinino, who in turn was acting for Filippo Maria Visconti. After a truce between the Papacy and Milan left Ordelaffi exposed, Sigismondo was joined by Francesco Sforza, sacked Forlimpopoli and recovered Forlì for his employer, only to discover that Eugenius IV was plotting with Ordelaffi against Sforza and, according to a captured and tortured papal emissary, against the Malatesta brothers as well. Eugenius IV was by then installed in Bologna and Sigismondo twice visited him at the head of his troops, to show support but also as a warning. Keen though Eugenius IV was to purge the Church of his predecessor's nepotistic legacy, the collective consciousness of the Papacy was *always* bent on recovering control of the Papal State. The Romagna lords might be honoured and showered with benefits, but any accommodation was circumstantial and the underlying relationship remained adversarial.

In 1437 Sigismondo did not renew his papal commission, which was taken up by Domenico, and he signed with Venice on condition that he should not be employed against the Papacy. His new commission brought him up against first-class opposition for the first time and in September, when under the command of Gian' Francesco Gonzaga, he suffered defeat and the loss of artillery and stores when their camp at Bulgaro, near Brescia, was attacked by Niccolò Piccinino and Gian' Francesco's son Ludovico. The marquis changed sides the following year, when Filippo Maria Visconti unleashed Piccinino against the Papal State. The back story to this crucial moment is, as usual, complex. The Duke of Milan had just made Piccinino a marquis and endowed him with a considerable estate at the expense of a number of lesser lords, but Piccinino wanted more: he picked a quarrel by objecting to the unrevoked betrothal of Filippo Maria's daughter, Bianca Maria, to Francesco Sforza, then flirted with the pope, letting it be known that the lordship of his home town of Perugia plus Assisi and Cità di Castello were on the table. Filippo Maria was obliged to grant him freedom of action in the forthcoming campaign and plenipotentiary powers to negotiate in his name.

Piccinino descended on Romagna and occupied Ravenna, Forlì, Imola and Bologna in a few months, none of which put up more than token resistance.* Faenza was spared because the Manfredi were already serving with him and the Polenti, Ordelaffi and Bentivogli hastened to seek terms; but Piccinino's treatment of the Malatesta brothers, both of whom were in enemy service, was curious. Domenico's men were stripped of their arms when Piccinino expelled the papal garrison from Bologna but Sigismondo's were permitted to keep theirs. Piccinino camped near Cesena and could have taken it, but refrained from doing so. Instead he marched up the Savio valley to the Viamaggio Pass and raided San Sepolcro in the Tiber valley. There is,

* The Alidosi never recovered Imola after being dispossessed by Visconti in 1424. Nominally papal from 1426, the town was several times awarded to Francesco Sforza to deny it to Filippo Maria (Appendix D).

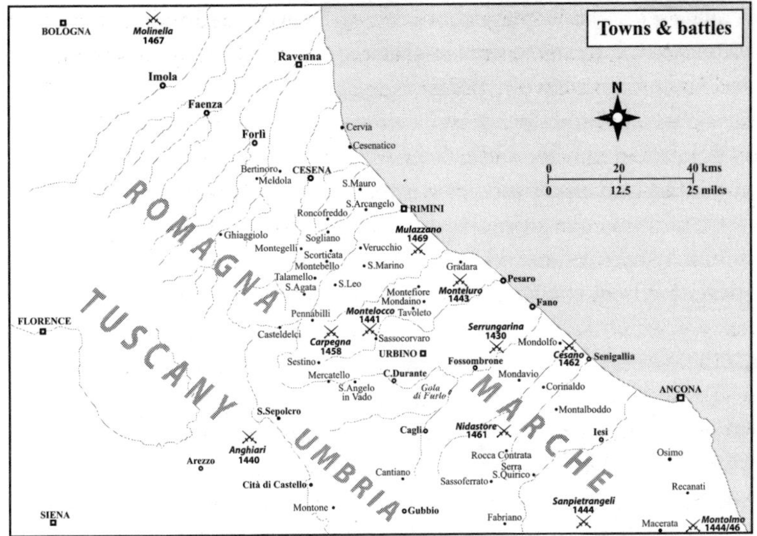


Map 8: THE COCKPIT 1430-70

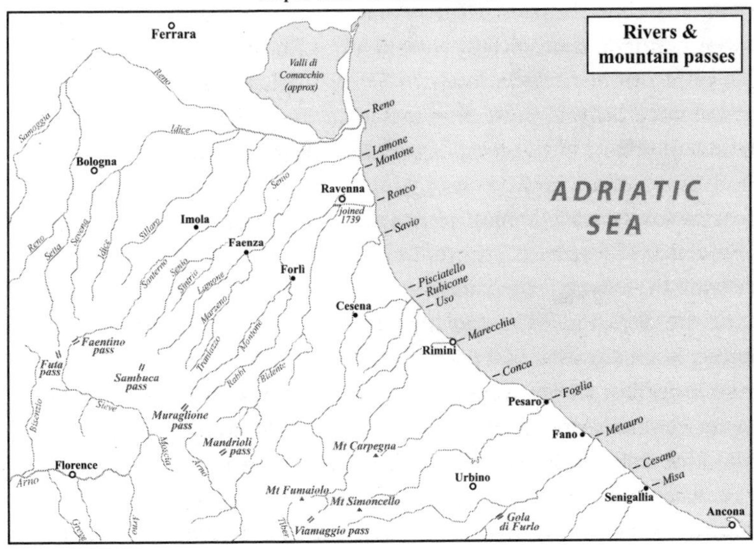

as the Spanish say, a cat shut up in this box. Pope Eugenius IV by now was offering Piccinino the world to fight against Sforza in the Marche, Filippo Maria also wanted him to campaign there, but instead Piccinino chose to cross the Apennines and attack a papal city coveted by Florence. In January 1439 Florence, Venice and the pope formed a league against Milan and gave the captain-generalcy to Francesco Sforza. It may be the league was inevitable once Filippo Maria invaded Romagna again, but it seems likely that Piccinino's aim was to preclude any reconciliation between Visconti and Sforza and to make himself indispensable – which he became during two years of epic campaigning across the whole of north-eastern Italy.

In all probability, therefore, Piccinino persuaded the Malatesta brothers to make an unprovoked attack on the Montefeltro domain in October 1439. After eight years of peace and despite his betrothal to Guidantonio's daughter, Domenico seized Castel d'Elci and the neighbouring forts in the Senatello (upper Marecchia) valley and it may be that part of the price demanded by Piccinino for sparing Cesena was that Domenico should provoke a war with the Montefeltri. The Malatesta brothers had their own reasons to fall in with the plan as they had done little to earn their money from Venice and the pope, and the Montefeltri were firm allies of Milan. Piccinino's motive would have been to create a situation in which he could make both parties look to him as their arbiter and benefactor. After the Montefeltri struck back and sacked Tavoleto, Sigismondo took the opportunity to recover lands lying between his own and Domenico's domains and previously part of the Sogliano Malatesta patrimony. He seized nine villages including Sogliano itself and Montebello, where he demonstrated for the first time his mastery of the use of field artillery to reduce a fortified place, and his ruthlessness by hanging fifteen captured soldiers outside the gates to emphasise the advisability of prompt capitulation.

The other shoe dropped when Piccinino arbitrated the conflict in March 1440. The parties agreed to return all lands taken from the other and the Malatesti signed an agreement that made them in theory the retainers of Filippo Maria, but which exempted them from fighting against Venice, Florence or the Papacy. They were, however, granted permission to recover the lands previously held by Carlo II Malatesta in the Marche, now in the possession of Sforza. The agreement was made public at the end of the month and in April Domenico and Sigismondo were received at Urbino with much public celebration. Everything changed in June when Piccinino, in pursuit of his ambition to become lord of Perugia and Assisi, was heavily defeated by Micheletto Attendolo at Anghiari. This was a rare example of a genuinely decisive battle. In the peace treaty of 1441 Florence obtained the title to San Sepolcro and the upper Tiber valley from the Papacy while Venice, as well as recovering all the *terraferma* towns previously lost to Piccinino, permanently evicted the Polenta family from Ravenna and held it until 1509.

**BATTLE OF ANGHIARI, 1441**

**Fought between a Papal–Florentine army under Micheletto Attendolo and a nominally Milanese but in practice a virtually free company led by the Piccinino brothers, each army numbering about 8000 men. A heavy cavalry engagement with relatively low casualties (seventy dead and 800–900 wounded), it ended with the rout of the Piccinini and the capture of twenty-two of their captains and 1400 other condottieri. The prisoners were soon released, but the victors massacred the peasants who had been following the Piccinini in the hope of loot.**

Niccolò Piccinino took refuge with Guidantonio at Urbino immediately after Anghiari and passed through Cesena on his way back to Milan. What assurances he gave Guidantonio Montefeltro and Domenico Malatesta we do not know, but they must have been persuasive because they remained loyal to Milan, whereas Sigismondo jumped ship and joined forces with Sforza. Again, too much has been made of this alleged treachery by Montefeltro-leaning historians: without the prospect of support from Piccinino and Milan, and sandwiched between Venice to the north and Sforza in the Marche, Sigismondo was very well advised to make a deal with them and nobody at the time thought any less of him for doing so. The same sources blithely perpetuated the accusation made by Pope Pius II that Sigismondo poisoned his young wife Ginevra in 1440, when it is clear she was always sickly (her twin Lucia died in 1437) and her father Niccolò III and successors (Ginevra's half-brothers) Leonello and Borso d'Este remained friendly with Sigismondo throughout his turbulent life.

In July 1441 Sigismondo became betrothed to Francesco Sforza's legitimated daughter Polissena and in September married her at Fermo in the Marche, although he did not bring her to Rimini until the following April. It became apparent how opportune the marriage was when in October he attended, in Cremona, the long-delayed wedding of his new father-in-law to Bianca Maria Visconti. Filippo Maria had no other issue besides Bianca and the union made Sforza the heir-apparent to the dukedom of Milan. Niccolò Piccinino had overplayed his hand during 1441 by demanding Piacenza before he would fight against Sforza, which prompted an outburst from Filippo Maria. 'These condottieri have now reached the stage when if they are defeated we pay for their failures, and if victors we must satisfy their demands and throw ourselves at their feet even more than if they were our enemies,' he said. 'Must the Duke of Milan bargain for the victory of his own troops, and strip himself to receive favours from them?' Niccolò Piccinino, who had tried so hard to prevent Sforza's marriage, died in 1444 not long after learning that his adopted son Francesco had been defeated and captured at Montolmo. Filippo Maria attended his funeral in the Milan Duomo but the monument over Niccolò's grave and all other signs of honour to his memory were destroyed by Francesco Sforza in 1455.

The years 1441–3 marked what hindsight reveals to have been the true apogee of Sigismondo's career. He had attached himself to the rising star of Francesco Sforza at a moment when this could be done without prejudice to good relations with the Papacy and Venice, and he had even produced a potential male heir by Vanetta dei Toschi, daughter of a patrician family from Fano. Her social rank qualified their son Roberto for formal recognition and ultimately, in 1450, for legitimation by the pope. Roberto may not have been born in February 1442, as claimed in the Bull of legitimation, but it was essential to assert that neither Vanetta nor Sigismondo was married at the time of his conception. The possibly perjured basis for the legitimation may have made Sigismondo hesitant about nominating his eldest recognised son as his heir, although as we shall see there were pressing personal reasons as well.

## THIRTEEN

# *Federico*

We left Federico in 1437, when after his spell at Vittorino da Feltre's Ca' Gioiosa he inherited a considerable force of armed retainers from Bernardino della Carda. It was also the year when he finally married Gentile Brancaleoni, his acting elder sister and fiancée since 1425, becoming lord of her freeholds in the Massa Trabaria and Count of Mercatello sul Metauro. The influence of Vittorino on Federico's character may have been matched by an incident that marked him for life in 1433, when he was eleven years old. He developed a boil on his left cheek that became infected and had him at death's door. Guidantonio sent for the best doctors but they could do nothing and the boy's life was saved by a peasant woman who applied a salve to the wound, which promptly healed. Ever afterwards Federico was fanatically concerned with personal cleanliness and insisted on scrupulous attention to hygiene by those around him, laying down strict instructions about hand-washing for his kitchen staff and his table and personal attendants in the detailed written 'Orders and Offices' that governed the conduct of his court.

The earliest alleged portrait of him is a fresco on the walls of the Oratory of St John in Urbino. The fresco is in poor condition but shows a decidedly pretty young man wearing Federico's customary scarlet cloak and hat over gilt armour – with long, wavy and golden hair. Federico had dark hair but the Montefeltri were generally blue-eyed and fair-haired, so the fresco may have been an attempt to reinforce his claim to the bloodline. This aside, we have no idea what he looked like before a jousting accident in 1451 shattered the bridge of his nose and destroyed his right eye – the reason why only he was always portrayed in left profile. He was of medium stature, dark-skinned, began to lose his curly hair early and was inclined to corpulence, physically the opposite of his rival Sigismondo. However Piero della Francesca's portrait of him (Picture section 2, p. 4) captures the impassive coldness of expression they shared – more striking, perhaps, in Federico's case because he was painted facing another portrait of his supposedly beloved second wife Battista. We may fairly wonder how much real affection can have been involved in the ruthless quest for a male heir that wore her out with eight full-term pregnancies and an unknown number of miscarriages in the twelve years before her death in 1472, aged only twenty-six.

Along with Bernardino's soldiers Federico received a commission from Filippo Maria Visconti and his first battle was under the command of Niccolò Piccinino in August 1438 at Rovato, west of Brescia, where the Venetians under Gattamelata defeated them. In 1439 when engaged in support of the Manfredi of Faenza in an obscure conflict with Antonio Ordelaffi of Forlì, Federico won a small cavalry battle against Pietro Giampaolo Orsini, Sforza's leading captain. When Guidantonio recalled him to Urbino after Domenico Malatesta captured Castel d'Elci, Federico led the counter-attack and sacked Tavoleto – an interesting choice, given that it was one of Sigismondo's towns, not Domenico's. The campaign continued with Federico seizing the fort of Rupoli near Fano while Sigismondo collected villages between the Marecchia and the Rubicon (Map 8).

We have seen how the episode can best be understood as an exercise in *furbizia* by Niccolò Piccinino, and when it all ended in fraternal embraces and the formal betrothal of Violante to Domenico at Urbino in April 1440 it seems Federico, nursing a wound received in the preceding exchange of unpleasantries, was not invited to join the festivities. It was his first independent campaign and he must have resented discovering that he had been a cat's-paw in a far deeper game – but what must have stung far more was that although his 'wicked stepmother' Caterina Colonna had died in 1438 he was still being kept at arm's length by his official father in favour of Caterina's son Oddo Antonio. Instead of attending the wedding party he rode with Piccinino across the Apennines into the upper Tiber valley and was fortunate not to be present at the Anghiari debacle. He fell back on Gubbio to defend it against a threat from papal forces under Cardinal Legate Ludovico Scarampo, who was soon to replace the disgraced Vitelleschi as Pope Eugenius IV's chief enforcer. Federico reportedly rejected Scarampo's appeal to defect from Visconti to papal service on grounds that his commission from Filippo Maria still had six months to run, and if this was all that took place between them it was a remarkably principled stand to take when the army of the anti-Visconti league was just across the Trabaria Pass from his own small domain. Given Federico's later contact with Scarampo it is more likely that he made a secret deal to defect at a more opportune moment. As it was, neither Federico nor Guidantonio paid any penalty for remaining loyal to Milan because the league fell apart after Anghiari, with the Papacy turning away to concern itself with the succession struggle in Naples, Florence militarily bereft by Micheletto Attendolo's refusal to renew his commission and Venice with more than enough on its hands trying to recover lost ground in Lombardy.

With the Sforzas also deeply involved in the struggle for the southern kingdom, all the cats were away and the mice decided it was safe to play. The occasion was the death in April 1441 of Pandolfo Malatesta, titular Archbishop of Patras, leaving his brother Galeazzo 'the Inept' as sole lord of Pesaro and Fossombrone. Within days of the archbishop's death 200 cavalry and 300 infantry under Federico marched into Pesaro to 'protect' it from Sigismondo, although there is no proof whatever that he planned a coup. Absent such evidence, the episode can be more readily explained as a pre-emptive act by Guidantonio Montefeltro to stake out a claim to his brother-in-law's estate, probably with the connivance of Galeazzo himself. It was no secret that Sigismondo wished to reunite the Malatesta domain, so, contrary to the usual interpretation that places the onus for renewed hostility on him, it was Guidantonio's provocation that broke the peace and threw down a challenge that no self-respecting lord could ignore.

In July 1441 Federico left Pesaro and marched to Faenza, where he joined forces with Francesco Piccinino and Guidantonio Manfredi to defend it against Antonio Ordelaffi, who was reinforced by troops sent by Sforza. Not long afterwards news came that Alberigo Brancaleoni, one of those who had taken refuge in Rimini after being dispossessed by Guidantonio a decade earlier, was loose with a small army in the old Brancaleone territory around Sassocorvaro and had taken the fortified villages of Santa Croce and Montelocco. With only the small force he had taken to Pesaro in April, Federico was sure he would be ambushed if he marched directly to Urbino and devised a stratagem to make the trap misfire. He created a pantomime of messengers supposedly arriving with news that his father had suffered an accident and was dying, then marched out of Faenza by day towards Urbino. During the night he doubled back and passed around Ordelaffi's Forlì to Cesena where he was warmly received by Domenico Malatesta, who lent him reinforcements and escorted him up the Savio valley to Montegelli. There was no threat from Ordelaffi beyond Cesena – the escort can only have been against Sigismondo.

During September, demonstrating the same cruel logic that we saw in the treatment of Linari during the San Romano campaign, Federico laid waste Santa Croce, which ceased to exist as a settlement, and besieged Alberigo Brancaleoni at Montelocco. While so engaged he received a letter from Sigismondo falsely protesting that he disapproved of Alberigo's activities and offering his help against him. Whether lulled into a false sense of security by this or because his scouts let him down, Federico was wrong-footed when troops provided by Sigismondo and led by Angelo d'Anghiari, Alberigo Brancaleoni's son-in-law, made a night attack on his three encampments. One encampment fell in the first rush and Federico was wounded by an arrow in the collapse of the second. He was rescued when sorely beset in the third encampment by the arrival of 3000 men led by Matteo da Sant'Angelo and two other condottieri recently hired by Guidantonio. Angelo d'Anghiari retreated and in the following days Alberigo Brancaleone was permitted to march out of Montelocco before Federico erased it from the map.

In October the fortress of San Leo fell to a daring night escalade, akin to Niccolò Montefeltro's feat in 1338, by Matteo da Sant'Angelo who climbed the cliff face with twenty men and hid until Federico made some unspecified demonstration that drew out the garrison, after which Matteo's men locked the gates against them, having first taken the precaution of chaining the doors of the houses in the town. There must have been some unrecorded *furbizia* involved, because the only approach to San Leo is along a narrow path with cliffs on either side, controlled by town gates that could have been held by a handful of men, while the fortress is on a higher promontory beyond the town. Precisely what Federico did to persuade the garrison to march stupidly out of the town gates is not known, but the presumption must be that he bribed the garrison commander. For whatever reason Federico seems to have reaped all the glory for the capture of San Leo and it may be significant that Matteo was never again directly employed by the Montefeltri.

Francesco Sforza called the mice to order in November 1441 after Sigismondo's marriage to his daughter and Sforza's own to Bianca Maria Visconti. Once again all conquests were restored – although San Leo was formally returned to the Church – and peace proclaimed between the families, followed by the June 1442 wedding of Domenico and Violante in Urbino. Following from this, later in the year, Sigismondo and Domenico signed the first of several written agreements, each supposed to resolve all differences between them, on this occasion brokered by Guidantonio Montefeltro and Francesco Sforza. There are a number of cats in this box also, as Sigismondo was by now Sforza's captain-general but Guidantonio and Domenico were still in the service of Filippo Maria, who had sunk his differences with Pope Eugenius IV and together with him sent the Piccinini to make war on Sforza's condottiere state in the Marche. Whatever wheels within wheels were involved, Federico was careful not to accept a commission from his old mentor Niccolò Piccinino and in October took service instead with Alfonso of Aragon against Sforza in the southern kingdom.

Federico's and Sigismondo's mutual loathing was cemented by the manner in which Federico seized power at Urbino. Federico's complicity in the murder of his half-brother, Oddo Antonio, must be apparent to anyone not wearing the rosiest of spectacles. Federico's hagiographers have portrayed Oddo Antonio as a monster of depravity, one furthermore manipulated by Sigismondo through the 'evil advisers' beloved of monarchist apologists, who was killed along with his advisers by the outraged husbands of women they had raped. There is no credible evidence that Oddo Antonio was anything more than young and excessively trusting, and a great deal that he was a kindly and generous young man highly thought of by all who knew him and particularly by Pope Eugenius IV, whose faith in human nature had long since eroded but who made Oddo Antonio Duke of Spoleto on his accession (Guidantonio's title had been for his lifetime only), also Vicar for Urbino, Gubbio and Cagli, Count of Montefeltro and Castel Durante and lord, among other places, of Cantiano, Sassocorvaro and San Leo. Federico had to wait through four papacies before finally being made Duke of Spoleto by Sixtus IV in 1474, when Federico's daughter married the pope's nephew, Giovanni della Rovere.

Oddo Antonio's sin, for such it was in a lord of the Romagna borderlands, was to be insufficiently ambitious. A revealing episode was his handling of the betrothal arranged for him by Guidantonio in 1439, when he was twelve, with fourteen-year-old Cecilia, daughter of Gian' Francesco Gonzaga. In documents not made public until 1897, by which time Oddo Antonio's reputation had been comprehensively blackened, correspondence between him, Cecilia and her father revealed that she adamantly refused to marry Oddo Antonio, not for any dislike of him personally but because she wished to retain control of her destiny. She was a student at Feltre's Ca' Gioiosa and a genuine feminist pioneer who appears to have been encouraged to defy her father by her mother, Paola Malatesta. Thereby hung the dynastic significance of the marriage, for Paola was sister to Galeazzo 'the Inept' of Pesaro, who had consented to Fossombrone forming part of Cecilia's dower estate if he were paid compensation equivalent in value to the rest of her dowry.

In 1442 the outraged Gian' Francesco wrote to assure Guidantonio that he would deliver Cecilia even if he had to bind her hand and foot, but Oddo Antonio replied defending her right to choose and wrote to her absolving her of any obligation – a delicacy of feeling impossible to reconcile with the reputation inflicted on him posthumously. Cecilia became a nun, joined by Paola after Gian' Francesco died in 1444, and was the subject of the sole Pisanello medallion of a woman, the obverse showing her taming a unicorn, the traditional prerogative of a virgin. In March 1444 Oddo Antonio married Isotta d'Este, daughter of Niccolò III and sister to Leonello, who succeeded his father as lord of Ferrara, Modena and Reggio in 1441. It seems their marriage was never consummated, but the imminent possibility of the couple producing a legitimate heir no doubt affected the timing of Oddo Antonio's assassination four months later. It is notable that the Este, who remained close to Sigismondo after he allegedly murdered Ginevra, took a long time to be reconciled with Federico.

The world's police forces may disagree on many aspects of methodology but all are guided by the sound principle that whoever benefits from a crime is the most likely perpetrator. When, as in the case of Oddo Antonio's murder, the principal beneficiary departed from Pesaro before the crime was committed and rode through the night in order to present himself at the gates of Urbino early the next morning, suspicion hardens into certainty. In addition Federico then went through a choreographed farce in which citizens' representatives presented him with a petition whose first item was a full pardon for the murderers, who just happened to be known associates of his. The text of the document survives and quite apart from the fact that it must have been prepared in advance, a more transparent piece of chicanery would be hard to find. Among the twenty clauses the fifth gives the lie to the charge that Oddo Antonio had increased taxes in order to pay for a profligate lifestyle: 'Further, that your lordship would deign to revoke all *donations* made since the death of the Lord Guidantonio, *in order the better to provide for your outgoings and expenses* [my italics].' Other clauses were people pleasers, promising to pay debts incurred by Guidantonio and Oddo Antonio 'as far as possible', to lower taxes and not to raise forced loans 'except in case of necessity'.

If, as seems likely, the petition was drafted in advance of the assassination, it provides us with a blueprint of how Federico meant to govern that speaks well of him. In no particular order he undertook to lower the tolls on the roads of the province to encourage trade, to restore certain aspects of ecclesiastical administration that had fallen into disuse and to restore the town Priors to the emoluments and to the hall of justice they had once occupied, which strongly suggests the Priors were involved in the conspiracy. Federico also promised to revoke all exemptions from general taxation, to restore a fixed third of all fines and awards for damages to public works and maintenance, and finally to appoint two physicians and a schoolmaster to serve all taxpayers. The petition just barely served the purpose of disguising a blatant *coup d'état* as a popular rebellion, but by dint of endless repetition it stuck – and that is all any politician can ask. As we have seen, there was nothing unusual about Romagna and Marche lords killing close relatives in the course of a power struggle. Federico's very particular problem was that his claim to the succession was doubly illegitimate: he was the beneficiary of the murder of the true heir and he was not, in fact, Oddo Antonio's half-brother.

Also looming over Federico's usurpation were the dynastic arrangements made by Guidantonio in the last years of his life. As already mentioned, the Este were alienated by Oddo Antonio's murder, a factor made more ominous by the marriage in April 1444 of Marquis Leonello, who succeeded his father in 1441, to the daughter of Alfonso of Aragon, now master of Naples as well as Sicily. Federico might also have incurred the enmity of the Gonzaga because Oddo Antonio's older sister, Agnesina, after a brief marriage to Guidantonio Manfredi, was promptly remarried to Alessandro, the unworldly second son of Gian' Francesco Gonzaga. However, Agnesina died in 1447, so whatever her feelings towards Federico they made no impact on events. He was even more fortunate that Guidantonio had kept Violante in Urbino and that devotion to Oddo Antonio held her there, because he was not only able to use her as a hostage in his dealings with the Malatesti but also to prevent her from strengthening their resolve to eliminate the Urbino usurper. Domenico was weak and if Violante had been by his side in 1444 it might have changed the course of events. Sveva, the last of Guidantonio's daughters by Caterina Colonna, was only ten years old in 1444 and was to play an ambivalent role in Federico's own dynastic combinations. All in all it took a great deal of *fortuna* as well as *furbizia* for Federico to affirm his dominion over Urbino.

Piero della Francesca's stylised and mysterious *Flagellation of Christ*, still on display at the Urbino palace, indicates that Federico was also troubled by a guilty conscience (Picture section 2, p. 6). The small panel was painted in 1454, on the tenth anniversary of Oddo Antonio's assassination, and the scarlet-robed, fair-haired youth in the right foreground with the thousand-yard stare is almost certainly Oddo Antonio himself. It follows that the shaven-headed older man to his left may be Guidantonio, but who the bearded scholar to his right might be, and what it all means, is impossible to deduce with certainty. The background appears to be an allegory for the fall of Constantinople in 1453, widely attributed to the sins of Christendom, and if so the foreground group is probably confessional. Federico had also recently survived a desperate illness that nearly left him blind. All we can say with certainty is that although the prince portrayed in the Oratory of St John fresco could have been Oddo Antonio's twin, the real Federico shared no family likeness whatever with the young man in Piero's *Flagellation*.

Not so Federico's lookalike brother Ottaviano degli Ubaldini, who was forced to remain at the Visconti court until Filippo Maria died in 1447 – probably the real reason why Federico kept faith with the unlovely Duke of Milan. Once free, Ottaviano travelled to Urbino and ran the day-to-day administration during Federico's long absences and was co-ruler of the state beyond his death, when he became the guardian of Federico's son, Guidobaldo. In addition to the face-to-face bas-reliefs already mentioned, Ottaviano is shown standing behind Federico to the right in Justus van Wassenhove's *The Institution of the Eucharist*, also in the Urbino palace, and in Francesco di Giorgio Martini's bas-relief bronze panel of the *Deposition from the Cross* from the door of the Santa Maria del Carmine church in Venice. They were so joined at the hip that the great architect Leon Battista Alberti referred to them as 'the two princes of Umbria'.

In sum they looked like brothers, behaved like brothers and did everything short of formally admitting it to let posterity know that they were brothers – and proud of it. There is no way of knowing how much of the artistic patronage, the palace designs and the more symbolic than practical military works associated with Federico's reign were a product of Ottaviano's influence because he was discretion personified and never put himself forward, choosing always to work behind the scenes. It may be that the verdict of Burckhardt *et al.* that Federico was the prototype Renaissance prince, combining all the virtues of peace and war, missed the crucial point about him: the historical personage they so admired was two men, and the aspect of Federico they liked best was the learned subtlety and artistic sophistication brought from Milan, at the time the richest and most brilliant court in Europe, by Ottaviano.

It is in this light that we can understand the scorpion-like counterattack by Federico when Sigismondo wrote to his father-in-law Francesco Sforza at length setting out the reasons why the Sforzas should have no dealings with the new lord of Urbino. Sigismondo's first charge was that Federico 'has always attacked and insulted your name and when he could has thwarted your political aims, and has never in peace or war been among your followers'. The second was that he was 'negligible and cowardly', akin to Cleopatra who deserted Mark Antony at the battle of Actium and that he should 'not even be entrusted with the baggage train'. The fourth declared that the honour of the Sforzas would be besmirched by association with this 'sewer of vice and by dealings with this laughable captain'. Harsh words, but no worse than the insults routinely traded by the princes of the Church. It was the third charge that went for the jugular: 'Who, possessed of any sense of humanity, can forget the treachery and crimes of the said Federico, who suspending all faith in God and divine justice and without regard ... for the sacred memory of those who bore, reared and fed him, recklessly has not shrunk from wielding iron against his own blood to take possession of the state.'

It is interesting that in this letter Sigismondo stressed Federico's fratricide as likely to be a more weighty consideration with his father-in-law, whereas in another letter to Cardinal Legate Ludovico Scarampo, whom we last saw negotiating with Federico at Gubbio after Anghiari and now Papal Governor of Romagna, he emphasised that Federico was not Guidantonio's son, thus his legitimation was fraudulent and his right of succession null and void. Scarampo sent a copy of Sigismondo's letter to Federico and his reply of 8 January 1445, copied 'on the record' to all the courts of Italy, survives in vitriolic full. Federico began by asserting that 'Lord Sigismondo by [exhibiting] his disordered passion ... has played into my hands'. Like a leper envious of the healthy, he continued, Sigismondo wished to drag him down to his own level.

> He wishes to say that I am the son of Bernardino and not of him whom I hold truly to be my father. But even if his calumny were true he should realise that that it is no great insult, as at least I would have been born of a famous gentleman unlike himself, who claims to be the son of Lord Pandolfo. The world knows that he is the son of the jester Marchisino, a villein of Bergamo, from whom my own ears have heard the disgusting manner and occasion in which he was engendered.

There followed the first mention of some of the unsupported allegations that Pope Pius II was later to make his own and that insufficiently sceptical historians have repeated ever since, among them that Sigismondo had stolen the dowry of Carmagnola's daughter and had beaten and poisoned his wife Ginevra d'Este because she would not submit to his unnatural lust. Next came an outpouring of overwrought details about alleged betrayals of the Church and dishonest dealings involving Sigismondo, his brother Domenico, Niccolò Piccinino and Francesco Sforza, before closing with a further allegation about Sigismondo's uncontrolled priapism. An anonymous young woman had been stripped naked and whipped to death because she would not surrender her virtue; he had turned an unspecified nunnery in Fano into a brothel and had impregnated eleven of the nuns; he had raped a Jewish virgin who later fled to Pesaro; he had killed a young man in Fano who prevented him from raping his sister; he had stolen the money and the beautiful wife of one Francesco de Guccio. Finally, by reference to Dante's *L'Inferno XXXIII*, Federico declared that Sigismondo had treated an (unnamed) faithful member of his own extended family like Ugolino della Gheradesca of Pisa, who was accused of treason in 1284, imprisoned and starved to death along with his sons and grandsons.

The end of the letter is decidedly rambling and gives the impression of being a true record of an exhausting outburst – although in fairness contemporary punctuation and syntax makes many letters of the period read like stream of consciousness. Given the provocation, Sigismondo's reply to Federico dated 21 February was restrained:

> Your lordship knows the differences that have existed between us for some time and if you judge rightly you will see that in this matter the right is with me. Patience is no longer an option for me and it seems you do not intend to alter your behaviour; to the contrary every day you increase the injuries you do me. You have once again written calumnies against me to the Court of Rome and caused ill to be spoken of me. I am determined to bear it no longer; rather to show with my person against yours that I am a braver man and you a bad one and that you do ill to insult me. I therefore send my chancellor ... with full authority to summon you to a duel. ... In

# FOURTEEN

## *Treachery*

If the propaganda war between Sigismondo and Federico was the first exchange in the war that defined their lives, the fulfilment of Guidantonio Montefeltro's plan to take possession of Fossombrone was the offence that made it inevitable. It is impossible to say which of the many injuries the clans had inflicted on each other over the preceding centuries did most to prepare the ground, but the poisoned seed was planted by the nepotism of Pope Martin V. Geopolitically the natural coastal outlet for the trans-Apennine state created by Guidantonio, thanks to the Colonna pope's indulgence, lay between the Metauro and Foglia rivers, encompassing Pesaro and Fano, and it would have been unnatural for him not to covet them. Half a century of barren or male heirless marriages between the clans also contributed a background of chronic frustration, but the final ingredient in the dynastic stew was the dense history of intermarriage between the Pesaro Malatesti and the Varani of Camerino.

By 1444, after Cecilia Gonzaga's refusal to marry Oddo Antonio Montefeltro had nullified Galeazzo the Inept's previous arrangement, legitimate claim to the Pesaro estate ran through Costanza, the daughter of Elisabetta Malatesta (only child of Galeazzo and Guidantonio Montefeltro's sister Battista) and Pier Gentile I Varano. In principle Costanza's older brother Ridolfo IV had priority but he waived his rights. It is likely he did so because Camerino was surrounded by the state the Sforzas had carved out of the Marche and it was prudent to fall in with their plans; however his decision was lubricated by the promise in 1444, jointly to Ridolfo IV and his young cousin Giulio

Cesare I, of the papal vicariate for Camerino, lost to the Varani since the 1434 massacre. Something was going on behind the scenes to make Costanza a dynastic prize that Alessandro, Francesco Sforza's younger brother, fervently wished to marry. That 'something' must be related to the tenuous link of legitimacy Costanza provided, without which the pope would not have had a fig leaf of justification to award Alessandro the Vicariate of Pesaro in return for a hefty bribe. Stitching the whole scheme together was Federico III Montefeltro, probably through his confidential liaison with Cardinal Legate Ludovico Scarampo. Oddo Antonio's lack of animosity towards the Malatesti posed an insurmountable obstacle, but once he was out of the way Federico rapidly brought the plan to fruition.

THE VARANO CONNECTION

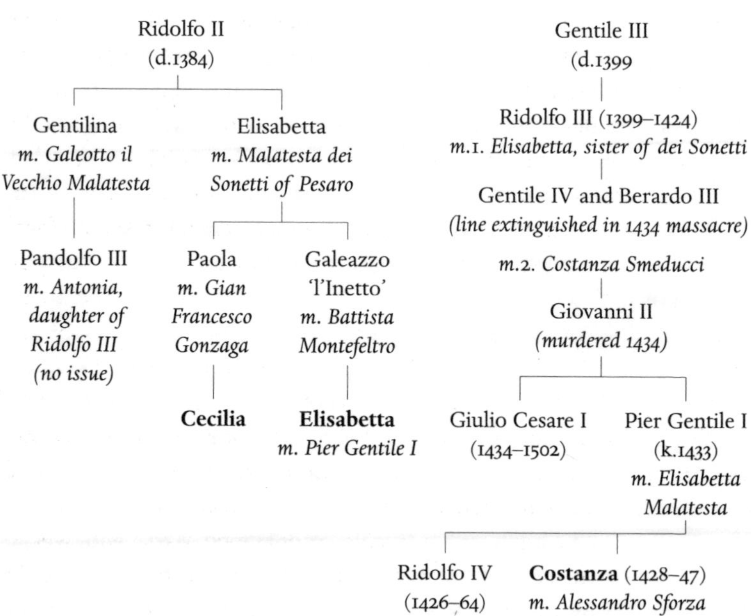


Philip Jones's great work on the Malatesti accepts that 'nothing was more natural than that the three lords whom Sigismondo had antagonised . . . should combine to frustrate his ambition. It was Federico, perhaps the least affronted, who took the initiative in bringing them together.' The sequence of events points rather to a plot at least partially inspired by the Papacy to create a rift between Sforza and Sigismondo, who together might have created complementary states that could have alienated the Marche on a permanent basis: nor would Urbino have been able to survive for long as an independent state in the face of such a combination. In Italy conspiracy theories more often than not are conspiracy facts, and to deny them is to exclude much of the rich complexity of a political culture that mirrored a restless and inventive society. To argue that Federico simply took advantage of Sigismondo's mistakes is to underestimate the man: Federico was a highly intelligent and devious individual who knew his enemy and forced errors on him.

The background to Federico's second coup, accomplished in 1444, was that Pope Eugenius IV, having broken up the anti-Visconti league, made an abject deal with Alfonso of Aragon in 1443 in which not only was Alfonso's right to Naples recognised and his bastard son Ferrante legitimated as heir to the kingdom (when Alfonso died in 1458 Aragon and Sicily reverted to his brother John), but the papal enclaves of Terracina and Benevento were surrendered to Alfonso as well. With the Aragonese in hand the pope now allied with Filippo Maria and together they sent the Piccinini, Domenico Malatesta and Federico Montefeltro (who was at this time Oddo Antonio's captain-general) against Sforza in the Marche, while Alfonso attacked his holdings in the Abruzzi. Within months Sforza's state was reduced to a triangle with the points at Ascoli, Fermo and the mountain fortress of Rocca Contrata. Sforza himself was forced to move to Fano, then to Rimini after Galeazzo Malatesta besieged Fano. Galeazzo's initiative was yet another example of the Pesaro Malatesti's chronic bad timing, for the Rome–Milan–Naples combination now fell apart. Alfonso had driven Sforza out of the southern kingdom and had obtained all he wanted, so he withdrew from the alliance with the prior agreement of Filippo Maria, with whom Alfonso had remained in step since they agreed in 1435 that Italy would best be ruled by the two of them. Filippo Maria, in turn, wanted to break up the League because he had lost Bologna in June to a revolt led by Antonio Bentivoglio with support from Venice and Florence, and in August the Milanese counter-attack was defeated at San Giorgio di Piano, just north of Bologna. It did not require political genius to see that the Venetian Eugenius IV would jump ship, so Filippo Maria beat him to it by giving up Bologna and forming a new alliance with Florence and Venice.

The defection of Naples and Milan left Piccinino and his captains supported only by the pope. Piccinino gambled on one last throw to break up the looming rapprochement between Sforza and Filippo Maria, moved his headquarters to Galeazzo Malatesta's Pesaro and advanced on Rimini. On 8 November Piccinino's fortified camp at Monteluro was furiously assaulted by Sforza's vanguard under Sigismondo, who led from the front and, despite being wounded, hacked his way through the throng and personally killed the camp commander. The rout was completed when Sforza's most trusted confederate, Antonio 'Ciarpellone' da San Severino, broke out of Fano and attacked Piccinino's army from the rear. Piccinino lost 2000 horses, all his infantry and his wagon train, and fled south with Domenico Malatesta while Galeazzo and Federico Montefeltro fell back on Pesaro. In the aftermath Sigismondo requested his employer's support to take Pesaro as a reward for his loyalty and in compensation for the damage done to his domain when he alone stood with Sforza. Sforza's interest was best served by pursuit of Piccinino and the recovery of ground lost in the Marche, and he was irritated by the delay. Pesaro refused to capitulate and Sigismondo settled for taking Gradara and Candelara in the Pesaro hinterland before marching south with Sforza. In December Sigismondo took Montalboddo by infiltrating the castle with soldiers disguised as merchants and by the end of the month he was besieging Sanpietrangeli deep in the Marche, outside of which he smashed a relieving army led by Francesco Piccinino and Federico Montefeltro in January 1444.

Instead of riding to further glory with his father-in-law Sforza, Sigismondo now turned his attention to his own domain and lost credit with his employer.* Sigismondo thrust into Urbino territory to take Montegaudio and Castel d'Elci in the Montefeltro and also took Pergola and Frontone in the Cesano valley, where he installed Giovanni Gabrielli to pose a threat to Gubbio's, Cagli's and Urbino's control of the Via Flaminia. In March Galeazzo Malatesta negotiated a truce, presumably at the sug-

* The deaths during 1443–4 of Sigismondo's cousins Gian' Francesco Gonzaga of Mantua and Guidantonio Manfredi of Faenza must also have diminished Sigismondo's diplomatic standing.

gestion of Federico. The clearest indication that Galeazzo was now in Federico's pocket is that he broke the truce in June as soon as Federico rejoined him at Pesaro. During the lull, in April Sforza sent Sigismondo to Venice to collect 35,000 ducats, which Sigismondo kept as owed to him for services rendered. This was the moment when it all began to go wrong – correct procedure was to deliver the money to Sforza along with his invoice. Sforza never denied that he owed his captain-general the money but the manner in which Sigismondo took it showed disrespect. The immediate effect, however, was that in June Oddo Antonio, rather than face the fully paid-up army of Rimini, agreed a six-month truce with Sigismondo and the mutual return of all places seized. The truce left Federico isolated in Pesaro and was probably the final nail in young Oddo Antonio's coffin.

Thoroughly confused by events following the ensuing assassination of Oddo Antonio at Urbino, Sigismondo ignored increasingly agitated demands by his employer that he join him in the Marche, where Niccolò Piccinino and Domenico Malatesta had been joined by a dozen hastily recruited condottieri and once more outnumbered the Sforzas. At the same time Sigismondo also demanded that he be given Senigallia and Mondavio, which had been taken by Sforza some years earlier. Although this was plainly an attempt to renegotiate his commission as captain-general in bad faith, so dangerous was Sforza's situation that he agreed to what were, in the circumstances, plainly extortionate demands. However the credit Sigismondo had built up over the preceding years was now seriously overdrawn. Sigismondo lost his remaining usefulness after Niccolò Piccinino was removed from the field when Filippo Maria recalled him to Milan, leaving Francesco Piccinino in command. At Montolmo, during the night of 18–19 August, Sforza attacked when Francesco had assembled his captains for a council of war and after their leaderless troops fled Francesco and eight of his captains were captured along with 4000 horses and the wagon train. Domenico Malatesta escaped with a handful of men.

At the end of September 1444 Eugenius IV admitted defeat and recognised Sforza's right of possession to most of the Marche, reserving for the Church only Ancona and the overland route from Umbria through Fabriano, Osimo and Recanati. In early October the pope lifted all anathemas and sanctions proclaimed against Sforza and his captains, and confirmed Sigismondo in all his vicariates on condition that he negotiate a settlement with Galeazzo. These concessions were in fact a smokescreen to distract Sigismondo while papal representatives negotiated secretly with the Sforzas, the Varani and Federico to agree the deal Federico had already made with Galeazzo Malatesta for the transfer of Pesaro and Fossombrone. When Sigismondo arrived at Fermo later that month to excuse his earlier absence he was stunned to find that Sforza, in agreement with the pope and Florence, had given Federico a year's commission for 400 *lance* and 400 foot in time of war, 800 cavalry and 100 infantry in peace, with an additional year of *rispetto*. This led to the first of the letters previously cited, at which time it seems Sigismondo did not appreciate the full extent of the dealings between his employer and his enemies.

Implicit in Federico's commission was that he would become Sforza's captain-general when Sigismondo's contract expired the following February. Sigismondo was not the only one shocked by the arrangement – it also offended Ciarpellone, generally regarded as the most competent condottiere employed by Sforza, who felt the captain-generalcy should be his. Ciarpellone had earlier urged Sforza to put Sigismondo on trial for treachery but when he learned of Federico's contract he secretly accepted a commission from Filippo Maria to become his captain-general in replacement of the recently deceased Niccolò Piccinino. Instead of slipping quietly away, however, Ciarpellone asked Sforza for permission to travel to Milan to deal with some matters relating to an inheritance. Sforza had learned the real purpose, probably from Filippo Maria whose aim all along may have been simply to unsettle his son-in-law, and in the ensuing confrontation he wounded Ciarpellone with a dagger. The unfortunate captain was imprisoned and gagged to prevent him revealing the details of Sforza's deal with Federico and the pope, then tortured until he confessed to crimes he had not, indeed could not have, committed, after which he was hanged, quartered and his remains exposed at the gates of Fermo.

On 8 December 1444 Alessandro Sforza and Costanza Varano, whose claim to Pesaro and Fossombrone was a crucial factor in the plot, were married at Camerino; she bore him Battista in 1446 and died bearing him an heir, Costanzo, in July 1447. It was not until the following January that the full details of Federico's elaborate arrangements became public. Galeazzo Malatesta sold Alessandro his rights to Pesaro and Fossombrone, and Alessandro in turn financed the cession of Fossombrone to Federico.

The two men took possession in March, by which time it had become clear that the monetary cost was the least of the expenses they would incur. After failing to provoke Federico to a duel Sigismondo challenged Galeazzo and was ignored. He then made overtures to Filippo Maria and Alfonso of Aragon, but on the expiry of his *condotta* with Sforza in February Sigismondo found employment instead with the Church, as captain-general and *Gonfaloniere*.

This was a startling reversal of policy even by the standards of Eugenius IV. It is hard to say what had happened between October 1444 and February 1445 to turn the pope against the rapprochement he had facilitated between Federico and the Sforzas. Possibly Scarampo, the keystone of Federico's plot, was from the start playing the age-old Curia game of ensuring that the lords of Romagna and the Marche were constantly at each other's throats. After the defeat at Montolmo the Pesaro–Fossombrone deal was the only way that the dangerous alliance between Sigismondo and the Sforzas could be broken up while new arrangements were made with Milan and Naples. With both of these objectives accomplished Scarampo may have calculated that it was time to ensure that the new combination of the Sforzas and Federico, potentially no less dangerous to papal interests, should be placed under pressure.

Federico's situation now became extremely exposed. The pope also gave Domenico Malatesta a commission, accompanied by reinforcements from Milan, while ships carrying troops and supplies came from Naples to Fano, Rimini and Cesenatico. Domenico demanded the release of his wife Violante and of the lands within the Vicariate of Urbino granted to her as a child by papal dispensation, as well as those outstanding from the dowry agreed by her father. The matter was submitted for arbitration to the Papacy, which in September 1445 pronounced Violante the rightful heiress of the entire county of Montefeltro and of several fortified villages including Montegelli and Savignano sul Rubicone – which from their location must have been disputed with the Sogliano Malatesti, not Urbino. Federico, that pillar of rectitude, held Violante captive in Urbino until she renounced the 1445 award. When at last she joined Domenico at Cesena in 1447 he had become crippled by 'varicose veins' – presumably phlebitis – and it was left to Sigismondo to uphold her rights in arms. Federico never honoured the terms of her dowry either, but Violante did not renounce her remaining claims until 1466, after the death of Domenico.

In mid 1445 Sigismondo was called back from an attack on Urbino by an invasion of his domain by Francesco Sforza, now allied with Florence and Venice, although the commitment of the Venetians to the new arrangement was purely formal – they kept Sigismondo on their payroll as insurance in case Filippo Maria tried to turn the new Church–Naples–Milan alliance against Venetian interests. Francesco Sforza took Pergola on the Cesano and entrusted it to Federico as a counter-threat to Sigismondo's ally Gabrielli at Frontone, then Alessandro Sforza pinched out the threat to Pesaro posed by the fortress of Candelara, seized by Sigismondo along with Gradara in 1443. By becoming the principal military instrument of the Papacy, Milan and Naples, Sigismondo had moved on to far shakier political ground than he had occupied during the heyday of his association with Sforza, as none of his new employers had any patience with his personal dynastic concerns. Thus, although he counter-attacked and drove Alessandro Sforza away from Fano in mid 1445, and went on to reconquer much of the Marche for the Papacy in the following eighteen months, he was unable to divert the necessary resources to take Pesaro and Fossombrone. He delegated the subsidiary campaign against Urbino to his distant cousin Carlo Fortebraccio, hired to take the place of brother Domenico whom Sigismondo preferred to keep by his side – not, we may be sure, because of brotherly love.

It seems that during 1445 Sigismondo was chastened by the consequences of having given priority to his own princely interests while serving Sforza and now devoted himself to the proper fulfilment of his duties as a condottiere. When he did so, it seems he was unbeatable: in September he struck south of Sforza's capital at Fermo and seized the town of Offida, and when Francesco marched to recover the town Sigismondo moved north again to take Sassoferrato, Osimo and Rocca Contrata, and even tried to take Ancona, whose prudent neutrality irritated Pope Eugenius. Carlo Fortebraccio, meanwhile, seized Piandimeleto in the heart of Federico's Massa Trabaria and rode around Urbino laying waste the countryside. In November Fermo rebelled against Sforza and Sigismondo made a triumphal entrance to the city with Domenico, then rode to Rome to receive the insignia of *Gonfaloniere* from Eugenius IV before returning to winter quarters and another triumphal parade at Rimini.

In preparation for the 1446 campaigning season Sigismondo set out with a small escort to confer with Filippo Maria in Milan. He was ambushed near Cotignola by a Florentine force led by Astorre II Manfredi, lord of Faenza since the death of his brother Guidantonio in 1443. Sigismondo escaped by hiding in a swamp and while immersed learned from conversations among the searchers that the purpose of the ambush was to kill, not capture him. It was brave of him to complete his journey to Milan as it is unlikely to be a coincidence that Astorre II Manfredi received a very generous commission from Filippo Maria the following winter. In February Sigismondo recovered Pergola and in March Federico Montefeltro uncovered a conspiracy promoted by Sigismondo among his captains. He beheaded three of them while the rest either fled to Rimini or declared for Sigismondo along with the castles entrusted to them. Among the defectors were the Prefetti di Vico brothers, who had held the complex at Castel d'Elci as Montefeltro retainers since their expulsion from Umbria in 1435, and whose debt of gratitude to Guidantonio and Oddo Antonio made them hostile to the usurper Federico.

Although the coup failed, in the following months things went badly for Federico and the Sforzas. In July Sigismondo besieged Federico at Urbino while another papal army under Cardinal Scarampo sealed off Alessandro Sforza in Pesaro, cutting Francesco Sforza off from his two most trusted subordinates. Although Federico lost strategically vital Sassocorvaro and nearby Montegrimano, as well as Monte Cerignone and with it control of the upper Conca valley, he did not seek terms. Alessandro Sforza made a separate peace and surrendered Pesaro to Scarampo, but to Sigismondo's fury Filippo Maria and Pope Eugenius IV offered Alessandro a commission and the pope even returned Pesaro to him as a vicariate, conditional on handing over his brother Francesco's wife and children and taking service against him. Alessandro bought time by promising to do both but instead spirited Bianca Maria and her children out of Pesaro. After Scarampo moved on to Urbino Alessandro emerged from Pesaro to recover some of the towns taken from him by Sigismondo.

The siege of Urbino and the ravaging of the surrounding territory seems to have been designed to force Federico to accept humiliating terms; possibly the town itself was too well defended to assault, but it is no less possible that Scarampo ruled it out and Sigismondo was compelled to obey. Sigismondo himself was drawn south to counter a foray led by Count Dolce d'Anguillara, now Francesco Sforza's leading captain, and in

October routed him at Montolmo, the scene of Sforza's great victory two years earlier. While thus occupied Sigismondo's own domain was attacked not only by Alessandro Sforza out of Pesaro, but also by a sizeable Florentine army led by Astorre II Manfredi from Faenza, and by the garrison of Urbino under Federico, who was released when Scarampo lifted the siege, without warning Sigismondo, and marched his army back to Rome. The circumstantial evidence is overwhelming that the cardinal set a trap for the captain-general and *Gonfaloniere* of the Church, and since Eugenius IV received Scarampo with open arms it follows he was doing the pope's bidding.

Thus a year that began with an attempt to assassinate Sigismondo by one of his employers ended with him betrayed by another into a military situation that would have crushed a less able commander. It's not paranoia when they really are out to get you, and Sigismondo's subsequent machinations should be viewed as the prudent behaviour of one who knew any hand extended in friendship might contain a dagger, rather than as evidence of the faithlessness of which he is so often accused. First he saved Gradara by coordinating a sally with his own relief activities, communicating via a secret passage that can still be seen in the slope below the castle (see p. 255). Manfredi negotiated a unilateral truce and marched swiftly back to Faenza, while Federico retreated to his own domain. Alessandro Sforza had been drawn away by what turned out to be a spurious offer of employment from Venice – again, unlikely to be a coincidence – and when Eugenius IV died in February 1447 he took to the grave the reasons for the persistent, if usually covert, malevolence he showed towards Sigismondo during much of his pontificate. There can have been few outside the pope's immediate circle who mourned him, but among them was Aeneas Silvius Piccolomini, later Pope Pius II and Sigismondo's nemesis, who first took holy orders in 1446 upon changing allegiance from the Antipope Felix V. He became Eugenius IV's representative in Germany, where he negotiated a comprehensive Concordat that at last ended the papal schism and which was signed by Eugenius IV on his deathbed.

We analysed the battle of San Romano as a proxy for campaigns we lack sufficient information to examine individually, and the unpeeling of the layers of deceit, treachery and 'Machiavellian' calculation wrapped round the imbroglio over Pesaro and Fossombrone likewise permits us to establish a benchmark against which to measure other military–diplomatic combinations to which we cannot devote such close attention. In general we may take it that any time A seemed to be allied with B against C, A and C were also conspiring against B, while C and B were plotting against A. None of the parties was ever happy to see an ally triumph totally over a rival because today's ally could, and probably would, become tomorrow's foe. This was, of course, a self-fulfilling prophecy. But once the closed circle of mistrust was established anyone who tried to break out of it would lose whatever benefit might have been gained by treachery without winning any compensating advantage from acting in good faith: nobody would believe it and all would assume it concealed a deeper *furbizia*.

# FIFTEEN

## *Isotta and the Tempio*

Without succumbing to sentimentality, the single fact that permits us to see through the mask of villainy projected on to Sigismondo by his enemies is that some time in 1445 he met an enchanting twelve-year-old called Isotta degli Atti and fell head over heels in love with her. Given everything else that was going on in 1445–6 it is astonishing how he found the time, but he courted her with a delicate passion that eventually overcame her reservations. Her wealthy family did not obstruct their lord's wooing: Isotta's mother died bearing her and her father died in 1448, having lived to see his son Antonio knighted by Sigismondo. Nonetheless Sigismondo did not take or buy Isotta – he won her love, thereby creating the intriguing contradiction with his public persona that has fascinated scholars ever since. The most charming of several medallions bearing Isotta's image made by Matteo de' Pasti (Picture section 2, p. 2) is dated 1446, the year she and Sigismondo became lovers, but was cast some years later, after the death of his second wife, Polissena Sforza. By then Isotta had borne him two sons: Giovanni, who died an infant in 1447 and was solemnly buried in Carlo II's sarcophagus in the church of St Francis; and Malatesta, born in 1448 and destined not to reach his tenth birthday.

From 1446 the real court of Rimini revolved around Isotta while Polissena, no longer politically useful, was neglected along with her daughter Giovanna, born in 1444 – an infant son, Galeotto, died in 1443. Sigismondo kept his mistress Vanetta dei Toschi in her own establishment at Fano, where she lived with her children Roberto and Contessina. Sigismondo also had two older children, Pandolfo and

Lucrezia, whose mother Gentile di Ser Giovanni had died in 1439, but where they lived and who raised them is not recorded. Even amid their grand passion Isotta was by no means the only woman breeding by the Lord of Rimini in the late 1440s and early 1450s. Gentile Ramessini, a lady from Bologna, bore him Sallustio, Valerio and Margherita, while other unidentified women bore him at least five other children even as he wrote poems and had medallions made of Isotta, gave her a chapel in the Tempio Malatestiano and named one of the towers of the new castle he built at Senigallia the 'Torrione Isotta'.

Isotta appears to have adopted Sallustio as though her own after the death of young Malatesta, although it is possible that Gentile Ramessini died earlier and Isotta took her children in. The dates are uncertain, but there is no doubt that several women knowingly shared Sigismondo at this time. It could be they had a tacit arrangement akin to Oriental polygamy, with Isotta becoming the senior consort in Rimini when Polissena died in 1449. Within this scheme it would not have been until she was formally married (the ceremony was private and we can only date it from her signature changing to *de Malatestis* in early 1457) that her 'seniority' over Vanetta dei Toschi would have been recognised. Although this is speculation built on very few precise details, it does offer an explanation why Sallustio and not the older and better-qualified Roberto became Sigismondo's heir-apparent.

The following is the second of three stanzas composed by Sigismondo during his courtship of Isotta. That his words in love were not matched by a deeper consideration for the well-being of his beloved is not remarkable in a male of any time or place, but they do illustrate an aspect of his personality impossible to reconcile with the image of a bloodthirsty tyrant:

| | |
|---|---|
| *O vagha e dolce luce, anima altera!* | Oh sweet and noble light, proud soul! |
| *Creatura gentile, o viso degno* | Kind being in whose worthy look |
| *o lume chiaro angelico e benegno* | Lit by the clear, angelic glow |
| *in cui sola virtù mia mente spera.* | Of virtue all my hopes repose. |
| *Tu sei de' mia natura alta e primiera* | You are most high and first to me |
| *anchora che men tier mio debil legno.* | And steer my fragile ship at sea. |
| *Tu sei del viver mio fermo sostegno,* | My dove so innocent and pure, |
| *turtura pura, candida e sincera.* | You are my life's stability. |
| *Dinanzi a te l'erbetta e i fior s'inchina* | Before you blooms and grass lie down, |

| | |
|---|---|
| *vaghi d'esser premi dal dolce pede* | Proud to be trod by your sweet foot |
| *e commossi del tuo ceruleo manto.* | And ruffled by your azure robe. |
| *El sol quando se leva la matina* | Vain the sun in the early morn, |
| *se vanagloria, e poi quando te vede* | But when he sees you, overcome |
| *sconficto e smorto se ne va con pianto.* | And pale he goes away in tears. |

Whether inspired by Isotta or simply because a man's fourth decade tends to be his most productive, most of the works of art that earned Sigismondo immortality were commissioned by him in the ten years after he met her. His greatest creation, however, began much earlier. Work on Castel Sismondo began in 1437 and during a brief sojourn at Rimini in 1438 the great Florentine architect Brunelleschi may have contributed some elements to its design and to other military works. The panels set into the walls of the massive keep proclaim it was finished in 1446 but in fact work went on at least until 1456. Sigismondo demolished the old Gattolo palace, along with the bishop's palace, two chapels and a nunnery, to make way for the new castle, and it was because he moved to alternative accommodation opposite the Atti residence in Rimini that he chanced to see young Isotta and was hit by the thunderbolt.

Castel Sismondo must have been awe-inspiring in its pomp. The twin towers covering the drawbridge (Diagram 8), demolished long ago, were green and red, the two colours of the chequerboard Malatesta livery, and residual plasterwork on the towering *mastio* (Picture section 2, p. 3) indicate that it was painted white. It may be the most written-about fortification in Italy not for its military significance, which is slight, but for the palpable aura of menacing grandiosity that clings to its ruins. But it was not so much Castel Sismondo that won the admiration of d'Annunzio, Pound, *et al.*: rather it was the open-handed patronage that Sigismondo dispensed to architects, writers, sculptors and painters in general. The document that 'hooked' Pound was a letter from Sigismondo to Cosimo de' Medici dated 7 April 1449, which reads in part:

> With reference to the Master Painter [probably Piero della Francesca], the chapels are still freshly plastered and not ready for painting – it would be a wasted effort. But I wish to state that my intention is to have him paint another [place] until the chapels are ready, which will give him and me the greatest pleasure, and so that he should be

> able to serve me invite him to write to me concerning the money he needs. For it is my intention to indulge him and to give him an annual salary, to make him feel secure and to give him whatever else he needs, and to treat him so well that he will wish to live and die in my lands – unless you, my lord,* should wish otherwise – to have him without making demands on him so that he can work as he likes or not, and will lack for nothing.

The terms of the letter may have reflected Sigismondo's desire to impress one of the richest men in Italy, but the fact remains that his tiny state not only attracted talent from all over Italy but also nurtured it among its own inhabitants, something not seen in Rimini since the days of the centenarian Mastin Vecchio. Carlo II had the distinction of awarding the great sculptor Lorenzo Ghiberti's first commission for work in the Gattolo palace, and is said to have built the tallest tower in Italy at Sant'Arcangelo. Although almost nothing remains of the work commissioned by Pandolfo III in his short-lived Lombard domain, we know he considered it vitally important to project an image of princely magnificence. Enough remains of the art and architecture created under Malatesta dei Sonetti of Pesaro to appreciate that he devoted significant resources to putting a splendid face on the declining viability of his little state. In today's vernacular this would be called *bella figura* – the desire to seem to be more than you are. But Sigismondo's patronage was in a different category. The works produced for him were devoted to expressing a very firm identity, at a time when he should have devoted all his resources to ensuring the survival of his house. In contrast the works of art commissioned by his rival Federico were a modest adjunct to the consolidation of his dynasty, only embarked upon when his own situation was secure.

The crucial difference, the one that makes Sigismondo a far more modern figure, is that he did not believe in an afterlife – he lived in the now and does not appear to have devoted any thought to what would befall his progeny. The charge of paganism levelled against him by Pius

* *Compater* – medieval Latin for godfather, patron or protector. In Sicilian dialect this became *compare*, which in turn led to 'goombah', the American slang term for a member of the Mafia.

II is of a piece with the rest of an indictment otherwise borrowed word for word from Federico's black propaganda – Sigismondo had no more genuine reverence for the gods of antiquity than he did for the god of Rome. The prospect of personal extinction weighed obsessively on his mind, however, and later in life he penned another poem that indicates a change of heart:

| | |
|---|---|
| *Io confesso a te, Padre, i miei peccati* | My Father, I confess my sins, |
| *e primamante i toi dieci precetti* | Your ten commandments above all |
| *io li ho più volte adulterati e infetti* | Too often soiled and infected |
| *con li mei vizi enormi e scellerati.* | By my monstrous, sudden vices. |
| *I delitti mortali ho tanto usati* | Mortal sins I have known so well |
| *che se non gratia tua nol remetti* | That by your saving grace alone |
| *io mi veggo cascar ne gli interdetti* | I may be spared the forbidden |
| *luoghi d'abisso o'sta i dannati.* | Abysmal places of the damned. |
| *I cinque sentimenti ho tanto pronti* | The five senses I have so close |
| *chi ode, vede, odora, o gusta, o palpa* | That hear or see, smell, taste or touch |
| *ogni vouttoso o vago ogetto.* | Every hollow or casual thing. |
| *Allumami, o Signor, ch'io son qual talpa* | Oh Lord I am a mole who needs |
| *per noi spargesti per quei cinque fonti* | Your light to feel in full the rich |
| *el prezioso sangue benedetto.* | And blessèd blood you shed for us. |

If the pagan trappings with which he transformed the church of St Francis can be seen more as the expression of an aesthetic than a religious sensibility, the citizens of Rimini have been right to call it the Tempio Malatestiano – it is a temple to the cult of Sigismondo, whose foremost practitioner was the man himself. Again, very modern – our own time has been polluted by personality cults, with submissives abjectly drawn like iron filings to the magnets of egomaniacs far more deadly even than Pius II's caricature of Sigismondo. The Tempio is qualitatively very different from the browbeating magnificence of Castel Sismondo and repays close study. When I last visited the Tempio I was fortunate to have to hand the interdisciplinary study by Pernis and Adams on the parallel lives of Sigismondo and Federico, and recommend it to anyone who wishes to explore the subtle allusions and cultural cross-references that make the structure a profoundly autobiographical statement by a highly cultivated narcissist.

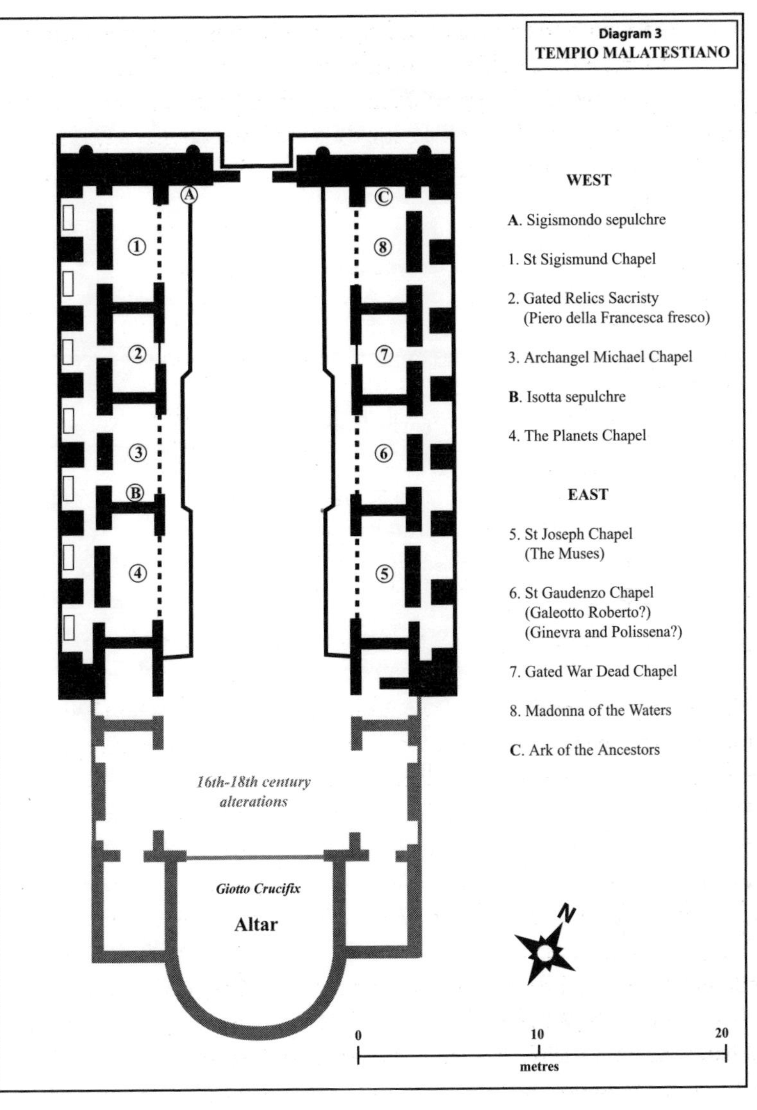
Diagram 3
TEMPIO MALATESTIANO
WEST
A. Sigismondo sepulchre
1. St Sigismund Chapel
2. Gated Relics Sacristy
(Piero della Francesca fresco)
3. Archangel Michael Chapel
B. Isotta sepulchre
4. The Planets Chapel
EAST
5. St Joseph Chapel
(The Muses)
6. St Gaudenzo Chapel
(Galeotto Roberto?)
(Ginevra and Polissena?)
7. Gated War Dead Chapel
8. Madonna of the Waters
C. Ark of the Ancestors
16th-18th century
alterations
Giotto Crucifix
Altar
N
0
10
20
metres

**LEON BATTISTA ALBERTI (1404–72)**

**Polymath and prototype Renaissance man, Leon Battista was born in Genoa to an exiled Florentine family, grew up in Venice and studied law at Padua and Bologna. His first employment was as a clerk at the papal court in Rome. He accompanied Pope Eugenius IV when he fled Rome for Florence in 1434 and was appointed a canon of the Duomo. The Tempio Malatestiano was his first major commission.**

The Tempio Malatestiano was the first design to be executed according to the principles of the great architect Alberti, who enclosed the old brick Gothic church in a new structure of marble. The dominant element in the completed part of the new design is the triple-arched façade, modelled on the Marecchia bridge in Rimini built by Emperor Tiberius *circa* AD 20. The white marble cladding of the new outer shell was taken from the silted-up Roman port works as well as from a stockpile assembled by the citizens of Fano to build a bridge over the Metauro. The porphyry (red and purple), serpentine (green) and black marble used in the interior were brought from the Abbey of San Appollinare di Classe near Ravenna. The seven external niches on the eastern side are empty, but on the western side they are occupied by neo-Roman sarcophagi. The first contains the remains of Basinio of Parma, Sigismondo's court poet, the second Giusto de' Conti, a songwriter and one of his councillors, and the fourth Roberto Valturio, his closest adviser and author of *De Re Militari* (the title taken from Vegetius's late fourth-century treatise on warfare), which Valturio dedicated to Sigismondo in 1455. The fifth and seventh honour medical doctors, the sixth has no inscription. The third sarcophagus contains the bones of the Byzantine philosopher Plethon, brought back in 1465 from Mystras in southern Greece. The Latin inscriptions on the sarcophagi, even for Plethon who is identified as 'prince of the philosophers of his time', dwell on their connection with Sigismondo. On the first pillar at both sides of the Tempio there is an inscription in classical Greek, which proclaims:

> Sigismondo Pandolfo Malatesta, son of Pandolfo, Bringer of Victory, having survived many and most grave dangers during the Italic Wars,

> in recognition of his deeds accomplished so felicitously and with such courage, for he obtained what he had prayed for in such a critical juncture, has erected at his magnanimous expense this temple to the Immortal God and to the City, and left a memorial worthy of fame and full of piety.*

The external inscriptions are merely bombastic – what sets the Tempio Malatestiano apart from any other structure with which mortals have sought to perpetuate their memory is the maniacally detailed self-worship of the interior decoration. The Franciscans, aghast at what Sigismondo made of their modest Gothic church, insisted on dedicating the inner chapels to Saints Sigismund, Joseph and Gaudenzo, the Archangel Michael and the Madonna of the Waters (Diagram 5). However, they were really dedicated to the cults of Sigismondo, Isotta, and to Sigismondo's dead offspring and ancestors, while the chapels nearest the altar are devoted to the Roman planet-gods and the Greek muses. It should be noted that the genuine Roman sarcophagus of Rimini's patron, St Gaudenzo, sits in a garden on the eastern side of the Tempio. Previously it was sheltered within the nearby monastery, from which the Franciscans certainly would have refused to let it be removed to be used as window dressing for the Tempio. The old monastery is now gone, demolished by the stick of bombs that destroyed the apse of the Tempio in 1944, hence the present-day location of St Gaudenzo's sarcophagus.

It would, anyway, have been incongruous for Sigismondo to honour St Gaudenzo when the whole message of the Tempio is that he was the only patron Rimini should revere. Before entering the building we must first ask why the year 1446 was so significant to him. It is the date on the dedicatory panels set into the walls of Castel Sismondo, and most of the medallions of Isotta, even those showing her looking decidedly middle-aged, bear the same date. One might suppose that this was simply another expression of egomania – that Isotta did not acquire quasi-divinity until she coupled with the Lord God Sigismondo – were it not that several medallions depicting an older Sigismondo are also dated 1446. It was of course the year that began with

* Translation from the article by Marilyn Aronberg Lavin in *Art Bulletin*, 56.3 (September 1974).

his very fortunate escape from an ambush intended to assassinate him and ended with his brilliant defence of Gradara against a combination of the Church, Milan and the Sforzas, and there may have been no more to it than the combination of his military success and the discovery of making love after years of less exalted copulation. But there may also have been another culmination involved, the moment when his astrological star (whatever it may have been) was at its highest celestial point above his horizon, or conceivably he had a vision of himself as the new Caesar taking his place in the pantheon. There is much in the decoration of the Tempio to suggest something along these lines, but nothing definitive.

Immediately on the right inside the Tempio is Sigismondo's tomb, a Greek sepulchre within an arch surmounted by two bas-relief busts wearing victor's laurels. The Latin epitaph reads 'I am Sigismondo of the Malatesta Blood and Clan Pandolfo my Father and Flaminia my Fatherland died the 7th of October aged 51 years three months and 20 days in 1468'. The tomb was originally adorned with Sigismondo's banners and a full set of ceremonial armour, since dispersed. Above the helmet were two horns and banners with the punning words in Italian 'I bear the horn that all may see / So big that you cannot believe'. When the tomb was opened in 1756 a large ossicle was found on the right temple of the skull (it would have been above the hairline), but of course the 'horn' also refers to the male sex member. The horn on Sigismondo's head must have been a closely guarded secret, because such evidence that he was Satan's spawn would certainly have featured in the ecclesiastical vituperation lavished on him. Whether the deformity inclined the man himself to devil worship is an open question – he had more than enough political reasons to regard the Church as his enemy.

Relics taken from the tomb in 1756 can be seen in the sacristy next to the first chapel on the right, which is nominally devoted to St Sigismund, the Burgundian king and martyr who became the patron saint of Bohemia when Emperor Charles IV moved his remains to Prague in the fourteenth century. The saint was, obviously, chosen as a proxy for Sigismondo himself, a blasphemous subterfuge made all the more provocative by the fresco in the sacristy (Picture section 2, p. 6). Painted by Piero della Francesca and dated 1451, it shows

Sigismondo, wearing the short cloak in which he was to be buried, kneeling in front of the saint depicted with the face of Emperor Sigismund, who knighted him when returning from his 1433 coronation in Rome. The round mirror/oculus behind Sigismondo shows a castle identified as Castel Sismondo, although it is not an accurate depiction, and there may be a (heretical) Manichaean reference in the white hunting dog facing towards the two human figures and the black one facing away. Showing religious reverence to the emperor was not something a mid fifteenth-century papal vicar who cared about good relations with the Church would even have allowed to cross his mind. Even if Sigismondo did not also publicly sodomise a papal nephew – which if not true, should be (as the Italians put it, *se non è vero è molto ben trovato*) – the fresco would have been sufficient by itself to provoke the annihilating hatred of a Papacy shaped by the struggle with the Holy Roman Empire.

An added provocation is to be found in the next chapel, nominally dedicated to the Archangel Michael but containing Isotta's elaborate sepulchre (Picture section 2, p. 2). The original inscription, rediscovered in 1912 and held between two angels on her sarcophagus, set high on the left-hand wall, read 'Isotta of Rimini Beauty and Virtue the Adornment of Italy 1456', the year of her marriage to Sigismondo. It was overlaid with a bronze plaque that read 'D. ISOTTAE. ARIMENSI. BM. SACRUM MCCCCL'. The 'D' might have stood for *domina* (lady) but the *sacrum* surely removes any doubt that it stood for *diva*, so the epitaph translates as 'Divine Isotta of Rimini Meritorious and Sacred 1450'. The word 'divine' was not one to use loosely in the late Middle Ages, least of all in a Christian church.

There is no way of knowing when the bronze plaque was inserted over the original inscription. Possibly it was the epitaph she chose for herself after Sigismondo's death, 1450 being the year she would have become the Lady of Rimini if he had married her after Polissena's death. The sarcophagus, held up by two Malatesta elephants, is surrounded by monograms in which the letters 'S' and 'I' are entwined, quartered with the Malatesta livery. Although experts on heraldry concur that the 'I' of the monogram, omnipresent in the Tempio and on all Sigismondo's works, was no more than the second letter of his name, in this place we may permit ourselves to believe it represented

Isotta. The sarcophagus is surmounted by a ceremonial helmet and above that two elephant heads with dragon-like dorsal sails and finally banners bearing the Latin words *Tempus Loquendo* and *Tempus Tacendo* (Time for Talking – Time to Cease Talking). It's anyone's guess what they mean. Maybe Isotta became a nag; indeed, we learn from the only surviving letter from her to Sigismondo (Appendix E) that she became intolerant of his philandering and that he told her to stop writing to him. If so, the words constitute self-criticism, because the most startling fact about the barbaric ensemble, far better suited to a warrior than to a gentle lady, is that it was all commissioned by Isotta herself.

Given the subtlety of allusion characteristic of the Tempio, there may be more than meets the eye in the sculpture of the Evil One being struck down by the condottiere-like Archangel Michael in the niche of Isotta's chapel, also perhaps in the joyous celebration by the angels (if indeed they are angels) carved on the chapel pillars. Liberation of the human spirit from religious oppression, perhaps? Next to Isotta's chapel is the Chapel of the Planets with the signs of the zodiac between the pillars, including a menacing Crab hovering over a depiction of Rimini. Across the aisle is a chapel unconvincingly dedicated to St Joseph, decorated with statues representing the Muses of arts and sciences. Although the two chapels nearest the altar celebrate pre-Christian Roman and Greek traditions, the screens separating them from the apse have an early Christian inspiration. Working back towards the entrance the next chapel is now dedicated to St Gaudenzo but was originally devoted to the cult of the Blessed Galeotto Roberto, Sigismondo's half-brother and predecessor as lord of Rimini. Sigismondo's first two wives and their children who died as infants are buried under the floor, which explains why it is decorated with bas-reliefs of sixty-one children chasing each other, riding dolphins and generally enjoying themselves. Next and opposite the sacristy is another enclosed and gated chapel with the names of Rimini's war dead on the walls, its original purpose unknown.

The final enclosure, to the left of the main entrance, is dedicated to the Madonna of the Waters, and a statue of the Virgin and Child dated *circa* 1400 occupies the niche over the altar. It is also known as the Chapel of the Sibyls and Prophets because the pillars are filled with statues of ten pagan sibyls and a mere two Christian prophets.

However, the chapel is dominated by the splendid Ark of the Ancestors set high in a polychrome alcove with sculpted curtains in the left-hand wall, found in 1756 to contain the bones of nineteen men, women and children. Most of the bones were jumbled, indicating a rather cavalier reinterment from other tombs, but two complete skeletons of a man and a fully dressed woman lay on top of the rest. Since the skeleton in Isotta's tomb was found unclothed there is speculation that this was her true resting place, perhaps to be close to her beloved son Malatesta who we know was buried in the sarcophagus of Sigismondo's uncle Carlo II. The 'ark' is so called because it was clearly intended to evoke the biblical Ark of the Covenant and is decorated on all four sides, indicating that it was intended to be free-standing. The bas-reliefs on the pillars held up by black marble elephants are perhaps the most powerful of all portrayals of Sigismondo; they are the work of Agostino di Duccio who along with the medallist Matteo de' Pasti was responsible for the internal decoration of the Tempio, much of it mediocre but overwhelming in the aggregate.

Pernis and Adams rightly emphasise the significance of the bas-reliefs on the front of the Ark. On the right is the Temple of Minerva and on the left the Triumph of the Roman general Scipio Africanus, who defeated the great Carthaginian Hannibal at Zama in 202 BC. Scipio may have been the greatest general of antiquity, but somebody should have remembered that the signature episode at Zama involved the panicking of Hannibal's elephants back through his own lines, hardly an event to celebrate in a chapel whose main pillars are upheld by Malatesta pachyderms. Sigismondo appears in both reliefs, as the man in Roman armour amid a crowd of men in togas at the foot of the goddess Minerva in the first, and as Scipio himself in the second. Lest we should misinterpret the references, the Latin inscription between the reliefs reads 'Sigismondo Pandolfo Malatesta Son of Pandolfo to the Ancestors and Descendants of his House Illustrious for Great Merit of Probity [Minerva] and Fortitude [Scipio]'.

It hardly needs saying that none of the decorations in the Tempio Malatestiano would have survived had the Protestant Reformation reached Rimini. Even the tolerance of the Roman Catholic Church, which wisely incorporated so many pagan anniversaries and symbols into its ritual, was tested to the limit by a church that barely, and

equipment. Over the following months the indefatigable Filippo Maria Visconti returned one last time to the game of scrambling everybody's expectations by seeking a rapprochement with his son-in-law. Francesco Sforza attempted to make it a condition of the reconciliation that Sigismondo should return Senigallia to him and restore the towns taken from Urbino. In what may have been no more than a scramble to find a better alternative than the Piccinino brothers, Filippo Maria gave Sigismondo a commission for the winter months and invited him to Milan, holding out the prospect of the captain-generalcy of his army. Sigismondo prudently travelled to Milan in the company of King Alfonso's viceroy, but after two months of negotiation declined the offer, possibly because it was conditional on acceding to Sforza's demands but also because Filippo Maria had by now hired Astorre II Manfredi, who had made two unprovoked attacks on Sigismondo during 1446. In March 1447 Sigismondo returned home via Ferrara, where he met with Venetian representatives to discuss joining the anti-Visconti league. Finally a truce was declared by which the Sforzas and Federico on one side and the Malatesta brothers on the other undertook to commit no acts of aggression against each other. Shortly afterwards, however, Filippo Maria signed a treaty with Sforza in which he accepted the conditions pertaining to Sigismondo, although lacking the means to enforce them. At the same time Venice turned cold towards Sforza after a thoroughgoing investigation by the Council of Ten uncovered evidence that many patricians, including the eldest son of Doge Francesco Foscari – the driving force of their war against Milan and conquest of the *terraferma* empire – were on Sforza's payroll.

In the meantime Pope Eugenius IV had died and his successor Nicholas V was elected with astonishing alacrity a mere eleven days later. A most intriguing man, devoted to books and determined that Rome should emerge resplendent from the filth and neglect into which it had fallen, Nicholas V was also, almost uniquely, free from the taints of avarice and nepotism. He ceaselessly urged the Italian states to peace and during his papacy they came close to recognising that their game of beggar-my-neighbour was pointless – although this owed much to the death in August 1447 of Filippo Maria, who for thirty-five years had kept the pot boiling. In May, with a Venetian army ravaging the Milanese hinterland, the ailing Filippo Maria was compelled to buy his

Sforza son-in-law's services at enormous cost, offering him 20,000 ducats in cash and 30,000 in letters of exchange. Sensing that the big prize was at last within his reach, Sforza freed his hands by surrendering Iesi and the rest of his Marche holdings to the pope in exchange for 31,000 ducats and made a hasty peace with King Alfonso and Sigismondo. Sforza's timing was just a little off: he had barely begun to equip 4000 cavalry and 2000 infantry assembled in Pesaro when he learned that Filippo Maria was dying, and had only reached Cotignola when news came of the duke's death on 13 August. Had he reached Milan in time it is most unlikely that the citizens would have dared proclaim the 'Golden Ambrosian Republic' – indeed, they were only able to do so because Sforza's supporters were held in check by an 'anyone but' coalition including many of Filippo Maria's captains. The Visconti–Aragon dream of sharing Italy between the two houses went up in the smoke of the Viscontean castle, burned and demolished by the citizens of Milan.

Milan was still beset by the Venetians, however, and in what was probably the best alternative open to the new republican leaders they increased the generous terms of Francesco Sforza's commission from the late duke. The upfront money was increased to 60,000 ducats in cash against a monthly stipend of 15,000, to be increased to 17,000 if he drove the Venetians back beyond the Adda river. From the start Sforza behaved like the de facto ruler of Milan, for example winning over Francesco and Jacopo Piccinino by offering them the lordships of Cremona and Crema (both east of the Adda) once these were secured from the Venetian threat. He crossed the Adda but was unable to provoke Micheletto Attendolo to battle, so he pulled back to besiege Piacenza, across the Po south of Milan, seized by Taddeo d'Este (one of Niccolò III's countless bastards) for Venice after the death of Filippo Maria. The siege of Piacenza was one of the most savagely fought in Italian history, with every artifice of late medieval warfare employed to overcome three lines of defence. When the city fell in December it was sacked for forty days, the final indignity coming when the 10,000 imprisoned male inhabitants were compelled to pay an indemnity before returning to their raped women and pillaged houses. In contrast Taddeo d'Este was treated with conspicuous courtesy, a left-handed compliment given that it aroused the totally unjustified suspicions of the Venetians, who poisoned him in June 1448 – one cannot dismiss the possibility that Sforza hoped for just such an outcome.

While his troops were sated with the sack of Piacenza, Sforza was able to dispense with the stipend from Milan, withheld by a faction demanding peace with Venice, which was joined by the Piccinino brothers when they belatedly realised that Sforza intended to restore all their father's holdings to their original proprietors – who naturally became fervent Sforzeschi. Sforza himself, now at the head of an army swelled by condottieri ready to serve for loot, embarked on perhaps the most devastatingly effective campaign prior to the French invasion of 1494. In July 1448 he blockaded the Venetian commander Andrea Querini at Casalmaggiore and forced him to destroy his own fleet to prevent capture, then marched on Caravaggio. The defenders held out against constant bombardment, mining and assaults through August, but the citadel had capitulated by the time Micheletto Attendolo and Bartolomeo Colleoni arrived to relieve it at the head of 12,500 cavalry and 5000 infantry. Sforza's army was by now somewhat smaller because the opportunists deserted when the expected loot was not forthcoming, but thanks to an ill-considered attack urged by Colleoni on the hesitant Micheletto Attendolo the Venetians were routed. Reports of casualties range from negligible to many thousands, but the completeness of the victory is attested by the fact that only 1500 Venetian cavalry escaped the debacle. In Venice the Council of Ten was reduced to offering 2000 ducats for Sforza's assassination – a ludicrously small amount that seems to have been calculated more to insult than to motivate anyone to make an almost certainly suicidal attempt on Sforza's life.

Let us leave Francesco and Bianca Maria (who had distinguished herself in the defence of Cremona earlier in 1448) at Pavia, where they occupied the Visconti palace and established a lordly court, and go back to Sigismondo and Federico. Needless to say they had not been idle while the fate of Lombardy was being decided. In July 1447 Sigismondo's emissaries signed a commission with King Alfonso for one year active service and another in reserve, the terms being 600 *lance* at 50 ducats (a minimum of 90,000 ducats) and 600 infantry at 4 ducats per head, with a personal stipend of 4000 ducats, the advance payment of 32,400 ducats to be paid in four tranches from the day Alfonso recovered certain sums owed him by the Papacy and Filippo Maria.

The details are important, because this commission was to be instrumental in the downfall of Sigismondo. In September there was a pro-Malatesta revolt in Fossombrone but the castle held out and when Federico arrived he drove out the rebels in three days of fighting. Clearly the townspeople had favoured the rebellion, because he then released his troops to conduct a murderous three-day sack. The rebellion seems to have been led by supporters of Galeazzo the Inept, who was now living in Rimini, but Sigismondo did not intervene. Possibly he held back because Nicholas V lifted Federico's excommunication and confirmed him as Vicar of Fossombrone in July, and Sigismondo did not want to offend the new pope. Some accounts allege that Federico was held back from counter-attacking Sigismondo's domain by a five-month commission from Florence, but this was for only 440 cavalry and 800 infantry, suggesting that he may not have been strong enough to attack Rimini anyway. He was tasked by Florence with clearing Aragonese invaders from southern Tuscany, where a number of villages around Volterra had surrendered to them.

Federico crossed the Apennines with a larger force (500 cavalry and 1000 infantry, half of them crossbowmen) than he had been paid for, raised entirely from his own lands hence paying no sub-commissions. He did not break off his campaign against the Aragonese even when he learned that in his absence the Fossombrone exiles had seized several villages in the name of Galeazzo. This may have been because he was so pushed for money that he simply could not risk forfeiting the Florentine commission; alternatively he may have been privy to the negotiations the Florentines were conducting with Sigismondo to detach him from the Aragonese cause. Sigismondo was also very much in need of money to pay for the immense programme of building and refortification he had undertaken, and it led him to commit the cardinal error of treating King Alfonso as he had Francesco Sforza in 1444 with regard to money owed him. The error was compounded in this case because Alfonso was not, in fact, dilatory in his payments to Sigismondo. The king had agreed to pay the advance in four tranches conditional on Sigismondo ratifying the terms, which he did not do, and on receiving repayment of loans only partially forthcoming from Rome and not at all from Milan, where Filippo Maria's death threw everything into confusion. Even so, at a time when Alfonso was maintaining two armies in Tuscany and a fleet offshore, he paid Sigismondo between 22,000 and 25,000 ducats. He also demanded that Sigismondo start earning it by marching to Tuscany, and when cringing emissaries arrived from Rimini bearing a letter in which Sigismondo refused, saying that he could accomplish more by attacking Urbino to draw Federico back to the Marche, the king threw them in prison. Oblivious of the offence he had given, Sigismondo felt justified in negotiating a new commission with the Florentines, and in a final act of disrespect pocketed a further 2000 ducats from Alfonso as he did so.

The commission Sigismondo accepted from Florence in December 1447 was for rather less than the terms he had negotiated with Naples, but appealed to his grandiosity by giving him the title of Captain-General of all Florentine forces – except Federico's contingent. The only obvious reason why he chose this moment to alienate an employer as potentially lucrative as Alfonso to throw in his lot with the shamelessly dishonest Florentines – who lived down their reputation by cheating both him and Federico at the end of their commissions – is that he thought Milan would be defeated by Venice. While he waited for the advance payment to arrive from Florence and co-payee Venice, he captured a few more villages from Federico and Alessandro Sforza, and Pietracuta from San Marino, until in March he crossed the Apennines with 2000 men. As soon as he departed, troops left behind by Federico attacked some of the lost villages, but Sigismondo had also left troops behind and they quickly countered the threat, the episode ending in yet another truce brokered by Florence.

In September, as we have seen, Venice suffered a ruinous defeat at Caravaggio, but things went better for Florence on the same day thanks to Sigismondo. King Alfonso's forces had been besieging Piombino (Map 3) by land and sea since the previous December, and both Federico and Sigismondo were sent to the relief of the town, which was held by Rinaldo Orsini, lord by marriage into the Appiani family, who was supported by Siena. In the preceding months Sigismondo had conducted a punitive ride through Sienese territory and the new alliance between old enemies Florence and Siena put him in the awkward position of having to account for all the cattle his men had rustled: the Sienese grudgingly accepted that they had all been eaten because the animals had, in fact, been sold to Florence.

There is disagreement over who deserves the greatest credit for the relief of Piombino, but the manner in which the attack by the relieving force was synchronised with a sortie by the garrison was so similar to Sigismondo's relief of Gradara in late 1446 that it is fair to assume his was the guiding intelligence. The Aragonese were forced to embark their troops and flee, leaving 2000 casualties behind along with all their siege equipment and stores. For the remaining ten years of his life King Alfonso nurtured the hope of forcing Sigismondo to eat the poems commemorating the relief of Piombino. In contrast Rinaldo Orsini won the king's good will by resisting the urge to gloat, accepting his nominal sovereignty and agreeing to pay an annual tribute of a golden bowl worth 150 ducats.

Following Piombino Sigismondo was sent to the aid of Venice in Lombardy and in November marched out of Rimini at the head of 3000 cavalry and 2000 foot, most of the latter hired by Florence under a separate commission. Federico, meanwhile, had a commission for 506 *lance* (a minimum of 1518 horse) and 300 infantry, for a monthly stipend of 3000 florins for six months during which he mopped up the remaining Aragonese garrisons in Tuscany. This was a unique occasion when we can compare the standing of Sigismondo and Federico in the condottieri hierarchy as measured by the Florentines, who understood money if nothing else. Sigismondo commanded more men and a higher price, but less than one would expect in a hiring that in itself did more than the victory at Piombino to relieve Florence of the Aragonese threat. It would appear, therefore, that the Florentines bought him relatively cheaply with the title of captain-general. He in turn may have calculated that the title would boost his standing, but when he passed to the service of Venice at the end of 1448 he negotiated a monthly payment of 7040 ducats (80,480 annualised) to cover 2000 cavalry, 400 foot *and* his own stipend, from which he had to pay subcontracts to make up the numbers. This was markedly less than the 1447 contract with King Alfonso, even though the Venetians were in such desperate straits after Caravaggio that they finally allied with Sforza against the Ambrosian Republic. It would appear, therefore, that Sigismondo's switch from Naples to Florence was not only a political miscalculation but also a very poor business decision.

During 1449, while Federico earned modest money for modest tasks in Tuscany, Sigismondo played for high stakes in Lombardy as Captain-General of Venice, at first in alliance with the Sforzas. The fact that Alessandro Sforza was also fully committed in Lombardy may explain why the year passed without overt hostilities in the Romagna borderlands, although Sigismondo spent more time intriguing to recover Pesaro than he did in fulfilling his commission, the lowlight of which was a poorly conducted siege of Crema where his siege works and bombards fell to a sortie in April. Crema capitulated to him in August but proved a hollow victory as Venice now switched back to an alliance with the Ambrosian Republic against the Sforzas. In December the Venetian army under Sigismondo and the Ambrosians under Jacopo Piccinino, seeking to break the blockade of Milan, clashed with Francesco Sforza at Monte di Brianza, north of Milan. Sigismondo and Piccinino had the worst of what was little more than a skirmish but the consequences were that riots broke out in famine-stricken Milan. In February 1450 Sforza was invited to enter the city as the new lord, perhaps the clearest example of how the *signori* invariably gained power when republican communes were unable to impose order.

Polissena Sforza died in June 1449. Sigismondo had obtained her legitimation from Pope Nicholas V in October 1448 and although many years later her father was to accuse him of poisoning her for the benefit of Pope Pius II's omnibus indictment, there is no reason to doubt that she died of the plague. Likewise false was the most notorious of the charges of rape made against Sigismondo, that in May or June 1450 he and fifteen of his men gang-raped a German noblewoman. The alleged victim was later described by Sforza as 'the wife of the Duke of Bavaria', although the matter seems to have escaped the notice of the Bavarian court. Mario Tabanelli has laid this canard to rest by pointing out the many inconsistencies in the oft-repeated accusation, as well as the suggestive similarity with an accusation made a century earlier against Bernardino da Polenta by his enemies. The final refutation is that the Venetians – although in 1452 they repeated the accusation against Sigismondo in correspondence with Emperor Frederick III – at the time conducted a thorough investigation, including the interrogation under torture of some of Sigismondo's alleged co-rapists whom he sent under guard to Venice, and concluded that no such incident took place.

There is every reason to believe the accusation was yet more black propaganda by Federico, because it coincided with a masterful piece of *furbizia* also designed to drive a wedge between Sigismondo and Venice. In December 1447 Sigismondo had tricked Federico and Alessandro Sforza into discussing joint attacks with each against the territory of the other, and then revealed to each what the other had been up to. Federico salvaged the situation by hastening to Pesaro to confer with Alessandro, and the two swore revenge. In May 1450 Federico made secret contact with Sigismondo and offered to let him into Pesaro – which Federico was garrisoning for Sforza – in exchange for the return of the towns Sigismondo had seized in the Montefeltro. Given their history it is hard to believe that Sigismondo fell for it; but he did, and demanded a release from his commission in order to hurry south. The Venetians were outraged that their captain-general should put his little dynastic interests above the great game they were playing in Lombardy and considered treating him as they had Carmagnola. Sigismondo soon found out that he had been duped but the damage was done and his lucrative commission with Venice was not renewed in November.

Oddly, Sigismondo's staunchest ally after the death of Eugenius IV was the Papacy. In August 1450 he was in attendance on Nicholas V at Fabriano, where the pope had fled to escape an outbreak of the plague in Rome, and was shown extraordinary favour. He and brother Domenico were jointly reconfirmed as vicars of Rimini, Cesena, Fano, Cervia, Bertinoro, San Leo and Sestino, for which their annual tribute was reduced from 6000 to 4000 florins. This was a remarkable concession: San Leo had been returned to the Papacy by Federico after his reputation-making capture of it in 1441, while Sestino controlled the upper Foglia valley and the Viamaggio Pass. In addition the pope confirmed Sigismondo's right to Senigallia, Gradara and Mondaino, disputed with the Sforza brothers, and to Pergola, Sant'Agata, Talamello, Castel d'Elci and Pennabilli, all lands Federico believed were his by right. The pope rubbed further salt in Federico's wounds by validating the Malatesta conquests in the Montefeltro, which were indeed due to Domenico through his marriage to Violante, and decreed that should Federico recover any through negotiation he must pay all costs incurred in their capture and maintenance. Finally, Nicholas V legitimated Sigismondo's sons Roberto and Malatesta, securing the succession.* A few months later Sigismondo and Domenico came to an omnibus agreement to rationalise the administration of the lands thus confirmed to them, in which Domenico ceded to his brother the lands and title of Count of Montefeltro that were his by marriage to Violante. From what we know of the lady we may assume that her primary concern was to deny the title to her brother's assassin, and since her disabled husband could not defend her rights she renounced them in favour of Sigismondo.

Any other lord might have concluded that if he did nothing else, he should show the utmost gratitude to the man and the institution that had so blessed him. Sigismondo, as we have seen, instead commissioned the highly provocative Piero della Francesca fresco of himself kneeling before the Emperor Sigismund. Under Nicholas and his short-lived successor Callixtus III he paid no penalty for his hubris, but after Pius II was elected in 1458 the long-suppressed resentment of the Curia burst over him. Whatever Pius II's faults and excesses, and they were many, any fair assessment must conclude that Sigismondo had it coming. He was also living far beyond the modest revenues even of his newly extended domain, making it doubly damaging that after he lost his commission with the Venetians he only won three more.

Federico, meanwhile, survived two incidents that would have killed a less robust man. In a tournament at Urbino in January 1451 his opponent's lance splintered through Federico's visor and shattered his nose and right eye socket, creating the profile by which he is known to history. While convalescing he was chagrined to learn that his employer Sforza, now Duke of Milan, had given Sigismondo a commission, and in October Federico signed a commission for 600 *lance* and 600 infantry with King Alfonso of Naples. He became Alfonso's captain-general in 1452 and remained in his employ for five years, through a serious illness in 1453–4 that at one point threatened the sight of his remaining eye. During the entire time of his service to Naples Federico was associated with only one noteworthy military achievement, when in August 1452 under the overall command of Count Everso dell'Anguillara he defeated Astorre II Manfredi for Florence at Montepulciano in the

* In November 1452 Nicholas V also legitimated Sigismondo's children Valerio, Margherita and Lucrezia.

southern Valdichiana. The glue binding Federico and Alfonso together was their mutual loathing of Sigismondo.

A detailed account of the military and diplomatic manoeuvrings preceding the Peace of Lodi would simply reinforce the points already made, and I cannot hope to improve on Philip Jones's summary of the situation as it stood in 1450:

> Between Sigismondo and his immediate neighbours the normal state of clandestine hostilities continued which, with the impending revival of war, and every power once more a prospective paymaster, developed into an issue of general concern. It was soon evident that the aims of Federico and his enemy were not those of the [powers] they were engaged to serve. To them a *condotta* and the pay it procured were means to fighting their own local feuds, and any government wishing to hire them had also to undertake to satisfy their private purposes.

Federico was notably more successful than Sigismondo, finding in Alfonso an employer whose interests were served by indulging Federico's own personal agenda. This was most clearly illustrated in April 1452 when a nearly successful attempt by Federico to storm Fano froze Sigismondo within his own domain when he should have been in Tuscany earning a commission from Duke Francesco Sforza, now allied with Florence against Venice and Naples. When Sigismondo did ride across the Apennines in August, now commissioned by Florence, it was because Federico was there at the head of the Neapolitan army. Sigismondo drove Federico out of Tuscany in a brilliant campaign of manoeuvre, but the Florentines were as usual dilatory in rewarding success and only paid him what he was owed when he renewed his commission in June 1453. They never paid him for the renewed period, even though he continued to give good service, and when the commission expired he sought employment with Venice and Naples.

Sigismondo drove so many nails into his own coffin that it is possibly futile to select one in particular; however, the negotiations he conducted with King Alfonso in late 1453 have a fair claim to being the tipping point, the moment when he wilfully gave up his last hope of salvaging a rapidly eroding situation. At this time the whole of

Christendom was aghast at the Ottoman capture of Constantinople, so long invulnerable (bar the Fourth Crusade) behind the mighty Theodosian walls. Pope Nicholas redoubled his efforts to bring peace to Italy and it is only in the light of this unique moment, coincident with Federico's near-fatal illness, that we can understand why Alfonso overcame his resentment to accept the mediation of Venice and make what appears to have been a sincere effort to achieve reconciliation with Sigismondo. He offered the remission of half the amount paid to Sigismondo in 1447, the post of Captain-General of Naples and also a marriage between his illegitimate granddaughter Eleanor of Aragon and Sigismondo's son Roberto, who was conducting the negotiations on behalf of his father. If ever there was a gift-horse whose teeth should have been left unexamined, this was it.

**THE THEODOSIAN WALLS**

**The symbolic importance of the awesome lines of fortification around Constantinople can be seen in the castles built by Edward I to subdue northern Wales. Edward imported a Savoyard master mason, James of St George, who copied his signature bands of red masonry from the walls built by Emperor Theodosius in the fifth century.**

Instead, and fatefully echoing his behaviour in 1447, Sigismondo prevaricated and even, under the circumstances insolently, proposed his own marriage to Alfonso's legitimate granddaughter. Alfonso angrily withdrew the offer he had made and now added swingeing interest to the capital sum outstanding. There must have been more involved, as not even Sigismondo can rationally have believed himself of sufficient stature to marry into one of the great royal houses of Europe. In the absence of any other explanation it is reasonable to suspect that Isotta's influence may have tipped the balance: Sigismondo had conspicuously failed to regularise his relationship with Isotta, despite being free to do so since 1449, and the marriage proposed by Alfonso would have made her rival Vanetta dei Toschi's son Roberto the heir-apparent to Rimini over her own son Malatesta, an unendurable prospect. How she prevented the match is no less open to speculation: possibly by inflating

Sigismondo's grandiosity and urging him to make the overweening demand that slammed the door on all hope of a settlement with Naples.

With exquisitely bad timing – for Sigismondo – Federico recovered from his illness and hastened back to Naples, where he now found the king fully receptive to the fabrications he had devised to blacken his enemy's reputation. In April 1454 Sforza, Venice and Florence signed a peace treaty at Lodi to which all the other Italian states were invited to adhere. All except Alfonso did so, and also agreed to a general league to last for twenty-five years, during which all disputes would be submitted to arbitration. Sigismondo signed in his own right and was included among the allies listed by Milan, Venice and Florence. However, the price demanded by Alfonso for joining the league was the exclusion of Sigismondo, of Astorre II Manfredi who also owed him money, and of the Genoese for base treachery in the lately concluded wars. None of the other signatories was prepared to intercede on Sigismondo's behalf: on the contrary they all, including the pope, urged him to settle his debt. This he undertook to do in a personal letter to Alfonso, but of course the whole point of the League of Lodi was to suppress the endemic warfare that offered him the only prospect of earning the necessary amount.

The sole conflict available was between Siena and Count Aldobrandino Orsini of Pitigliano. Considering what a buyer's market it was the Sienese were generous to offer Sigismondo a commission of 16,000 ducats and the title of captain-general. Separately commissioned were his son-in-law Giulio Cesare Varano and the condottiere Giberto da Correggio, and together they besieged Orsini in the fortress of Sorano. Because the Sienese archives are so well preserved we know much about their dealings with condottieri. To say that they were generally unfortunate in these matters is a considerable understatement: they were almost invariably treated with contempt by the soldiers they hired, perhaps because the Sienese in turn were so paranoid. In this particular case there is a sub-plot involving the Sienese commissioner being caught in the act with one of Correggio's pageboys by a Malatesta retainer, after which he and his suite were roughed up by Sigismondo's men. The commissioner then claimed that the boy had been in his tent to steal, a face-saving formula that was accepted by Correggio, no doubt along with a substantial bribe, given that sodomy was punishable by death. Together they concocted a tale of treacherous dealings between Everso dell'Anguillara (a branch of the Orsini family) and Sigismondo in order to muddy the waters.

Intent on their fabrication, they failed to detect the real dealings taking place between Sigismondo and the besieged Count Aldobrandino. In December, when Sorano was close to capitulation and after receipt of 12,000 ducats from Siena to continue the siege beyond the campaigning season, Sigismondo agreed a one-month truce with Count Aldobrandino, who gave him a son as hostage, and lifted the siege. The outraged Sienese sent a commissioner to intercept the courier carrying Sigismondo's correspondence with Rimini, which contained nothing they could use but which they could not return without admitting their own wrongdoing. It thus remains in the Siena archives as the most illuminating documentary source on Sigismondo's life, also providing our sole insight into his relationship with Isotta (Appendix E). He, meanwhile, marched to the Tuscan coast on a looting expedition in Orsini territory. At some point his Varano son-in-law broke away and, returning home through Siena, told a friend about Sigismondo's activities. This duly reached the ears of the Councillors, who ordered Correggio to intercept and kill Sigismondo. In February at a bridge near Giuncarico, midway between Siena and the coast, Correggio's men ambushed him and captured his baggage train.

What followed simply does not fit with the canonical version of events. Sigismondo formally requested and was granted leave to return to Rimini, which he did through Florentine territory, and in due course the Sienese apologised to him for their behaviour: they did not, however, advertise this to the courts of Italy, to which they had earlier sent letters denouncing his alleged perfidy. The reason for this volte-face is that in May Count Aldobrandino signed a capitulation with Siena in which he agreed to pay tribute for Pitigliano and Sorano, and returned two villages in the coastal area ravaged by Sigismondo, whose seizure had been the cause of the war in the first place. From this it emerged that Sigismondo had not, in fact, betrayed Siena, and the Councillors awoke to the trick played on them by their own commissioner and Correggio, whom by now they had appointed captain-general in place of Sigismondo. In September 1455 Correggio rode into Siena to a hero's welcome, but once inside the Palazzo Pubblico one of the Councillors revealed that they had documentary proof of his treachery, including an agreement he had made with Jacopo Piccinino to devastate the Sienese countryside. Correggio leapt on his accuser and bit off his nose, after which the other Councillors threw the condottiere out of a window. The crowning touch is that Correggio was then buried in the cathedral with all the honours due his rank so that the citizens should not realise how he had tricked their rulers.

It is impossible to say whether or not there were corrupt dealings between Sigismondo and Count Aldobrandino. The surrender of one of the count's sons as a hostage argues against it, and it was perfectly within the norms of contemporary warfare for a condottiere to break off a siege in winter and to profit from looting enemy territory. The Sienese put themselves in the wrong by stealing Sigismondo's correspondence and although it is a fine point whether the lands seized by Orsini from Siena should have been looted, to have sent Correggio to assassinate their own captain-general was outrageous. Correggio, intent on robbing his employers, certainly did little to bring about Orsini's capitulation and his fate plus the fact of the Sienese apology strongly suggests that the sordid sub-plot involving the commissioner and the pageboy was indeed the cause of the whole imbroglio. The trouble was that Sigismondo was now a dog with a bad name, of whom the worst was readily believed, and that the rulers of Siena had every reason to conceal the truth in order to spare their own blushes.

The result was that Sigismondo was discredited as a condottiere and so was unable to repay King Alfonso, and when the Sienese Pius II became pope he believed Sigismondo was the principal villain of the story. His account of the affair exposes the undependability of his memoirs as a source for anything other than his own state of mind:

> ... the Sienese had been engaged in a war with Ildebrando, Count of Pitigliano, in which they had hired two captains notorious for their perfidy, Roberto Corrigiano [*sic*] and Sigismondo Pandolfo Malatesta, the prince of all wickedness, both of whom promised Piccinino to desert to him. Roberto was summoned to the palace where he was murdered forthwith and flung through a window into the Piazza. Sigismondo, the poison of all Italy, who was reserved for greater crimes, saved himself by flight.

## SEVENTEEN

# *Endgame*

The career of Jacopo Piccinino, Niccolò's younger son and real heir, is tightly threaded into the vendetta between Federico and Sigismondo. Among the letters seized by the Sienese was one between Sigismondo and Jacopo, which revealed some discussion of a matrimonial alliance and a joint attack on Pesaro. Jacopo was now the principal loose cannon rolling about on the unsteady deck created by the Peace of Lodi. He commanded a following to which many others gravitated whose livelihood was threatened by peace. Although the speech by him as the epigraph of this book is taken from the autobiographical *Commentaries* of Pius II and their attribution is therefore highly suspect, the words undoubtedly encapsulate the views of the men-at-arms faced with the prospect of severely reduced revenues in what was a declining market even before Lodi. A peace-seeking pope, desire for a period of consolidation by the Medici and Sforza, and Venice's turn away from *terraferma* to a belated effort to salvage her trading empire in the Levant had left only the southern kingdom's war against Genoa as a steady source of employment. As Captain-General of Naples Federico was therefore not only the most favoured condottiere in Italy but also perfectly placed to sabotage any attempt of reconciliation between his employer and Sigismondo.

The Peace of Lodi did not last. The death of Nicholas V in 1455 and his succession by the corrupt and nepotistic Borgia Pope Callixtus III opened the door to renewed hostilities, with the Curia reverting to its traditional role of stirring up trouble in the hope of recovering lost domains. The Papacy's desire to divide and rule was most blatantly

Pisanello's 1436 portrait of Sigismondo's first wife Ginevra: her mother Parisina Malatesta was executed for adultery by her husband Niccolò III d'Este in 1425.

Matteo de' Pasti's 1446 medallion of Isotta degli Atti, with the heraldic Malatesta elephant on the obverse.

Isotta's magnificent sepulchre in the Tempio Malatestiano, showing the bronze plaque dated 1450 overlaid on the original inscription dated 1456.

Piero della Francesca's 1451 portrait of Sigismondo Malatesta, in which a restorer overpainted Sigismondo's auburn hair.

The imposing *mastio* of Castel Sismondo, with the Malatesta coat of arms and Sigismondo's name in gothic script on a panel by Matteo de' Pasti, repeated on the gatehouse beyond.

Piero della Francesca's 1465 diptych of Battista Sforza and Federico da Montefeltro, showing the scar of the infection on his cheek that nearly killed him in 1433, and the damage to the bridge of his nose from the jousting accident that destroyed his right eye in 1451.

The view as one enters the courtyard of the ducal palace in Urbino; the top line proclaims 'Federico Duke of Urbino, Count of Montefeltro and [Castel] Durante'.

Pedro Berruguete's 1481 portrait of Federico and his son Guidobaldo; note the insignia of the English Order of the Garter, the collar of the Neapolitan Order of the Ermine and the richly inlaid helmet top left, a gift from Ottoman Sultan Mehmed the Conqueror.

Exquisite marquetry (*intarsia*) incorporating illusionistic techniques in Federico da Montefeltro's private study (*studiolo*) at Urbino; above it there are 28 portraits of the wisest men in history, including his schoolmaster Vittorino da Feltre.

Piero della Francesca's provocative 1451 fresco in the sacristy of the Tempio Malatestiano: Sigismondo Malatesta kneels before Emperor Sigismund, thinly disguised at St Sigismund, with Manichaean dogs behind him and Castel Sismondo displayed in the oculus behind them.

Piero della Francesca's enigmatic *Flagellation of Christ*, painted in 1454: the two right-hand figures in the foreground are probably Guidantonio da Montefeltro and his heir Oddo Antonio II, who was murdered by Federico da Montefeltro ten years earlier.

Piero della Francesca's huge altarpiece, painted 1472–4 for the Osservanti di San Donato church in Urbino; when Federico (kneeling) died in 1482 it was moved to accompany his sepulchre in the church of San Bernardino.

Part of Benozzo Gozzoli's 1460 *Journey of the Magi* fresco in the Palazzo Medici-Riccardi, Florence, showing (left foreground) a properly red-haired Sigismondo Malatesta riding beside young Galeazzo Maria Sforza, heir apparent to the dukedom of Milan.

The dying Pope Pius II at Ancona, looking out for Christian warships that never answered his call for a crusade; from Pinturicchio's 1502–8 fresco cycle in the Piccolomini Library, Siena.

The della Rovere gang in Melozzo da Forlì's 1477 fresco for the Sistine Library: Pope Sixtus IV with nephews (left to right) Girolamo Riario, Giovanni della Rovere, Giuliano della Rovere – later Pope Julius II – and Raffaele Riario; the humanist Bartolomeo Platina kneels to be appointed the first Prefect of the Library.

revealed in one of Callixtus's last acts before he died in August 1458, two months after King Alfonso. The pope declared invalid the succession at Naples of Ferrante, who had been legitimated by Eugenius IV and recognised by Nicholas V. Callixtus declared the line of Aragon extinct and reclaimed Naples as a papal fief, which for added mischief he awarded to René of Anjou–Provence. Yet another ferocious civil war ensued in the southern kingdom, which lasted through the Papacy of Pius II. The further backdrop to the events we shall examine in this chapter was the contradictory but sincere effort of the Church to unify Christendom against the Ottoman conquest of the Balkans. Finally, Jacopo Piccinino's colourful career did not come to an end until he was treacherously captured and murdered by Ferrante in June–July 1464. Some nine months earlier, in a magnificent ceremony in Milan, Piccinino had married Francesco Sforza's daughter Drusiana. The Duke of Milan was notably unmoved by the death of his son-in-law, and there is little reason to doubt Drusiana's accusation that her father was the author of the murder and had used her marriage to lull Piccinino into a false sense of security. In sum, after the shock of the fall of Constantinople wore off it was business as usual in Italy.

The downfall of Sigismondo was accomplished in three stages. The first was a combined operation by Federico Montefeltro and Jacopo Piccinino in 1457–8, financed by King Alfonso, which ravaged the Fano hinterland and laid siege to Senigallia. An attempt by Borso d'Este to break up the alliance between Piccinino and Federico in May 1457 included arranging a meeting between Sigismondo and Federico at Borso's country estate at Belfiore, attended by representatives of Venice and Naples. The meeting ended in recriminations and drawn swords, for which Borso – the last dependable ally of Rimini – held Sigismondo primarily responsible. Meanwhile Alessandro Sforza of Pesaro discovered the adultery of his wife, Sveva, Oddo Antonio's sister married off to him by Federico in 1448, with one of his lieutenants. Alessandro claimed that it was part of a plot by Sveva and Sigismondo to overthrow him and the charge is credible. Sveva shared her sister Violante's hatred of Federico and later proved her capacity for leadership by rising to become the abbess of the nunnery to which she was consigned.* It is

* She was beatified as Sister Serafina in 1754.

by no means improbable that she seduced Alessandro's lieutenant in order to undo the web her brother's murderer had spun around Sigismondo. Whether Borso, who had his own problems with Alessandro, was also privy to the plot is less easy to say. It was, however, Sigismondo's last chance to recover Pesaro (which he may have falsely promised to cede to Piccinino) that made his failure to lull Federico into a false sense of security at the Belfiore meeting a fatal lapse from the level of *furbizia* the scheme required.

Sigismondo enjoyed a brief respite thanks to a quarrel between Federico and Piccinino following some indiscriminate looting by Piccinino's men, although they reunited to trounce Sigismondo's captain Antonello da Forlì at Carpegna in July 1458. The defeat knocked Sigismondo's kinsman Count Ramberto Malatesta of Carpegna out of the war, but apart from a few minor losses around Fano the lord of Rimini weathered the storm reasonably well in territorial terms. He was, however, compelled to suspend his programme of construction and to raise taxes repeatedly in order to defend his domain and, as we have seen, the real purpose of any war between a greater and a lesser power at this time was to bankrupt the lesser. This was clearly King Alfonso's intent, as confirmed by the escalation of his financial demands on Sigismondo to include the cost of Federico's and Piccinino's campaign. An indication of Sigismondo's desperation is that in November 1457 he bought a 20,000-ducat diamond from a Venetian merchant, for which he borrowed 5000 ducats; Rimini and Fano underwrote the balance. Intended as a peace offering to Alfonso, the jewel became simply another item added to the Neapolitan invoice by Alfonso's son Ferrante when his father died in late June 1458.

Rimini greeted the news of Alfonso's death with unseemly celebration and when this was followed by Pope Callixtus III's invalidation of Ferrante's succession Sigismondo's cup of joy, along with that of every other condottiere in Italy except Federico's, was filled to overflowing. Earlier in 1458 Federico and his brother Ottaviano also suffered the devastating loss of their sons Buonconte and Bernardino, who died of the plague at the Neapolitan court. The death of Buonconte, legitimated by Pope Nicholas V, left Federico without an heir – he had another illegitimate son, Antonio, but he was only eight years old and for reasons unknown Federico never had him legitimated, although he sponsored him to a highly successful career as a condottiere. Federico's first wife Gentile died in 1456, but he did not take another until 1460, when he married fifteen-year-old Battista, Alessandro Sforza's daughter by his first marriage to Costanza Varano, and she did not bear him a male heir until 1472. Meanwhile Sigismondo had married Isotta but they too suffered the irreparable loss of their only son Malatesta in 1458. Accordingly the endgame of their rivalry was fought out between two deeply embittered men who had reason to believe their bloodlines would die with them.

The second stage in the undoing of Sigismondo came about as a result of his attempts to exploit the disputed succession in Naples. Whatever chance there might have been to win from Ferrante a reconsideration of the crushing terms demanded by his father was thrown away by Sigismondo's contacts with Jean, René of Anjou–Provence's son, and with Count Gian'Antonio del Balzo Orsini, Prince of Taranto. There were two successions in play because Isabella, Balzo Orsini's eldest niece and presumptive heiress, was married to Ferrante. On the death of Gian' Antonio, therefore, Ferrante would acquire the enormous and quasi-independent principality of Taranto unless previously forced to renounce Isabella's inheritance. It was certainly imprudent of a minor princeling like Sigismondo to think he could deal himself a hand in the intricate dynastic affairs of kings, and also surprisingly naïve of him to believe his dealings with Ferrante's rivals would remain secret. When Sigismondo's emissary arrived at Naples with formal condolences for the death of Alfonso the man was severely beaten and sent back to Rimini with coarse suggestions about what Sigismondo might do with his condolences.

During the papal interregnum Piccinino made peace with Sigismondo and marched into Umbria to conquer a principality for himself. Assisi, Gualdo Tadino, Foligno and Nocera Umbra opened their gates to him and he besieged Spoleto. Confronted with the prospect of fighting Sigismondo face to face, Federico sought a truce and became the go-between for Ferrante and the new Pope Pius II. They concluded a secret alliance to renew Alfonso's strategy of taming the troublesome Piccinino with the prospect of a principality to be carved out of Sigismondo's domain, while overtly Pius offered to mediate between Naples and Rimini. All the other Italian powers were anxious to lance the festering boil of the Montefeltro–Malatesta vendetta once and for all, and since Federico was so well supported they chose to overlook the manifest bad faith of the pope. To concentrate fire on Sigismondo, in late 1458 Pius II bought back the towns seized by Piccinino for 30,000 ducats, while early in 1459 Ferrante commissioned Piccinino for 3000 cavalry and 500 infantry, and appointed him lieutenant-general at the fabulous annual salary of 96,000 ducats. Federico's role in all of this won him higher esteem in the eyes of his peers than any military success might have done.

If military prowess were the measure of a ruler Sigismondo's performance in 1459–61 would have been his apotheosis. Bankrupt, with many enemies and no real friends, he and his people put up a heroic last stand against the combined forces of Naples and the Papacy, led by Piccinino and guided by the deadly intelligence of Federico. During the early winter months of 1459 Piccinino and Federico marched almost at will through the Rimini hinterland, capturing fifty-seven villages. Only twenty surrendered without a fight; the rest were sacked and burned in accordance with the custom of the time. In May Sigismondo was finally compelled to accept the pope's mediation, which unsurprisingly confirmed Ferrante's impossible financial demands. Pius II ruled that Sigismondo should surrender Senigallia, Montemarciano, Mondavio, Morro d'Alba, Pergola and Sassocorvaro to the Church until he had paid the debt, and rubbed salt in the wound by requiring him to surrender a dozen towns to Federico to compensate him for the cost of his campaign against Sigismondo, plus interest. These included Castel d'Elci, Certaldo, Monte Cerignone, Montesecco and Pietrarubbia in the Montefeltro, and San Costanzo on the Metauro–Cesano watershed between Senigallia and Fano. There were popular rebellions against the settlement, the most significant at Pietrarubbia where the massacre of the Montefeltri in 1298 was still a treasured folk memory. It is likely that Venice and Milan interceded to prevent the pope carrying out his plan to complete the destruction of Sigismondo's state at this time, although one would not guess it from Pius's description in his autobiography:

> The Pope, though he had the power to make any decision he pleased about Sigismondo, nevertheless considered it disgraceful to consider

victory rather than justice and for a long time strove to settle the quarrel to the satisfaction of both sides. When he failed, he released both the king and Sigismondo from their agreement, uncertain whether a war of this kind or peace was more advantageous for the Church, since it was common knowledge that Piccinino could not keep quiet and if he were freed from the war with Sigismondo, he would probably turn his arms against the Church. Pius therefore came to the conclusion that it was God's will that peace could not be arranged.

### GEORGE 'SKANDERBEG' CASTRIOTI (1405–68)

**Skanderbeg, the national hero of Albania, was among those drawn into the war of succession in Naples. Like Jan Hunyadi of Hungary and Vlad Dracula of Wallachia, Skanderbeg had received financial support from Alfonso and Ferrante to resist the Ottoman advance in the Balkans. Skanderbeg repaid his debt by crossing the Adriatic to fight for Ferrante against the Anjou–Provence pretender and was instrumental in tipping the balance in Ferrante's favour.**

Attention did indeed now shift back to Piccinino, who had neither received the salary nor the lands promised to him by Ferrante and consequently enlisted in the cause of Anjou–Provence. Federico was badly shaken by the refusal of the inhabitants of Malatestaland to accept his authority, which he complained to the pope was the result of Sigismondo's recalcitrance, but he could not ignore Ferrante's order to combine forces with Alessandro Sforza and prevent Piccinino from marching south. They failed to do so and in July 1460 Piccinino and Balzo Orsini stormed Sarno, only thirty miles east of Naples. Later that month they brought Federico and Alessandro to battle at San Fabiano in Puglia, where for seven hours some 10,000 cavalry milled about inconclusively until Piccinino made belated use of his greater number of infantry to claim the day for Anjou. During much of the battle Federico was in bed with a back injury sustained in an earlier skirmish, but although unable to wear armour because of the pain, he successfully led the Aragonese reserves to cover the retreat.

The struggle for the southern kingdom ended when Jean of Anjou and Balzo Orsini ran out of funds early in 1461. No money no Piccinino, who deserted the Angevin cause and set out on an independent looting expedition. The decisive battle in the war was probably the defeat of René of Anjou at faraway Genoa in July 1462, but Balzo Orsini did not drop out until defeated by Alessandro Sforza and Skanderbeg near Troia in August 1462. Finally, at Arce in August 1463 (where he supposedly spoke the epigraph of this book), Piccinino was brought to bay outnumbered nearly two to one. Even so he was able to negotiate an agreement with Naples, Milan and the Papacy to appoint him joint captain-general with Federico, at an annual salary of 45,000 ducats. In addition his right to the domain he had conquered in the Abruzzi was recognised, his nominee was appointed Chancellor of Naples and he was given Sforza's daughter in marriage. For the next eighteen months Jacopo Piccinino was outrageously flattered, mainly by Sforza, until he made the fatal error of delivering himself into Ferrante's hands.

While the struggle for the south was unresolved Sigismondo made a last effort to recover his position. Pius II's outrageous bias had extended to casting doubt on the legitimacy of Violante's claim to the Montefeltro and for once the Malatesta brothers stood together against a hostile world. There were also old ties of friendship between Piccinino and Domenico, and when the three men met at Cesena in January 1460 they secretly agreed to throw in their lot with Jean of Anjou. Before marching south Piccinino surrendered his conquests to the brothers, an act that drove Pius II over the edge. The pope now added a demand for unpaid tribute to the burden already laid on Sigismondo, a measure regarded as patently unjustified by every ruler except Ferrante. It was at this point that Pius's malice passed over into the realm of the ridiculous, finally making him a *brutta figura* even in the eyes of Federico and undoing the consensus that Sigismondo was the principal obstacle to peace. That title clearly now belonged to Piccinino and the pope's insistence that Sigismondo was still the curse of Italy brought him into disrepute.

With some Angevin money to hand Sigismondo began his 1460 campaign by throwing Federico's men out of Uffigliano, which they were fortifying although the pope had not yet awarded it to Urbino. That was, however, the only move he made specifically against Federico or Alessandro Sforza, which in the circumstances suggests unwonted *furbizia* – perhaps some tacit pact among them. Instead he made war against the Church authorities, taking back Montemarciano, reconquering Mondavio and besieging Senigallia, where to his chagrin the fine defences he had built now stood against him. He also intervened to exacerbate a local conflict between Ancona and Iesi, crown jewels of the papal Marche. The pope's appeals for assistance fell on deaf ears – even Duke Francesco Sforza, who hated Piccinino but feared the Angevins, urged Pius to moderate the demands that had driven Sigismondo into rebellion. Pius somehow found the funds to field a papal army against Sigismondo, led by the middle-ranking condottiere Ludovico Malvezzi, who enjoyed some minor success around Senigallia and Ancona in 1460. Malvezzi was joined by another force led by Pietro Paolo Nardini in early 1461, but even with 3000 cavalry and 2000 infantry to Sigismondo's 1300 and 1000, they were not eager to advance on Rimini. Pausing to pawn his household gold and silver, Sigismondo sought them out instead and in July near Nidastore, in the Cesano valley, stormed their camp and utterly routed them, killing Nardini and capturing their stores, the papal banners blessed by Pius II himself and all their horses except forty, on which the remaining papal officers fled.

Sigismondo did not follow up the victory, expecting the pope to come to terms. Both were now without funds but excommunications and pronouncements freeing Malatesta subjects from obedience to their lords poured out of Rome, as in the good old days. These having no effect, at Christmas 1461 a solemn farce was enacted at Rome where a papal advocate presented the College of Cardinals with a list of charges against Sigismondo including rapine, wilful fire-raising, slaughter, rape, adultery, incest, parricide, sacrilege, treason, lèse-majesté and heresy. The advocate prayed His Holiness to listen to, in Dennistoun's words, 'the suppliant voices of those who could no longer endure the tyrant's cruel yoke, and to avenge them by at length freeing Italy from a foul and abominable monster, in whose cities no good man's life was safe'. Federico Montefeltro and Alessandro Sforza then joined the proceedings, 'alleging that many of the culprit's worst enormities had been passed over; that his treacheries equalled the number of his transactions, that none ever trusted him without being betrayed, that he scoffed not at one or another point of faith, but at the whole evangelical system, in utter ignorance of religion'.

The Duke of Milan also weighed in with a written accusation that Sigismondo had murdered Polissena in 1449 and had led the gang rape of the 'Duchess of Bavaria' in 1450. Having achieved Sigismondo's condemnation to death for heresy by the College of Cardinals, Pius now invented a unique ceremony of canonising him to hell, that is declaring him as surely elected to the company of Satan as the saints were to the entourage of God. This was followed by the burning of effigies on the steps of the Roman cathedrals, with scrolls issuing from their mouths reading 'Here am I, Sigismondo Malatesta, son of Pandolfo, king of traitors, foe of God and man, condemned to the flames by the sentence of the Sacred College'. Even Federico and Alessandro cringed to be involved in such petulance and the damage done to the pope's authority was not confined to Italy. At the end of Pius II's life, three years later, when he sat on his throne at Ancona looking out over the Adriatic in vain for the response of Christendom to his convocation to a Crusade (see Pinturicchio's fresco, Picture section 2, p. 8), it was supremely ironic that the only Christian lord at that time fighting the Ottomans was Sigismondo, decanonised from hell and carrying a papal banner.

One of life's certainties is that when you are down additional troubles jostle with each other to add to your burdens, and so it was with Sigismondo. On receipt of a flattering letter from Sultan Mehmet II, the conqueror of Constantinople (the simplest Ottoman correspondence was extremely flowery), he sent Matteo de' Pasti with a reply and a manuscript copy of his councillor Roberto Valturio's *De Re Militari*, a treatise on warfare dedicated to Sigismondo and widely circulated in Europe even before it was printed in 1472. In November 1461 the Venetian authorities in Crete arrested Pasti and confiscated the letter and the book. They found nothing untoward in either and released Pasti in December, but the episode gave birth to far-spreading rumours that Sigismondo had appealed to the sultan for assistance against the pope and had sent him a military map of Italy. We need look no further than the pages of the popular press in our own time to see that there is an assumption of guilt whenever someone is arrested, and that a subsequent release without charges never has the same resonance. Against which it would have been only prudent for Sigismondo to have refrained from correspondence with the great ogre of Europe or at least to clear it first with Venice, his ally of last resort: but discretion never stood a chance in any contest with his vanity.

At some point in 1462 Sigismondo wrote a despairing letter to Federico saying there was no reason for either to seek the overthrow of the other at the behest of the pope, 'who wished to see both destroyed'. It was far too late for that, but other Romagna lords saw their own interests threatened. In August, accompanied by the future Pino III Ordelaffi of Forlì and Count Gian' Francesco Pico della Mirandola, Sigismondo again besieged Senigallia, which capitulated with suspicious alacrity on the 12th. His moment of triumph was short-lived: at the urgent request of the pope Ferrante released Federico to salvage the situation in the Marche. Federico came too late to prevent the fall of Senigallia but arrived outside its walls with a far larger force than Sigismondo and his associates commanded. Not waiting to be trapped inside the city, they escaped in a night march towards Fano on the 15th, but were caught by Federico's cavalry when crossing the Cesano river. Pico della Mirandola and his men were captured, and Ordelaffi escaped alone, saved by his exceptionally large and powerful horse. Sigismondo was harried all the way to Fano and lost most of his men.

This time Federico was determined to finish him off. He was joined by the Malatesta Count of Sogliano and by contingents from San Marino, from minor Marecchia lords including the Bagni, and by the peasant condottiere Antonello da Forlì, once Sigismondo's most trusted captain but hired away from him by Francesco Sforza in July 1461. All Sigismondo's holdings between the Foglia and the Conca with the exception of Gradara fell to Federico in August, as did Scorticata and San Giovanni in Galilea to his Sogliano cousins and Talamello to Antonello da Forlì. In October–November he lost the vital fortresses of Savignano, Sant'Arcangelo and, the unkindest cut of all, Verucchio. The ancestral heart of Malatestaland and the key to the Rimini coastal plain fell when Federico, using a copy of Sigismondo's personal seal provided by a Rimini exile, sent the commander of the Verucchio garrison a letter advising him that a troop of reinforcements would soon be arriving from Rimini. The 'reinforcements' were twenty of Federico's men, led by defectors from Sigismondo's army who were familiar with the current passwords, and once inside the gates they quickly overpowered the garrison.

Sigismondo, meanwhile, left the defence of Fano to his son Roberto and sailed to Apulia, where he made a desperate appeal to Jean of Anjou and Jacopo Piccinino. They, however, had recently suffered defeat at Troia and were faced with the imminent defection of Balzo Orsini, so they could offer Sigismondo nothing. On his way back Sigismondo was blown by a storm to Ragusa and continued overland to Venice, where he arrived at the end of October. The republic fired a diplomatic warning shot across Pius II's bow at this time, not for any love of Sigismondo but to indicate that they felt their own interests – specifically with regard to Montemarciano, sold to them by Sigismondo – were not being sufficiently considered. The Venetians also promised to guarantee Domenico Malatesta's core domain in exchange for the valuable salt flats at Cervia, long claimed by the Church.

In November Domenico's men struck a blow at the jackals closing in on the brothers. Astorre II Manfredi of Faenza, by now acutely anxious to get off Ferrante's blacklist, made a deal with Pius II to attack Domenico's domain if the pope would prevail on Ferrante to forgive him. Astorre's men seized the Rocca delle Caminate and laid waste the lands around Meldola, until Domenico's garrison sortied from Bertinoro and routed the invaders. Pius II was not dissatisfied with the outcome: his purpose had been to complete the isolation of Sigismondo and Venice now requested a truce on Domenico's behalf, which permitted the pope to make a show of magnanimity. Pius II also kept his word to Astorre, who thereby dodged the axe that the House of Aragon had long yearned to apply to his neck.

Federico completed a clean sweep of the Montefeltro in the spring of 1463, reducing Sigismondo's holdings to Rimini, Fano, Senigallia, Gradara, San Costanzo and Mondolfo. Even now, *in extremis*, Sigismondo was able to promote a rebellion in Pesaro in March, but that was his last kick. Conceivably he might have saved more from the wreck had he been able to inflict a severe reverse on Federico, because now not only the Venetians but also Sforza in Milan had become convinced that Pius II's intention was no longer to punish Sigismondo but to create a state for his own family. They were not wrong. In the final settlement the pope gave Senigallia and Mondavio to his 'nephew'

Antonio Piccolomini. The pope also wished to give his nephew Fano but was thwarted by the College of Cardinals, where he had exhausted much of his credit with the farce of Sigismondo's canonisation into hell.

In advance of the final settlement the Venetians took possession of Cervia and declared that Domenico was under their protection, which the enraged pope was forced to accept. Senigallia and Fano held out for Sigismondo well into 1463 before capitulating, after which Federico showed how very far-sighted he was by treating Roberto with the greatest courtesy, even granting Sigismondo's son an honour guard when he departed from Fano. Alessandro Sforza was bitterly disappointed not to get Senigallia in the division of spoils and felt cheated when he only received Gradara, which he believed was already his by right. San Marino, the Count of Sogliano, the Bagni and others received some rewards, but the big winner was Federico. He was recognised as lord of the whole of the Montefeltro, most of the Marecchia valley and all the territory between the Conca and the Metauro rivers except the coast.

Thanks to the intercession of Venice Sigismondo was allowed to keep Rimini and its immediate environs for his lifetime against an annual tribute to Rome of 1000 florins, but first he and his subjects were required to confess their heresy, beg for pardon and receive absolution. Sigismondo firmly rejected Pius II's demand that he go to Rome – he would have been insane to do so – but after a three-day fast and a public act of contrition in Rimini, at the feet of a cardinal legate sent from Rome as the pope's proxy, he was pardoned on 2 December 1463. He does not appear to have been as devastated by the experience as one would expect. Three days after his act of contrition Sigismondo wrote to Piero de' Medici asking him to send some hunting dogs. The only reference to his situation came at the end of the letter where he wrote, 'I find my situation to be the opposite of the popular saying that he who has few possessions has little to think about; I am left with few possessions and much to think about.'

## EIGHTEEN

# *Strange Crusade*

Although the rest of Sigismondo's life was dramatic enough to stand out in the career of any normal man, for him it was tragically anticlimactic. In March 1464 he won a two-year commission from Venice with a monthly salary of 300 ducats to lead an expedition of 3000 horse and 5000 foot, including 1200 of his own cavalry, against the Ottomans in Morea (the Peloponnese), where the last outpost of the Byzantine Empire had capitulated in 1460. Venice still held a string of islands and held several mainland fortresses along the southern coast of Morea (Map 9). The key to Morea was the Isthmus of Corinth and in 1463 Bertoldo, nephew of Marquis Borso d'Este, led 13,000 men to Nauplia and took Argos before marching on Corinth. There he rebuilt the demolished Examilion Walls across the isthmus, said to have been comparable to the Theodosian Walls at Constantinople. The walls were not complete when the inevitable Ottoman counter-attack arrived and Bertoldo was mortally wounded defending them. Local command devolved to the Venetian admiral. Sigismondo's command was originally intended to reinforce the Examilion front but by the time he sailed in June 1464 the Venetians had lost the walls, so he was sent to Kalamata in southern Morea to open a second front.

What could have been his moment of redemption became instead a sad coda of wasted heroism and spitefully frustrated endeavour. In 1462 Sigismondo had married off his pregnant mistress, Aritrea (see Appendix E), to the Venetian oligarch Andrea Dandolo with the promise of a generous dowry, but amid the collapse of his domain he was unable to pay it. For reasons that will become apparent when we examine the political backdrop, the Venetians appointed Dandolo as *provveditore* (comptroller) for Sigismondo's expedition and he did everything in his power to ensure that it should fail, while blackguarding Sigismondo in confidential dispatches. Richly though Sigismondo earned his humiliation in 1462–3, one would have to be very hard-hearted to deny sympathy for his plight during the Morea campaign. Despite only receiving half the promised men and with Dandolo withholding supplies and even the soldiers' pay, he still managed to shake the Ottoman hold on southern Morea. If Sigismondo had been backed properly he might have given Venice a few more cards to play in their centuries-long game of geopolitical poker with the Ottoman Empire.

**Map 9**
**THE MOREA CAMPAIGN**
**1464-65**

The political background to the episode is that the Venetians only prevented Pius II from foreclosing on Sigismondo because they wished to establish themselves more solidly in Rimini with an eye to taking possession of the city for themselves. Pius II, of course, wanted Sigismondo gone to secure Rimini for his own family. Both the Venetians and the pope thought they would only have to deal with Isotta and her favourite stepsons Sallustio and Valerio, and overlooked the able and intelligent Roberto Malatesta. Roberto quietly cultivated Sforza in Milan, from whom he obtained a commission, also his uncle Domenico in Cesena who seems to have intended to appoint him his heir, and even the Medici in Florence. At some point, too, Roberto made confidential contact with Federico Montefeltro, which was to flower into an alliance to thwart both the Venetians and the Papacy. There appears to have been a genuine liking between Federico and Roberto, perhaps because each had been the less-favoured son, and in Roberto the Malatesta clan recovered the *furbizia* whose lack had contributed so much to the downfall of his father. While Sigismondo lived, however, Isotta ran Rimini and skilfully navigated the dark currents of conspiracy and treachery that swirled around her.

During 1464–5 it seemed possible that Sigismondo might yet redeem the family fortunes, particularly after Pius II died in August 1464 and was succeeded by the Venetian Paul II. The new pope, a nephew of Eugenius IV, was determined to undo Pius II's nepotistic legacy. Paul II was also initially inclined to encourage Humanist studies, but after he reversed course in 1466 one of those who landed in prison was Bartolomeo Platina, later the Vatican librarian (Picture section 2, p. 8) and author of *Vitae pontificum*, the first biographical study of the popes. Platina depicted Paul II as a vain and effeminate pederast, which may not have been far from the truth. Paul II liked to dress up in a decidedly 'camp' style and liked the company of young boys, but he was also a determined papal imperialist who brought an end, among others, to the troublesome Orsini of Anguillara dynasty. In addition, he moved swiftly to take possession of Cesena after Domenico Malatesta died and would have done the same in Rimini after Sigismondo died if Federico and Roberto had not secretly combined against him.

When Sigismondo finally disentangled himself from Morea he travelled to Rome three times during 1466 and on the second occasion was stunned to be told by his son-in-law Giulio Cesare da Varano that the pope intended to make him surrender Rimini in exchange for Spoleto and Foligno. This was presumably a trial balloon because when Paul II learned that Sigismondo had reacted with murderous rage the pope chose not to press the issue, yielding to Sigismondo's tearful entreaty and even granting him a small pension. The canonical accounts have Sigismondo falling ill on his way home, at last a broken man, and never recovering. In fact he travelled to Rome again later in 1466 and once more in June 1468, when he was awarded a 4000-florin commission by the pope. Sigismondo's final illness took hold when returning home with this late, if small, reaffirmation of his worth. A possible explanation for the aborted offer to exchange Rimini for Spoleto and Foligno is that Paul II thought Sigismondo, who was physically diminished and visibly ill, was no longer strong enough to hold Rimini. Convinced by Sigismondo's passionate commitment the pope gave him the means to resist Venetian blandishments instead. It would have been wiser to have Sigismondo killed, as either Paul II's predecessor or his successor would have done without hesitation.

Although Sigismondo did not die in the Morea the malaria he brought back from the campaign, which was arguably his most remarkable military achievement, ultimately killed him. The capital of Morea was Mystras, near ancient Sparta, now a hilltop ruin and a UNESCO World Heritage Site but in its time one of the most important cities of the Byzantine Empire and a centre of scholarship second only to Constantinople. Its most famous recent resident had been the neo-Platonist philosopher Plethon, who captivated Sigismondo in 1439 when returning from a failed ecumenical meeting in 1438 between the Orthodox and Roman Catholic Churches. It was, therefore, doubly a magnet for Sigismondo, who after a failed siege of the Ottoman fortress at Mitilene midway between the Venetian ports of Kalamata and Modon, set about clearing the Maina peninsula.

### GEORGE GEMISTHOS 'PLETHON' (1355–1452)

**Plethon was exiled from Constantinople by Emperor Manuel II at the urging of the Aristotelian George Scholaris, later Patriarch Gennadius II. In 1438 Plethon and Scholaris accompanied Emperor John VIII to the Council of Ferrara, an attempt to effect the union of the Eastern and Western Churches. During the visit Plethon was invited to teach at Florence by Cosimo de' Medici, who founded the *Platonica Accademia* in his honour.**

Unfortunately Sigismondo's unpaid soldiers behaved brutally towards the Greek population with the result that far from supporting their fellow Christians, they implored the Ottomans to rescue them. Sigismondo was compelled to hang twenty of his men and put a further hundred or so in chains, and shipped some unruly Venetian captains back to Venice for punishment. With order restored and in the absence of pay he sent his men to raid Ottoman settlements for loot, until finally in late August he led an assault on Mystras. The town fell to him but the citadel held out and he was soon besieged in turn by the Bey of Morea. Sigismondo did not let himself be trapped inside the walls and led an active defence against greatly superior forces until his ranks were winnowed by malaria and he himself fell ill. Having first smuggled the remains of Gemisthos Plethon through the enemy lines he led a breakout in late December and made a fighting retreat to Modon, where he used up his last energies to get Dandolo recalled and then collapsed to remain at death's door for many weeks.

News of his imminent demise caused the Venetians and the Papacy to unmask their guns. By the terms of Sigismondo's commission Venice had already sent 150 men-at-arms to Rimini and now sent 200 more, unsolicited, to support Isotta and Sallustio. Paul II found that his predecessor's Piccolomini nephew at Fano controlled the papal contingency plan to occupy Rimini upon the death of Sigismondo and scrambled to create an alternative. Intriguingly, neither the old nor the new papal plan to secure Rimini included any significant role for Papal Captain-General Federico Montefeltro. Roberto Malatesta, meanwhile, set out from Milan at the head of a troop supplied by Sforza and joined forces with his uncle Domenico at Cesena, ready to intervene. Sigismondo had wisely taken the eldest sons of forty leading Rimini families with him to Morea as hostages, but news of his death emboldened some of the Rimini notables to show their hands. Isotta swiftly stamped out the flickers of rebellion by having one of Sigismondo's counsellors, who imprudently let it be known that he favoured the succession of Roberto, tortured and publicly executed. However, it was not until news of Sigismondo's recovery arrived that the forces poised to intervene from Fano, Cesena and Venice dispersed.

As 1465 progressed it became increasingly apparent that Venice wished to make as little investment as possible in Sigismondo's Morea expedition, which in combination with the otherwise inexplicable appointment of his enemy Andrea Dandolo as *provveditore* to the expedition confirmed that the real purpose all along had been to keep Sigismondo away from Italy, maybe permanently. Despite this, Sigismondo led two attacks out of the Coron peninsula towards Corinth, seized Mantinea as a base and with only 1000 men successfully attacked an Ottoman camp of about the same number of soldiers, coming away with hundreds of horses, cattle, mules and swine, much additional booty and 2000 eunuchs – the Ottoman army did not believe in roughing it. He was finally given permission to break his commission in November, returning to Rimini with only thirty or forty men in December, his safe arrival greeted with spontaneous popular celebrations not only in Rimini but also across many parts of Malatestaland now in the hands of others.

When Domenico Malatesta felt his death was imminent in August 1465 he sent for Roberto, who was promptly released by Sforza and took up residence in Cesena. Domenico died in November and Roberto, with the full support of his newly widowed aunt Violante, proclaimed himself the heir to Cesena and Bertinoro. Paul II acted swiftly and ordered Federico to enforce the agreement made in 1462, whereby Domenico's domain reverted to the Church upon his death. Federico made a display of military force outside Cesena but pressured the pope into giving Roberto a small estate between the Bidente and Ronco rivers including Meldola and the Rocca delle Caminate, 2500 ducats for the munitions stored in Cesena castle and an annual stipend of 3000 ducats. There was no reason for the pope to make any concession whatever and the generosity of the settlement argues that Paul II knew he could not depend on Federico. As a quid pro quo when Violante entered a nunnery the following year she surrendered her claim to the Montefeltro lands due to her by inheritance and dowry to Federico, the man who had dispossessed her, and not to the Church in whose bosom she spent the rest of her life.

In March 1466 Francesco Sforza died and was succeeded by his twenty-two-year-old son Galeazzo Maria, a man with no military experience or inclination who seems to have inherited a taste for opulence and cruelty from his Visconti mother. The circumstance awoke the ambition of Bartolomeo Colleoni, the brilliant Venetian captain-general, to seize Milan for himself. During 1466 he conspired with a band of wealthy Florentine exiles who wanted to use him to overthrow

Piero de' Medici, but also with the dispossessed Anguillara clan and with Galeazzo Maria's uncle Alessandro of Pesaro, plus a number of others who had designs on the Papal State. For the condottieri of Italy it was 'happy days are here again'. Early in 1467 the Venetian Senate gave Colleoni its blessing and, joined by Ercole, Duke Borso d'Este's half-brother and future successor, by Giovanni II Bentivoglio and some disgruntled Visconti, he embarked on a campaign in Romagna that culminated at Molinella in July, when he fought a Papal–Florentine–Milanese army led by Federico. The forces involved were more than double the size of any other battle in the 1460s, perhaps 7000 cavalry on either side, but Colleoni had 6000 infantry to Federico's 3500 and also employed massed artillery for the first time in Italian military history. Despite these advantages the battle was a draw and some accounts credit counter-attacks by Astorre II Manfredi and by Ercole d'Este, who was severely wounded, with saving Colleoni's army from outright defeat.* After nightfall Colleoni and Federico met to agree on an untroubled disengagement; a little later reinforcements arrived from Naples for Federico, Colleoni fell ill and his 'glorious enterprise' evaporated. Somehow the great survivor Astorre II Manfredi, although attacked by Colleoni at the start and by Federico at the end of 1467, emerged with his domain intact. Although Roberto had a commission from Federico he played little part in the campaign, emphasising how peripheral the Malatesti had become to the politics of Romagna.

Unlike Domenico, long an invalid, nobody expected the potent Sigismondo to be removed from the chessboard so young (he was only fifty-one when he died in October 1468) and he himself made no great effort to assure the succession of the Sallustio and Valerio faction. Possibly this was because of his grandiosity and lack of interest in life after death, but a more likely explanation is that he saw himself in Roberto and knew there was little he could do to thwart the triumph of the fittest. Sigismondo's death ushered in a display of *furbizia* at its most refined by Roberto and his secret ally Federico. Federico was now the pre-eminent condottiere, commissioned Captain-General of the Church, then Naples and then Florence in 1465–8 and refusing a very

---

* Despite this a large but sadly deteriorated fresco of the battle, attributed to Romanino, is in the courtyard of Colleoni's Malpaga castle at Cavernago in Bergamo province.

generous offer and the same rank from Venice. In September 1468, probably on learning that Sigismondo was unlikely to recover, Federico did not renew his papal commission and became Captain-General of Milan. Roberto remained in Rome, under commission to the Church, and reached back into family memory to revive the *furbizia* of Guastafamiglia in 1331: on receipt of a letter from Isotta and Sallustio begging him to return to Rimini to defend the city against papal forces, he took the letter to the pope and requested permission to take Rimini for the Church. Paul II fell for it, promised to give him Senigallia and Mondavio (at the expense of the Piccolomini) and gave him 1000 florins. Roberto marched into Rimini, evicted the Venetian garrison from Castel Sismondo and then wrote to Rome:

> Holy Father, no divine or human law can oblige a man, through his own submission, to deliver up his own. It is true that I have promised to act in such a way as to take possession of Rimini and I have done so; but the Holy Father will forgive me if I do not now hand it over to him; I ought not and had no right to promise to do so. I remain the faithful vassal and good son of the Holy Seat; but Your Holiness will approve [!] that I should live and die within the walls of the city, where I was born and where the remains of my father and my ancestors repose.

One would have liked to be a fly on the wall when Paul II opened that missive, and again when he discovered that Federico had stitched up an informal agreement among Milan, Naples and Florence to preserve the independence of Rimini. In 1469, after concluding an alliance with Venice, the pope put together an army of 5000 men, half cavalry and half infantry, under Alessandro Sforza of Pesaro and Napoleone Orsini, a claimant to Tagliacozzo (a large domain at the frontier between Naples and the Papal State) in rivalry with the Colonna. This was *furbo:* Duke Galeazzo Maria would be hesitant to deepen the rift with his uncle, who was also Federico's father-in-law (he had married Alessandro's daughter Battista in 1460) and Ferrante of Naples favoured the Orsini over the Colonna. Roberto had only a few hundred men-at-arms and Venice was not letting through any supplies by sea, so when the papal army arrived at the gates of Rimini its commanders must have thought the city would capitulate at the mere sight of them. Their confident complacency was soon dispersed by a ferocious sortie that left fifty dead and twice as many wounded, and they settled down to a formal siege, looking over their shoulders at Federico's army camped to the south of San Marino. In July Federico's commission as Captain-General of Milan was renewed for another year and after eighteen squadrons of cavalry joined him from Naples in early August he marched down to the coastal plain and took possession of Cerasolo, near Coriano, one of the few places left to Rimini in the 1463 settlement. The significance of the move, however, is that it placed Federico across Alessandro Sforza's line of communication with his Pesaro domain and as such could not have been more provocative.

Most accounts date Federico's apotheosis as the premier condottiere of Italy to the reduction of rebel Volterra in 1472, but it was at Mulazzano on 30 August 1469 that he won the title of *furbissimo*. Constrained by peremptory instructions not to initiate hostilities, he needled his opponents by going forward with a small party to make a display on a hill near their lines. The traditional 'mooning' by his troops and trumpet raspberries had the desired effect and when Alessandro sent a detachment to avenge the insults Federico fell back from the hill and lured them into an ambush led by Roberto, who had broken out of Rimini earlier. As the fighting escalated Federico fed reinforcements to Roberto until the papal forces fell back on their camp at Mulazzano. It is intriguing that although his paymasters knew very well that Federico had engineered the whole thing, they accepted that the papal forces had drawn first blood and that he was therefore entitled to counter-attack. This he did in an all-day assault led by Roberto that ended with both the papal captains wounded, many of their condottieri captured and the loss of all their baggage and artillery, which Federico turned over to Roberto.

Thus equipped, Roberto rapidly induced nine papal *castelli* in the Rimini hinterland to capitulate, including Montescudo, Monte Colombo and Saludecio, while Federico handed over Cerasolo to him and marched south to capture thirty more villages around Fano, which he also handed over to Roberto. In due course Roberto gave them back to the Church in exchange for recognition of his hereditary right to Rimini, which was what Federico intended all along: he wanted Rimini to be independent, but not strong enough to threaten his own domain. At the time, however, the threat to Alessandro Sforza's Pesaro from Roberto in the north and Federico to the south was patent and led to a rebuke in January 1470 from Galeazzo Maria for putting the interests of Urbino over those of Milan. This gave Federico the excuse he was looking for to resign his commission as Captain-General of Milan and, in May, to accept a better offer from Venice. Since this, very clearly, signalled that Venice would not now move against Roberto, the apoplectic pope was forced to negotiate.

During 1470 Sallustio and Valerio were murdered, the first allegedly by a relative of the Bagni – highly unlikely, given that the Bagni were among Roberto's most determined enemies. According to Roberto's account of the incident, incriminating evidence was found in the man's house and he, Roberto, was unfortunately unable to arrive in time to prevent an angry crowd from hacking the suspect to death. He was less circumspect about Valerio, who was murdered near Longiano by hired assassins, but he did give both his half-brothers splendid funerals. As he did Isotta when she died in 1474: rumours that Roberto had her poisoned persist, but there is no reason to doubt that she had no desire to live bereft of all power and with Roberto's mother Vanetta dei Toschi, who only outlived her for less than a year, triumphant.

Roberto was formally betrothed to Federico's young daughter Elisabetta in April 1471 at an elaborate ceremony in Urbino attended by most of the Romagna and Marche lords, and representatives from Naples, Milan and Venice. Elisabetta was one of seven girls born to Federico and Battista Sforza, and if they had not at last had a boy, Guidobaldo, in 1472, the dynastic significance of a Malatesta marriage might have fundamentally altered the history of their little corner of Italy. Pope Paul II died in July and was succeeded after a short conclave by Cardinal Francesco della Rovere, who took the name Sixtus IV. Had his immediate successors not included the infamous Rodrigo Borgia (Alexander VI) and his many children including the deadly Cesare and the much-defamed Lucrezia, Sixtus's claim to being the most nepotistic pope of all time would have been secure. Federico cemented a dynastic alliance with the Rovere by the marriage in 1474 of his eldest daughter Giovanna to papal *nipote* Giovanni, Duke of Sora in the southern Papal State, and was himself made Duke of Urbino by Sixtus IV. Later in 1474

Federico assured in arms his new son-in-law's possession of Senigallia and Mondavio, which remained in the possession of the Rovere family until 1624. No doubt the Piccolomini Pope Pius III, elected in 1503, would have reversed the situation, but he died within a month and was succeeded by Julius II, the most famous Rovere of them all.

Only after Guidobaldo was born and the Rovere alliance secure did Federico permit the marriage of Roberto and Elisabetta in June 1475. Roberto served the Church, sometimes as a loyal lieutenant of Federico and sometimes independently, until February 1479 when he and other condottieri resigned from papal service citing unpaid commissions and other acts of disrespect. While probably true, the more certain reason why they now switched their allegiance to Florence was because the Medici were in deep trouble and offered them very generous inducements – in Roberto's case the rank of captain-general and double his previous salary to 44,000 florins in time of war and 36,000 in time of peace. A very strange campaign followed in which Roberto led one of two Florentine–Venetian armies and Federico one of two Papal–Neapolitan armies, and they contrived not to fight each other. In June at Passignano on Lake Trasimene Roberto defeated the second enemy army led by Matteo di Capua and captured the whole Neapolitan wagon park of 1400 carts, while in September Federico defeated the second Florentine army at Poggibonsi. To the surprise of his captains Federico failed to pursue the fleeing enemy soldiers, permitting them to join Roberto at San Casciano (Map 7). Arguing that his road to Florence was blocked, Federico applied the sledgehammer of his large army to the fortified village of Colle di Val d'Elsa, which saw him through to the end of the campaigning season. There is no proof of collusion between the two men to bring about a mutually profitable stalemate, but the circumstantial evidence is strong.

To backtrack a few years, on 26 December 1476 Galeazzo Maria Sforza was stabbed to death in the church of Santo Stefano by an odd trio, one each from the noble Lampugnani and Visconti families and the third, Gerolamo Olgiati, a republican who appears to have believed he was the reincarnation of Brutus. Lampugnani was lucky to be killed on the spot; the other two were cruelly executed a few days later. Galeazzo Maria's seven-year-old son Gian' Galeazzo succeeded under the tutelage of his mother, but power gravitated towards his swarthy uncle Ludovico, known as 'the Moor', who finally took over the regency in 1480. Perhaps inspired by the assassination of Galeazzo Maria, during 1477 the pope's nephew Girolamo Riario, with his uncle's knowledge and support, plotted to decapitate the Florentine state by assassinating the brothers Lorenzo I and Giuliano de' Medici in order to seize the principality for himself. What is known to history as the Pazzi conspiracy was in fact the Salviati–Rovere conspiracy: the Salviati were the papal bankers and they involved the Pazzi, another Florentine banking house, in the financing of a complicated deal involving the marriage of Girolamo Riario to Gian' Galeazzo's half-sister Caterina Sforza, who was legitimated by the pope, and the creation of a new principality of Imola-Forlì for the groom.* The pope also appointed Francesco Salviati to the archbishopric of Pisa and gave the Pazzi family the monopoly of the alum mines at Tolfa, the only Italian source of the dye-setting mineral, which was essential to the textile trade on which much of Florence's prosperity depended. All these measures were overtly anti-Medici.

In 2004 an encrypted letter in the Ubaldini archives at Urbino was deciphered by Marcello Simonetta, using a book on diplomatic codes written by one of his ancestors. It revealed that Federico da Montefeltro was a full participant in the conspiracy and had agreed to station 600 troops near Florence, ready to take control of the city once the Medici were dead. On 26 April 1478 during High Mass at the Duomo the assassins, who included a priest, killed Giuliano but only wounded Lorenzo. The leaders of the Salviati clan, including Archbishop Francesco, failed to seize the Palazzo della Signoria and were disembowelled and hanged from its windows, while the Pazzi elders were lynched in the street by the mob. Girolamo Riario wisely stayed in Rome but his younger brother Cardinal Raffaele was in Florence and was only saved from a similar fate by the personal intervention of the wounded Lorenzo. The gesture bought Lorenzo no favour from Sixtus IV, who with breathtaking cynicism denounced the killing of the archbishop, placed the city under interdict and enlisted Ferrante of Naples to attack Florence. It was during the ensuing war that Federico and Roberto danced around each other until Lorenzo I de' Medici boldly sailed to

---

* Federico ousted the feuding Ordelaffi and installed Girolamo in Forlì in late 1480.

Naples and put himself in Ferrante's hands. The two rulers found much in common, in particular their loathing for the Rovere clan, and the ensuing diplomatic revolution saw Naples allied with Florence against the Papacy and Venice. In Milan, Ludovico sensed that the tide had turned and moved first to neutrality, then to hostility towards the Rovere dynastic project.

Such were the vagaries of condottiere warfare that in the new war Roberto was appointed Captain-General and *Gonfaloniere* of the Church, while Federico became the captain-general of an anti-Venetian league formed by Florence and Milan to prevent the Venetians from taking Ferrara from Duke Ercole d'Este, supposedly to add it to Girolamo Riario's principality. We may fairly doubt that Venice would have been so altruistic and Federico had every geopolitical reason to oppose the further extension of the Venetian *terraferma* empire. He must also have had reservations about the meteoric career of his son-in-law to become 'Roberto il Magnifico' and second only to himself in the condottiere market. However Federico was only sixty years old in 1482, with every expectation of living to see his young son reach maturity, and failing that he had the comfort of knowing that Guidobaldo would be in the safe hands of Ottaviano, who had been running the administration of the dukedom while Federico made a fortune as a condottiere. Cecil Clough estimates his military income to have been an average of 50,000 ducats a year between 1468 and 1482, when the annual profits of the Medici bank at its peak in 1441–52 was 20,000 florins and a year's salary for the Doge of Venice was only 3000 ducats. Federico was so rich that he had no hesitation in refusing a Venetian offer of 80,000 ducats merely to refrain from fighting for anyone in 1482.

But did he refuse the offer? Federico's last campaign (at a salary of 60,000 florins) on behalf of the anti-Venetian league might lead one to suspect that his heart was not in it. The Venetian army was led by the able and extremely ambitious Roberto da San Severino, who got the 80,000 ducats Federico had refused and was the target of several Sforza-inspired assassination attempts. The two commanders got into a protracted competition involving the digging of channels and causeways in malarial swamps in the vicinity of Melara, a Mantuan fortress on the Po that fell to San Severino in May, and Ficarolo, a Ferrarese fortress downstream from Melara occupying a strategic dogleg on the northern bank of the Po, which fell in July. Counter-attacks were led not by Federico but by Duke Ercole d'Este. The fieldworks were immensely expensive undertakings seemingly designed to exhaust both sides, but if it was a case of collusion it misfired disastrously because both Federico and San Severino came down with malaria. San Severino recovered but Federico, battered by the many wounds, accidents and illnesses that had punctuated his life, died in Ferrara on 10 September.

On the Papal–Neapolitan front, Roberto was welcomed as a redeemer when he entered Rome in July, with cardinals lining his route and lodging provided by Sixtus IV in the basilica of Santa Maria Maggiore. Sixtus also appointed him *Gonfaloniere* over his own nephew Giovanni della Rovere, who had married Federico's eldest daughter in 1474 and stood next in line for the dukedom of Urbino should Guidobaldo fail to survive or produce an heir. The murderous Girolamo Riario was appointed Roberto's deputy. In August Roberto marched out of Rome at the head of thirty-four squadrons (about 150 men each) of cavalry, two squadrons of mounted crossbowmen and 9000 infantry to confront King Ferrante's son Alfonso, Duke of Calabria, who had advanced as far as the Alban lake less than fifteen miles from Rome. Alfonso had only 2500 cavalry and 1500 infantry, among the former a squadron of Ottoman Turks who had joined the Neapolitan army after their brief occupation of Otranto in 1480, cut short by the death of Sultan Mehmet the Conqueror the following year. Although the battle was between the Papacy and Naples, the bitterness of the fighting that followed owed much to the fact that the Orsini were present in force in the papal army and their blood enemies, the Colonna of Paliano, were lined up with Alfonso.

The one-sided battle that took place on 21 August near Velletri on a field aptly named Campomorto was possibly the bloodiest and certainty the most annihilating victory of the century, with over 1200 dead and an enormous haul of prisoners. Forty-eight named condottieri fought under Roberto including many Malatesta retainers, six Orsini and a Mirandola, four Varani, two Piccinini, two Tolentini and a Castracane. Alfonso's army contained 352 named condottiere and we owe the complete roll-call to the fact that all except twenty-five of them were captured. Alfonso made good his escape with an escort of only a hundred men. The captured Turks, who had previously provided

Alfonso's bodyguard, cheerfully joined the papal army where they gave good service for many years as fearsome mounted scouts. Roberto led from the front and had a horse shot under him, but he took a risk too many when he had dinner with Riario in early September. Almost disabled by severe abdominal pains, he returned to Rome but was obliged to take part in a triumphal procession by Sixtus before he could seek medical attention. He took refuge in the palace of Stefano Nardini, Cardinal-Archbishop of Milan, but died on 10 September, the same day as Federico Montefeltro. I would be happy to sell Tower Bridge to anybody inclined to believe this was simply an amazing coincidence.

Let me close our narrative by introducing one last useful Italian word: *faccia*, roughly 'bare-faced' as in 'bare-faced lie'. Pope Sixtus IV had the almighty *faccia* to bury Roberto in the cellar beneath St Peter's basilica, traditionally reserved for popes, in an absurdly over-the-top funeral ceremony that would have been enough, even without the circumstantial evidence, to confirm the pope's guilt. Among the banners adorning Roberto's catafalque was one that read *Veni, vidi et vici, victoriam Sixto dedi, mors invidit gloriae*. A rough translation would be 'I came, I saw, I conquered, I gave victory to Sixtus and death was envious of my glory'. For 'death' read 'the della Rovere clan' and the epitaph could not be more accurate.

# NINETEEN

## *Epitaph*

The tone I have taken in recounting this long story of unbridled lust, treachery and murder sprinkled with great works of art may seem quaintly 'judgemental' and perhaps it is: the wild doings of our protagonists were, after all, mere peccadilloes compared to the horrendous crimes committed against language, art, intelligence and humanity during our own supposedly enlightened age. Without a moral compass, however, it is impossible to sort the shades of grey that envelop human existence. The condottieri were villains but in the context of their lethally chaotic time they were generally more sinned against than sinning and there is also something almost endearing about their shamelessness. The lay and spiritual princes who employed the condottieri were casually cruel tyrants and many of them were monsters, but kindliness and forbearance were often suicidal flaws in a late medieval ruler and at least, some leading churchmen excepted, they did not seek to camouflage their drive for power and dominance with the pretence that it was for the greater good of humankind.

Of all the serried ranks of warriors who have marched across the pages of this book Federico da Montefeltro has come down to us as the exception that proves the rule: he is the virtuous condottiere, the brave captain, the lover of arts, letters and justice, the devout son of the Church loved by his people and respected by his noble peers in Italy and abroad. In sum, a prince among men. And so he was – but as we have seen, goodness had very little to do with it. In 1373, near the end of his life, Petrarch wrote that a lord should support distinguished scholars (such as Petrarch) and frequent their company so that their praise should ensure the lord's lasting fame. Cecil Clough's clear-eyed study of Federico's patronage of the arts points out that although during the last fifteen years of his life he had more wealth available for patronage than any other prince in Italy, indeed possibly in all of Western Christendom, still:

> the artists selected were rather of the second rank, such as Giovanni Santi, Giovanni Angelo di Antonio da Camerino, and even Justus of Ghent. They were chosen, one may believe, because they finished their work on time, their services were not being bid for elsewhere, and they were cheaper than their more sought-after colleagues ... such was the potential of his patronage that he achieved fame from the eulogies of scholars, without having to pay, and without having to suffer their boring society. ... While [he] was the most brilliant exponent of the princely order of his day, his patronage was not disinterested. Shrewdly, with his eye on the best value for money, Federico invested in tangible things – this because he thought it was fashionable to do so, and because it benefited his dynasty. He can be compared, therefore, to the typical *nouveau riche*.

To which one must add that although Federico became a cultural ideal emulated by other Italian princes, his lifelong ambition was to surpass Sigismondo Pandolfo Malatesta and what he did once his rival was gone can be seen as continuing competition with the shade of the man he had so thoroughly humbled in life. It is to Sigismondo that we can trace the revival of Roman-style profile portrayals in the medallions of Matteo de' Pasti and in the fresco and portrait painted by Piero della Francesca in 1451 – twenty years before Piero painted the famous diptych of Federico and his wife Battista now in the Uffizi. It was soon after working for Sigismondo in the design of the Tempio Malatestiano that Alberti wrote in *De Re Aedificatoria:* 'men of public spirit approve and rejoice when you have raised a fine wall or portico, and adorned it with portals, columns, and a handsome roof, knowing you have thereby not only served yourself, but them too, having by this generous use of your wealth gained an addition of great honour to yourself, your family, your descendants and your city.'

Alberti's words could be boiled down to 'more commissions, please', but there is nothing wrong with that. As I commented about the explosion of Roman Baroque in *Crescent and Cross,* 'artists respond to money as heliotropes to the sun' – and so do scholars. Federico devoted little more than 10,000 ducats to them, about the same as he spent on tapestries, mainly to copy classical works to build up a library of about 1000 volumes. By comparison the Gubbio palace cost in the region of 35,000 ducats and the elaborate fortifications at any one of Cagli, San Leo, Mondavio and several other places must have exceeded this considerably. It was Cosimo de' Medici who set the trend of building magnificent structures as acts of political propaganda, beginning in the late 1430s, but that was also when Sigismondo set about building Castel Sismondo, the most browbeatingly ostentatious structure of all. Sigismondo and even more so his brother Domenico were also trendsetters with regard to libraries, and the Biblioteca Malatestiana built by Domenico as an adjunct to the Franciscan convent in Cesena remains the principal glory of the city after the splendid castle on the hill that overlooks it. If not the first in the world, the Biblioteca Malatestiana is the oldest public library in Italy, in continuous operation since its inauguration 550 years ago, and is on the UNESCO 'Memory of the World' register.

For all that he was a fratricidal usurper and no match for Sigismondo man-for-man, one still warms to Federico more than to his great rival, principally because of the fondness he showed towards his little son Guidobaldo in several of the paintings that have come down to us (see Picture section 2, p. 5). Given the precedent of Federico's complicity in the Medici assassination it is possible, even likely, that he was also a party to the Rovere plot to kill Roberto Malatesta, and Federico may have died consoled that his brother Ottaviano would shield young Guidobaldo from lesser predators. Nobody could have foreseen that Ottaviano's excessive care for his nephew was to be what doomed the Montefeltro–Ubaldini line to extinction. When Guidobaldo married the talented Elisabetta Gonzaga in 1489, Ottaviano insisted the marriage should not be consummated until the horoscope was propitious, deepening the young man's anxiety to the point that he was never able to perform. The people of Urbino in due course judged that Ottaviano had put a curse on the couple, which in a sense he did, and Ottaviano died in exile. Elisabetta went on to become immortalised as the gracious hostess in Baldassare Castiglione's *Il Cortegiano* (*The Book of the Courtier*), a discussion of what makes a whole man published in 1528 but notionally dated to 1507. Given the unfortunate circumstances of Elisabetta's marriage it is poignant that one of the key passages in the book is a discourse on Platonic love by the Venetian scholar and future Cardinal Pietro Bembo. *Il Cortegiano* defined the ideal gentleman, who should be learned and graceful, able to turn an elegant phrase, to draw and paint but also adept at the arts of war, and withal modest and unshowy. Vittorino da Feltre in his Joyous House would not have changed a word – nor would Rudyard Kipling when composing the poem 'If' in 1895.

Roberto's son, Pandolfo, born to his mistress Isabetta Aldobrandini in 1475, the year he married Federico's daughter Elisabetta (by whom he had no children), grew up to exhibit all the traits associated with boys brought up by a doting mother without the balance of a father. Known contemptuously as 'Pandolfaccio' he was evicted by Cesare Borgia in 1503 and despite several efforts to return, including one engineered by his own son Sigismondo in 1527, he had exhausted the charisma of the Malatesta brand and the people of Rimini would not have him back, preferring the Venetians and, remarkably, even the Church. It was as though all the life force in the Montefeltro and Malatesta lines was consumed in the struggle between Federico and Sigismondo, and the failure of both their lines resulted in the rule of the Montefeltro della Rovere clan over both their domains until Duke Francesco Maria II died heirless in 1623.

### CESARE BORGIA (1475–1507)

**Cesare was originally destined for the Church but after the assassination of his elder brother in 1497 he resigned the cardinalate to become the focus of their father Pope Alexander VI's secular dynastic ambitions. Cesare seized Camerino, Imola, Faenza, Forlì and Pesaro as well as Rimini and Urbino in 1502–3, murdering the rulers who fell into his hands. The plan was to create a Borgia duchy but the death of his father and the succession of Julius II della Rovere undid the scheme.**

It is difficult to summarise the long Malatesta–Montefeltro saga. Perhaps the most startling theme to emerge from it all is that people living in Italy during the late Middle Ages would put up with almost any bizarre eccentricity and even pathological behaviour from their lord so long as he preserved civil order. It was not the venality of the Church that made the citizens of the Papal State prefer almost any other ruler, but rather its chronic failure to keep the peace. It was what permitted the Romagna borderland lords to flourish for so long and, when they were finally evicted from their little domains, it was what kept their memory fresh through the centuries-long nightmare of papal misrule. As John Larner so aptly puts it:

> While they survived the lords of Romagna were able to give their fellow-citizens the one thing they desired above all others: local independence. They gave their subjects a pride and a sense of belonging, almost impossible for us to imagine in a world of giant states – the pride that comes from being a citizen in a community small enough to allow the individual to identify himself intimately with its interests.

If the preceding pages have done nothing else they must surely have highlighted the profoundly corrupting effect of secular power on the Church of Rome, a veritable curse that lay upon it until finally driven out of the lands it exploited so pitilessly for so long. With the collapse of what I have called, with deliberation, the Communist Caliphate, we are now left with only a few countries where secular and religious (or pseudo-religious) power is combined. It is no surprise that they are socially stagnant and irredeemably corrupt – so it will always be when Church and state become promiscuously entwined.

I began by saying that no other cohort of soldiers has attracted anything like as much attention as the condottieri, and that this could be because although it was an age when belief in life after death was strong, men also pursued secular glory in the hope that future generations should remember them. I have also unfashionably suggested that women may have been less inclined to seek ostentatious glory not merely because of 'patriarchy' but also because childbearing is a more certain guarantee of immortality. It seems to me the chapel of Isotta degli Atti da Malatesta in the Rimini Tempio Malatestiano might be a place of pilgrimage for feminists of both sexes, and a reminder that the English word 'brave', today associated almost exclusively with courage, comes from the Italian *bravo/brava*, which means talented, clever and capable.

In closing, I hope the imperative of driving the narrative through three centuries in which almost every page could have been expanded relatively easily into an article, and every chapter into a book, has not sacrificed any necessary complexity – the random 'what if' moments when history could easily have followed another course. The process that produced Burckhardt's 'universal men' meandered like a river around huge historical formations such as the population boom and bust of the fourteenth century, the failure of the Holy Roman, the extinction of the Byzantine and emergence of the Ottoman Empires, and the sinful pride followed by the humbling of the Roman Catholic Church. But the river also altered course because some dynastic marriages were barren and others excessively fecund, because some individuals were fortunate to live in a time that suited their talents and others were not, but above all because of the unremitting pressure of circumstances at a time when communications were slow and uncertain, which often drove rulers to take ill-considered action in an attempt to gain some control over the 'noise' that threatened to overwhelm them. In sum, the contingent nature of history, from which hindsight permits us to mine a coherent narrative but which to those involved was a deluge of events whose significance was usually unclear and whose consequences were unknowable and in many cases unimaginable.

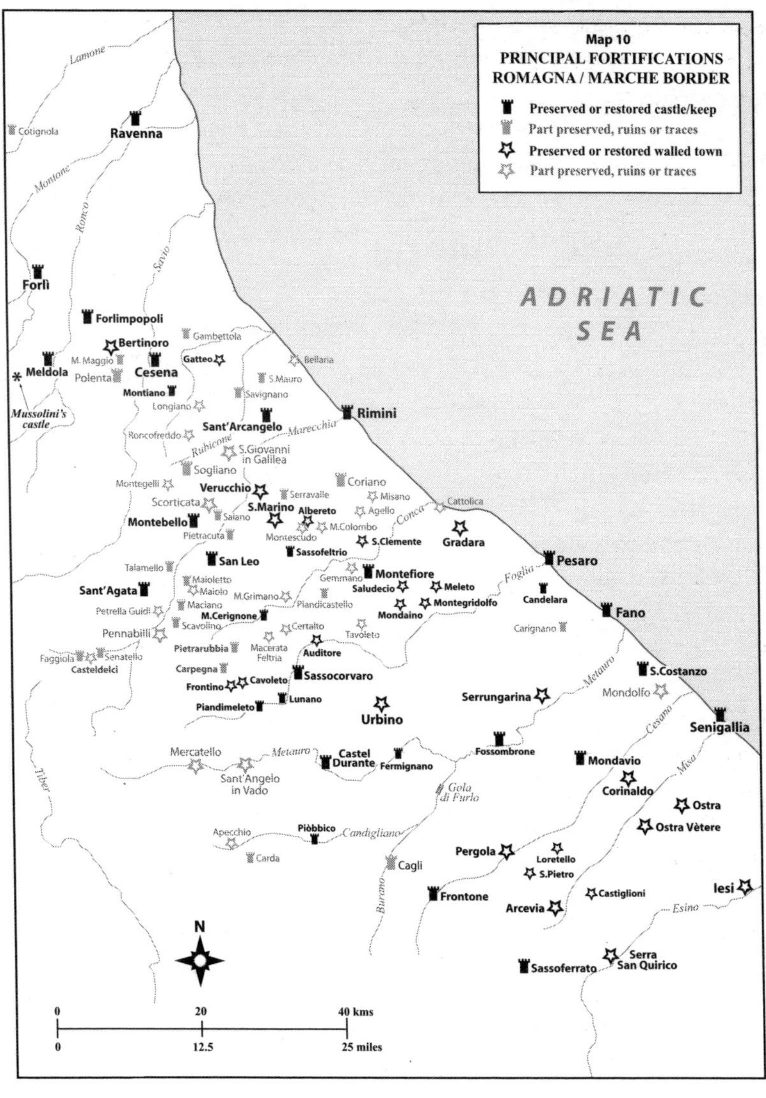

Map 10
PRINCIPAL FORTIFICATIONS
ROMAGNA / MARCHE BORDER
Preserved or restored castle/keep
Part preserved, ruins or traces
Preserved or restored walled town
Part preserved, ruins or traces
ADRIATIC SEA
Lamone
Cotignola
Ravenna
Montone
Ronco
Savio
Forlì
Forlimpopoli
Gambettola
Bertinoro
M. Maggio
Meldola
Polenta
Cesena
Gatteo
Bellaria
S.Mauro
Montiano
Savignano
Mussolini's castle
Longiano
Rimini
Sant'Arcangelo
Marecchia
Roncofreddo
Rubicone
S.Giovanni in Galilea
Sogliano
Coriano
Montegelli
Verucchio
Serravalle
Misano
Scorticata
S.Marino
Albereto
Agello
Cattolica
Conca
Montebello
Saiano
M.Colombo
Montescudo
Gradara
Pietracuta
S.Clemente
Sassofeltrio
San Leo
Pesaro
Talamello
Gemmano
Montefiore
Foglia
Maioletto
Maiolo
Saludecio
Meleto
Sant'Agata
M.Grimano
Candelara
Maciano
Piandicastello
Montegridolfo
Fano
Petrella Guidi
Mondaino
M.Cerignone
Scavolino
Certalto
Tavoleto
Carignano
Pennabilli
Pietrarubbia
Macerata Feltria
Auditore
Faggiola
Senatello
Casteldelci
Carpegna
Sassocorvaro
S.Costanzo
Frontino
Cavoleto
Metauro
Mondolfo
Lunano
Serrungarina
Piandimeleto
Urbino
Senigallia
Cesano
Fossombrone
Mercatello
Metauro
Castel Durante
Fermignano
Mondavio
Sant'Angelo in Vado
Misa
Gola di Furlo
Corinaldo
Ostra
Tiber
Ostra Vètere
Apecchio
Piòbbico
Candigliano
Pergola
Loretello
Carda
Cagli
S.Pietro
Burano
Castiglioni
Iesi
Frontone
Arcevia
Esino
N
Serra San Quirico
Sassoferrato
0
20
40 kms
0
12.5
25 miles

# CODA

# *Touring the Borderlands*

You cannot explore the borderlands of Romagna, the Marche, Tuscany and Umbria without being struck by the layers of humankind's efforts to shape the region, with Roman engineering works still in use and hilltops crowned with medieval castles *(rocche)* or walled villages *(castelli)* nestling around churches often built on sites that were once pagan places of worship. Even in Italy, where a hole dug almost at random will find evidence of civilisations stretching back thousands of years, there are few more historically evocative regions. The region is still largely agricultural and the lower population required to cultivate the fields today has left room for a host of new occupations to fit comfortably within the confines of medieval settlement.

The signature feature of the region is the intense identification of the people with their history, manifest in the loving revival, preservation and restoration of many places eroded by time or shattered by warfare. Although attitudes vary from municipality to municipality, broadly based prosperity in the latter half of the twentieth century has permitted many little rural communes to refurbish their historical environment. Perhaps the most striking example of this can be seen at Cotignola, the small town west of Ravenna where Muzio 'Sforza' Attendolo was born in 1369. In 1376, when Pope Gregory XI returned to Rome from exile in Avignon and needed to bind leading condottieri to his cause he appointed Hawkwood 'the Sharp' as lord of Cotignola. Hawkwood refortified the town and converted the church bell tower into a lookout post, which was demolished along with the rest of the town by the Germans in 1945. In an impressive display of civic pride

*Imola castle with detached outwork remnant in the foreground*

the historic centre was rebuilt, where possible using original materials.

Although more famous for its mountainous southern border area, the principal wealth of Romagna lies in the broad River Po alluvial plain, known as Lower Cisalpine Gaul to the Romans (Map 4). A natural starting point for a visit is Bologna airport, from which one can bypass the city to take the autostrada parallel to the Via Emilia. The old Roman road runs in a dead-straight line south-east with the Apennine mountains looming to the south through Imola, Faenza, Forlimpopoli and Forlì, all with drum-towered castles dating from 1470–80. At Forlimpopoli a series of arches have been cut in one wall, which successfully incorporate the work into the city centre. The most instructive is Imola where one can see how sections of the medieval walls were protected by a very early detached ravelin, a triangular outwork built so that its flanks could be raked by fire from the towers.*

North-east of Imola is the triangle formed by Cotignola, Bagnacavallo and Barbiano, birthplace of several great condottieri. Nearby the complex castle at Lugo is a visual manual of successive styles of medieval fortification, from the time of Uguccione della Faggiuola in

* Although the Italians call any angled bastion that juts out from the main work a *rivellino*, the term 'ravelin' is elsewhere reserved for open-backed, detached triangular outworks.

the early thirteenth century to Borso d'Este in the fifteenth. Predappio, south of Forlì, is where perhaps the most famous Romagnol of all was born and is buried. High above his natal village Benito Mussolini built the bombastic Rocca delle Caminate on the site of a Malatesta castle, where his wife lived while he shared his life with mistresses – the last of whom, Clara Petacci, was shot and shamefully hung by her ankles alongside him for execration by the mob in Milan in 1945. Returning to the plain from Predappio one passes the lovingly restored medieval keep at Meldola, from which a further detour takes one up the steep hill crowned by the walls and towers of Bertinoro. Further south the ruins of the castle at Polenta are a *sic transit gloria mundi* memorial to the clan of that name, which once dominated Ravenna, one of several families to descend from the hill country to rule over the prosperous cities of the plain.

All the previous stops serve as aperitifs for the spectacular castle crowning the hill at the heart of Cesena, the first of the great Malatesta fortresses we shall encounter. Although the outer defensive works have disappeared and the main work is obscured by dense woods, it is worth an overnight stop if only to enjoy the illumination of the Episcopal Palace, which dates from the post-Malatesta era of ecclesiastical rule, with the tower-bastion of the castle glowing high above. In addition the city is graced by the handsome Biblioteca Malatestiana, the oldest public library in Italy, built by Domenico Malatesta. Unfortunately the interior of the castle has been vandalised by dumping fill in one corner to create a podium for popular entertainment, while the rusting bars in the windows of the older keep *(mastio)* bear witness to its use as a common jail in the nineteenth and early twentieth centuries. The second and taller of the two central keeps is whimsically known as the *femina*, a play on words (*mastio* sounds like *maschio*, which means male) at odds with its rampant domination of the city.

Cesena is an exception to the rule that gunpowder artillery made medieval castles obsolete: to the south, the only practicable approach, an attacker would have faced layered counter-battery fire from the walls and from long-gone earthworks. The defences were never put to the test, probably because nobody believed a formal siege was practicable. A steep street along the eastern side of the castle commemorates the massacre of 1377, infamous even in a very bloody time,

Mastio *and* femina *towers at Cesena castle*

when mercenary troops under the direction of Cardinal Legate Robert of Geneva, who inappropriately took the name Clement VII when he became antipope a year later, butchered 4000 inhabitants, burned the town and demolished the old castle. The main perpetrators were the Breton company under Jean de Maléstroit, avenging the death of 300 of their number in a riot sparked by their brutal behaviour a few days earlier. They were abetted by Hawkwood's company, including the future 'saviour of Italy' Alberico da Barbiano.

Between Cesena and Rimini, like Julius Caesar in 49 BC, one crosses the Rubicon. It is a most disappointing trickle but the historically minded cannot refrain from muttering *alea jacta est* (the die is cast) before entering one of the zones of densest fortification in all Europe. The area on either side of the Rubicon was the domain of the Malatesta Counts of Sogliano, who salvaged and increased their holdings when their distant cousins at Cesena died out and at Rimini went down to defeat and dispossession in the 1460s. The Counts of Sogliano fell to a popular uprising that destroyed their palaces, followed by papal repossession, in 1640. There is little left of the Malatesta fortifications at Massa, Monleone, Montecodruzzo, Montepietra, Monte Tiffi, Perticara, Pietra dell'Uso, Savignano di Rigo, Sogliano itself, Strigara,

Rontagnano and Turrita, but the remaining works at Roncofreddo and San Giovanni in Galilea are worth visiting. Beyond the Uso we enter an area with several notable medieval works, of which the best preserved is the castle above Sant'Arcangelo di Romagna, today a private dwelling owned by the Colonna of Paliano family and the headquarters of the Associazione Sigismondo Malatesta, devoted to interdisciplinary cultural research and discussion. Once reputedly the tallest tower in Italy, built by Carlo II Malatesta early in the fifteenth century, Sant'Arcangelo was reduced in height and a curtain wall built round it by Sigismondo in 1447. The Latin plaque over the gate states that he rebuilt the work 'for the benefit and guardianship of its inhabitants and for posterity'.

Sant'Arcangelo is the first of the castles built on the rocky outcrops characteristic of the Marecchia (Roman *Ariminus)* valley. The features are enormous boulders of calcareous rock exposed by erosion of the surrounding marl and, being highly porous and fissile, are about as unsuitable a base for major construction as geology provides. In 1700 Maiolo was abandoned after a rock slide carried away much of the village, while the castles at Verucchio, Carpegna and Sant'Agata Feltria have all lost sections to similar rock failures. Extensive reinforcement at several other sites testifies to the imprudence of building to the edge of the cliffs, although the practice did create the pleasing illusion that the castles are natural extensions of the rocks on which they stand. Other works built on these unstable formations include: San Giovanni in Galilea; the three towers on soaring Monte Titano in San Marino; the tower at Scorticata (now Torriana); Pietracuta; Talamello and Maciano; the twin keeps of Pennabilli and of Faggiuola and Senatello at Castel d'Elci. The largest of the outcrops are the Sasso Simone and Simoncello mountains in the Montefeltro and Mounts Fumaiolo and La Verna at the headwaters of the Marecchia, Savio and Tiber rivers.

All the works mentioned are worth a visit although if time is short San Marino, overbuilt, overcrowded and smug, can readily be dispensed with – the towering cliff of Monte Titano, the rock on which San Marino stands, is best appreciated from the south anyway. From Sant'Arcangelo a narrow, winding ridge road leads to Scorticata/ Torriana, where some optimistic soul has built a restaurant behind the twin drum towers of the gate works, all that remains of the castle in whose dungeon lame 'Gianciotto' Malatesta, murderer of his adulterous wife Francesca and brother Paolo 'il Bello' in 1285, is believed to have been put to death in 1304. The ridge road continues to the well-maintained castle at Montebello, which has been in the continuous possession of the Bagno family since the Middle Ages and which, like Sant'Arcangelo, can be visited only by prior arrangement. The contrast between historic properties where people still live and the dead shells of state ownership, here as anywhere else, bears witness to the 'tragedy of the commons'.*

Returning through Scorticata, the road down into the Marecchia valley goes past the round tower at Saiano, dating from 1183, before climbing the southern flank of the valley to Verucchio, the base from which Mastin Vecchio mounted his successful campaign to become lord of Rimini in 1295. Exhibits in the town museum illustrate that this was an important settlement long before that date. The Latin plaque inside the palace-fortress on the Sasso peak reads 'Sigismondo Pandolfo Malatesta son of Pandolfo to keep enemies at a distance walled these rocks around with an external and an internal wall and built a citadel 1449'. The citadel under reference, on nearby Pasarello peak, is gone and although the town walls leading up the Sasso have been carefully restored, the fortress has lost one of the two octagonal towers that covered the only practicable approach and the older upper works are in ruins. The setting overlooking the coastal plain is magnificent and on a clear day the view from the walls encompasses much of 'Malatestaland'.

Returning to the valley road (Provincial 258) a quick side trip to the ruins of Pietracuta provides another *sic transit gloria* moment. The traces remaining after centuries of use as a quarry for building material indicates that this must have been a major work, controlling as it did one of the approaches to the fiercely independent commune of San Marino, whose historic identity, like Switzerland's, was based on highly defensible topography and universal military service. San Marino bought Pietracuta valley in 1375 for 35 gold ducats but lost the castle to

* A phrase popularised in a 1968 article by the passionate neo-Malthusian Garrett Hardin, who in accordance with his beliefs died by his own hand, joined by his wife, in 2003.

*Castle at Verucchio*

Sigismondo in 1448. The work was promptly assaulted by 300 men sent by San Marino's ally Federico Montefeltro, but they were beaten off and pursued as far as Frontino in the Conca valley. It passed into the possession of Federico in 1463, but after that date the castle seems to have been wrecked and abandoned, perhaps as a gesture to show that the Republic of San Marino, granted its modern borders by the Papacy the same year, had nothing to fear from the new master of the Marecchia valley – nor he from them.

Not far beyond Pietracuta a winding mountain road turns off to San Leo, our first encounter with the theatrical extravaganzas built by Francesco di Giorgio Martini for Federico Montefeltro after Federico had crushed his lifelong rival Sigismondo and was enjoying vast revenues from his greatly increased domain and as Italy's foremost condottiere. The Romans called the feature *Montis Feretrius* (Feretrius = Fulminator = Jove/Jupiter), from which derived the name and diocese of Montefeltro. In 270 Saints Leo and Marino fled persecution in their native Dalmatia and founded monasteries on the peaks that bear their name, while their companion in exile, St Agata, perched on a rock at Perticara in the Uso valley. San Leo alternated between ecclesiastical and Montefeltro rule until the Papacy expropriated all the family hold-

*Ruins of the Pietracuta* rocca

ings in 1370. In 1376 Gregory XI awarded it to the Malatesti, who held it until Federico's forces took it in 1441 with a daring escalade of the sheer cliffs that surround the town. The place reverted to the Papacy and in 1450 Nicholas V gave it to Sigismondo Malatesta, who lost it definitively to his rival in the settlement of 1463. The dramatic palace-fortress built for Federico by Martini was always a military absurdity because once an attacker gained control of the lower town the garrison could not hope for relief and must surrender. Its intention was to vaunt, magnificently, an illusion of permanent Montefeltro power over the Marecchia valley.

With its delightful eleventh-century pre-Romanesque church of Santa Maria Assunta and the cathedral, built in 1173 with funds provided by Count Montefeltrano I, San Leo is the appropriate base from which to explore the Montefeltro. The little town itself drips with history: it was the final seat of Berengar II, last of the Frankish kings of Italy, who surrendered the citadel of San Leo to the Holy Roman Emperor Otto I in 963 after a long siege. After the Malatesta–Montefeltro duel San Leo's principal claim to fame is that the populariser of freemasonry and fraudster 'Count' Alessandro Cagliostro, previously a guest at the Bastille in Paris and Castel Sant'Angelo in Rome, died there in 1795.

*Martini's fortress at San Leo*

For the last three years of his life, condemned to death by the Inquisition but cruelly spared execution, he was buried alive in the 'little well', set into the first floor of the fortress. No doubt others before him died in this dreadful cell, walked over by those going about the mundane activities of a life denied to the miserable captives below.

From San Leo a short drive along a usually mist-shrouded mountain road leads to Montecopiolo, the sub district around tall Mount Carpegna and the epicentre of the Malatesta–Montefeltro vendetta. The title deed of the Montefeltri invested their forefather Udalric as Count of Carpegna and Pietrarubbia. The latter is a village in the Apsa valley blessed with the eleventh-century church of St Arduino under a hill on which the square thirteenth-century Falcon's Tower stands. In 1298 the citizens of Pietrarubbia hacked to pieces Count Corrado Montefeltro, his infant son, his brother Filippo and sister Giovanna, and held his widow prisoner until sure she was not pregnant – 'that his seed should not remain'. The town name means 'ruddy stone', not because of the bloodshed but with reference to the colour of a nearby deposit of iron ore, whose scarcity in Italy led Mussolini to sign the disastrous 'Pact of Steel' with Hitler in 1939. In 1996, excavations uncovered the remains of the most complete medieval ironworks so far discovered, while the town itself, after a long decline, has revived around the artistic metalwork centre founded by local sculptor Arnaldo Pomodoro, whose works can be seen in the castle as well as the main squares of Milan, Copenhagen, Brisbane, in front of Trinity College Dublin and in the courtyard of the Vatican museum.

*The Martini/Ubaldini tortoise at Sassocorvaro*

Leaving Montecopiolo, after a loop to visit the great castle at Monte Cerignone and the partially walled town of Macerata Feltria, one exits the Montefeltro and descends into the Foglia valley to be greeted by the extraordinary palace-fortress of Sassocorvaro. Martini built it to a tortoise-shaped trace for Ottaviano degli Ubaldini in 1474. Originally part of the Gaboardi and then the Brancaleoni domains, it was much fought over by Sigismondo and Federico after the latter took possession of the upper Foglia and Metauro valleys in the name of his first wife, Countess Gentile Brancaleone. In 1441 Federico suffered his first serious wound in a battle with Sigismondo's proxy over the nearby village of Montelocco, of which only the name remains. The old castle at Sassocorvaro was burned and collapsed when Sigismondo sacked the town in 1446, and the work with which he replaced it was so strong that in 1458 Federico was compelled to reduce it to rubble with siege artillery. Again rebuilt by Sigismondo, it passed to Federico in 1463 and was ceded by him in turn to Ottaviano in 1470. Sassocorvaro sits astride the main road between the Montefeltro and Urbino, but once the Malatesta threat was neutralised its strategic significance vanished, which probably explains why Federico permitted his court architect and Ottaviano to indulge their shared taste for the esoteric in building the new work. Further up the Foglia valley at Piandimeleto can be seen another oddity with much the same explanation: the palace-fortress of the Counts of Oliva was rebuilt at about the same time as Ottaviano's Sassocorvaro, its ornamental, militarily obsolete design demonstrating that the Oliva expected to live in peace under the lord of Urbino.

Heading back towards Montecopiolo with the national park of Sasso Simone and Simoncello looming on the left, side roads lead to the walled villages of Frontino and Cavoleto: hard to believe they survived the breaching of the nearby Gothic Line in 1944. At the seat of the Counts of Carpegna, who separated from the main Montefeltro clan in 1140, the rock on which the castle stood crumbled in the early 1600s and there are few traces of what was once a considerable work. Worth a stop all the same, if only for the excellent prosciutto. Pennabilli, the last town on the circuit, was the birthplace of the Malatesta clan. Originally there were two towers on the twin peaks of Penna and Billi, and the town filled the valley in between. Little of either castle or of the strong town walls rebuilt by Sigismondo around Penna remain: only a gatehouse and a few sections, including the bases of three or four octagonal towers and the square bastion at the end of Piazza Malatesta, from which an L-shaped staircase descends. A plaque on the wall of a B&B establishment in the old town records that the American Modernist poet Ezra Pound stayed there in 1923, when he was gathering material and inspiration for his strange *Malatesta Cantos* and cultivating the hatred of the unheroic petty bourgeoisie that was to lead him to treasonous embrace of Fascism during the Second World War.

Returning to Provincial 258 down the Marecchia, the castle and village of Maioletto-Maiolo loom over the valley, the former blown up in 1639 when lightning struck the powder magazine and the latter destroyed by a rock slide in 1700. Exploration of the Montefeltro would not be complete without side trips through Petrella Guidi to Sant'Agata Feltria in the upper Savio valley and further up the valley to Castel d'Elci on the Senatello tributary of the Marecchia, both covering what used to be the main trans-Apennine route from central Italy to Cesena and Ravenna (the modern E 45 swings west past Bagno di Romagna but required two long tunnels). The village walls at Petrella Guidi are intact and over the gateway of the ruined castle can be seen the heraldic crests of the Malatesta, the Oliva (clients of the Malatesta in the fourteenth century), and the Papacy. The main work, however, an imposing tower with some of its original white plaster still in place, was built by the Tiberti, a clan that moved to Cesena in the thirteenth century. The narrow road continues across the Marecchia–Savio watershed to Sant'Agata, acquired by Federico in 1463 and refurbished by Martini as the dowry for Federico's illegitimate daughter Gentile when she married Agostino Fregoso in 1466. Before that the castle was modernised by Sigismondo, who lost it in 1459 and regained it briefly in 1462, but the work one sees today bulging over the sides of the 'Wolf's Rock' owes its exaggerated proportions to later additions by the Fregoso family and to a partial collapse in 1835. Of interest are the pits inside the castle, whence the name and unique flavour of the local cheese *(formaggio di fossa)*. The pit cheese is a survival from medieval times, when the garrison might have little time to bring fresh provisions into the castle before a siege.

Sant'Agata once formed part of the patrimony of Uguccione della Faggiuola, the ferocious leader of the Romagna Ghibellines and friend to the exiled Dante. Uguccione's family (a distant branch of the Montefeltro clan, dating from around 1200) took its name from the steep hill above Castel d'Elci. There were two castles here, Faggiuola and Senatello, and of each there remains only a tower, one of them now the bell tower of the town church. The narrow track winding west from Castel d'Elci leads to the headwaters of both the Marecchia and the Tiber, whose great valley runs through the heart of Italy to Rome.

Before continuing, a review of the development of fortification is advisable. English-speakers tend to think of round towers as 'Roman', square as 'Norman' and more complex geometrical shapes as 'Renaissance', but the crucial factor was height over the surrounding ground. Tall towers served as lookout and signalling posts, although in time their height also became urban status symbols, most clearly seen in the evidence of medieval one-upmanship jutting above San Gimignano, south of Florence. When such towers were joined to enclose a settlement the walls were also tall to discourage escalade by besiegers, with crenellation along the top to provide cover for archers. The parapet jutted out to create the 'murder holes' of machicolation, permitting

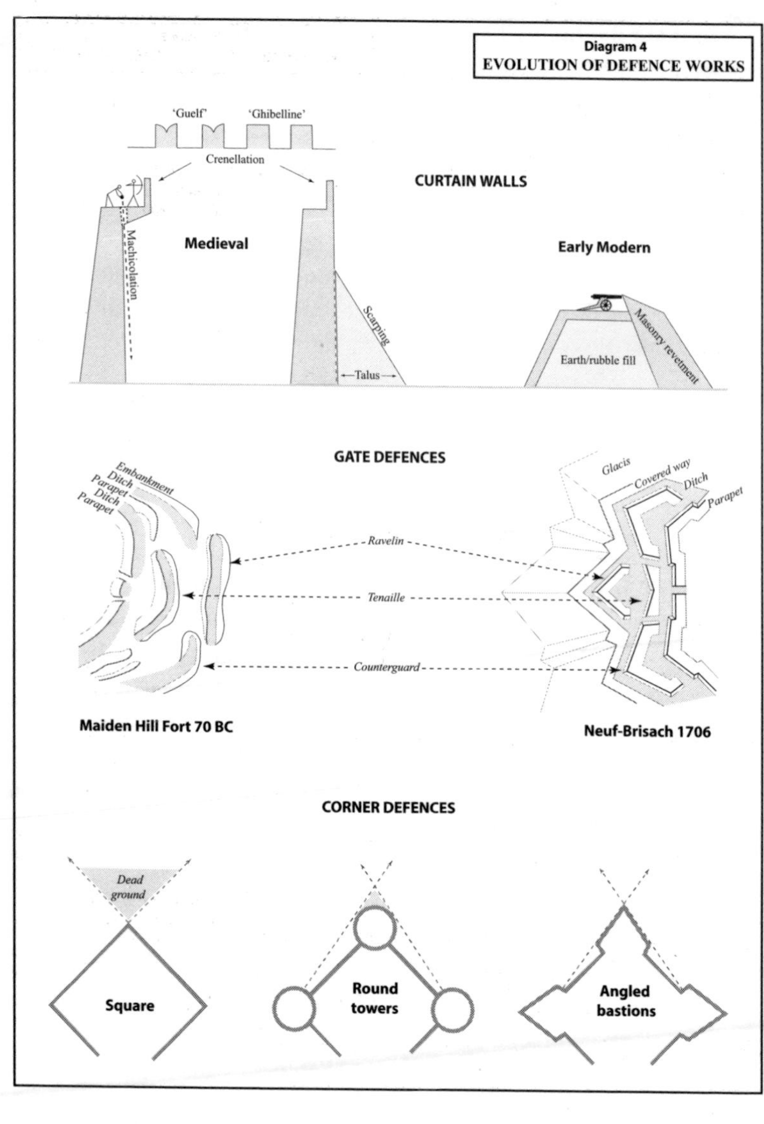
Diagram 4
EVOLUTION OF DEFENCE WORKS
'Guelf'
'Ghibelline'
Crenellation
CURTAIN WALLS
Machicolation
Medieval
Scarping
Talus
Early Modern
Masonry revetment
Earth/rubble fill
GATE DEFENCES
Embankment
Ditch
Parapet
Ditch
Parapet
Glacis
Covered way
Ditch
Parapet
Ravelin
Tenaille
Counterguard
Maiden Hill Fort 70 BC
Neuf-Brisach 1706
CORNER DEFENCES
Dead ground
Square
Round towers
Angled bastions

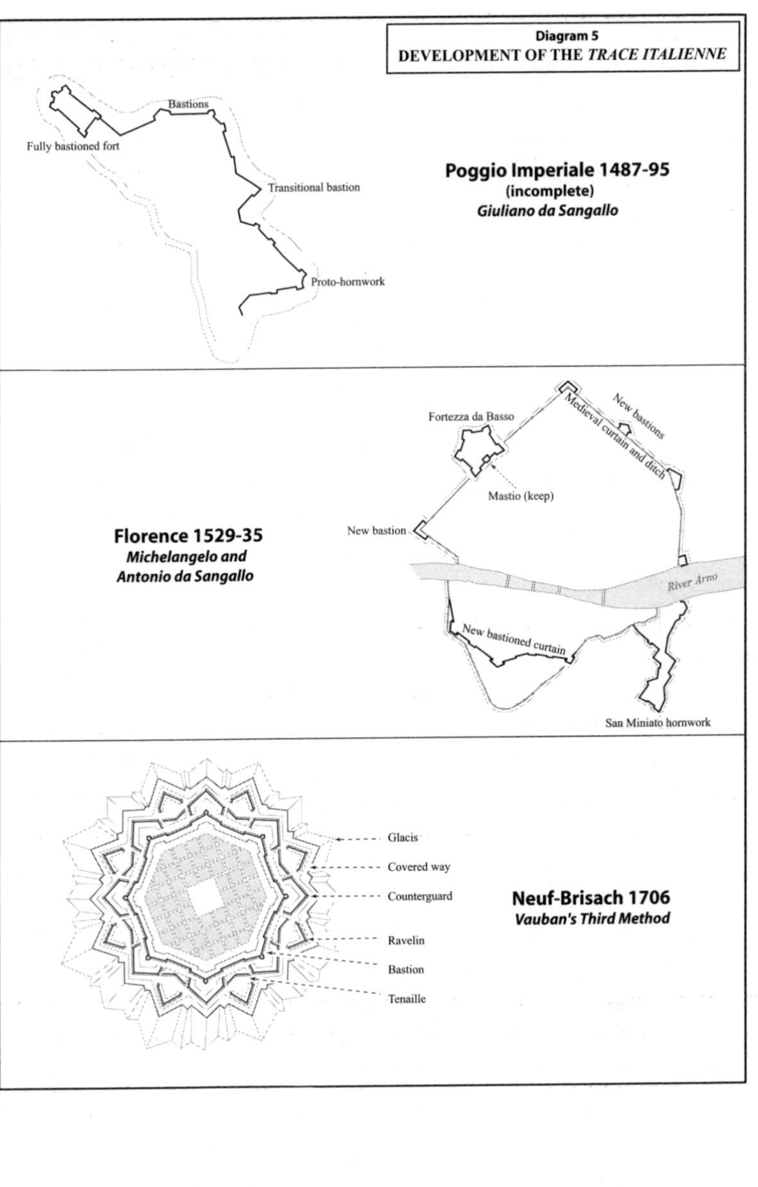
Diagram 5
DEVELOPMENT OF THE TRACE ITALIENNE
Bastions
Fully bastioned fort
Transitional bastion
Proto-hornwork
Poggio Imperiale 1487-95
(incomplete)
Giuliano da Sangallo
Fortezza da Basso
Medieval curtain and ditch
New bastions
Mastio (keep)
New bastion
Florence 1529-35
Michelangelo and
Antonio da Sangallo
River Arno
New bastioned curtain
San Miniato hornwork
Glacis
Covered way
Counterguard
Ravelin
Bastion
Tenaille
Neuf-Brisach 1706
Vauban's Third Method

defenders to drop rocks or pour the proverbial boiling oil, from cover, on those seeking to bring down the wall by battering or mining the base. Machicolation would not deter an attacker equipped with stone-hurling siege engines or rolling assault towers and in time the base was scarped, that is pushed out to create a sloping abutment (talus) that at once greatly strengthened the base and made it impossible to roll a siege tower against the wall. The survival of machicolation along the parapets of scarped castle walls was stylistic – it served no practical purpose whatever.

The advent of gunpowder artillery 'batteries', the term explicit as to their purpose, changed the rules. The older, mechanically powered siege engines hurled stones in a parabola to hit the same spot on the wall until it came down, but the equipment was vulnerable to counter-fire from similar engines in the castle towers or from archers on the walls. Cannon could fire at greater range but were less ballistically predictable: for best effect they needed to be in protected emplacements close to the walls, against which a gun on high could not reply because firing with the muzzle depressed would, among other things, shatter the top-straps holding the barrel in the carriage. Accordingly the towers were brought down to the height of the walls, and both walls and towers became much lower and broader to accommodate more and bigger counter-batteries able to fire on a flat trajectory, and were protected by ravelins. In time the whole work was taken out of line of sight by building up the earth around it in a sloping rampart (glacis). The height needed to deter a surprise infantry assault was retained by surrounding the work with a broad ditch, covered by infantry firing from fortified positions within it (caponiers) or from guns mounted low at the base of the arrow-shaped bastions of the main work, by which any approach could be taken under crossed fire. The new bastions were also better able to deflect artillery fire and abolished the problem of dead ground that was the Achilles' heel of round towers (Diagram 4).

It was not gunpowder artillery but the prohibitive cost of defending against it that put minor warlords out of business all over Europe. As can be seen from a comparison of the Iron Age earthworks at Maiden Hill and the 1706 apogee of the *Trace Italienne* at Neuf-Brisach, the principles of gate defences were as old as fortification. The revolution brought about by cannon, once metallurgy developed to the point that siege guns could be made light enough to move overland at a reasonable pace, was that height over the surrounding countryside went, in a few decades, from being the sine qua non of fortification to being its greatest vulnerability. Ironically, earthworks were a better response than masonry, but although cheaper to build they were more expensive to maintain – and they totally lacked the element of grandeur, the vaunting of lordly power and wealth that was always the crucial element of castle design. As Sir John Hale wrote of Francesco di Giorgio Martini:

> while a case can be made from his [writings] that he was abreast of current practice he was not ahead of it, and his drawings and actual buildings show that he was diverted from dealing with simple, mutually dependent low-lying forms by a scholar's exuberant interest in ideal geometrical patterns, and by the relish for vertical mass he derived from church and palace, the staple of his architectural work.

The inheritance of medieval works also worked against innovation – it was vastly cheaper to modify an existing structure than to build anew in a more appropriate location and, even if relocation could be contemplated, the settlements that had grown up around the castles could not be moved as easily. The first work to incorporate a fully bastioned fortress was the new build at Poggio Imperiale in Tuscany, which failed because the townspeople of Poggibonsi refused to move from the valley to the greater security of the new development (Diagram 5). Every work in the Romagna borderlands is either plainly medieval or transitional, as indeed was the style of warfare practised by Sigismondo and Federico. Sigismondo, in particular, was a bold innovator who, as well as scarping and broadening the walls of a large number of the castles within his domain, invented the hand grenade and introduced the use of iron cannonballs to increase the impact of the relatively small-bore cannon that could accompany his fast-moving forces. But neither he nor Federico, during their period of mortal rivalry, possessed the time or the means to refortify their castles from scratch.

Sigismondo's reputation was won by his gunner's eye for the correct emplacement of artillery even before he won fame by personally leading an assault on the earthworks around an enemy camp at Monteluro in 1443. Federico's apotheosis as Europe's foremost soldier was won in 1472, when on behalf of the Medici he forced the well-defended rebel city of Volterra to capitulate by digging the zigzag of approach trenches leading to heavy artillery emplacements that were to become the staple of warfare in Europe for the next 350 years.* Although the French brought the Hundred Years War to a close by rapidly reducing the English castles in Normandy with cannon, and the last battle, at Castillon in 1453, was the first in which field artillery was decisive, Federico's feat had greater resonance because Italy was regarded as the laboratory of warfare and Volterra was a major city. However, the fortress built by the Medici at Volterra after 1472 was a drum-towered work, indicating that even the well read and wealthy had not yet adjusted to the new reality. The pendulum had swung from manoeuvre, with a premium on relatively small, fast-moving armies, surprise and trickery, to the ponderous deployment of large forces against which mere cleverness could not prevail – and against which the older forms of fortification could no longer hope to hold out until winter brought the campaigning season to an end.

Returning to our tour, Provincial 258 runs out of the Marecchia valley and continues over the Apennines at the Viamaggio Pass before descending to the upper Tiber valley. We stay in the valley only to drive past San Sepolcro before recrossing the mountains on Provincial 73, a steep switchback road that crosses the Apennines at the Bocca Trabaria Pass and runs on to the Adriatic along the Metauro valley. Here begins the area known as Massa Trabaria, Federico's domain even before he had his half-brother murdered and inherited Urbino. Federico ceded the territory and the title of Count of Mercatello to his Merlin-brother Ottaviano, and amid the many treasures of medieval art housed in the church-museum of St Francis in Mercatello sul Metauro can be seen two bas-relief marble tondos of Federico and Ottaviano, which celebrate their strong family resemblance. Further down the valley, inside

* Although the principles survived in the trench warfare of World War One, the last formal siege conducted in this manner was at Brussels in 1830.

the Porta Albana gateway of Sant'Angelo in Vado, there is a well-lettered inscription that reads 'The creed of the bourgeois is egoism – the creed of the Fascist is heroism'. Someone has thrown red paint at it, but it must have been done when the gate was last painted and clearly no attempt has been made to remove it: a reminder that Fascism was strongest in the rural areas, which provided a disproportionate share of the soldiers and casualties in Italy's disastrous participation in World War One and was a revolt against both the reserved-occupation industrial workers and their war-profiteering employers.

It is worth making a side trip south from Sant'Angelo to Piòbbico, in the Candigliano valley. The town is overlooked by the fourteenth-century palace-fortress of the Brancaleoni, which contains 130 rooms and is built around a large garden-courtyard with the name and date of the person who carved it incised on every door and window. The work includes a small village *(borgo)* that sheltered all the family retainers in houses with tiny entrances, over which are carved three faces looking to the past, present and future. The clock tower, built in 1510, ran counter-clockwise and a tradition of perversity persists. In the town there is a statue of a decidedly plain individual looking in a mirror, unveiled during the annual Festival of the Ugly in 2006 staged by the International Ugly Club, founded in the nineteenth century, whose motto is 'Ugliness is a Virtue, Beauty is Slavery'. Further up the Candigliano valley are Apecchio and Carda, the domain remaining to the Ubaldini after their traditional heartland in the Tuscan Mugello was blotted out in the fourteenth century.

The principal Brancaleone stronghold was back in the Metauro valley at Urbania, then Castel Durante, named for Cardinal Legate William Durand who at the end of the thirteenth century heavily refortified the town of Castel del Rippe during a long campaign to wrest control of the area from the Brancaleoni and their Montefeltro allies in Urbino. Ironically Durand's riverside keep was occupied and much built upon by the Brancaleoni until 1430, when Federico's father took possession. The interior was remodelled in the 1460s by Luciano Laurana, who designed a similar courtyard in the ducal palace at Urbino. Urbania is one of two local places (Monte Adrualdo, now Fermignano, is the other) claiming to be the birthplace of Bramante, designer of St Peter's basilica in Rome, and was one of the few

*Castel Durante*

manufacturing towns in the Duchy of Urbino – it still offers a riotous selection of Baroque ceramics.

The most striking feature of the area around Urbino, at the Metauro–Foglia watershed, is the scarcity of the hilltop villages otherwise characteristic of the Borderlands. This is hard, unproductive land and Urbino became a significant population centre solely because of its strategic location. The town was made glorious – today a UNESCO World Heritage Site – by the determination of the Montefeltri that it should be so. An indication of its original insignificance is that the taller of the two hills now covered by the town was not even fortified before Cardinal Albornoz built a citadel there during the papal repossession of the 1350s, while the angled bastion wall round Urbino dates from about 1515, when Duke Francesco Maria della Rovere refortified it. The outstanding feature of the ducal palace, atop the lower hill, is that it was designed to be open to the citizens, even though several previous Montefeltri were expelled by popular rebellions and two assassinated. The palace embodies the sophisticated political thinking of Federico, who knew that no fortress could hold down the town in which it stood by force alone and chose to impress, not by overt power, but by majesty. Once inside the modest gate, however, visiting citizens were reminded

*Urbino palace*

how lucky they were to have such a ruler by the two-tiered neo-Latin inscriptions around the courtyard (Picture section 2, p. 4):

I. Federico, duke of Urbino, Count of Montefeltro and Castel Durante, standard-bearer of the Holy Roman Church, and commander of the League of Italian States, constructed from its foundations this palace, which was erected to his own glory and future renown.

II. He fought in war many times, rallied the standards six times, overcame the enemy eight times, and increased his dominion as victor in all his battles; his justice, mercy, generosity and piety equalled and adorned his victories in peacetime.*

Descending from Urbino back to the Metauro, one joins the route of the Roman Via Flaminia (roughly, today's E 78), the backbone of the Montefeltro domain, at Fossombrone. The town was a Malatesta

* My thanks to Philip Ford, Professor of French and Neo-Latin Literature at Cambridge University, for this authoritative translation.

possession from 1304 until 1445, when Galeazzo 'the Inept' of the Pesaro branch sold it to Federico in the deal which also saw Pesaro alienated to Alessandro Sforza, and which precipitated the final showdown with Sigismondo. The outward appearance of the fortress on the hill at the centre of the town, where Malatestino Novello and his young son Guido were murdered on the orders of their aptly nicknamed cousin Malatesta 'Family Devastator' in 1336, is much as it was before the change of ownership – Federico built the separate Corte Alta as his seat. It is not easy to disentangle oneself from the complex E 78 highway interchange to find the minor road that follows the line of the old Via Flaminia to the Roman bridge at Calmazzo, but if you succeed the reward beyond is the spectacular pass at Gola di Furlo and the short tunnel bored through a granite outcrop in AD 73, during the reign of Emperor Vespasian.

The Via Flaminia runs along the Candigliano–Burano rivers towards Cagli, before which one can admire the Y-shaped Roman bridge over the Bosso torrent, in use until the 1950s. Only a single support tower remains of the great work built by Martini at Cagli, which we know from illustrations was a seriously practical fortification consisting of broad drum-towers flanking a large ravelin. Recrossing the Apennines we reach the Montefeltro stronghold of Gubbio, like Urbino today well off the beaten track. However, its strategic location at the confluence of the main road running from Spoleto–Umbria to the Adriatic coast at Fano, and the secondary route through Sassoferrato to Senigallia explains its significance in the creation of the Duchy of Urbino. As at Castel Durante and Urbino, the Laurana-designed palace at Gubbio is built round a courtyard. The intricate wood inlay *(intarsia)* panelling of Federico's private study *(studiolo)* at Urbino is still in place, but the equivalent workmanship that used to grace his study at the Gubbio palace is now in the Metropolitan Museum in New York. The Met exhibit is in many ways better displayed – as a discrete work of art – than the marquetry at Urbino, but of course it lacks the intimacy and the enhancing context of its original setting.

There is no coherent itinerary to explore the area between the Metauro and Esino rivers, which constituted the southern part of Federico's domain. Worth visiting are the castle at Frontone, the almost

San Leo-like prominence of the walled town of Arcevia, once Rocca Contrata, the clever gate works at Loretello and the neat little fortified country estate at Nidastore, where in 2005 someone was busily refurbishing the interior of one of the towers to create a unique dwelling. The most significant fortifications are at Mondavio, one of the three fully preserved works unequivocally attributed to Martini, and the outstanding fortified town of Corinaldo. Mondavio is the home of the Crossbow Association of Italy and when I was there they were firing, very accurately, from the lower works at a target on the main tower. The work is an architect's plaything, in substance no stronger than any medieval castle but wonderfully shaped to explore geometric forms and attractive complexity. Corinaldo, by contrast, boasts one of the most complete medieval perimeter wall and tower complexes in the Marche, and one of the finest examples of the transitional tower-bastion in all of Italy. It is scarped, angular and juts out from the main walls to cover them with flanking fire: but it is twice the height of the walls, themselves very tall at this point. The machicolation and 'Guelf' crenellation are the product of a whimsical twentieth-century restoration.

The Adriatic coast road is crowded, ugly and dangerous, and it is best to use the E 55 to hop from town to town. Archaeologists have cut into the wall of the drum-towered della Rovere palace-fortress at Senigallia to show how the work now visible was erected over the original castle built by Sigismondo. This was the seat of secular power created for his family by Pope Sixtus IV, better remembered for the Sistine Library and Chapel in the Vatican, the latter made eternally glorious by Michelangelo for Sixtus's grandson Pope Julius II. Sixtus and his 'nephews' *(nipoti)* are shown together in the Sistine Library fresco by Melozzo da Forlì (Picture section 2, p. 8). The future Julius II stands in front of Sixtus, while on the left in red is Girolamo Riario, whom Sixtus made lord of Imola and Forlì. If Lorenzo I de' Medici had been assassinated along with his brother Giuliano in the Pazzi conspiracy of 1478, Sixtus would have made Girolamo lord of Florence as well. The prelate behind Sixtus is Cardinal Raffaele Riario, who was nearly lynched along with Archbishop Salviati of Pisa following the failure of the Pazzi conspiracy, and the man kneeling is Bartolomeo Platina, the first Vatican librarian. Next to Girolamo is Giovanni della

*Martini's* mastio *at Mondavio, with crossbow target*

*Angular* rivellino *at Corinaldo*

*Archaeologists' cut at Senigallia showing addition by Francesco della Rovere to Sigismondo's work.*

Rovere, whom Sixtus made lord of Senigallia and who married Federico's daughter Giovanna, whose son Francesco became Duke of Urbino after Federico's heir Guidobaldo died childless in 1508.

*Old and new walls at Fano*

Further north at the Malatesta fortress in Fano there is a fine juxtaposition of angular bastion and medieval wall, but sadly the huge tower built by Sigismondo's father Pandolfo III, which once controlled the port (at the corner of the work beyond the section illustrated), was utterly destroyed in 1944. The keep was extensively rebuilt by Sigismondo between 1438 and 1452, and another bombastic neo-Latin plaque in the wall proclaims that he found 'minimal remains of the old [city] walls and the tower and walls of this castle [and] most opportunely rebuilt them by sea and land 1452'. In the church of St Francis there is a funerary chapel 'dedicated in 1460 by Sigismondo Pandolfo Malatesta to his father, the Lord and most Merciful Prince Pandolfo'. On reading these two inscriptions it first occurred to me that the key to Sigismondo's behaviour as man and lord was a highly ambivalent competition with the shade of his father: how else to explain the manifestly false description of the, now lost, tower as 'minimal remains', coupled with the father-worship explicit in every plaque? By claiming that other inherited works he modified were built 'from the foundations', Sigismondo seems to have been telling posterity that, apart from the everlasting glory due to Pandolfo III for having produced such a son, his father's legacy was ephemeral.

*Shrapnel damage at Pesaro*

The drum-towered della Rovere palace-fortress at Pesaro shows the effects of Allied bombing in 1944 – just so must the walls have looked after the ranging shots of siege artillery before the breaching battery got down to business. Across the Foglia we are once more into the dense fortification characteristic of Malatestaland. Pesaro was the eastern end of the Gothic Line and it is astonishing how many works in the hills beyond survived Allied sea, air and artillery bombardment during the grinding 1944 assault, particularly the great work at Gradara, which commands the coast road. It is somewhat over-restored, a small price to pay for an archetype of the medieval walled town, with massive walls and towers and even a couple of resident ghosts – the spirits of Dante's doomed lovers Francesca and Paolo Malatesta, alleged on no authority at all to have been murdered by husband and brother Gianciotto in one of the castle bedrooms.* Gradara was a key acquisition by Mastin Vecchio in 1283, projecting Malatesta power down the coast towards Pesaro, Fano (first secured in 1306 by inviting the leading

* Much the most likely crime scene was the family Gattolo palace in Rimini.

citizens to dine and drowning them) and Senigallia, which cut off the Montefeltri from the outlet to the sea they needed to complete their control of the Foglia valley.

*Gradara, with excavated secret sally port in foreground*

Inland from Gradara the hill villages of Meleto, Mondaino, Saludeccio and jewel-like Montegridolfo (below which South African Lieutenant Gerard Norton won the Victoria Cross on 31 August 1944) were spared, but Martini's work at Tavoleto was flattened. Unlike little Montegridolfo, which has been restored with strict concern for historical accuracy, the great Malatesta palace-fortress at Montefiore Conca, where they went to escape the coastal heat in summer, now looks like a cardboard box with random holes punched in it. Never of much military significance, the gloating spitefulness of Pius II in depriving the Malatesti of their country retreat is immortalised by the Piccolomini coat of arms mounted above the Porta Curina. To no avail: in the town square the Cafè dei Malatesta proclaims the abiding loyalty of the inhabitants to the lords who put their little town on the map. Beyond the Conca things did not go so well for the hill villages in 1944, with Agello, Misano, Monte Colombo and Montescudo irreparably damaged. Along with Coriano and Sassofeltrio, the latter one of so many places claiming to have been rebuilt by Martini, they were part of the original Montefeltro patrimony, long held by the Malatesti and recovered with deep satisfaction by Federico.

And so to Rimini, the end of the tour and the spider in the Malatesta web that once spread as far as San Sepolcro in the upper Tiber valley, north to Cesena and the valuable salt flats of Cervia, and south into much of the Marche. Rimini is where the Via Flaminia met the Via

*Bizarre reconstruction at Montefiore Conca*

Emilia and the Via Popilia, a strategic choke point on the coastal plain created by Monte Titano, where the aggrieved citizens of San Marino erected a monument to those fallen in 1944 when the Allies bombed what was possibly the finest artillery observation post in Italy despite the nominal neutrality of the little ecclesiastical state. Rimini/Ariminum was one of the most important settlements of ancient Rome, first as a military outpost guarding against the Gauls of the Po valley and then as the base for the conquest of northern Italy. The forum (now Piazza Tre Martiri to honour three partisans hanged there by the Nazis) where Julius Caesar made his appeal to the legions in 49 BC, the great Arch of Augustus (27 BC) that marks the end of the Via Flaminia and the five-arched Bridge of Tiberius (*c.* AD 20) across the Marecchia, which marks the start of the Via Emilia and still sustains heavy traffic, bear witness to the town's key role in the early history of imperial Rome.

Sigismondo was strongly influenced by the Roman heritage of his family's core possession. Because it was never completed (there was to be an extended apse and a prominent transept crowned by a dome), we can see how Alberti designed the Tempio Malatestiano to create a symbiosis between pre-existing and new elements. The inscription on the façade states that the church was built – not rebuilt – by Sigismondo in 1450, but only a few feet above these words the brickwork of the old church peeps between the unfinished pillars of what was to have been a miniature Arch of Augustus. The ensemble provides an irresistible metaphor of how greatly Sigismondo's desire for grandeur and eternal glory exceeded the means at his disposal.

Flanked by remnants of the medieval city walls, Castel Sismondo was built to be a palace as well as a fortification but the military aspects overwhelmingly predominate (Picture section 1). Only the nucleus around the *mastio* (second, third and fourth storeys) was spared when the outworks were demolished and the ditch filled in 1826, and Diagram 6 is based on medallions and old maps. Over the main gate there is a splendid cruciform marble inlay. The central panel, said to be the work of Matteo de' Pasti, shows the Malatesta coat of arms on an angled jousting shield, above which there is a ceremonial helmet surmounted by the tusked head of an angry elephant with a dragon's dorsal sail. The lateral panels are inscribed with Sigismondo's name in Gothic script. A lower panel in neo-Latin, repeated with minor variations on two other walls, bears the words 'Sigismondo Pandolfo Malatesta, son of Pandolfo, erected and constructed this great new structure from the foundations to be an ornament to Rimini, and decreed the castle should be called Sismondo after his own name 1446'.

Although the great Florentine architect Brunelleschi may have contributed to the design of this and other fortifications during a brief stay in 1438, the principal architect was Sigismondo himself. Apart from his name and parentage, the text of the tablet is misleading: Castel Sismondo was constructed on the site and in part with materials from the demolition of the old Gattolo palace-fortress begun by Mastin Vecchio in the late thirteenth century; the new structure was nowhere near complete in 1446; and the eastward orientation of the main tower and the north and east bastions makes it clear that his intention was to browbeat the citizens of Rimini, although they had not rebelled against the Malatesti since they became lords of the city in 1295. Perhaps the *mastio* is, after all, the horn 'so big that you cannot believe' boastfully proclaimed on the banner that once draped Sigismondo's sepulchre.

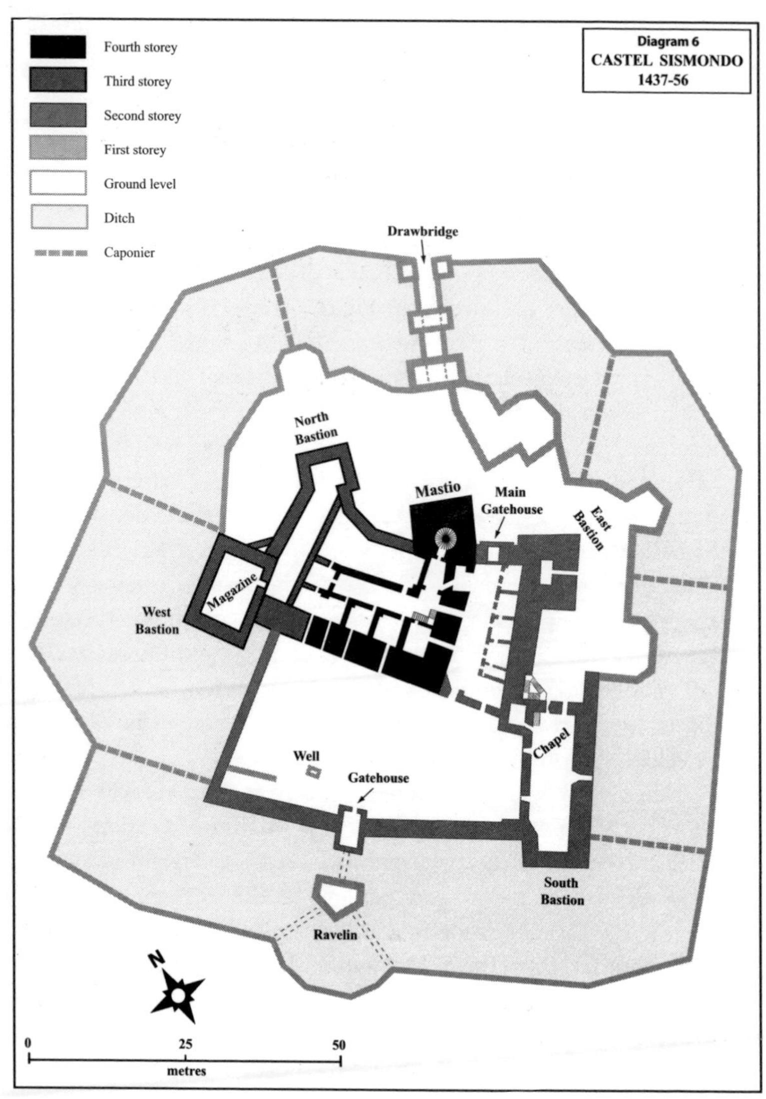
Fourth storey
Third storey
Second storey
First storey
Ground level
Ditch
Caponier
Diagram 6
CASTEL SISMONDO
1437-56
Drawbridge
North Bastion
Mastio
Main Gatehouse
East Bastion
Magazine
West Bastion
Chapel
Well
Gatehouse
South Bastion
Ravelin
N
0
25
50
metres

# APPENDIX A

# *Popes, Emperors and Rulers in Italy 1050–1500*

## Popes/*Antipopes*

| | |
|---|---|
| 1049–54 | St Leo IX |
| 1058–61 | Nicholas II |
| 1061–73 | Alexander II |
| 1073–85 | Gregory VII |
| *1080–1100* | *Clement III* |
| 1088–99 | Urban II |
| 1099–1154 | Nine popes & *seven antipopes* |
| 1154–59 | Hadrian IV |
| 1159–81 | Alexander III |
| *1159–80* | *Four antipopes* |
| 1198–1216 | Innocent III |
| 1216–27 | Honorius III |
| 1227–41 | Gregory IX |
| 1243–54 | Innocent IV |
| 1254–61 | Alexander IV |
| 1261–64 | Urban IV |
| 1265–68 | Clement IV |
| 1271–76 | Gregory X |
| 1277–80 | Nicholas III |
| 1281–85 | Martin IV |
| 1294–1303 | Boniface VIII |

**Avignon Popes**

| | |
|---|---|
| 1305–14 | Clement V |
| 1316–34 | John XXII |
| 1334–42 | Benedict XII |
| 1342–52 | Clement VI |
| 1352–62 | Innocent VI |
| 1362–70 | Urban V |
| 1371–78 | Gregory XI |

**Western Schism**

Rome *Avignon* [*Pisa*]

| | |
|---|---|
| 1378–89 | Urban VI |
| *1378–94* | *Clement VII* |
| 1389–1404 | Boniface IX |
| *1395–1415* | *Benedict XIII* |
| 1404–06 | Innocent VII |
| 1406–15 | Gregory XII |
| [*1409–10* | *Alexander V*] |
| [*1410–15* | *John XXIII*] |

**Unified Papacy**

| | |
|---|---|
| 1417–31 | Martin V |
| 1431–47 | Eugenius IV |
| 1447–55 | Nicholas V |
| 1455–58 | Callixtus III |
| 1458–64 | Pius II |
| 1464–71 | Paul II |
| 1471–84 | Sixtus IV |
| 1492–1503 | Alexander VI |
| 1503–13 | Julius II |

## Holy Roman Emperors

**Salian (Frankish)**

| | |
|---|---|
| 1046–56 | Henry III |
| 1084–1105 | Henry IV |
| 1111–25 | Henry V |

**Hohenstaufen**

| | |
|---|---|
| 1155–90 | Frederick I |
| 1191–97 | Henry VI |
| 1209–18 | Otto IV |
| 1220–50 | Frederick II |

**Luxembourg**

| | |
|---|---|
| 1312–13 | Henry VII |
| 1328–47 | Louis the Bavarian |
| 1355–78 | Charles IV |
| 1433–37 | Sigismund |

**Hapsburg**

| | |
|---|---|
| 1452–93 | Frederick III |
| 1493–1519 | Maximilian I |

## Southern Kingdom

**Hauteville**

| | |
|---|---|
| 1057–85 | Robert Guiscard |
| 1071–1101 | Roger I (Sicily) |
| 1085–1111 | Robert Borsa |
| 1101–05 | Simon (Sicily) |
| 1105 | Roger II (Sicily) |
| 1130–54 | King of Two Sicilies |
| 1154-94 | William I, II & III |

**Hohenstaufen**

| | |
|---|---|
| 1194-97 | Henry VI |
| 1198–1250 | Frederick II |
| 1250–54 | Conrad |
| 1254–58 | Conradin |
| 1258–66 | Manfred |
| 1266–68 | Conradin |

**Anjou (Naples) Aragon (Sicily)**

| | | |
|---|---|---|
| Both | 1268–82 | Charles I |
| Naples | 1282–84 | Charles I |
| Sicily | 1282–85 | Peter I |
| Naples | 1285–1309 | Charles II |
| Sicily | 1285–1337 | Frederick III |
| Naples | 1309–1343 | Robert |
| Sicily | 1337–42 | Peter II |
| Naples | 1343–82 | Joanna I |
| [1352–62 | Louis of Taranto] | |
| Sicily | 1342–55 | Louis I |
| Sicily | 1355–77 | Frederick IV |
| Sicily | 1377–92 | Barons' rule |

Naples 1382–86
Charles of Durazzo
Louis I (Anjou-Provence)

| | | |
|---|---|---|
| Sicily | 1392–1409 | Martin I |

Naples 1384–1417
Louis II (Anjou-Provence)
Ladislas of Hungary

| | | |
|---|---|---|
| Sicily | 1409–10 | Martin II |

Naples 1414–35
Joanna II
Louis III (Anjou-Provence)

**Aragon**

| | | |
|---|---|---|
| Sicily | 1411 | Alfonso V |
| Naples | 1435–58 | Alfonso V |
| Sicily | 1458–79 | John II |
| Naples | 1458–94 | Ferrante I |
| Naples | 1495–96 | Alfonso I |
| | 1496 | Ferrante II |
| | 1496–1504 | Federico |

Ferdinand II of Aragon
Sicily (1479) & Naples (1504–16)

## Milan

| | |
|---|---|
| 1076–1115 | Countess Matilda |
| 1115–97 | REPUBLIC |
| 1197–1277 | Della Torre clan |

### Visconti Counts

| | |
|---|---|
| 1277–94 | Bishop Ottone |
| 1294–1302 | Matteo I |
| *1302–11* | *Della Torre interlude* |
| 1311–22 | Matteo I |
| 1322–29 | Galeazzo I |
| 1329–39 | Azzone |
| 1339–49 | Luchino |
| 1349–54 | Archbishop Giovanni |
| 1355 | Matteo II |
| 355–78 | Galeazzo II (Pavia) |
| 355–85 | Bernabò (Milan) |

### Visconti Dukes

Gian Galeazzo
Pavia (1378), Milan (1385)
Duke 1395–1402

| | |
|---|---|
| 1402–12 | Gian Maria |
| 1412–47 | Filippo Maria |
| 1477–50 | Ambrosian Republic |

### Sforza Dukes

| | |
|---|---|
| 450–66 | Francesco I |
| 466–76 | Galeazzo Maria |
| 494–99 | Ludovico il Moro |
| *499–1512* | *French occupation* |
| 512–15 | Ercole |
| 521–35 | Francesco II |

## Florence

| | |
|---|---|
| 1076–1115 | Countess Matilda |
| | REPUBLIC |
| 1343 | Collapse of Bardi and Peruzzi banks |
| 1378–81 | Ciompi rebellion and aftermath |
| 1382–1434 | Albizzi clan |

### Medici Financiers

| | |
|---|---|
| 1360–1429 | Giovanni di Bicci |
| 1389–1464 | Cosimo |
| 1416–69 | Piero |

### Medici Autocrats

| | |
|---|---|
| 1469–92 | Lorenzo I |
| 1469–76 | Giuliano |
| 1492–94 | Piero |
| *1494–98* | *Second Republic* |
| *1498–1512* | *French Occupation* |
| 1513–21 | Pope Leo X |
| 1513–19 | Lorenzo II |

## Ferrara/Modena

| | |
|---|---|
| 1076–1115 | Countess Matilda |
| 1115–70 | REPUBLIC |

### Este of Ferrara

| | |
|---|---|
| 1170–1212 | Azzo V |
| 1212–15 | Aldobrandino |
| 1215–22 | Azzo VI |
| 1240–64 | Azzo VII |

### Ferrara and Modena

| | |
|---|---|
| 1264–93 | Obizzo II |
| 1293–1308 | Azzo VIII |
| *1308–17* | *Angevin/Papal rule* |
| 1317–26 | Aldobrandino II |
| 1326–35 | Rinaldo II |
| 1335–44 | Niccolò I |
| 1335–52 | Obizzo III |
| 1352–61 | Aldobrandino III |
| 1361–83 | Alberto I |
| 1383–88 | Niccolò II |
| 1388–93 | Alberto II |
| 1393–1409 | Niccolò III |

### Ferrara, Modena & Reggio

| | |
|---|---|
| 1409–41 | Niccolò III |
| 1441–50 | Leonello |

**Este Dukes**

Borso
Duke of Modena & Reggio 1452
Duke of Ferrara 1471

| | |
|---|---|
| 1471–1505 | Ercole |
| 1505–34 | Alfonso I |

# APPENDIX B

## MONTEFELTRO CLAN

**UDALRIC** invested Count of Carpegna and Pietrarubbia in 962.
Descendant was first **Count of Sogliano**, title passed by marriage 1255 to **Giovanni di Ramberto Malatesta**.

**ODDO ANTONIO I** had three sons who divided the inheritance in 1140:
1. Guido (d. 1216?) Count of Carpegna*
2. Galeazzo (d. 1190?) Count of Pietrarubbia.
3. ANTONIO I

**ANTONIO I** (d. 1184?) Count of Montecopiolo, invested Count of Montefeltro 1150.
1. MONTEFELTRANO I
2. Cavalca
3. Buonconte

**MONTEFELTRANO I** (*c.*1135–1202) Count of Montefeltro, inherited Pietrarubbia.
1. BUONCONTE
2. TADDEO I
3. Rolando, Bishop of Montefeltro.

BUONCONTE (*c.*1170–1242) Count of Montefeltro, invested joint Count of Urbino 1226.
1. MONTEFELTRANO II
2. Ugolino (d. 1252) Bishop of Montefeltro 1232, excommunicated and deposed 1245.
3. Taddeo, Franciscan friar.
4. **Cavalca** from whom the line of **Lords of Bagno**.
   - **Galasso** (*c.*1240–1303).
     - Ricardo and Galeotto Novello fought on opposite sides at battle of Ferrara 1333.

**TADDEO I** (*c.*1175–1251) Count of Pietrarubbia, invested joint Count of Urbino 1226.
1. Taddeo (d. 1284) Count of Pietrarubbia.
   - **Corrado** (k. 1298).

---

* Long allies of the Malatesti, through marriages *circa* 1400 took the family name.

- Agnese (k. 1298) m. **Tino Malatesta** 1288.
- Taddeo Novello (k. 1299).
  - Malatesta m. widowed Simona, youngest child of **Malatesta da Verucchio** 1324.

2. Arrigo (d. 1307?) **Count of Faggiuola** by marriage.
3. Ranieri **Count of Castel d'Elci**.
   - illegitimate descendants of Arrigo or Ranieri included **Uguccione** and **Neri della Faggiuola**.

**MONTEFELTRANO II** (*c.*1195–1255)
1. TADDEO II
2. GUIDO
3. Feltrano 'Feltruccio' (*c.*1240–85?).
   - **Speranza** (1270–1345) led anti-papal association 'Friends of the Marche'.

**TADDEO II** (*c.*1220–82)
1. Roberto (d. 1285) Bishop of Montefeltro, deposed and imprisoned 1284.

**GUIDO** (1223–98) m. Manentessa di Ghiaggiolo.
1. Buonconte (*c.* 1257–89).
2. FEDERICO I
3. Corrado (1259–1319) Bishop of Urbino.

**FEDERICO I** (*c.*1258–1322)
1. Guido Novello 'Tigna' (d. 1343?).
2. Ugolino (d. 1363) Bishop of Fossombrone.
3. NOLFO
4. **Galasso** (1296–1350).
   - Guido (d. 1350)
5. Feltrano (d. 1366?) m. daughter of Marquis Spinetta Malaspina of Verrucola.
   - illegitimate **Niccolò** (1319–67) led the Company of the Hat.
   - Spinetta (d. 1369?).
6. Enrico (d. 1361?) m. daughter of Teodorico Ordelaffi of Forlì.
7. Francesco (k. with father 1322).
8. Anna m. **Ferrantino Novello Malatesta**.

**NOLFO** (*c.*1290–1364) *c.*1327 m. daughter of Cante Gabrielli I of Gubbio.
1. Paolo (d. 1370).
2. **Federico II** (d. 1367?) m. (A) unknown; (B) 1361 Teodora Gonzaga of Mantua.
   - (A) ANTONIO II
   - (A) Nolfo II (d. in prison 1380) in 1377 m. daughter of Cante Gabrielli II of Cantiano.
   - (A) Galasso (d. 1398).
   - (A) Guido (d. in prison) Venetian patrician.
   - illegitimate Niccolò.

**ANTONIO II** (1348–1404) m. Agnesina de' Prefetti di Vico.

1. GUIDANTONIO
2. in 1395 Anna (1378–1434) m. **Galeotto 'Belfiore' Malatesta** lord of Pesaro.
3. in 1405 Battista (1384–1448) m. **Galeazzo 'l'Inetto' Malatesta** lord of Pesaro.

**GUIDANTONIO** (1377–1443) m. (A) 1397 Rengarda (1380–1423) barren daughter of **Galeotto Malatesta**; (B) 1424 Caterina (d. 1438) niece of Pope Martin V.

1. in 1420 illegitimate Aura m. **Bernardino degli Ubaldini**.
   - Ottaviano (1423–98).
2. illegitimate FEDERICO III declared legitimate by Pope Martin V in 1424.
3. (B) Agnesina (1425–47) m. (1) 1442–3 Guidantonio Manfredi; (2) 1443 Alessandro Gonzaga.
4. (B) ODDO ANTONIO II
5. (B) in 1442 Violante (1430–93) m. **Domenico Malatesta** of Cesena, joined Poor Clares 1466.
6. (B) in 1448 Sveva (1434–78) was second wife of Alessandro Sforza, made to join Poor Clares for adultery 1457, Abbess of Corpus Christi Abbey in Pesaro 1475, beatified as Sister Serafina 1754.

**ODDO ANTONIO II** (1427–44) in 1444 m. Isotta (1425–56), legitimated daughter of Niccolò III d'Este.

**FEDERICO III** (1422–82) m. (A) 1437 Gentile (d. 1456) heiress of Count Bartolomeo Brancaleone; (B) 1460 Battista (1446–72) daughter of **Alessandro Sforza** of Pesaro and Costanza da Varano.

1. in 1454 illegitimate Buonconte (1442–58) declared legitimate by Pope Nicholas V.
2. illegitimate Antonio (1450–1500).
3. in 1466 illegitimate Gentile (1458–1529) m. Agostino Fregoso.
4. (B) seven daughters of whom:
   - in 1474 Giovanna (d. 1514) m. **Giovanni della Rovere** Duke of Sora and lord of Senigallia.
   - in 1475 Elisabetta (d. 1521) m. **Roberto Malatesta** of Rimini.
   - in 1483 Agnese (d. 1522) m. Duke Fabrizio Colonna of Paliano.
5. (B) GUIDOBALDO

**GUIDOBALDO** (1472–1508) in 1489 m. Elisabetta Gonzaga (1471–1526).

Succeeded by **Francesco Maria** (1490–1513) who took in 1504 the name 'da Montefeltro della Rovere d'Aragona'; Duke of Sora, lord of Senigallia and Pesaro (1512), son of Federico III's daughter Giovanna and Duke Giovanni.

# APPENDIX C

## MALATESTA CLAN

**MALATESTA 'Antico'** (d. 1195) of Pennabilli m. Berta da Pietro Traversari of Ravenna.

1. Malatesta 'Minore' (d. 1197) m. Alaburga?
   - MALATESTA 'della Penna'.
2. **Giovanni** (1185–1221?) m. Donissa Ravegnani of Cervia.
   - Ramberto (d. 1249) m. Rengarda daughter of Count Brandolini of Bagnacavallo.
     – Giovanni di Ramberto (d. 1299) became **Count of Sogliano** by marriage 1255.

**MALATESTA 'della Penna'** (1183–1248) m. Adalasia?

1. MALATESTA DA VERUCCHIO

**MALATESTA DA VERUCCHIO 'Mastin Vecchio'** (1212–1312) m. (A) 1248 Concordia Arrigheto daughter of Imperial Vicar of Romagna; (B) 1266 Margherita Paltanieri of Monselice.

1. (A) GIOVANNI 'Gianciotto'.
2. (A) PAOLO 'il Bello'.
3. (A) MALATESTINO 'dall'Occhio'.
4. (A) Ramberto (1260–98) chaplain to Pope Boniface VIII.
5. (B) PANDOLFO I
6. (B) in 1275 Maddalena (d. 1313) m. Bernardino da Polenta.
7. (B) in 1285 Rengarda (d. 1309) m. Francesco I Manfredi.
8. (B) in 1324 widowed Simona (d. 1355) m. Count Malatesta of Pietrarubbia.

**GIOVANNI 'Gianciotto'** (1249–1304) m. (A) 1275 Francesca daughter of Guido da Polenta (k. 1285); (B) 1286 Zambrasina Zambrasi of Faenza.

1. illegitimate Tino (d. 1319) in 1288 m. Agnese (k. 1298) daughter of Count Corrado of Pietrarubbia.
   - Giovanni (d. 1375) from whom **lords of San Mauro**. He had seven sons, of whom:
     – Ramberto (d. 1430) whose son **Giovanni di Ramberto** (d. 1435?) tried to seize Rimini in 1431.
2. (B) **Ramberto** (1307–30) lord of Roncofreddo and Castiglione.

**PAOLO 'il Bello'** (1250–85) in 1269 m. Orabile (1257-1304) to become **Count of Ghiaggiolo**.

1. **Uberto** (1270–1324) m. daughter of Count Guidi of Dovadola.
   - Ramberto (d. 1367) m. Rengarda?
     – Francesco (d. 1351) and Niccolò (1355-76).

**MALATESTINO 'dall'Occhio'** (1254–1317) *c.*1270 m. Giacoma de' Rossi of Rimini.

1. **Ferrantino** (d. 1353) m. Beluccia Baligani of Iesi.
   - **Malatestino Novello** (k.1336) m. Polentesia daughter of Guido Novello da Polenta.
     – Guido (k.1336); **Ferrantino Novello** (d. 1352) m. Anna sister of **Nolfo Montefeltro**.

**PANDOLFO I** (1267–1326) m. Taddea? (d. 1362).

1. MALATESTA 'Guastafamiglia'.
2. GALEOTTO Vecchio'.
3. in 1329 Caterina m. Luigi I Gonzaga.

**MALATESTA 'Guastafamiglia'** (1297–1364) in 1324 m. Constanza Ondedei of Saludecio.

1. PANDOLFO II
2. **Malatesta 'Ungaro'** (1327–72) m. (A) Concordia Pandolfini; (B) 1363 daughter of Alberto I d'Este.
   - (A) in 1362 Costanza (k.1378) m. Ugo d'Este.
3. in 1338 Taddea and Caterina m. brothers Giovanni and Lodovico Ordelaffi; sons included Sinibaldo I (below).
4. *c.*1340 Melchina m. Roberto Alidosi; son Azzo ruled Imola 1363–72.
5. illegitimate Leale (*c.*1323–1400) legitimated 1363 by Pope Nicholas V, Bishop of Rimini 1374–1400.

**GALEOTTO 'il Vecchio'** (1299–1385) m. (A) 1324 Hélise (d. 1366) niece of Amelio de Lautrec Rector of the Marche; (B) 1367 Gentilina (d. 1385) daughter of Ridolfo II da Varano, widow of Gentile Orsini.

1. (A) Rengarda (d. 1366) m. Maso Tarlati of Pietramala.
2. (B) CARLO II
3. (B) PANDOLFO III
4. (B) ANDREA
5. (B) **Galeotto 'Belfiore'** (1377–1400) in 1395 m. Anna (d. 1434) sister of **Guidantonio Montefeltro**.
6. (B) in 1393 Margherita (d. 1399) m. Francesco I Gonzaga; son Gian Francesco ruled Mantua 1407–44.
7. (B) in 1396 Gentilina (d. 1455) m. Gian Galeazzo I Manfredi; son Guidantonio ruled Faenza 1417–43.
8. (B) in 1397 Rengarda (1380–1423) m. **Guidantonio Montefeltro**.

**PANDOLFO II** (1325–73) in 1362 m. Paola (d. 1371) daughter of Bertoldo Orsini.

1. MALATESTA 'dei Sonetti'.
2. in 1372 Elisabetta (d. 1405) became first wife of Ridolfo III da Varano.
   - Gentile IV, Berardo III and 8 siblings.

3. Paola Bianca (d. 1398) m. (A) 1379 cousin Sinibaldo I Ordelaffi; (B) 1388 cousin Pandolfo III (below).

**MALATESTA 'dei Sonetti'** (1368–1429) in 1383 m. Elisabetta (d. 1405) daughter of Ridolfo II da Varano.

1. **Carlo I** (*c.*1390–1438) in 1416 m. Vittoria Colonna (d. 1463?) niece of Pope Martin V.
2. **Pandolfo** (*c.*1392–1441) Archbishop of Patras.
3. in 1409 Paola (1393–1449) m. Marquis Gian' Francesco I Gonzaga; son Ludovico ruled Mantua 1444–78.
4. Galeotto (1398–1414).
5. **Galeazzo 'l'Inetto'** (d. 1457) in 1405 m. Battista (1384–1450) sister of **Guidantonio Montefeltro**.
   - in 1425 Elisabetta m. Pier Gentile I da Varano.
     - in 1444 Costanza da Varano (1428–47) m. Alessandro Sforza.
     - in 1460 Battista Sforza (1446–72) m. **Federico III Montefeltro**.
6. in 1423 Taddea (d. 1427) m. Ludovico Migliorati lord of Sulmona.

**CARLO II** (1368–1429) in 1386 m. Elisabetta (d. 1432) sister of Francesco I Gonzaga.

**PANDOLFO III 'il Grande'** (1370–1427) m. (A) 1388 cousin Paola Bianca Malatesta of Pesaro (above); (B) 1421 Antonia da Varano (d. 1423); (C) 1427 Margherita di Conti Guidi. In 1428 Pope Martin V legitimated sons by (D) Allegra de' Mori and (E) Antonia Barignano (d. 1471) both of Brescia.

1. (D) **Galeotto Roberto 'il Beato'** (1411–32) in 1429 m. Margherita daughter of Niccolò III d'Este.
2. (E) SIGISMONDO PANDOLFO
3. (E) **Domenico 'Malatesta Novello'** (1418–65) in 1442 m. Violante daughter of **Guidantonio Montefeltro**.

**ANDREA** (1373–1416) m. (A) 1390 Rengarda Alidosi (k. 1401); (B) 1403 Lucrezia Ordelaffi (k. 1404); (C) 1409 Polissena Sanseverino, niece of King Ladislas of Naples.

1. (A) in 1408 Antonia (1393–1416) m. Duke Gian' Maria Visconti.
2. (A) Galeotto (1395–1414) in 1413 m. Nicolina (d. 1429) daughter of Ridolfo III da Varano. In 1421 widowed Nicolina m. Braccio da Montone; their son was Count Carlo Fortebraccio of Montone (1421–79).
3. (A) in 1414 Elisabetta (d. 1434) m. Obizzo da Polenta of Ravenna.
4. (B) in 1418 Parisina (beheaded 1425) m. Niccolò III d'Este.
   - in 1433 Ginevra (1419–40) m. **Sigismondo Pandolfo**. Twin Lucia (d. 1437) m. Carlo Gonzaga of Mantua.

**SIGISMONDO PANDOLFO** (1417–68) m. (A) 1433 Ginevra d'Este (above); (B) 1442 Polissena (1428–49) illegitimate daughter of Francesco Sforza; (C) 1456 Isotta degli Atti (1433–74). Nicholas V in 1450 legitimated Isotta's son Malatesta and Roberto by (D) Vanetta dei Toschi (1426–75); in 1452 he legitimated Sallustio, Valerio and Margherita by (E) Gentile Ramessini, and Lucrezia by (F) Gentile di Ser Giovanni (1411–39).

1. (F) illegitimate Pandolfo (1434–90) m. daughter of Ridolfo III da Varano (above).
2. (F) in 1456 Lucrezia (1436–68) m. Alberto d'Este.

3. (D) ROBERTO
4. (D) in 1474 illegitimate Contessina (1444–1515) m. Stefano Nardini of Vignanello.
5. (B) in 1451 Giovanna (1444–1511) m. Giulio Cesare da Varano.
6–7. (C) Giovanni (1447); Malatesta (1448–58).
8. (C) in 1481 Antonia (1453–83) m. Rodolfo Gonzaga; beheaded for adultery.
9–10. (E) Sallustio (*c.*1448–70); Valerio Galeotto (*c.*1451–70).
11. (E) in 1456 Margherita m. Count Carlo Fortebraccio (above).
12. in 1462 Alessandra (1462–8) by Aritrea Malatesta (*c.*1444–1501) married Andrea Dandolo.
13–15. (unknown) Galeotto m. daughter of Ridolfo III da Varano; Elisabetta (1458–1517); Umilia (1464–1517).

**ROBERTO 'il Magnifico'** (1442–82) in 1475 m. Elisabetta (d. 1521) daughter of **Federico III Montefeltro**.
1. PANDOLFO IV (by mistress Isabetta Aldobrandini).
2. Carlo (1482–1508) in 1505 m. into Venetian patrician Gradenigo family.

**PANDOLFO IV 'Pandolfaccio'** (1475–1534).
1. Sigismondo (1498–1553)

# APPENDIX D

# *Other Clans*

## OTHER CLANS

| **Alidosi (Imola 1291–1424)** | **Manfredi (Faenza 1313–1502)** | **Polenta (Ravenna 1275–1441)** | **Ordelaffi (Forlì 1295–1504)** |
|---|---|---|---|
| Alidosio<br>1291–3 | | Guido 'Vecchio'<br>1275–1310<br>*1275 daughter Francesca m. Gianciotto Malatesta, & son Bernardino m. Maddalena Malatesta* | Scarpetta<br>1295–1315 |
| Litto II<br>1346–51 | Francesco I<br>1313–27<br>1340–3<br>*m. Rengarda Malatesta* | | Francesco I<br>1315–31<br>*Sinibaldo I*<br>1331–7 |
| Roberto (1350–62)<br>*m. Melchina Malatesta* | Alberghetto<br>1327–9 *(beheaded)* | Lamberto II<br>1310–15 | Francesco II (1337–59)<br>*sons Giovanni & Ludovico m. Taddea & Caterina Malatesta* |
| Azzo<br>1365–72 | Riccardo<br>1339–40 | Guido Novello<br>1315–30<br>*daughter Polentesia m. Malatestino Novello* | Papacy<br>1359–76 |
| Bertrando<br>1365–91 | Giovanni<br>1340–56 | Ostasio III<br>1330–46 | Sinibaldo II<br>1376–85<br>*m. Paola Malatesta 1379 deposed by sons and killed* |
| *Daughters Rengarda m. Andrea Malatesta 1390, Giovanna m. Bartolomeo Brancaleone 1415** | Astorre I<br>1379–1405 *(beheaded)* | Guido III (1346–90)<br>*deposed and killed by sons* | Pino II 1386–1402<br>Francesco III 1402–5<br>*in 1404 killed daughter Lucrezia for conspiring with her husband Andrea Malatesta. He was killed by his sons including:*<br>Giorgio 1411–23 |
| Ludovico (the last)<br>1391–deposed 1424 | Gian' Galeazzo I 1410–17 *m. Gentile Malatesta*<br>Guidantonio 1417–43<br>*m. Agnesina Montefeltro* | Pietro (d. 1404)<br>Aldobrandino (d. 1401)<br>Ostasio (d. 1396)<br>Bernardino (d. 1399) | |
| Visconti<br>1424–6 | Astorri II 1443–68<br>Taddeo (Imola) 1467–73 | Obizzo<br>1404–31 | Teobaldo<br>1423–5<br>Antonio<br>1433–48 |
| Church from 1426 granted to Francesco Sforza in 1434, 1438 and 1470 | Carlo II<br>1468–77 | Ostasio IV<br>1431–41 | Francesco IV<br>1448–66<br>Pino III<br>1466–80 |
| Dowry to Girolamo Riario<br>1477–88 *(assassinated)* | Galeotto 1477–88<br>*killed by wife* | | Civil strife: Sinibaldo III and uncle Francesco V |
| Ottaviano Riario<br>1488–92 *(deposed)* | Astorre III 1488–1500<br>*raped/killed 1502* | Venice<br>1441–1509 | Papacy/Visconti<br>1488–99 |
| Cesare Borgia<br>1499–1503<br>Papacy from 1503 | Cesare Borgia<br>1500–3<br>Papacy from 1503 | Papacy from 1509 | Cesare Borgia<br>1499–1503<br>Papacy from 1504 |

* Only surviving child Gentile (d. 1356) Countess of Massa Trabaria married Federico III da Montefeltro 1437.

| **Gonzaga (Mantua 1328–1708)** | **Bentivoglio (Bologna 1401–1506)** | **Sforza (Pesaro 1445–1512)** | **Varano (Camerino 1266–1542)** |
|---|---|---|---|
| | | | Gentile I<br>1266–84 |
| | | | Ridolfo I (d. 1326)<br>Berardo I (d. 1329) |
| Ludovico I<br>1328–60 | | | Gentile II<br>1332–55 |
| Guido<br>1360–9 | | | Ridolfo II<br>1355–84 |
| Ludovico II<br>1369–82 | | Muzio Attendolo 'Sforza'<br>1369–1424 | Giovanni I<br>1384–7<br>Gentile III<br>1385–99 |
| Francesco I (1382–1407)<br>*m. Margherita Malatesta* | Giovanni I<br>*killed at Casalecchio 1402* | ***Dukes of Milan Appendix A*** | Ridolfo III<br>1399–1424<br>*(1) Elisabetta Malatesta*<br>*(2) Costanza Smeducci* |
| **Marquis from 1432**<br>Gian' Francesco<br>1407–44<br>*m. Paola Malatesta* | Anton Galeazzo<br>*assassinated 1435* | **Lords of Pesaro**<br>Alessandro 1445–73 | (1) Gentile IV (k. 1434)<br>(1) Berardo II (k. 1434 *along with six sons)*<br>(2) Giovanni II (k. 1434 *by* Gentile and Berardo) |
| Ludovico III<br>1444–78 | Annibale I (1438–45)<br>*m. Donina Visconti* | Costanzo I<br>1473–83 | (2) Pier Gentile I (k. 1433)<br>*m. Elisabetta Malatesta* |
| Federico I<br>1478–84 | Sante<br>1446–63<br>*m. Ginevra Sforza* | Giovanni<br>1483–deposed 1500 | Giulio Cesare<br>1444–1502<br>*and son Venanzio killed by Cesare Borgia* |
| Francesco II<br>1484–1519 | Giovanni II (1463–1506)<br>*also m. Ginevra Sforza* | Cesare Borgia<br>1500–3 | Cesare Borgia<br>1502–3 |
| **Duke of Mantua from 1530**<br>**Marquis of Monferrat from 1533** | Papacy<br>from 1506 | Giovanni<br>Restored 1503–10<br>Costanzo II<br>1510–12 | **Duke of Camerino from 1515** |
| Federico II<br>(1519–40) | | Rovere family<br>from 1512 | Giovanni Maria<br>1503–27 |

# APPENDIX E

## CORRESPONDENCE INTERCEPTED BY THE SIENESE

From Mario Tabanelli, *Sigismondo Pandolfo Malatesta* (Faenza 1977)

Only the second of two folios survives in the Sienese archives, but it provides a wonderful insight into the range and detail of the matters Sigismondo was dealing with even when on campaign across the Apennines. The most politically sensitive document was a copy of a letter from Jacopo Piccinino to his own chancellor, setting out a plan for a joint attack with Sigismondo on Pesaro and hinting at a far wider military agreement. There was, too, a wide range of letters dealing with administrative matters, including the payment of a pension to Sigismondo's mother with apologies for the delay in sending her the money and a begging letter from Vanetta de' Toschi in Fano. There were also instructions to Matteo de' Pasti to use the words proposed by Roberto Valturio for a plaque over the new gate at Carignano and to the chief of works about another plaque made by Pasti to be placed over the gate of Senigallia. The most personally illuminating correspondence is a very formal letter from his six-year-old son Malatesta thanking him for the gift of a horse (which Ezra Pound quoted in the *Malatesta Cantos*) and the following from Isotta, dated 20 December 1454:

> Magnificent and potent lord, lord Sigismondo Pandolfo Malatesta, my most special lord.
>
> My Lord, I have received your letter in which Your Lordship [Y.L.] swears to me a sacred oath that you love me more than ever. Of course, my Lord, I believe you; I would believe this oath even more if an end could be put to the matter that has always made me angry; I would

then be even more certain of your feelings. With regard to whatever more Y.L. requires of me, I ask indulgence of Y.L., if you do not want it for yourself, that for my love, and Y.L. wishing my life and my peace of mind, should want it and give concrete form to it as soon as you can.* With regard to what Y.L. writes to me, that I should not write as a person who is always suspicious and jealous of you, I had come to know of a certain betrayal of me by Y.L., to wit with the daughter of S.G.,† and for this reason and my other worries it seemed to me within my rights to write a little, and for that reason my letter may have seemed a bit brusque. With regard to the fact that you may tell me not to write any more, tell me after you have read this: I lack nothing more to be totally wretched. And I beg you, if you truly love me as you say, not to deprive me of writing to you, which is my happiness. Not being able to see you in person, at least may I see your letters: may it be your will to have compassion on poor little me! Our own Malatesta is well and has received with great contentment the horse [you sent]. All our other boys and girls are well. No more than this for now. I commend myself to Y.L. a thousand times.

From your Lady maidservant

*Yxotta Arimenesse* [signature in different handwriting]

In a cover letter Dorotea de Malatesti, wife of the Count of Ghiaggiolo, explained:

> Today My Lady Isotta has had me write [to you] about the daughter of Mr Galeazzo. My Lord, it is well said that young hens make thin broth! We have been close to this one/about this matter these days. All in all I have suppressed nothing and disguised nothing. In sum, my Lord, Isotta has told you, as I see it, her mind . . .

The 'young hen' was ten-year-old Aritrea, orphan daughter of Galeazzo Malatesta of Pesaro, who was Sigismondo's ward. In 1462, pregnant by him, she was married to the Venetian Andrea Dandolo. Sigismondo was ruined and never paid her dowry, which came back to bite him when Dandolo was appointed the *provveditore* of the expedition to Morea he undertook under commission from Venice in 1464.

* The 'matter' being that they were not married although he had been free since 1449.

† See following letter.

# BIBLIOGRAPHY

## INTERNET

I could not have written this book without daily recourse to a wide range of internet sites, in particular the wealth of biographical information in:

- 'Condottieri di Ventura' at *www.condottieridiventura.it*. Roberto Damiani, bless him, has put together data from a wide range of sources including the previous mother lode, Ercole Ricotti's rare four-volume *Storia delle compagnie di ventura in Italia* (1845).
- Davide Shamà's 'Genealogie delle Famiglie Nobili Italianae' at *www.sardimpex.com*
- 'The Dark Age' at *www.thedarkage.com/genealog.htm*
- 'Foundation for Medieval Genealogy' at *fmg.ac/Projects/MedLands/Contents.htm*

The Society for Medieval Military History site at *www.deremilitari.org* is a delight and for background information I found *historymedren.about.com* useful – for example, it contains the full text of Niccolò Machiavelli's *History of Florence*. The Web Gallery of Art at *www.wga.hu* is also priceless. For Boccaccio, Brown University's online 'Decameron Web' is superb, the full text of Jacob Burckhardt's *The Civilization of the Renaissance in Italy* is available at *www.idbsu.edu/courses/hy309/docs/burckhardt/burckhardt.html*, Longfellow's translation of Dante's *Divine Comedy* is at *www.everypoet.com/Archive/poetry/dante*, and so on and on.

I suppose I'm showing my age by chirruping about the cornucopia of research goodies available online, but it does make writing so much easier to be able to refresh the memory or to seek clarification of some point or other with a few mouse-clicks. But in addition one of my great joys has been to discover that if you browse the name of an obscure little village and have the patience to work through the ads trying to sell you hotel rooms, holiday homes and flat-shares, you can sometimes find a site where a local historian with no chance of being published has posted information on his *paese*, which it is prudent to cross-check but that may illuminate small but significant details that together go to make up the late medieval mosaic.

## BOOKS
(** = INDISPENSABLE; * = PARTICULARLY VALUABLE)

### English

* Abulafia, David, *The Western Mediterranean Kingdoms 1200–1500* (London 1997)

* Ady, Cecilia, *The Bentivoglio of Bologna* (Oxford 1937)

Anderson, Bonnie & J. Zinsser, *A History of their Own*, 2 vols. (London 1989)

Arnold, Thomas, *The Renaissance at War* (London 2001)

Baxandall, Michael, *Giotto and the Orators: Humanist Observers of Painting in Italy and the Discovery of Pictorial Composition 1350–1450* (Oxford 1986)

* Bertelli, Sergio and others, *Florence and Milan: Comparisons and Relations – Acts of Conferences at Villa I Tatti 1982 & 1984*, 2 vols. (Florence 1989)

Blomquist, Thomas & Maureen Mazzaoui (eds.), *The 'Other Tuscany': Essays in the History of Lucca, Pisa and Siena in the 13th, 14th and 15th centuries* (Kalamazoo 1994)

* Bowsky, William (ed.), *The Black Death: a Turning Point in History?* (New York 1971)

* Bradbury, Jim, *The Medieval Siege* (Woodbridge 1992)

Bueno de Mesquita, Daniel, *Giangaleazzo Visconti, duke of Milan 1351–1402* (Cambridge 1941)

Caferro, William, *Mercenary Companies and the Decline of Siena* (Baltimore 1998)

Cilliers, Jakkie & Peggy Mason (eds.), *Peace, Profit or Plunder? The Privatization of Security in War-Torn African Societies* (Pretoria 1999)

* Clough, Cecil, *The Duchy of Urbino in the Renaissance* (London 1981)

Cole, Bruce, *Italian Art 1250–1550: the Relation of Renaissance Art to Life and Society* (New York 1987)

* Contamine, Philippe (trans. Jones), *War in the Middle Ages* (Iowa 1984)

Creveld, Martin van, *The Transformation of War* (New York 1991)

Cunningham, Andrew & Ole Grell, *The Four Horsemen of the Apocalypse* (Cambridge, 2000)

Deiss, Joseph, *Captains of Fortune* (London 1966)

Dennistoun, James, *Memoirs of the Dukes of Urbino*, vol.I (London 1909)

* Fagan, Brian, *The Little Ice Age: How Climate Changed History* (New York 2002)

* Gabel, Leona (ed.) (trans. Gragg), *Secret Memoirs of a Renaissance Pope: the 'Commentaries' of Aeneas Sylvius Piccolomini, Pius II* (London 1988)

Gordon, Dillian, *The Italian Schools before 1400* (London 2001)

Green, Louis, *Castruccio Castracane: a Study in the Origins and Character of a Fourteenth-Century Italian Despotism* (Oxford 1986)

Gundersheimer, Werner, *Ferrara: the Style of a Renaissance Despotism* (Princeton 1973)
Hale, John (ed.), *Renaissance Venice* (London 1973)
* Hale, John, *Renaissance Fortification: Art or Engineering?* (London 1977)
* *Renaissance War Studies* (London 1983)
* *War and Society in Renaissance Europe 1450–1620* (Leicester 1985)
* *Artists and Warfare in the Renaissance* (New Haven 1990)
* *The Civilization of Europe in the Renaissance* (London 1993)
* Hall, Bert, *Weapons & Warfare in Renaissance Europe* (Baltimore 1997)
* Housley, Norman, *The Italian Crusades: the Papal–Angevin Alliance and the Crusades against Christian Lay Powers* (Oxford 1982)
*Crusading and Warfare in Medieval and Renaissance Europe* (Aldershot 2001)
Howard, Michael, *War in European History* (Oxford 1976)
Jacob, Ernest (ed.), *Italian Renaissance Studies: a tribute to the late Cecilia M. Ady* (London 1960)
Jardine, Lisa, *Worldly Goods: a New History of the Renaissance* (London 1996)
** Jones, Philip, *The Malatesta of Rimini and the Papal State* (Cambridge 1974)
Karlen, Arno, *Plague's Progress: a Social History of Man and Disease* (London 2001)
Kirshner, Julius (ed.), *The Origins of the State in Italy 1300–1600* (Chicago 1996)
* Larner, John, *The Lords of Romagna* (London 1965)
** Mallett, Michael, *Mercenaries and their Masters: Warfare in Renaissance Italy* (London 1974)
Mallett, Michael & John Hale, *The Military Organization of a Renaissance State: Venice 1400–1617* (Cambridge 1984)
Martines, Lauro (ed.), *Violence and Civil Disorder in Italian Cities 1200–1500* (Berkeley 1972)
*Power and Imagination: City-States in Renaissance Italy* (London 2002)
*April Blood: Florence and the Plot Against the Medici* (London 2004)
McNeill, William, *The Pursuit of Power* (Chicago 1984)
Mockler, Anthony, *Mercenaries* (London 1970)
Murrin, Michael, *History and Warfare in Renaissance Epic* (Chicago 1994)
Paret, Peter, *Imagined Battles* (Chapel Hill 1997)
* Partner, Peter, *The Lands of St Peter* (London 1972)
* Pernis, Maria & Laurie Adams, *Federico da Montefeltro and Sigismondo Malatesta: the Eagle and the Elephant* (New York 2003)
* Porter, Bruce, *War and the Rise of the State: the Military Foundations of Modern Politics* (New York 1994)
Rubinstein, Nicolai (ed.), *Florentine Studies: Politics and Society in Renaissance Florence* (London 1968)

* Setton, Kenneth, *The Papacy and the Levant*, 4 vols. (Philadelphia 1976–84)
Shearer, David, *Private Armies and Military Intervention* (New York 1998)
Simon, Kate, A *Renaissance Tapestry: the Gonzaga of Mantua* (London 1988)
Smail, Raymond, *Crusading Warfare 1097–1193* (Cambridge 1995)
* Stonor Saunders, Frances, *Hawkwood: Diabolical Englishman* (London 2004)
Taylor, Frederick, *The Art of War in Italy 1494–1529* (London 1993)
Thomson, Janice, *Mercenaries, Pirates and Sovereigns* (Princeton 1994),
Tickler, Peter, *The Modern Mercenary: Dog of War or Soldier of Fortune?* (London 1987)
Trease, Geoffrey, *The Condottieri* (London 1970)
* Verbruggen, J. F. (trans. Willard & Southern), *The Art of Warfare in Western Europe during the Middle Ages: from the Eighth Century to 1340* (New York 1977)
Waley, Daniel, *Condotte and Condottieri in the Thirteenth Century* (London 1976)
*The Italian City-Republics* (London 1988)
Waugh, Scott & Peter Diehl, *Christendom and its Discontents: Exclusion, Persecution and Rebellion 1100–1500* (Cambridge 1996)

## Italian

* Argiolas, Tommaso, *Armi ed eserciti del Rinascimento Italiano* (Rome 1991)
Bagatin, Pier Luigi (ed.), *Le tarsie dello studiolo e del palazzo ducale di Urbino* (Treviso 2003)
Cerboni Baiardi, Giorgio & others (eds.), *Federico di Montefeltro: lo stato, le arti, la cultura,* vol. 1: 'Le Arti' (Rome 1986)
Cesari, Luca (ed.), *Ezra Pound: Cantos Malatestiani VIII–XI* (Milan 1998)
* Chiaretti, Angelo, *Un tesoro di Montegridolfo: la cassa dotale di Isotta degli Atti* (Morciano di Romagna 2003)
Cipolla, Carlo, *Storia Belle signorie Italiane dal 1313 al 1530 (Milan 1881)*
Covini, Maria Nadia, *L'esercito del duca: organizzazione militare e instituzioni al tempo degli Sforza 1450–1480* (Rome 1998)
Dominici, Luigi, *Il Montefeltro e i suoi Tiranni nella Divina Commedia* (Lanciano 1926)
Donati, Claudio, *L'Idea di nobilità in Italia: secoli XIV–XVIII* (Rome 1988)
Franceschini, Gino, *Figure del Rinascimento Urbinate* (Urbino 1959)
** *I Montefeltro* (Varese 1970)
** *I Malatesta* (Varese 1973)
** Ghisalberti, Alberto (ed.), *Dizionario biografico degli Italiani* (Rome 1960–)
Jones, Philip (ed.), *Studi Malatestiani* (Rome 1978)
Mariano, Fabio (ed.), *Le fortificazione di Corinaldo* (Urbino 1991)
Mauro, Maurizio (ed.), *Rocche e bombarde fra Marche e Romagna nel XV secolo* (Ravenna 1995)
Michelini Tocci, Luigi, *Storia di un mago e cento castelli* (Pesaro 1986)

Morachiello, Paolo, *Programmi umanistici e scienza militare nello Stato di Federico da Montefeltro* (Urbino 1972)

Pasini, Pier Giorgio, *I Malatesti e l'arte* (Cinisello Balsamo 1983)

*Malatesta Novello: Magnifico Signore* (Bologna 2002)

*Piero e i Malatesti* (Cinisello Balsamo 1992)

*Tempio malatestiano* (Milan 2000)

Pieri, Piero, *Il Rinascimento e la crisi militare italiana* (Turin 1952)

Rendina, Claudio, *I capitani di ventura* (Rome 1999)

Rimondini, Giovanni, *L'araldica Malatestiana* (Verucchio 1994)

* Roccasecca, Pietro, *Paolo Ucello: le battaglie* (Milan 1997)

Rocchi, Loretta (ed.), *Rocche e castelli nelle terre dei Malatesti di Sogliano* (Rimini 2002)

Rossi, Giovangirolamo de' (ed. Bramanti), *Vita di Federico di Montefeltro* (Florence 1995)

Sassi, Marco, *Castelli in Romagna: l'incastellamento tra X e XII secolo nelle province romagnole e nel Montefeltro* (Cesena 2005)

Settia, Aldo, *Chiese, strade e fortezze nell'Italia medievale* (Rome 1991)

* Tabanelli, Mario, *Sigismondo Pandolfo Malatesta* (Faenza 1977)

* Tartaglia, Gaspare Broglio (ed. Luciani), *Cronaca Malatestiana del secolo XV* (Rimini 1982)

Tomassini Pietramellara, Carla & Angelo Turchini (eds.), *Castel Sismondo e Sigismondo Pandolfo Malatesta* (Rimini 1985)

Treppo, Mario del (ed.), *Condottieri e uomini d'arme nell'Italia del Rinascimento* (Naples 2001)

Ugurgieri della Berardenga, Curzio, *Avventurieri alla conquista di feudi di corone 1356–1429* (Florence 1963)

Valazzi, Maria Rosaria, *La rocca di Gradara* (Rome 2003)

** Various, *Biblioteca Malatestiana*, 20 vols. (Rimini 1998–2006)

## * ARTICLES

Bueno de Mesquita, Daniel, 'Some Condottieri of the Trecento', *Proceedings of the British Academy*, vol. 32 (1946)

Canestrini, Giovanni, 'Documenti per servire alla storia della milizia Italiana dal secolo XIII al XVI', *Archivio Storico Italiano*, vol. XV (1851)

Clough, Cecil, 'Federico da Montefeltro and the Kings of Naples', *Renaissance Studies*, vol. 6 (1992)

Griffiths, Gordon, 'The Political Significance of Uccello's Battle of San Romano', *Journal of the Warburg and Courtauld Institutes*, vol. XLI (1978)

Housley, Norman, 'The Mercenary Companies, the Papacy and the Crusades 1356–1378', *Traditio*, vol. 38 (1982)

Isenberg, David, 'Soldiers of Fortune Ltd.', *Center for Defense Information Monograph* November 1997 (*www.cdi.org*)

McGlynn, Sean, 'The Myths of Medieval Warfare', *History Today*, vol. 44 (1994)

Smith, Eugene, 'The New Condottieri and US Policy: The Privatization of Conflict and its Implications', *Parameters*, Winter 2002

# INDEX

Figures in **bold** refer to illustrations.